Legitimate
Acts
and
Illegal
Encounters

Smithsonian Series in Ethnographic Inquiry

Ivan Karp and William Merrill, Series Editors

Ethnography as fieldwork, analysis, and literary form is the distinguishing feature of modern anthropology. Guided by the assumption that anthropological theory and ethnography are inextricably linked, this series is devoted to exploring the ethnographic enterprise.

Advisory Board

Mindie Lazarus-Black

LEGITIMATE ACTS

AND

ILLEGAL ENCOUNTERS

Law and Society
in Antigua and Barbuda

SMITHSONIAN INSTITUTION PRESS

Washington and London

Copy Editor: Karin Kaufman
Production Editor: Jenelle Walthour
Designer: Alan Carter

Library of Congress Cataloging-in-Publication Data
Lazarus-Black, Mindie.
Legitimate acts and illegal encounters : law and society in
Antigua and Barbuda / by Mindie Lazarus-Black.
    p.   cm.
Includes bibliographical references and index.
ISBN 1-56098-327-2 (cloth : alk. paper). —ISBN 1-56098-326-4
(paper : alk. paper)
1. Kinship (Law)—Antigua and Barbuda. 2. Customary law—
Antigua and Barbuda. 3. Ethnological jurisprudence. 4. Sociological
jurisprudence. I. Title.
KGK43.L39   1994
349.72974—dc20
[347.2074]   93-11005

British Library Cataloguing-in-Publication Data is available

Manufactured in the United States of America
01 00 99 98 97 96 95 94   5 4 3 2 1

∞ The paper used in this publication meets the minimum requirements
of the American National Standard for Permanence of Paper
for Printed Library Materials Z39.48-1984

For

BILL

❧

❧ Contents

❧ List of Tables

❧ Preface

THROUGHOUT CARIBBEAN history, kinship, class, and state formation have been interwoven processes commanding and repelling the power of law. Beginning with the colonial slave era and continuing through to modern times, the origin, development, and present character of kinship, class, and gender in the English-speaking Caribbean lies in the continuing struggle between lawmakers and ordinary men and women who, in the course of their daily lives, alter in practice the purpose and meaning of lawmakers' law. In the earliest days of colonization, local laws, dramatically different from English statutes of the same period, were tools men used to create and maintain a slave-based plantation economy. In the activities and practices that forged these new societies, former assumptions and conceptions about the "natural" hierarchy of persons, marriage, legitimacy, property, pagans, Christians, and the natures of men and women were reassessed and reinterpreted. From slavery to freedom, beliefs about social hierarchy, labor, gender, justice, and family embedded in local legal ideologies and processes shaped, even as they were shaped by, a commonsense understanding of love and marriage, sex and sin, and the legal and illegal.

This narrative, a historical anthropology, unfolds in a three-island nation within the Leeward chain in the Caribbean, known generally as Antigua and consisting of Antigua, which covers 108 square miles; Barbuda, comprising 62 square miles; and tiny uninhabited Redonda, 1.25 square miles. In the main low lying, Antigua is also generally flat, except for the southwestern section, which is the site of the highest point, Boggy Peak (1,330 feet). The coastline has many beautiful white sandy beaches, some protected by dense bush, and many natural harbors. The vegetation is evergreen and deciduous forest and evergreen woodland. Barbuda lies some thirty miles to the northeast. It is a coral island, mostly uninhabited, and rather wild. Feral cattle, deer, guinea fowl, and hogs roam freely through the bush. The vegetation is dry, mostly open scrub and scrub forest (Berleant-Schiller 1977a:300). Its unsafe harbors contributed to Barbuda's isolation over the centuries, with regular air service from Antigua beginning only in 1961.

Antigua and Barbuda's climate is characteristically Caribbean: warm and sometimes hot and humid. The average temperature is 82 degrees Fahrenheit. Trade winds temper the heat but also blow away the much-needed rain clouds. Both islands suffer frequent and terrible droughts. The average yearly rainfalls are forty-six inches for Antigua and thirty-nine inches for Barbuda, but can fall as low as twenty-five inches in some years. At times there is not enough water available to bathe properly or to wash clothes. The government frequently cuts all the city water supplies for several hours, and sometimes for days, to preserve dwindling supplies.

In 1991, the total population of the two islands was 60,840 persons, of whom only 2 percent lived in Barbuda (Antigua and Barbuda, 1991 Population and Housing Census: Preliminary Report 1991:3).[1] The majority of Antiguans and Barbudans are African-Caribbean people. Other groups include the few remaining descendants of British colonists, the progeny of Portuguese indentured servants, sons and daughters of Syrian and Lebanese people, and West Indians from other islands. A small group of expatriates from the United States, Canada, and England reside there as well. Most recently, there are emigrants from Italy and China. In contrast, Barbuda is home almost exclusively to the descendants of the slaves of Christopher Codrington.

English is the standard language, although there is a creole dialect that Antiguans call "our bad language" (Reisman 1964:48, 1970:136–37). Most islanders are literate and most consider themselves Christian. The Anglican church, once the church of the state but legally separated from government since 1873, has the largest following. Other large congregations include the Moravian, Methodist, Catholic, Seventh Day Adventist, Pilgrim Holiness, and Pentecostal churches.

Antigua and Barbuda gained independence from Great Britain in 1981. It is a parliamentary democracy with a bicameral legislature and an elected prime minister. Belonging to the Commonwealth, Antiguans speak very warmly about the Queen, and the occasion of her visit in 1985 sparked numerous parades and celebrations and much needed road repair. At independence, the government proclaimed a nonaligned foreign policy but maintains strongest political and economic ties with Britain, Canada, and the United States. The Antigua Labour party (ALP), led by V. C. Bird, Sr., has been politically dominant since 1946 with the exception of the period between 1971 and 1976, when George Walter's Progressive Labour Movement (PLM) gained control. Another political party, the Antigua Caribbean Liberation Movement (ACLM) formed in 1973. It attracts a numerically small following but is very outspoken in its criticisms of many government programs, policies, and officials.

For most of their history, Antiguans have worked in sugarcane fields. Reliance on this monocrop economy prevented the colony from achieving economic self-sufficiency. Today, the agricultural sector remains in general decline, despite a variety of efforts to revive it. The last large sugar estates closed in 1972, but there are periodic attempts to revive the industry. The government now owns nearly 60 percent of the available land, and the practice of offering short-term leases to individuals has not proved conducive to land improvement. Agricultural production is moving away from plantation crops, such as sugar and cotton, and toward a more diversified system that includes fruits, vegetables, and grains (World Bank 1985:15–16). Antigua exports cotton, pineapples, live animals, rum, tobacco, and animal and vegetable fats and oils. Many provision crops are consumed locally, with surpluses passed on to family and friends or sold for extra cash. The middle class depends heavily upon imported foods.

The manufacturing and industrial sector is developing slowly. Until a few years ago, Antigua exported some petroleum products, but the oil refinery is now closed. Industrial activity includes processing of local agricultural produce, some manufacturing of clothing, furniture, and household goods, and production of rum and nonalcoholic beverages. In 1983, manufactured exports represented about 85 percent of total domestic exports (ibid.:20). A handful of firms produce more than half of the output and employ at least half of the industrial work force. Crude oil, machinery, automobiles, luxury consumer items, and clothing are imported.

For the past two decades, tourism has been the most important economic activity in Antigua. Its direct value now accounts for approximately 21 percent of the gross domestic product, and at least 12 percent of the labor force is directly employed in this sector (ibid.:24). Still, living and working in St. John's, the capital, in 1985–87, I was not constantly aware of the extent to which Antiguans depended upon tourism. There were shops catering to the tourist trade, but very few restaurants. Large hotels claimed some of the larger beaches, but most of these were miles from St. John's. No doubt the poor quality of the highways deterred visitors; they took a quick tour of the city, ventured out to see the sights at Nelson's Dockyard, and then returned to the confines of their holiday retreat. Except on those occasional days when a cruise ship docked and spilled forth sunburned, camera-laden couples—many of them indecently clothed by Antiguan standards—tourists did not overrun the city of St. John's in the mid-1980s.

Facts and figures about the structure and organization of the Antiguan labor force were hard to come by (ibid.:x). According to a 1979 report on the employed labor force, 33 percent of all workers fell within the composite category of "community, social, and personal service industries." The second largest group of occupations, listed as "distributive trades, restaurants, and guest houses," included 22 percent of the work force. "Construction" and "transport" each accounted for 11 percent. "Agriculture" and "manufacturing" employed 9 percent and 7 percent, respectively (V. Richards 1982:33). A World Bank report found the government employs about 30 percent of the total number of working persons (1985:4). Unemployment remained at about 20 percent through the first half of the 1980s (*Statistical Yearbooks* 1982, 1983, 1985).[2] Multiple jobs and job sharing were common for both men and women (cf. Comitas 1964; Senior 1991:112). The per capita yearly income was estimated at about U.S. $1,070 in 1982 (*Caribbean Resource Kit for Women* 1982:A-1).

St. John's covers an area of about three square miles. By 1991, almost 37 percent of the population lived in the city, with another 23 percent residing in the surrounding parish (Antigua and Barbuda, 1991 Population and Housing Census 1991:3). The city is home to most government buildings, the island's largest commercial and retail stores, law offices, the prestigious high schools, the National Archives, the museum, and the library. "Town" is busiest in the mornings before the temperature rises. The streets are crowded with people walking to work, shoppers, and higglers (peddlers). Drivers in Japanese imports delight in honking their horns, whether to warn meanderers to move aside or to greet their friends.

High Street and Market Street meet at one of the city's busier intersections. The buildings and activities that take place on these two streets reveal some of the most important features of life in the West Indies. To walk these streets is to observe and experience the contradictory signs that are legacies of Antiguan history. For example, near the top of High Street sits the Arch of Independence, a sculpture commissioned to mark the birth of the nation, but as any cab driver will tell you, immediately provoked heated debates about government spending and the merits of local artists. High Street also has the High Court and most of the banks. (The only locally owned bank is on another street.) The courthouse building is a practical cement-block structure painted institutional green. The foreign banks are more modern and attractively designed, but their service is decidedly tropical; it is not uncommon to wait forty minutes to deposit a check. Further down High Street, near the deepwater harbor, are some perfume and gift shops. Everything in these stores is imported, including souvenirs made in Dominica but labeled "Antigua." The items for sale in these stores are beyond the means of almost all the local people.

Law and order, foreign banks, and tourist shops dominate High Street. Market Street, in welcome contrast, is a cornucopia of local colors and cloths, wit, and words. The internal economy of the island drives the smells and noises of Market Street. Women sit along crooked curbs with ice chests and trays between their knees. They sell single sticks of gum and single cigarettes, pop and tamarind juice, fried fish balls, and roasted peanuts. Behind them are single-story, cramped, dry-goods stores operated by the sons of men from the Middle East. Fifty years ago their fathers and grandfathers carried bolts of cloth to sell in the villages. Today, the villagers come to town. Many of the household items available in these shops were made in Japan, exported to the States, and reexported to Antigua. At one end of Market Street is the great market, comprised of open-air stalls and a massive structure enclosing the butchery and fish market. Market is open every day, but it is especially spectacular on Saturday mornings. People shop for fresh fruits, vegetables, fish, and meat. Available vegetables include plantains, okra, eggplant, yams, onions, green beans, and peas. Seasonal fruits include mangoes, bananas, and pineapples. Most citrus fruits are imported from Dominica and sold by Dominican women. People who remain on the island for any length of time find "their" higgler who remembers her clients' preferences. Tarpon, kingfish, barracuda, blue fish, red snapper, and mullet are popular fishes. Barbuda is famous for its lobster (actually large crawfish). The locally grown beef is chewy. In addition, Antiguans regularly consume "rice and peas" (white rice and red beans), frozen chicken wings and legs, salt fish, macaroni, and blood pudding. The national dish is a pepper pot stew.

Few people live at the center of the commercial district, but many people dwell just at its borders. In 1985–86, I lived near Pope's Head Street, which got its name from the seventeenth-century custom whereby English colonists regularly cut off the head of an image of the pope (Smith and Smith 1986:96). I rented an apartment in a two-story family home that had been converted into several units. My neighbors and I shared a courtyard and two cisterns that provided us water to wash and lines on which to dry our clothes. Depending upon the resources of the family, homes in St. John's are constructed of brick, cement, wood, or corrugated iron. Most people in town have electric lights, although the government frequently cuts off the current to reserve power and there are regular malfunctions at the main station that further limit service. Many people remain without indoor plumbing. Younger men use the public showers; they sing as they shower, and passersby tease them good-naturedly. There is still a long waiting list for a private telephone. Any discussion of the quality of city services causes Antiguans to suck their teeth in disgust. Still, everyone also agrees that great progress in education, public health, and the availability of consumer products has been made in the past two decades.

Almost all of the 1,200 persons in Barbuda live in Codrington Village. In the early 1970s, there were 234 households in Codrington (Berleant-Schiller 1977b:256). Although Antiguans sometimes joke about Barbuda's backwardness, Barbudans take great pride in their independent history and insist upon their communal ownership of land outside the village. A 1977 act established the Barbuda Council, the local governing body. The government regularly employs about a hundred people in a variety of service and agricultural tasks, most of them part time. Barbudans still depend upon the cultivation of provision grounds. Among other crops, men and women grow cassava, maize, peppers, beans, sweet potatoes, yams, squash, and peanuts. Men also fish for subsistence and sometimes sell their surplus. In the main, men accumulate cash and prestige by cattle keeping and lobster diving (Berleant-Schiller 1977a, 1977b). Many Barbudans also keep goats and sheep. Deer, wild pig, and guinea fowl are sometimes hunted for food. Both sexes make charcoal for cash (Berleant-Schiller 1977a, 1977b; Watters 1980). In 1986, I observed women breaking stones for concrete making and house construction. One very expensive and private resort employed about 80 Barbudans seasonally. There is a post office, a public school for children, and a modern health clinic. The police station, home to four or five constables, is converted into a courthouse approximately four times a year. During my fieldwork, Barbuda had a few stores carrying consumer goods and souvenirs, several popular rum shops, two banks, and an open air "disco" that opened and closed according to local demand. In addition to the Anglican church, there are several small fundamentalist churches that provide religious instruction and social and recreational activities for members. Barbudans found my question about whether there were any "social classes" in Barbuda very humorous. Two or three Barbudans are quite well-to-do; everybody else shares a very similar and simple way of life. Equal access to lands and resources shared in common promotes equality among Barbudans (Berleant-Schiller 1988:121). Most communication "off island" is by mail. Phones were being installed as I left. During my stay, the police radio was used in emergencies. Most peoples' radios, however, were tuned to cricket matches or the calypsos of singers Short-Shirt, Obstinate, Chalice, and Mighty Sparrow.

By 1992, St. John's had become much more cosmopolitan. It had a new deep-water harbor complex whose shops' advertisements boasted about the best, brightest, and most advanced commodities. There was a gambling casino, and fast food was readily available. The number of cars and taxi drivers seemed to have doubled. Barbudans had moved beyond the old walls of Codrington Village, expanded their enterprises, built some guest houses, watched new hotels open and close, and enclosed their disco. (I got caught up on all the news when my day's visit turned into an overnight because the plane from Antigua could not land.)

Some of this "progress" is to the historian's chagrin; some of it means more comfortable living conditions for Antiguans and Barbudans. Five years is a long time. Thankfully, friendships and the sea endure.

❧ Acknowledgments

SUPPORT FOR this long-term venture came from several sources and many people. The Tinker Foundation made possible my initial visit to Barbados, Antigua, and Barbuda in the summer of 1984. A Fulbright Grant from the Institute of International Education and an Inter-American Foundation Fellowship funded the major field project in 1985–86. The Inter-American Foundation also supported a supplementary visit to these islands in the summer of 1987. The American Association of University Women and the William Rainey Harper Fellowship Committee at the University of Chicago provided financial assistance in 1987–88 to give me the time to turn my hand-written field and library notes into a dissertation. A National Endowment for the Humanities Fellowship for College Teachers allowed me to return to Antigua and Barbuda in 1992 to finish this story and begin another. The Institute for the Humanities at the University of Illinois provided a Grant for Faculty Research to make it possible for Lone B. Black to transcribe some of my interview tapes and for Kim Breger and Dan Pavlakovic to gather references. Lisa Lazarus-Black kindly spent some of her weekends helping me check sources. I am grateful to the American Bar Foundation in Chicago, for work, space, time, and its intellectual community over the past four years, but in particular, Lisa Frohmann, Susan Hirsch, Nancy Matthews, Beth Mertz, Bob Nelson, Susan Shapiro, and the director, Bryant Garth. Colleagues at the University of Illinois at Chicago heard pieces of this story and offered encouragement in our offices, on the telephone, and over dinner. Thank you for listening. Patrick McAnany, department chair, made release time available so I could return to Antigua.

I want to address personally many friends in Antigua, Barbuda, and Barbados. You helped me grow intellectually, but in so many ways, as a person. Thank you, especially, John Barzy, Dada Baynes, Millicent Beazer, Cutie Benjamin, Alison Bohne, Ricky Bohne, Steadroy Browne, Dennis Byron, Lucella Campbell, Tessa Chaderton-Shaw, Sydney Christian, Marcel Commodore, Karen DeFreitas, John Fuller, Ralph Frances, Tony Hadeed, Ashley Hanley, E. Anne Henry-Goodwin, Iris Hinds, Sue Joseph, Vernon Joseph, Florence Lake, Louis Lockhart, Lona Lynch-Wade, Julie Martin, Kudjo Martin, Junie Norde, David Paterson, Bernie Payne, Monica Payne, Merle Perry, Jiel Perry, Rawlston Pompey, James Punter, Olivette Punter, Clare Roberts, Justin Simon, Ralph Thorne, Sharon Walter, and Leslie Watkins. Since 1985, Secki Lewis has been my friend, a sensitive listener, and a patient teacher. She has been my guide along many paths. In 1992–93, Pep Perry provided me space at his office so I could get things done using twentieth-century technology. I looked forward to coffee breaks with him, Cherry Perry, and Nigel Pilgrim during those months in residence. My sincere thanks, too, to the lawyers, magistrates, and judges who took the time to help me with my research, and to the staffs at the St. John's magistrates court and the High Court without whom I could not have located most of the records on which this study depends. In Antigua, I was also assisted by Dr. Edris Bird, and later Dr. Ermina Osoba, of the Department of Extra-Mural Studies, University of the West Indies, Mrs. Harris and the staff at the National Archives, and Mrs. Gwendolyn Tonge, Director of the Women's Desk. Mr. Lindberg Dowe, Clerk to Parliament, Mrs. Phyllis Mayers of the Antigua Public Library, and Mr. Desmond Nicholson of the Antigua Archaeological and Historical Society recommended important references to me.

The Antiguan and Barbudan litigants who allowed me to listen to their cases, and the men and women who patiently told me their life histories, brought this history of life and law into the present. Thank you for sharing your experiences. I sincerely hope that you will find that I have done justice to what you have told me. I also interviewed several ministers of religion, members of Parliament, and government officials, all of who must remain anonymous but have my appreciation. Mr. John Dyrud, Head Librarian at the Law School in Barbados, generously gave me my first instruction in legal research. Several of his assistants, including Colin Hinkson and Joyce Robertson, were most kind. In Barbados, I also used the university library and the resources of the Institute for Social and Economic Research. I both enjoyed and learned from conversations with Dr. Christine Barrow, Dr. Woodville Marshall, Dr. Joycelin Massiah, and Dr. Monica Payne.

I would like to thank several teachers, some fellow students and friends, and other special people who have lent much encouragement or editing suggestions. I developed my love of anthropology from Gil Kushner. He was, and remains, someone with whom I feel free to imagine. I want to thank Raymond Smith for all he taught me about the Caribbean and for insisting that I keep writing until the work got better. I am grateful to John Comaroff for leading me to the law (while understanding so well its possibilities and pitfalls) and for his willingness to listen as I learned. The insights I gained from discussions with Bernard Cohn, Rayna Rapp, David Schneider, and George Stocking will be obvious to most anthropologists. Arthur Stinchcombe read my completed dissertation and I benefitted from his testing of my arguments and careful editing. Love and thanks are due to Shellee Colen, Leah Feldman, Ken Leiter, and Sarah Maza, who read parts or all of the almost finished manuscript for me and didn't have to. Credit is due, too, to Frank Munger, O. Nigel Bolland, anonymous reviewers, Daniel Goodwin at Smithsonian Institution Press, and my editor, Karin Kaufman. Some of the history of Antiguan kinship legalities and part of the tale of why women take men to magistrates' court were previously published in *Law & Society Review* and *Ethnology*. Finally, I always knew I could call on (and frequently did) Irene Crofton, Lisa Douglass, Wendy Espeland, Kathy Hall, Susan Hirsch, Teddi Locke, Susan Lowes, Dorothy and Bernie Mozinski, Yvonne Seng, Dennis Torreggiani, and my sister, Jan Kaplan.

Most importantly, now, as in the past, my work is possible because of my parents, who taught me to work hard, and with courage, at something I loved. Bill Black has always understood and practiced the freedom to explore and the willingness to share. I also had the love and laughter of my daughter, Lisa, who, as a very young child with an undergraduate mother majoring in anthropology, walked into the kitchen one day smiling brightly and asked: "How ya doin' Mar-gar-reet-Mead?" She still teases me unmercifully, for which I am most grateful.

🐎 Notes on Sources, Methods, and the Terminology of Race and Class

I CHOSE Antigua and Barbuda as the site for this study on several accounts. First, with the exception of eight months in 1672 when they were captured by the French, these islands remained under continuous British rule until their independence in 1981. This consistency permitted a more rigorous analysis, because I had only to investigate the similarities and differences between legislation in the colony and British statutes of the same period. Second, Goveia's *Slave Society in the British Leeward Islands at the End of the Eighteenth Century* (1965) provided an invaluable foundation for analyzing the development of Antiguan society. I hope this project contributes to the later history of the Leewards, about which very little has been written. Third, though now one nation, Antigua and Barbuda comprise an especially interesting research setting because they have somewhat different histories and are today very different places. Antigua became the seat of the Crown's representative in the Leeward Islands in the early colonial period. Barbuda, in contrast, belonged to a single family and was without written law until it was formally incorporated under the jurisdiction of St. John's parish in 1859. Today, St. John's is the site of the busiest magistrate's court. In Barbuda, court meets just three or four times a year for two or three days. These contrasts allowed me to investigate the role of law in contemporary familial relationships in an urban place, where people have ready access to the courts, and in a rural setting where they do

xxi

not. Finally, Antigua and Barbuda gained independence in 1981, just a few years prior to my fieldwork. As a new nation, it has the opportunity to use law to effect social change in new directions. I wondered if contemporary leaders would reinvent its kinship codes.

The paucity, disarray, and general unavailability of Antiguan records makes it difficult to construct an anthropologically rich Antiguan history for all periods. There are few published historical sources on Antigua, almost no secondary material regarding its legal history, and little information about the social and kinship organization of Antiguan and Barbudan slaves (see also Gaspar 1985a:97; Lowes 1993:22–27). I have had to rely on primary legal records, a few contemporary accounts, scattered descriptions by visitors to the island, and a few excellent dissertations. The University of the West Indies Law School, Cave Hill, Barbados, holds a complete collection of statutes written in Antigua between 1668 and 1900 and sent to the Colonial Office for Royal Assent, as well as copies of more recent superseded and current legislation. The Antigua and Barbuda Government Archives, the University of Chicago Library, New York Public Library, and the Research Institute for the Study of Man furnished other secondary sources about life in colonial Antiguan society. Legal briefs illuminating how lawyers and judges formulated their cases and rendered their decisions during colonialism are rare. In sum, to investigate life and law in the first two historical periods under investigation, during slavery and in the postemancipation period, I drew on available primary legal materials, secondary sources, and family and church records.

My first field trip included three months of archival research in Barbados, followed by ten months in Antigua and two months in Barbuda (January 1985 to March 1987). To investigate formal legal codes and institutions, I observed for eight months all cases of bastardy and maintenance brought to the St. John's magistrate court, attended village courts on both islands, followed divorce and adoption cases at High Court, and gathered courthouse statistics. I interviewed two-thirds of all practicing lawyers, magistrates, and judges to record their experiences in handling kinship matters, patterns the professionals had discerned about their cases and clients, examples of unusual kinship cases, and views about the past and present role of law in family life. I also spoke with lawmakers and law enforcers: the attorney general, the solicitor general, members of Parliament, the bar association president, court clerks, bailiffs, and policemen. Litigants discussed with me their case histories and suggestions for legal reform. When one or both parties agreed to a lengthy interview, I gathered biographical information and data about the litigants' families, work lives, the length and quality of the relationship to the opposing party, their reasons for taking the case to court, and how they felt about their experience.

Thus, as much as possible, I treated a court case as a moment in the history of a dispute (cf. Epstein 1967; Gluckman 1967; Nader and Yngvesson 1973; Van Velsen 1967). These kinship cases mark crises in the lives of individuals, but they also highlight the strains and contradictions within the social system at large (cf. Cohn 1965; Comaroff and Roberts 1981; Epstein 1967; Gluckman 1967; Gulliver 1969; Moore 1978, 1986, 1989; Richards 1971). During a three month follow-up study in 1987, I reinterviewed litigants to determine what had transpired during the year following their court case. I completed reading the court records for the year 1987 in 1992.

To better understand familial and household organization, to investigate the meaning of family, to grasp people's ideas about gender, labor, the exchange of goods and services and inheritance, and to discover the interaction between local ideas and law, I used participant observation and interviews in St. John's and Codrington Village. I spoke with men and women of diverse ages, marital statuses, religious affiliations, and socioeconomic backgrounds who had never been to court. I sampled patterns of membership, labor, and exchange in some fifteen households. Interviews with ministers shed light on the continuing influence of the churches, as did attendance at services, baptisms, weddings, and funerals. I learned about "life and living" in Antigua, too, as I formed friendships, sat on stoops, cooked, cleaned, did the laundry, learned the words to calypso tunes, danced in discos, and walked by the sea. I learned about life in Antigua as a white woman, an American from Chicago, married with one daughter, but living on my own as I pursued what Antiguans correctly described as my "course." [1]

A note on racial terminology. In histories and anthropologies of the West Indies, colors are important signifiers. For example, a study of historical Trinidad gives us one very typical description:

> The word "coloured" will be used to describe an individual of mixed European and African descent, probably light-complexioned. A "black" is understood to be a person of unmixed African descent, or predominantly African descent, whose complexion is dark. "African" is used only to describe persons born in Africa. (Brereton 1979:2)

A conflation of phenotype, genotype, geography, and culture, these color categories were and remain "real" and "realized" for West Indians and students of their histories. Historically, they have marked social and legal possibility on the body. The ease with which scholars continue to use the categories "white," "black," and "brown" is part of the problem of representation in history. The terminology is colonial, partly a function of our historical sources. As Wells explains:

> The terms "black," "Negro," and "slave" are used interchangeably by colonial census takers; whites were generally called just that, though occasionally the term "Christian" was used instead of "white." Apparently the key distinction in the mind of the colonists was between slaves and all others. Although white servants were

present in many colonies, often they were not recorded separately from free whites. . . . [moreover,] at least some of the census takers seem to have been puzzled as to how to record free blacks. Before the second half of the eighteenth century, the few free blacks in a colony were occasionally listed as whites rather than Negroes, but the censuses taken after about 1750 began to distinguish free blacks and mulattoes from slaves and whites. (1975:39)

To cite one last example, a scholar of Antigua's early history distinguished "free Negroes (freedmen of unmixed Negro ancestry) from other free persons of color," because records from the first few decades of the eighteenth century show freedmen of mixed ancestry were allowed to own more land than free Negroes, and if they qualified as freeholders, they were allowed to vote (Gaspar 1985a:166).

The terminology of Caribbean scholarship has reflected Caribbean reality: it codes a history of colonialism and racism. I use these color terms occasionally, and also *people of color* and *nonwhite,* aware that they do not make my text less biased.[2] That so many academics continue to distinguish people by the color of their skin, without drawing attention to the implications of that fact, is deeply problematic.[3]

Equally troublesome is the category "social class." In the early days of colonialism, Antiguans did not view themselves as members of different "classes." Historians often use *ranks* and *social groups* to describe social hierarchy in the slave era, and I use that terminology here.[4] Discussions of social organization in the contemporary Caribbean, on the other hand, generally divide these societies into upper, middle, and lower classes, or sometimes into proletarians, peasants, and bourgeoisie. Antiguan society reflected the former three-tiered schema only in the period from emancipation to the late 1960s, when the last of the resident planters departed (Henry 1985:184–86). In my experience, the contemporary social structure consists of two broad classes, middle and lower, which can be further differentiated into smaller "strata" based on their members' socioeconomic status and ability to wield political power.

At the top of the present hierarchy, then, is a small local elite that holds elected political authority. In contrast to the days when sugar dominated the economy, this local elite is Antiguan born, descended from the working class, and increasingly educated in the Caribbean. Within this same stratum are also foreign businessmen and expatriates who play important roles in the economy, enter into business arrangements with the local elite and socialize on occasion with them, but who are noticeably absent from the official political process. The homes, cars, leisure activities, and ideas about family of the local elite, however, are virtually indistinguishable from those of people in Antigua's "middle" middle class. These similarities, in turn, help explain why middle-class persons almost always told me that Antigua had only two classes. They included politicians, lawyers, major landowners, teachers, clergymen, large retailers, government officials, members of the civil service, and the few industrialists in the middle class. People in these occupations are Antigua's "big people."

The working class is in some respects more heterogeneous. The upper stratum of this class consists of a petty bourgeoisie, "people who own small amounts of productive resources and have control over their working conditions in ways that proletarians do not" (Rapp 1982:180). Men of this class are often jacks-of-all-trades. They may own some land, raise a few cattle or goats, and work a job or two for weekly cash. Bourgeois women run their own small shops or work from their homes as seamstresses or hairdressers. In contrast, members of the working class have little or no property to speak of and only their own labor power to sell. They include agricultural workers, fishermen, domestics, hotel workers, and common laborers. Lower-class Antiguans commonly distinguish "the working class" from "the really poor" and "the riffraff." Embedded in these divisions are moral evaluations about labor, laziness, and the rights and responsibilities of individuals. People also have different expectations about the "class" from the "country" in contrast to those who live and work in "town." The unemployed and indigent "get by" with the help of their families and credit at small shops. Only a few persons, most of them Barbudans, suggested to me that there were no classes in their nation. History proves otherwise.

❧ Introduction:
Life and Law
in the Common Order

THIS BOOK is first an account of the colonists, servants, and slaves who created a new society in Antigua under, around, and through the rule of law.[1] It is about legalities, living, laboring, and loving in the past. But it is also an ethnographic study of how ordinary men and women make their legal system work for them today and how they resist state intervention in their everyday lives. I investigate class, kinship, gender, and state formation over three broad periods.

Beginning with Antigua's earliest kinship statutes and continuing through to recent legal reforms, I document critical changes in the law's content in conjunction with evolving social, economic, and political organization. I argue that kinship and gender patterns in these islands reflect continuously changing cultural arrangements of order, hierarchy, and justice that were first instituted in the seventeenth century during colonialism and slavery, altered momentously by emancipation in 1834, and transformed again after Antigua gained independence in 1981. Viewed historically and ethnographically, these changes not only mark the evolution of the legal definition of family and the functions the state assigns kinship law but also signal changes in the character and forms of resistance to state power in each of the three periods under consideration.[2] (cf. Foucault 1979; Abu-Lughod 1990).

1

My focus on law's role in constituting class, kinship, and gender relations over time corrects a significant omission in earlier research about families in the English-speaking Caribbean.[3] Studies of Caribbean kinship for the most part have ignored the power of government to define and alter the meaning of kinship and its legal effects for men and women of different classes. Although the state's ability to structure these relationships is never without challenge, we see clearly in the case of Antigua that the state has power to expand or contract rights and duties between members of different classes, within families, and between men and women, and may, over time, extend its power to matters formerly considered "personal" and extralegal.

My analysis also contributes to understanding how colonial orders are constructed and change with the passing of time and the ways in which local beliefs and practices alter the meaning, functioning, and consequences of formal laws and institutions.[4] I am concerned with how and to what extent the power of law is used to structure class, kinship, and gender relations and how those relationships, in turn, alter dramatically the content and processes of law.[5] The historical nature of my argument enables me to address the relationship between the political and economic dominance of particular groups and legislated rules and to contend with how such statutes interact with, but do not fully displace, norms and normative practices.[6] As did Stoler (1985, 1989), I investigate law as part of the process of European domination and as an instrument constituent of class and gender relations.[7] The small size of Antigua and its continuous domination by the British for most of its history enables me to focus on legal change in one locale over an extended period and allows for a detailed analysis of the effects of local ideologies[8] and practices on law (Lazarus-Black 1992:865).

Central to the argument developed here is Foucault's distinction between "systems of legalities" and "systems of illegalities" (1979:82). A system of legalities is easily identified; it is composed of the symbols, signs, and practices of formal law, together with its specialized activities, institutions, and discourse.[9] Everywhere in the British Caribbean colonies, settlers produced codes, courts, judges, juries, and jails. Antigua's system of legalities, for example, grew to include a host of formal institutions: legislating assemblies, governors' councils, parish vestries, and common courts. Within a few years, a formidable number of rules and regulations lay collected in the local registry. Officially these relied on metropolitan models; in practice they adjusted to the circumstances of life in the colony. Moreover, in the seventeenth and eighteenth centuries, the English Parliament dealt primarily with economy and the slave trade, not with the internal affairs of its West Indian colonies (D. Hall 1971:147). As a result, a local "legal sensibility," a regionally crafted method and manner of conceiving how things ought to be, and what to do if they are not (Geertz 1983:215), emerged in the colonies.

Foucault reminds us, however, that social orders also are possessed of systems of illegalities. The components of a system of illegalities are less easily observed and comprehended, necessarily so because they are illicit and punished by the state. Illegalities, Foucault observes, can take a variety of forms: breaches of codes, nonapplication of rules, explicit tolerance of illicit behavior, or tacit encouragement to defy the law (1979:82–84). No assumptions about morality are implied in the opposition of legalities and illegalities; the opposition is a function of the state's ability to classify and enforce certain social, economic, and political arrangements. Moreover, systems of illegalities formulate their own structures of domination.[10]

I argue that the circumstances and politics of colonialism set in motion forms and forces that made Antiguan law, family life, and social and gender hierarchy indigenous—creole.[11] From the beginning, the process of creolization entailed a dialectical interplay of legalities and illegalities that challenged each other as they changed over time and forged New World legal sensibilities. My position accords with Bolland's view that "our understanding of creolization as a central cultural process of Caribbean history should lead to a reconceptualization of the nature of colonialism and colonial societies, as social forces and social systems that are characterized by conflicts and contradictions, and that consequently give rise to their own transformation" (1992b:53). attention to the legal, the illegal, and, sometimes, the extralegal allows us to explore a variety of contested domains.

The prominence of legalities in early Antiguan society was manifest in law, buildings, public rituals, and the dress of the inhabitants. Governor's House and the stately High Court, for example, surpassed in size and expense most of the "big houses" of the masters of sugar production. The "common gaol," debtors' prison, and the "cage" for runaway and disobedient slaves, on the other hand, testified to the unrelenting misery of those who violated the law. As was common wherever the British settled, the system of legalities made rituals of voting, running for office, and attending the assizes. Elections and courts legitimated the political order with pomp and circumstance (cf. Hay 1975; Corrigan and Sayer 1985:34–35, 62, 104). Certain men regularly participated in events to make and process law; others could not.

Still, everyone was involved in legalities to some extent because formal rules governed monetary exchanges, credit, military duty, the hours for selling goods at the public market, what kinds of activities could take place on Sundays, and even the persons with whom one could have sexual intercourse. Moreover, itinerant courts held by specially appointed magistrates became occasions for educating and entertaining as well as disciplining the masses. Legalities pervaded costumes too, commanding the white wigs and black robes of barristers, the color and ornamentation of dress slaves might wear to funerals, and, later, the meticulously detailed uniforms of police constables. In short, the symbols, forms, and processes of the system of legalities were everywhere.

Legalities were critical to the development of the class, kinship, racial, and gender hierarchies of the English-speaking Caribbean. And yet law's presence and participation in the making of those hierarchies was so naturalized—hegemonic—that it has been virtually ignored.[12] In the British West Indies, kinship law originated in the mutually reinforcing doctrines of the Anglican church, the English state, and local laws. But in both British and Antiguan law, kinship encompassed relations of power over persons and things. Its rules and processes comprised the "official" model of the system of affinal and consanguineous relationships—the representation of the group for and of itself (Bourdieu 1977; Geertz 1973). Kinship in law represented and remains a particular organization of domination, wielding a powerful formative influence over familial relationships within and between the social classes in Antigua.[13]

Simultaneously, however, systems of illegalities spread throughout the British West Indian colonies. These invaded local economies in forms such as banditry, piracy, black markets, and theft, as Foucault would have predicted, but they also penetrated relationships between the sexes within and across social ranks. For colonists and slaves, illegalities included illicit unions, bastardy, miscegenation, fornication, and concubinage. These practices either blatantly violated the law or fell between its cracks, yet despite condemnation by church and state, they became commonplace. Their regularity encouraged the development of norms that were known and shared across the ranks of these societies. These other ideas about men, women, and life in families, including obeah[14] and other beliefs developing in the slave quarters, emerged alongside the rules and processes of law within the common order.

The phrase *common order* captures a way of life that is ordinary and especially characteristic of the nonruling classes, except that life in the common order is punctuated continually by the actions and declarations of those who manage the state and the means of production. Practices within the common order include everyday activities such as doing laundry, going fishing or to market, discussing who children look like, deciding whether or not to go to work, and dressing in white for a baptism but in purple or black for a funeral. In these activities, men, women, and children—rich, poor, or somewhere in between—are engaged in "life and living."

Life in the common order is characterized by commonsense knowledge and a commonsense understanding of the world (Schutz 1962:3–47). As Schutz explains, each person lives his or her life through a "biographical situation"

4

that determines how the individual perceives and interprets the world at any given moment. The biographical situation has as its central feature the fact that each person, each "actor," has a "stock of knowledge at hand." This knowledge includes typifications about the commonsense world, such as what motivates human beings, how others can be expected to behave, and what the results of certain actions will be. Using commonsense understanding, actors interpret the motives and actions of others with reference to their own biographical situations. They suspend doubt that the world might be other than the way it appears to be and assume that an objective reality is shared by all observers. As they go about their daily lives, actors readily distinguish between what is normal and commonplace and what is novel. Commonsense knowledge, then, is generated by action in the world, a concatenation of life experiences in a socially informed and structured community. It is not necessarily, however, clearly articulated by the actors in the common order (cf. Bourdieu 1977).

Commonsense knowledge, of course, includes norms regarding class, kinship, and gender. People voice these ideas when they talk about family and put their norms into practice. In Antigua, family provides the rationale for a number of social, economic, and political practices. The question of who lives where, for example, is mostly resolved by family norms, not family law. Recognition of who is and who is not family is also partly governed by pragmatic concerns and individual preferences and circumstances. Thus family norms incorporate local ideas about human equality, gender, and alliances, as well as principles of justice, order, and hierarchy that are distinct from, and sometimes critical of, those found in law. Antigua's normative kinship order includes some kinship legalities but leaves room for the specifically illegal and the extralegal—beliefs and practices to which the state has not attended or cannot attend.

Commonsense knowledge about family is also conditioned by collective representations from the past. Many people in Antigua and Barbuda told me, for example, that Barbudans differed from Antiguans because Barbuda was once a "stud farm" for slaves. There is no known historical support for this contention (Lowenthal and Clarke 1977), but it continues to enjoy great popularity. The story attests to Barbudans' virility, accounts for the informality of their unions, and projects and protects a history and identity separate from that of Antigua.

The myth that makes Barbudans a separate people teaches us that Schutz's discussion of commonsense knowledge underestimates how historical consciousness and ideas about gender shape commonsense understanding.[5] Schutz did not investigate the processes through which the past is made part of commonsense knowledge or how the interpretation of the past changes in different social groups. Yet this is a crucial issue for studies of West Indian

5

family organization, because ideas and' images from the past are essential components of Caribbean kinship beliefs (cf. R. Smith 1978, 1982a, 1982b, 1987, 1988; Alexander 1973, 1984; Austin 1979, 1984; Douglass 1992). Schutz's concept of the biographical situation only begins to address the consequences of a differential distribution of knowledge. Moreover, because Schutz does not pay any attention to gender, he fails to develop the ways in which commonsense knowledge differs for men and women and precludes the notion that their "structures of relevance" may be radically different. He ignores how gender shapes commonsense meaning but is itself shaped by the reality that so many people find gender hierarchy "natural."[16]

As Cohn and Dirks contend, commonsense understanding, or in their case Bourdieu's *habitus*, "is generated not only out of small scale networks of practice but also out of the legitimation project of the state" (1988:227). One function of the state's project is to define the people under its control (creating the external boundaries of the system) and to differentiate between them (creating internal boundaries within the system). The dual capacity of this function makes it possible for us to discuss the Antiguan family, gender ideology, and structure while distinguishing beliefs and practices that are more or less characteristic of and prevalent in different classes.[17] We find some class differences with respect to familial norms because different classes have different access to and relationships with society's political, legal, and economic institutions. A major concern of this study is to examine the ways in which the discourse of the common order selects, appropriates, and transforms rules and rituals of the official model of kinship and alters them to conform to norms regarding how men and women should interact, how children should be cared for, what constitutes appropriate behavior in marriage, and the like. As we shall see, family ideology expresses the dynamics of class relations and the exercise of power, but it also speaks to resistance to formal, institutionalized legalities. The means of that resistance varies, but sometimes it involves manipulation of the very symbols, procedures, and rules of the power wielders (e.g., de Certeau 1984:13; J. Comaroff 1985:2, 11–12; Comaroff and Comaroff 1991:5–6, 11–12; Hirsch and Lazarus-Black 1994).

Kinship in the English-speaking Caribbean

Kinship has dominated Caribbean studies since the 1940s, when West Indian families were first perceived as constituting a social welfare "problem" due to low marriage rates, high rates of illegitimacy, and female-headed households (R. Smith 1982a). Initial efforts to explain the diverse social and kinship organization of the region centered upon the disruptive effects of slavery (e.g.,

Curtin 1955; Goveia 1965; Henriques 1953; Patterson 1967, 1982; M. Smith 1966). Herskovits (1958) and Mintz and Price (1976) pioneered research on the retention and influence of African customs and traditions in the Caribbean. Community studies inspired by British structural functionalism, in turn, produced a variety of cultural, social, biological, psychological, economic, and demographic variables to account for local West Indian patterns (e.g., E. Clarke 1966; Gonzalez 1970; Goode 1960, 1961; Kunstadter 1968; Rodman 1971; Rubenstein 1976; M. Smith 1965a). In general, these works concentrated heavily on synchronic analysis of family organization, thereby minimizing the problem of origins and the direction of future change. Many studies were guided by the concept of the developmental cycle of domestic groups (Fortes 1970), which, for all its advance over earlier typologies, ultimately relied upon "European common-sense categories" (R. Smith 1978:338).

More recently, historians and anthropologists such as Bush (1990), Craton (1978), Gaspar (1985), Massiah (1986), Morrissey (1989), Olwig (1981), and R. Smith (1982, 1984, 1987, 1988), among others, have challenged the notions that West Indian slave families were highly unstable (M. Smith 1962:260), that they consisted solely of women and offspring, or that men were marginal (Goveia 1965:235; Patterson 1967:167–68, 1982:140). Higman (1973, 1976, 1977) corrected the view that the Jamaican slave family was disorganized or formed promiscuously. Similar findings were reported for Jamaica (Craton 1978), Trinidad (Craton 1979; Higman 1979), and St. John, Danish West Indies (Olwig 1981). Analyses of slave households concluded that slaves lived mainly in "nuclear" rather than predominantly female-headed units (Craton 1979; Higman 1973, 1976, 1977). Demographic accounts based on plantation records,[18] however, do not reveal the principles by which slaves founded these units, the kinds of relationships that obtained within them, or even if the records correspond with the slaves' own understanding of familial arrangements (Higman 1984a:60–61, 76).

Still, most historical or historically sensitive works ignore the salient fact that European settlers brought with them kinship codes and practices that would affect, and be affected by, the New World experience. With a few notable exceptions—Martinez-Alier's study of nineteenth-century interracial marriage in Cuba (1974), Higman's use of slave court testimony to examine kin terminology and mating (1984a), and R. Smith's research on the tenacity of the marriage system in Jamaica and Guyana (1982a, 1984, 1987, 1988)—there is little written on family law and conjugal practices in the English-speaking Caribbean from a long-term historical perspective. Yet the contributions of scholars who combine a concern for legal processes with a historically informed approach to the investigation of familial patterns is evident.[19]

Some studies of Commonwealth Caribbean kinship speak to more recent law and legal processes. Reviewing the literature, I encountered astute, albeit sometimes contentious, discussions of family land tenure and inheritance (Besson 1987; Carnegie 1987b; E. Clarke 1966; M. Smith 1965c; R. Smith 1955), of marital stability and conflict and integration on Guyanese plantations, (Jayawardena 1960, 1963; R. Smith and Jayawardena 1959), and an illustration of how contemporary disputes index intra- and interclass antagonisms in two neighborhoods in Jamaica (Austin 1984:133–45). Durant Gonzalez (1982), Forde (1981), Jackson (1982), Moses (1976, 1981), and Senior (1991:135–39) consider the consequences for women of recent changes in kinship laws.[20]

To fully appreciate the significance of these new legal indexes of social transformation, and their relation to systems of domination, a broad historical perspective is required. As R. Smith states, "Kinship and the family are prime areas for the study of race, class, and gender, for it is here that all the forces that reproduce the social order converge" (1992:274). Questions about how and why kinship beliefs and behaviors reproduce class structures and ideologies begin to be addressed in works by Alexander (1977a, 1977b, 1978, 1984), Austin (1979, 1984), Douglass (1992); R. Smith (1978, 1982a, 1982b, 1984, 1987, 1988), and B. Williams (1991). Austin, for example, analyzes Jamaicans' talk about kinship as part of a vocabulary about class and race (1979, 1984). Given a history of slavery, "illegitimacy represents for Jamaicans a paradigmatic social subservience which was realized simultaneously between classes, cultures and races" (1984:156).[21] Using gender as an analytical category, Douglass's (1992) study of the Jamaican elite shows how these families preserve power and hierarchy, reproducing historical patterns between men, women, and their "inside" [legitimate] and "outside" [illegitimate] children, and using legal distinctions once thought germane only to the middle and lower classes.

I argue that kinship studies should encompass simultaneously the legal forms and forces of the state and the commonsense understanding of kin that evolves in local communities (Lazarus-Black 1991:119). My research reveals that judicial codes and processes played a formative role in early Antiguan class, kinship, and gender organization. As we shall see, locally crafted marriage, fornication, bastardy, and inheritance laws influenced the evolution of familial and gender patterns in Antigua because they established particular meanings, associations, and consequences for marriage and parentage. Law discouraged marriage between persons of different ranks, blatantly denied contractual unions to some, and tried to create an alternative system among slaves. Colonial law's legacy was a hierarchical social world in which men and women were cast into rigid social ranks and men ranked higher than women. Ignoring the salience of legalities means ignoring the ways in which kinship encompasses state power and the state mediates class and gender hierarchy.

The Centrality of Law

I contend that the law played a central role in the formation of British West Indian societies and in the development of Caribbean social organization, and that it did so for several reasons.

First, contrary to local assumptions, laws relevant to the social status, welfare, and kinship organization of the inhabitants of these islands rarely replicated English laws of the same period. As Blackstone noted in his *Commentaries on the Laws of England*, "Colonists carry with them only so much of English law as is applicable to their own situation and the condition of an infant colony" (in D. Morrison 1979:46). The statutory and common law that arrived with the colonists from England provided only the base from which local courts and assemblies built a creole jurisprudence; the received law did not dictate the subsequent development of local law (Patchett 1973:67). Because life in the colonies did not replicate life in England, West Indian law and legal sensibilities could never duplicate those of Great Britain. Beliefs and practices were transformed in the interaction of men and women confronting a new environment, a plantation economy, and a radically altered system of social hierarchy that included slavery. Lawmakers used law "strategically," in de Certeau's sense (1984:35–36),[22] but sometimes with unexpected and unintended consequences.

Second, Caribbean people played a pivotal role in the transformation of capitalism in the West (R. Smith 1988:3). An analysis of the development of West Indian law and legal institutions, then, contributes to the broader issues raised by Weber about the nature of legal development in the West and the relationship between law and capitalism. Antigua's laws provided the ground rules, further instructions, and excuses for establishing and regulating an early form of capitalism. They created categories of persons for whom specific rules applied. Law concretized these social groups as it named them, gave each a purpose, and defined their respective relationships to the social body as a whole. Marriage and kinship laws proposed not only to control human reproduction but also to reproduce the hierarchical social and economic structures of capitalism.

Third, law is "not only practice and process but also discourse, code, and communication" (Lazarus-Black 1989:11). Because it is the text in which some West Indian people crafted their societies, it reveals lawmakers' assumptions and decisions about social order, the nature of humankind, and the different natures of men and women. Law provides insights into the moral order that presupposes contractual arrangements and allows us to uncover a society's particular organization of consent (Durkheim 1964:206–19). Of course, a nation's statutes also capture the central discourses of each era; they reveal the dramas of war and peace, drought and famine, religious and racial conflict, bastardy and poverty.

Fourth, law always encodes a history of power (Starr and Collier 1989).[23] Law is a place where power is invented, negotiated, distributed, and consumed (Lazarus-Black 1989:8). This concept found particular expression in the British-settled colonies, for the English law brought to the Caribbean concerned itself as much with domination and subordination between gentlemen and the masses as it did with property. There was, moreover, a "peculiar genius" to English criminal law:

> It allowed the rulers of England to make the courts a selective instrument of class justice, yet simultaneously to proclaim the law's incorruptible impartiality, and absolute determinacy. ... Discretion allowed a prosecutor to terrorize the petty thief and then command his gratitude, or at least the approval of his neighbourhood as a man of compassion. It allowed the class that passed one of the bloodiest penal codes in Europe to congratulate itself on its humanity. (Hay 1975:48–49)

Equally remarkable to the student of West Indian history is the power of colonial law to command the respect of the people it enslaved and the sex it subordinated. We shall see that the imagery and forces of "majesty," "justice," and "mercy" (ibid., 26) were as essential to creating the hegemony of law in the New World as in the Old. The peculiar genius of West Indian law and judicial processes inspired some commitment to kinship codes as well as to criminal statutes.

That is to say, legal texts and processes are not merely tools fashioned by elites for their own purposes.[24] The history of power that Antiguan law encodes shows that the poor and the disadvantaged regularly used legalities to resist the power wielders' attempts to stray beyond the legal limits they set for themselves, to check the elites' assumptions about the social world, and to demand a "justice" born of their own experiences. That West Indians used these courts increasingly and with unceasing persistence has not been fully appreciated.[25] The research presented here shows that investigating law is as invaluable to the social history and anthropology of the powerless as it is to the study of the elite. Indeed, court records and participant observation in legal arenas allow us to explore the intersection of these groups and to see how they create each other. As Glassman (1991) argues in an African context, slavery entailed a politics of inclusion and exclusion in which the marginalized and enslaved struggled to gain access and admission to the vital institutions of their society. "Slave resistance, then, often took the form of struggle for fuller rights of social inclusion, or for fuller access to local community institutions. Through such struggle, slaves sought to open up the rules governing inclusion, that is, to redefine dominant culture" (1991:284). Courts were one such institution manifesting the politics of inclusion and exclusion.

Finally, at different times and places, law and legal institutions alter the definitions of kin relationships and what institutional support they provide for kinship. What is meant by *family* and *support*, how much of it is given, to whom, and according to which principles, are questions for empirical investigation in this volume. I find, for example, that the Antiguan state changed regularly the meaning, type, and degree of assistance it offered families and that it intervened very differently in the lives of families of different classes. Moreover, the legal language of domestic relations helped to shape the form and content of those relations by furnishing the terms for discussion and controversy (Grossberg 1985:302).[26]

In short, a historical and ethnographic investigation of law and legal institutions has much to offer the ongoing debate about the character and development of class, kinship, and gender in the English-speaking Caribbean. To date, however, few scholars have explored in depth the role of law in the formation of West Indian societies or in the evolution of their kinship structures. In the main, West Indian histories concentrate on the slave codes in their discussions of "law," and scholars of the postemancipation period emphasize how law protected special interests.[27] I ask how Antiguan laws encoded familial rights, duties, and responsibilities, created boundaries between social groups and set limits to their interactions, directed the formation of certain domestic relationships, differentiated men from women, and defined bonds between individuals and the state. As one component of the sociocultural order that emerged in the British West Indies, law reflects the processes by which creole societies were formed and thus offers one means for investigating those processes. Nevertheless, as I have explained, the presence of legalities always presupposes the existence of illegalities, and dramatically complicates our research. We turn next to the legal, social, and economic context of the island's settlement.

Settling a Colony

Establishing colonies was one of the crucial ways in which states "stated" (Corrigan and Sayer 1985:3). The British Crown's colonies enabled it to increase the size of the realm and furnish commodities for the English home market. After a while, they also served as a remedy for local social problems. In the late seventeenth century, for example, many believed that the English population was outgrowing employment opportunities and that as it did, social unrest would be the consequence (Sheridan 1973:75–76).[28] At this time, England possessed one of the most vicious and repressive penal codes in all of Europe, which assured a steady and convenient supply of paupers, criminals, and other unemployed riffraff to be transported to the New World at the "mercy" of the courts.[29]

Antigua was settled during the "long wave" of political consolidation and economic instability that marked the years following the Tudor revolution (Corrigan and Sayer 1985:55).[30] Edward Warner, who headed the first expedition in 1632, was a gentleman out to make his name and fortune. His father had settled St. Christopher, now St. Kitts, the first permanent English colony in the Caribbean. Warner's party planted the flag, said a prayer, and declared the laws of England in effect. They immediately encountered severe water shortages and resistance from Carib Indians who used Antigua as a hunting and fishing ground. Edward's wife, Cynthia, and their two children were abducted by the Caribs in 1640. Edward rescued them in Dominica, the site of the Caribs' principal villages, but the Caribs attacked again in 1653, 1654, and 1666. In the last battle, the Caribs had French assistance, resulting in the only occupation of Antigua by non-British Europeans. French soldiers remained eight months before the island was returned to England by treaty.

Colonists from Antigua set sail for Barbuda in 1661. Their farming met only limited success, and they suffered heavy losses during Carib raids in 1681 and 1684. Over the next few decades, these small-crop farmers deserted the island. The Crown leased Barbuda to the Codrington family in 1685, 1705, and 1804, for a payment "unto her Majesty yearly and every year one Fat Sheep if demanded" (D. Hall 1971:59). The Codringtons used the island as a supply depot, manufacturing center, and occasionally as a slave "seasoning" area. Sometimes slaves gathered the jetsam from ships torn apart on the treacherous reefs off Barbuda's coast.

Dutch ships probably brought the first sugar cane to the Leeward Islands in the 1630s, but Antigua's sugar industry got its first real boost in the 1670s when Colonel Christopher Codrington migrated from Barbados with his slaves (Gaspar 1985a:65, 66). Barbados and the Leewards were the first of Britain's sugar mines, but most of the Caribbean islands evolved similar socioeconomic structures and served similar functions for the empire.[31]

To the early British settlers, it was "natural" that there be different ranks of men, that men be ranked by the labor they performed and the property they held, and that men rank higher than women. Not surprisingly, the first social divisions demarcated in Antiguan law were those of age, sex, nationality, religion, and ownership of real property. The spread of slavery and plantation agriculture, however, fueled by the insatiable eighteenth-century demand for sugar, encouraged Antiguan lawmakers to impose new principles of social order. Slavery was not the initial cause of racism,[32] but it changed forever how black and white men conceived of each other and the way they organized their societies (cf. Jordan 1968). Skin color signified legal and social rank in these islands. Slavery and racism were expressed in legal endogamy.

Plantation slavery produced a distinct organization for labor, changed the process of laboring, and created new perspectives about workers. The design of the sugar plantation, for example, included a new architecture for labor. Plantation fields were revealing; they were precursors to Samuel Bentham's panopticon and infinitely more lucrative for their inventors.[33] Fields were arranged in grids that allowed masters and overseers to observe and discipline the work force. In Barbuda, I stood on the hill from which Codrington's overseers surveyed rows of slaves working subsistence crops. They were imprisoned in the walled village at night.

Work was not only more visible but also acquired new connotations and new rhythms. In the seventeenth century, Europeans believed they were not physically fit to labor in tropical climates. The extremely high mortality rates that plagued early expeditions to the West Indies and Africa seemed to prove that the tropics were a "white man's grave" (Curtin 1964:85, 177–79; Dunn 1972:302). Once African slaves were available in sufficient numbers in the islands, and until emancipation, there was little reason to reexamine the hypothesis. West Indian planters were never persuaded that the equation "labor equals civilization" (Curtin 1964:62) applied to themselves. Instead, they strove to make sugar production—an agricultural, cyclical, and task-oriented activity subject to nature—into a mechanical, regimented task subject only to the will of men.[34] Like London's merchant capitalists, plantation owners experimented with labor time. They found new ways to save it, spend it, delay it, and lie about it. In the West Indies, however, laws and lashes served in place of the clocks and bells that would later discipline laborers in England's factories (cf. Thompson 1967).[35]

I argue that the formation of the legally constructed social hierarchy in Antigua transformed ideas and practices of everyday life and, concomitantly, shaped commonsense understanding of gender and personhood. A creole sense of person, family, and gender was worked out, in large part, in terms of categories of labor. In England, *labourer* referred to an adult male, generally a married man, who resided in his own abode away from the master who employed him (Laslett 1977:61–62). As we shall see, in the West Indies the category included some women and lost its connotations of freedom, adulthood, and marital status.[36] West Indian ideas about the individual and gender also depended on racial descent. Moreover, in British Caribbean slave societies the concept of "the citizen" was very weakly developed. Except for two brief periods in Jamaica, coinciding with the outburst of the American Revolution and the abolition of the slave trade (E. Brathwaite 1971:68–73), one rarely finds

British West Indian colonists hotly debating the virtues of republicanism and the rights of individuals.[37] The fiery rhetoric of the North Americans is missing.

To the North American colonists who revolted against the British in 1776, the English family patriarch and the family laws that buttressed his power appeared feudalistic, antidemocratic, and antiegalitarian (Grossberg 1985). Over the course of the next hundred years, they rewrote colonial laws in accordance with an ideology that reflected America's republican spirit, a commitment to individual rights (for white men), and a belief in the freedom of contract. Over time, the courts expressed increasing concern for the welfare of children and the equality of women. Judges reworked a distinctly American family law.[38]

The history of Antiguan kinship law reveals a very different tale. Antiguan family law supported rigid divisions between the social ranks, marital endogamy, and the subordination of women. Antigua's early family laws were more the products of avarice and the control of labor than the consequences of frontier spirit. The concern for the equality of all persons waited for the development of a late twentieth-century bourgeoisie, one whose roots lay in the working class.

In the West Indies, then, society was imagined differently (B. Anderson 1983; Comaroff and Comaroff 1991). The British version of colonialism, plantation agriculture, and the enslavement of African peoples profoundly changed ideas about class, labor, individuals, and the law. It was only a matter of time, and very little time at that, before Caribbean classes, familial organization, and gender hierarchy assumed their own forms and meanings.

Summary and Synopsis of Forthcoming Chapters

I analyze the development of kinship, class, and gender in Antigua as they relate dialectically to systems of legalities and illegalities. The object, ultimately, is to explain social transformation within a wider historical context: to understand such processes as they are shaped by the interaction between the local sociocultural order and the external forms and forces that impinge upon it (J. L. Comaroff 1980:86; 1982:146). My aim is not to present a mere chronology of significant political and economic episodes but to provide the necessary background that enables me to focus on class formation, family ideology and structure, and gender hierarchy within the wider contexts of slavery, postemancipation society, and independence.

My first task is to demonstrate how the political structures of colonialism, the underlying assumptions contained in British law, and the sociology of slavery combined to create a distinctly creole society. Forces both internal and external to the colony spawned local Antiguan laws, which were the consequences of structural relations between contentious metropolitan centers, between some settlers and the metropole, between contiguous island elites, and between rival categories of persons within the new society. Chapters 2 through 5 explore kinship and labor codes as part of a broader agenda to create an ordered, and orderly, society. These chapters also give instances of people's resistance to law and evidence for the origins of Antigua's system of illegalities.

Antiguan colonists established a viable political economy and a hierarchical social order by the end of the eighteenth century. After slavery was abolished in 1834, local kinship law and the administration of familial relations were tied increasingly to the politics of direct intervention by the state through management of labor contracts, poor laws, and other social welfare legislation. In the nineteenth century, the state "policed" (Donzelot 1979) as much as it "governed" families. About the same time, churches began to wield a more powerful ideological and practical influence in the common order. The combined efforts of the ministry, a newly imposed Crown-colony government, and the changing composition of the class structure helped sustain much of the structure and ideology of family begun in an earlier era. The Antiguan case lends strong support to Fox-Piven and Cloward's argument (1971) that welfare legislation is designed to regulate the poor while accommodating shifts in capital's need for labor. In contrast to the American case, however, Antigua's poor relief arrangements were expanded even before political unrest threatened the state (Lazarus-Black 1992:866–67). Chapters 6 and 7 examine legalities and illegalities in the common order after slavery was abolished.

Lastly, I turn to people's use of family law in contemporary courts, the manner in which local norms inform established judicial processes, and the events surrounding the making of the nation's newest kinship statutes. Chapters 8 and 9 analyze who uses courts for familial matters, for what purpose, and how frequently. I ask why men and women use, or choose not to use, their legal system to order reproduction, marriage, and child care. Some common patterns in the life histories of litigants, in events leading up to kinship cases, and in the effects of court orders provide us with examples of family norms and practices with which magistrates and judges contend, even if the law denies their "legitimacy." I also discuss the continuing practice of obeah, which remains illegal. Chapter 10 details events surrounding the radical revision of Antiguan kinship laws in 1987. As becomes clear, changes in the family practices within a society sometimes occur without any changes in its kinship codes, but the reverse is also true (E. Clarke 1966; Lewin 1981, 1987; M. Smith 1965c; R. Smith 1955).

In 1974 Mintz wrote: "It seems to me immensely important to maintain an insistence on the sociopolitical significance of the tyranny of everyday life—whether we analyze the contemporary black power movements, slave revolts, or the growth of a nation" (1974:32). This volume also seeks to understand better the tyranny of the everyday, past and present, and how women and men courageously resist.

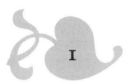

I

Fashioning a Creole Society

THIS CHAPTER introduces the political, social, economic, and legal context from which Antiguans fashioned a creole society. It records the development of a new social formation and illuminates the consciousness of local lawmakers and the practices of the people they governed. It demonstrates, in particular, the weight and pervasiveness of legalities in the early Antiguan common order, exploring the ways in which life and law conditioned each other and were influenced by external, intra- and interisland events, processes, and structures.

We begin with some fundamental, although contradictory, tendencies in British mercantile policies and practices that made law a constitutive force in the new creole society. Historical and statutory evidence suggests, for example, a certain laxity on the part of the home office in reviewing local laws from Antigua, perhaps inevitable given the distance between England and the Caribbean, constant warfare between the European powers, difficulties in communication, bureaucratic inertia, some tendency on the part of British authorities to humor or ignore minor irregularities committed by wealth-producing constituencies,[1] and the colonists' own stubborn determination to govern themselves. Although England tried repeatedly to rule the Leeward Islands as a single political entity, the settlers quickly recognized the islands' different social and economic interests and by 1682 had passed An Act To Settle Generall Councills and Generall Assemblies For The Caribbee Leeward

Islands In America, And To Secure To Each Particular Island Their Owne Peculiar Laws And Legall Customs.

Consequently, by the time slavery dominated life in these communities, each of the Leewards, except the smallest and poverty-stricken Anguilla, maintained its own separate legislature, executive authority, vestry boards, courts, militias, and agents in England. Antigua's own system of legalities, described in section 2, included all of these formal political and juridical institutions, as well as a prolific local assembly. One marvels at the sheer number of bills devoted to the "better administration of justice" and to the organization of persons and property in the island. Political and juridical offices were distributed to men who not only would never have achieved such positions of power and authority in England, but who also faced circumstances for which there was little or no precedent in English law. Much of day-to-day government, therefore, reflected indigenous and self-taught practice.

How Antiguan law authorized and furnished power for certain groups but not for others is critical to understanding the island's early and later class, kinship, and gender organization. The final sections of this chapter describe the principal sociological characteristics of Antigua's population and their legal status as the island emerged as one of Britain's foremost sugar-producing colonies. It was a society in which participation in varying forms of labor, religion, ethnicity, color, gender, and the kind and amount of one's property determined people's social positions and opportunities to achieve upward mobility. Speaking generally, the common order was divided into three social ranks corresponding most directly to the division of labor: free persons, servants, and slaves. Law innovatively demarcated these social ranks and differentiated each group's relationship to power, yet law was itself shaped by the tensions of life in the common order, by the diversity of the population, by the unusual household organizations of the settlers, and by the mundane routines and consequences of mercantile practice that often go unremarked in analyses of Caribbean social, kinship, and gender organization.

Political and Legal Contradictions in British Mercantile Practice

British mercantilism varied greatly over time and in different places, but two contradictory tendencies in the seventeenth century helped shape the form and content of early Antiguan law, local judicial institutions, and the emerging legal sensibilities of the island people. On the one hand, successful British expansion into the New World necessitated the development and control of certain relations of dependency between the metropole and her colonies and between the colonies themselves. Methods for constructing these relations included organizing formal political institutions responsible to central boards in England, appointing Crown officials to local offices to carry out British directives, and passing specific trade laws that prevented political and economic self-sufficiency (Goveia 1965:51–81; D. Hall 1971:146–49; Henry 1983b:286–90, 1985:22–26). On the other hand, several conditions mitigated against this desired discipline. Britain's own guidelines for establishing New World colonies, the decentralized organization of colonial political institutions, assumptions and principles of English common law, and the exigencies of establishing a viable life in a wilderness promoted local autonomy and encouraged novel ideas and practices.[2] Creole law, juridical institutions, and legal ideologies originated in the struggle to contend with these contradictory forces.

Britain instituted early a political organization to manage colonial autonomy. Boards and committees supervised the New World communities and advised the Crown on their progress. The first Colonial Board was replaced by the Councils for Trade and for Foreign Plantations in 1660. These councils consisted of twenty-eight members drawn from the Privy Council, other offices of government, and men of some experience in trade and planting. After 1675, a permanent secretary and staff were appointed to the Privy Council committee in charge of the colonies. This committee provided the foundation for the modern Colonial Office (Watkins 1924:67–68). These councils, however, functioned only in advisory capacities; they sent suggestions, made inquiries, received reports, and kept track of revenues and external defense.

In Antigua, Carib Indian and French attacks caused a perpetual state of siege and contributed to the development of a strongly militarized and dependent government (Henry 1985:23–24). The Carib Indians, for example, frequently attacked the Antiguan colonists. A sustained assault on their stronghold in Dominica in 1683 reduced their number, although the Caribs continued to harass the settlers until the very end of the century (Oliver 1894–99:vol. 1, lii; Nicholson 1983:27–28; Henry 1985:14–15). Moreover, the British failed to secure their position in the Leeward Islands against the French until Admiral Rodney's victories in 1782.[3] Constant warfare fostered a recognition of dependency among the colonists that is evident in preambles to bills devoted to feeding, clothing, boarding, and drilling the militia and the King's soldiers.[4]

The French and Indian menace assured that the colonists would follow certain directives from the home office, but British instructions for formulating colonial laws within each island were surprisingly obscure. In lieu of specific legislation for establishing political and judicial order in the New World, three general principles guided seventeenth-century English settlers. *Calvin's Case* (1608) permitted a Christian land conquered by British forces to be ruled by its own laws until the king changed those laws.[5] The statutes of any territory ruled by infidels, on the other hand, were abrogated and replaced. In a land without inhabitants—or at least with relatively few of them, as was the case in Antigua—the statutory laws in force in England at the time of settlement prevailed.[6] When a 1722 case reopened questions about the political autonomy of the colonies, the council ruled "acts of Parliament made in England, without naming the foreign plantations, will not bind them" (cited in Greaves and Clarke 1897:2). Fifty years later, *Campbell v. Hall* (1774) reaffirmed the distinction between settled and unsettled territories and Parliament's right to grant each a representative legislature, after which the Crown's power of general legislation was lost (Patchett 1973:17). Thus the Caribbean settlers retained those statutes they found relevant to their new life but thereafter they were not subjected to other British legislation unless it was specifically framed for them by Parliament on special occasion, by the Crown before a local assembly had convened, or by their own assembly (ibid.:32).

In Antigua's case, Parliament confined direct legislation to issues such as trust regulations, collection of debts, coinage, felony laws, procedures for establishing courts and assemblies, and maritime codes. A nineteenth-century legal authority put the matter succinctly: "As Parliament has rarely had any motive to make laws for the interior government of the colonies, except in cases relative to navigation or trade, the instances of acts extending to them in other cases are not extremely numerous" (C. Clarke 1834:68, 74–81).

The British paid greater attention to West Indians' legislative activities in the late eighteenth century, especially after the humanitarian movement had turned the tide against the slave trade.[7] Even then, however, "the affairs of individual colonial territories scarcely sounded in the halls of Westminster" and "one of the functions of the Secretary of State for the Colonies was to ensure that colonial problems were settled, as far as possible in his office rather than in Parliament" (D. Hall 1971:147, 148). Moreover, the power of the secretary, who held the authority to withhold royal assent of a colonial law, "was modified by the well-understood dangers of too frequent refusal; and by the fact that his powers were almost entirely negative. He could refuse to accept . . . but he had no power to make laws" (ibid.:148).[8] In reviewing all of the Antiguan legislation sent to the Colonial Office between 1672 and 1900, I found less than a dozen bills disallowed by Great Britain.[9]

Clearly, some features of the British mercantile system intended to promote political conformity in the colonies and continuity between the legal traditions of the Old World and the New inadvertently encouraged nonconformity. This absence of definitive constraints upon local political and legal practice combined with three additional factors to give local politicians and lawmakers wide-ranging power. First, the decentralized political organization of inter- and intraisland government created a plethora of offices distributed to a small group of propertied white men who shaped those offices to serve their mutual interests. Second, the internal logic of English law and the principle of *stare decisis* further encouraged legal autonomy. Finally, the unusual social characteristics of the colonial labor force engendered vexing circumstances for which English law offered little or no assistance. The colonists responded to those situations with a sense of pragmatism rooted in their day-to-day experiences and their determination to succeed in the purpose for which the majority had come: to make their material fortunes.

Government as Indigenous Practice:
Political and Legal Structures

Historians commonly describe, sometimes in painstaking detail, the structure and function of political institutions in the New World colonies. It is one thing, however, to read and understand the forms and functions of bureaucratic offices and quite another to grasp the full range, weight, and power of political and legal institutions on life in the common order. What follows, therefore, is a description of Antigua's political and legal institutions, the larger purpose of which is to acquaint the reader not only with local political arrangements but also with the institutions that shaped, and were shaped by, Caribbean families.

In the seventeenth and eighteenth centuries, Antigua and Barbuda were part of England's "Leeward Charibbee Islands." Initially, the jurisdiction included Antigua, Barbados, St. Kitts, Nevis, Montserrat, Anguilla, and the British Virgin Islands.[10] Executive authority rested in the governor-in-chief or captain general and his assistant, the lieutenant general.[11] In addition to the governor's position, the Leewards shared the offices of surveyor general, receiver general of the Casual Revenue, attorney general, and solicitor general. The executive authority within Antigua was the lieutenant governor; the council president was in charge in his absence.[12]

The power to write law in the Leeward Islands was dispensed at two levels: a General Legislature regulated areas of concern to all of the Leewards, and a bicameral government within each island administered intraisland affairs. Two delegates from each island attended the General Legislature, which convened as business warranted. The Antiguan legislature consisted of an assembly of twenty-five elected representatives and a council of twelve men appointed by the lieutenant governor to advise and assist him. An assembly was elected in Antigua by 1668, the same year that its courts of justice were established. The assembly's laws were in force for two years until they received royal assent or were disallowed.

Like the laws framed by Parliament for its West Indian colonies, the statutes of the General Legislature were mainly concerned with defensive and economic measures. The General Legislature passed bills pertaining to military assistance, rules of war, the organization of militias, terms of trade, coinage, and procedures for establishing separate assemblies in each island (*Laws of Antigua* 1791–04:1–36).[13] In 1705, however, it voted to secure "for each island the right to its own peculiar Laws and legal Customs" and then did not reconvene until 1798, when Great Britain threatened to abolish the slave trade (Microfilm No. 1; *Laws of Antigua* 1864:2–3). In all, the General Legislature passed a total of 36 acts during its lifetime, of which only 5 were in force in Antigua by 1864. In contrast, there were 1,263 bills passed by the Antiguan assembly between 1668 and 1864 (*Laws of Antigua* 1864:preface).

In theory, the reins of political power were held tightly in Britain. Yet despite the presence of the General Legislature and the governor general's power to appoint men of his choosing to office, executive power "was significantly modified by the decentralization which was characteristic of the Leeward Islands government" (Goveia 1965:60). Insularity, competition, and petty jealousies marked the political behavior of the individual Leeward Islands from the beginning (ibid.:53). The General Legislature for all the islands, as we have seen, never enjoyed popularity and met only periodically between 1690 and 1798.

Day-to-day management of each parish fell to the vestry boards, operative as early as 1688. The boards collected taxes, distributed poor relief, constructed and maintained churches, roads, and bridges, and kept records of baptisms, marriages, and deaths (Microfilm No. 1; Goveia 1965:69).[14] Board members were elected from among qualified freeholders but always included the rector of the Anglican church. The vestry boards were another arena in which free men wielded power in Antigua. After slavery was abolished, these boards played a role in the governing of families.

Finally, a multitude of courts and legal officers divided the administration of law and justice. At the end of the seventeenth century, Antigua had a Court of Chancery, a Court of Error and Appeal, a Court of King's Bench and Grand Sessions, a Court of Common Pleas, a Court Ordinary, a Court Merchant, and a Court of Admiralty. After 1784, a Court of King's Bench and Grand Sessions governed the trial of criminal slaves (Microfilm No. 1; Edwards 1819:487; Howard 1827:vol. 1, 394–97; Goveia 1965:62). Itinerant justices of the peace heard complaints between servants and masters and masters and slaves.

The Court of Chancery met intermittently to adjudicate matters pertaining to Crown revenues. At first the governor presided alone, but due to "Great Corruption, Delays, and other Inconveniences by Courts of Chancery being held in this Island by one Person," a bill of 1715 made the governor and five or more of his council eligible to sit as judges for the court (Microfilm No. 1). These same men presided over the Court of Error and Appeal. Their majority decision was binding unless it was overturned by the king in council. The next tier in this judicial hierarchy, the Court of King's Bench and General Sessions, met biannually to hear criminal matters. The lieutenant governor, members of the governor's council, justices of the Court of Common Pleas, barons of exchequer, and justices of the peace sat as judges in criminal cases. Civil cases involving more than one thousand pounds of sugar or tobacco or other property valued at more than six pounds "current money of the island" were heard by the Court of Quarter and Petty Sessions. Courts of Common Pleas met several times a year in the towns of Falmouth and St. John's to try cases involving less than six pounds of property (Microfilm No. 1). Admiralty Courts resolved disputes originating on the high seas, and a Court Merchant decided matters pertaining to transients and intra- and interisland traffic and trade. A court ordinary, attended by the governor alone, granted marriage licenses, probates of wills, and letters of administration (Howard 1827:vol. 1, 393–97).

Another century would pass before Antigua's courts would feel the influence of a professional bar. [15] Left largely to their own devices and unencumbered by the finer points of law that might weigh upon men of letters, the Antiguans freely rejected or ignored legislation passed in Britain after 1632, the date they "received" English statutory law. They clung, however, to certain principles of the common law that encouraged a distinctly creole legal system. These principles included the cherished belief in the right of English men to govern themselves through their own assemblies and in courts of their peers, the crucial adage that "law ought to be adaptive to local conditions," the premise that a judge is bound to rule, first and foremost, in the interests of justice, and the method of *stare decisis* (Blackstone in Morrison 1979:46).

English common law evolves through cases that establish precedent on points of law. Though lower courts generally follow the decisions of higher courts, the law contains within itself the capacity for further development according to perceived changes in the society. The principles of law are construed so as to allow the development of local law in local courts. For example, judges rule according to their interpretation of law as given in the higher courts. However, a judge is also bound to try a case in the interests of "justice," even if in doing so he fails to observe the ruling of a higher court. As Friedman explains for the American case: "In theory, judges drew their decisions from existing principles of law; ultimately these principles reflected the living values, attitudes, and ethical ideas of the English people. In practice, the judges relied on their own past actions, which they modified under the pressure of changing times and changing patterns of litigation" (1973:17).[16]

England's benign neglect of local matters in the Caribbean colonies, the decentralized character of the Leeward Islands' political structure, the tenets and principles of the common law, and the fact that Antigua's legal system functioned in the hands of self-taught lawyers and judges combined to promote an indigenous system of legalities. Of at least equal importance to the developing kinship ideology and organization was the fact that the social characteristics of Caribbean peoples and the plantation economy that dominated their lives differed remarkably from the peoples and the industrializing economy of England.

A Ranking of Men and Women: Local Law and Social Structure

The sparsely populated Leeward Islands encouraged rapid European penetration, which in turn resulted in nearly complete destruction of Indian peoples' precapitalist order. Settlers in Antigua found no indigenous economy to integrate into the world market and no indigenous political or cultural systems to regulate; but neither was there an indigenous work force (Henry 1985:16). The colonists, therefore, hammered out a way to organize labor and time, and the means to secure commodities. They developed methods for production, exchange, and consumption using local material and ideological resources, or those that could be cheaply and easily imported. At first these settlers were explorers, self-interested adventurers, former soldiers from the king's regiments, and farmers. There wasn't a lawyer among them. In the seventeenth century, indentured servants made up a surprisingly large proportion of the population. Later, of course, there were more and more slaves. The slaves, and then a new cast of characters, people of color, had to be constituted legally. As they experimented, lawmakers produced and refined hierarchical categories of persons and amended the criteria for membership within different ranks.

The effect of constant European warfare, meager capital, assaults from the Caribs, and a lack of fresh water left the earliest colonists in a state of "perpetual crisis" (Dunn 1972:118). The Antiguans needed settlers to defend the settlement, clear the land, and plant the crops. To entice "suitable" immigrants, and to encourage wayfaring soldiers and sailors to remain on their shores, lawmakers turned to a conventional tactic: they offered new settlers ten acres of land with freehold status and voting privileges. Each of these "ten-acre men" also gained a barrel of beef, a bag of flour, a three-pound loan (if desired), and a tax exemption for three years. Their land could not be alienated for debt, but if a settler deserted or died without leaving an heir, it could be redistributed (*Laws of Antigua* 1690–1790:128).

Efforts to lure colonists brought a diverse lot to Antigua; the first settlers differed in their national and religious affiliations, economic statuses, and political loyalties. The earliest migrants were mainly English, but after the English Civil War (1642–49) the sources and character of emigration to the West Indies changed. Scotsmen, Irishmen, "a few Royalists of distinguished lineage," political prisoners, felons, and vagabonds found their way to the Leeward Islands (Sheridan 1973:236). The original plantocracy included some men of the professions and members of wealthy families who migrated from Dutch Suriname (ibid.:191–92).

Internal strife between these settlers was common. Indeed, early lawmakers were sometimes caught between the necessity of promoting white solidarity in the face of hostile French, Indians, and slaves and their desire to privilege English, Welsh, and Scottish Anglicans above all other persons. Initially, they attempted to control the white minorities on the island—the "aliens," "papists," and "Jews"—by using law to limit their opportunities for upward mobility, civil rights, and access to authority and power in the common order. Because local laws expired after only two years (Microfilm No. 1), the colonists had considerable freedom to change their minds about different groups as the spirit or some event moved them.[7]

A bill of 1681, for example, extended freehold status to settled "foreigners" but denied them the privilege of holding office. And although foreigners were promised freedom to practice religion "in their owne Severall Languages, according to the Severall Rights and Ceremonies of the Protestant religion used in their owne Countrys" in 1699, they were also required to swear that they believed in the "presence of God, Jesus and the sacrament of the Lord's supper" and not in the mass of the Church of Rome (Microfilm No. 1).

It is not clear how this act affected Jews, but a bill of 1694 already forbade Jewish merchants from trading with slave peddlers and allowed magistrates to try suspected Jews using "any such evidence as the said Justices shall judge sufficient in their own judgments and consciences."[18] "Papists" had even a more difficult time in Antigua; in fact, in 1702 they were all deported.[19] Other "aliens," approved by the governor, were allowed to purchase land, but their number was restricted to "one fourth of the number of English, Scotch, Irish and Criole Subjects." Aliens could not hold high-ranking political, judicial, or military offices, although their children were not so disqualified (Microfilm No. 1). Thus the legal record suggests there was considerable tension among free colonists in the common order.

In addition to farmers, king's soldiers, and fortune hunters, three types of white bondsmen came to Antigua: political prisoners incarcerated in the Civil War and the wars with Scotland and Ireland, other convicts released on condition that they serve as indentured servants in the West Indies, and poor people who agreed to work in return for their passage. The idea that both England and the colonies would benefit if recalcitrants and the indigent were sent overseas was common in England in the sixteenth and seventeenth centuries. It was widely held, for example, that poverty was due to idleness. A British act of 1531 therefore distinguished between persons with obvious disabilities and "sturdy beggars." The latter were to be "tied to the end of a cart naked and . . . beaten till [their bodies] be bloody." After that, they were put to work. Similarly, a 1547 law allowed vagabonds to be branded and enslaved for two years.

Such brutality was not uncommon. In fact, sixteenth-century English law prescribed the death penalty for so many transgressions that juries became loath to convict offenders. In 1617, the Privy Council decided some reform was necessary and announced that henceforth it would be "both humane and expedient" to transport some of the condemned (Richardson 1987:36–37). Recruitment of other indentured laborers proved extremely profitable in England, and when volunteers were scarce recruiters sometimes resorted to illegalities. During the 1660s, many British merchants were prosecuted "for kidnapping and inveigling servants away from the realm" (Beckles 1984:17).[20] There was sufficient abuse to warrant passage of a law in 1670 to punish kidnappers with death without benefit of clergy (Watkins 1924:18).

Indentured servants constituted a middle rank in early creole society. They could not vote, hold office, or regulate the daily conditions of their labor. Nevertheless, local statutes provided for minimum clothing, food, and shelter for them, fixed the terms and duration of their service, and standardized the bounty payable at the expiration of their contracts—if they lived that long (Microfilm No. 1). An act of 1698 suggests the poverty of their circumstances:

> Each Servant, during his servitude . . . shall have, and be allowed, from their Master, or Mistress, six pounds of Fish or Flesh per week, and Bread kind suitable, and shall have one Coat or Jackett, Three Shirts, three pair of Drawers, three pairs of Shoes, one Hatt, two pair of Stockins for each Year, and convenient Lodging during their term, and a Woman Servant proportionable. (Microfilm No. 1)

Persons under age sixteen were indentured for seven years; adults for four years. Laws of 1716 and 1740 reenforced the legal obligations between masters and servants, made provisions for complaints to be investigated by magistrates, and increased the penalties for either masters or servants who disregarded the law (*Laws of Antigua* 1690–1790:319–20).

Indentured servants played an important intermediary role in the early economy and social organization of Antiguan society. We shall find later, for example, that they were subject to their own fornication, bastardy, and marriage laws. By the early decades of the eighteenth century, however, the profits from producing sugarcane on large estates worked by slaves had become apparent and the era of indentured-servant labor waned.[21]

Once the change from tobacco and cotton to sugar occurred, farmers with small properties could not compete with the owners of the large plantations. As profits dwindled, they emigrated to less-populated islands and to North America. Nor was there any reason for an indentured servant to remain in the fields of another once his contract had expired. His gratuity, set in 1716 at four hundred pounds of sugar or tobacco or fifty shillings, a gun, and a cartouch (cartridge) box, enabled him to begin anew in places where cheap land was still available and small farmers and their families were welcomed (Microfilm No. 1). Antiguan planters welcomed instead thousands of slaves. In the new economic order, Britain supplied both African peoples and manufactured goods to the West Indian colonies; the Leewards sent sugar, rum, and molasses to England and the mainland colonies. The central features of the Caribbean economy were now in place: "It was a plantation economy founded on the effective ownership of its resources by metropolitan-based corporate institutions adapted to the overriding purpose of exploiting imported labor and natural resources for metropolitan profit and rationalized in the economic literature of the time in terms of the theory of the mercantilist division of international labor" (Lewis 1983:69).

The Free Minority: Profit and Prosperity, Pathos and Poverty

In 1675 Antigua was reported to have "40,000 acres, 1052 armed men, 100 horses, and 570 negroes" (Oliver 1894:vol. 1, li). Governor Stapleton's 1678 census listed 1,600 English (800 men, 400 women, and 400 children), 610 Irish (360 men, 130 women, 120 children), and 98 Scottish settlers (76 men, 14 women, and 8 children). They owned between them 2,172 slaves: 805 men, 868 women, and 499 children (ibid.:vol. 1, lxi). Fifty-four percent of the colonists' households contained no slaves, 28 percent between 1 and 4 slaves, 7.5 percent 5 to 9 slaves, and less than 6 percent 10 to 19 slaves. Less than 5 percent of the colonists held 20 or more slaves (Wells 1975:223).

Antigua's population changed dramatically in the first half of the eighteenth century: the number of free settlers hardly increased while the slave population tripled. Overall, the island's population grew from 4,480 in 1678 to 34,863 in 1756 (Wells 1975:209). Although British colonists comprised 51.5 percent of Antigua's population in 1678, the percentage of settlers from Britain or other European places fell to 9.9 percent in 1756 and to 6.5 in 1774 (Wells 1975:212; Gaspar 1985a:83). The free white population was only 3,672 in 1720, and it peaked at 5,200 in 1724 (Watkins 1924:19–20; Gaspar 1985a:80).[22] By that time, the island colony also included a small group of free nonwhite persons subjected to a variety of forms of special discrimination prescribed in law.

Despite the small size of their group, constant warfare, and periodic drought, eighteenth-century Antiguan planters reaped unprecedented fortunes. Interestingly, the most successful of these planters were rarely recruits from the English aristocracy; they were men from the professions, mercantile trade, administration, and plantation management (Sheridan 1973:387–88). They built strong kin networks on the island and abroad that enhanced both their wealth and their social life. Sheridan's study of the Antiguan elite between 1730 and 1775, for example, shows "the 65 families who dominated the island had among them 29 local merchants, 27 government officials, 18 doctors and 14 lawyers" (ibid.:377). These men used their influence to gain appointments, which in turn gave them further influence. When Governor Shirley swore in officers in Antigua in 1781 he found that the president of the council was the chief justice, that eight of twenty-four justices of the peace were members of the council, and that eleven of these councilmen also served in the assembly (Goveia 1965:86).

Leeward Island proprietors who could afford to do so eventually abandoned their estates and returned to England to "real" society, leaving their plantations in the hands of estate attorneys, overseers, and bookkeepers. Those who remained in the island shared a style of life that encouraged ostentation in personal habits, dress, and entertainment, and deprecated all labor except for the supervision of slaves. The wealthy free white population of the eighteenth century exercised legal privileges, participated in representational government, accumulated unrestricted amounts of property, and willed that property to their heirs. They were distinguishable from the petty merchants, clerks, bookkeepers, overseers, and artisans who could vote and serve as jurors but who were unlikely to have been elected or appointed to office (Goveia 1965:85, 203–17; Watkins 1924:19; Sheridan 1973:388).

Differences in the life-styles between wealthy and poor whites, including indentured servants, were dramatic materially and socially. The disparity between rich and poor was evident in the practices of the common order, the daily activities of work and play, and the events that marked the seasonal and social calendars. Yet the possibility and the example of upward social and economic mobility existed for the free poor. The small size of the white population and their overwhelming fear of the black majority increasingly made color an important status marker. This feature of West Indian social organization promoted acceptance of "commoners" in the company of better men—and some unusually liberal gatherings by English standards of the time (Flannagan 1967:vol. 1, 212 and vol. 2, 193–200; Goveia 1965:201–6).

The composition of the households of free persons in St. John's was also decidedly different from that of typical English households (Laslett 1965:1–21; Wells 1975:329; Macfarlane 1986:79–102).[23] A "List of the Inhabitants of the Island of Antigua" prepared by the governor-in-chief in 1753 describes the "familys"[24] in the town of St. John's and the surrounding parishes. Each "family" is identified by the name of a man or a woman followed by the number of men, women, boys, and girls in the household. As Table 1 shows, of 701 families listed for St. John's, 240, or 34 percent, were female headed.[25]

A remarkable number of women fended for themselves in Antigua in 1753. More than 50 percent of the female-headed households in St. John's consisted of a woman living alone, and another 28 percent included women with children. Unfortunately, the relationship of the female head of household to the other adults and children listed as part of their "familys" remains unknown. They may have been grown sons or daughters, other relatives, or servants. A second characteristic of these female-headed groups was their small size. Of households with children, 63 percent contained only one child, 21 percent two children, and 4 percent three. Only 11 percent of these households included more than three children. Indeed, children always comprised a rather small proportion of Antigua's white population, only 27 percent in 1756 (Wells 1975:215).

Small female-headed households were "normal" in the sense that they were commonplace in mid-eighteenth century St. John's, as they were elsewhere in the Leeward Islands (cf. Wells 1975:225, 317). Who these women were and how they earned their livelihoods is obscured by the paucity of the historical record. No doubt some were former indentured servants left on their own after completing a period of servitude. Others may have been recent immigrants who supported themselves by domestic work or petty trading. Goveia mentions, for example, that by the end of the century there were "poor whites of low status in the towns of the islands, who were chiefly engaged in the huckstering and victualling trades"—occupations often performed by women in the Caribbean (1965:210).[26] In 1790, one observer, Dr. Adair, reported that "the women of this class were of light virtue and the men mostly petty thieves" (ibid.:210), suggesting some were prostitutes. Others may have been mistresses of married men.

Many female household heads were also poor, although they might own slaves. A statute passed two years after the 1753 household census is An Act For . . . The Ease And Relief Of Many Poor And Indigent Women, Who Have Large Families, And Whose Sole Support Depends On A Few Slaves Only. The law gave women a special dispensation exempting them from certain taxes if they owned fewer than ten slaves upon whom they depended for their livelihoods (*Laws of Antigua* 1690–1790:323). A similar situation evolved in

TABLE 1   Female-Headed "Familys" of Free Settlers in St. John's, 1753

Composition of Family	Number of Families	Percentage of Families
One woman only	122	51
One woman and children	67	28
One woman and one man	2	1
One woman, children, and man or men	2	1
One woman and two men	2	1
Two women	15	6
Two women and children	15	6
Two women and one man	3	1
Two women, children, and man or men	1	0
Three women	3	1
Three women and children	4	2
Four women	1	0
No information	3	1
Total	240	99

SOURCE: Adapted from Oliver 1894–99:vol. 1, cix–cxiii. Percentages do not add up to 100 percent because figures have been rounded off.

Barbados, where 27 percent of households were headed by women as early as 1715 (Wells 1975:248). Magistrate Colthurst noted the poverty of these women in Barbados and St. Vincent immediately after emancipation; those who had relied upon the earnings of a few slaves were left completely indigent when those slaves were freed (Marshall 1977:211–16).

Life in the common order yielded a significant number of women who headed their own households. It generated as well a new category of persons whom legislators situated legally: free people of color. Initially they included women and their racially mixed children, slaves freed by their masters or by acts of assembly in reward for special deeds, and Carib or Arawak Indians. The entire group consisted of only a few hundred people in Antigua at the end of the eighteenth century; a total of twenty-five hundred to three thousand persons in all of the Leeward Islands. Later, the Indians disappeared almost completely, and free persons of mixed descent became distinguished in the community and in law as a distinct social enclave.

Free people of color were subjected to discriminatory laws that limited their mobility and economic security and excluded them from public office and juries. In 1702, for example, all free mulattoes, blacks, and Indians who did not own land in Antigua were required to attach themselves to white patrons, to "be owned by them, and with whom they shall live, and take their Abode, to the Intent that their Lives and Conversations may be known, to be called to their respective Duties." Those who were fit were bound as apprentices for seven years. Their patrons were legally responsible for their conduct and employment. The same law noted that any nonwhite person striking a white servant was to be severely whipped (Microfilm No. 1). As Gaspar remarks: "The change of wording from *white person* to *white servant* indicated a trend toward a refining of distinctions between social groups, towards a finer tuning of class and race relations" (1985a:165).

Lawmakers used statutes to protect employment opportunities and supervisory and managerial jobs for white men and to prevent the free colored population from achieving social mobility. Statutes requiring a fixed proportion of white persons in relation to black slaves on the plantations hindered free nonwhite men from finding employment on estates.[27] Most preferred to live and work in the towns (Goveia 1965:228). Yet within the towns, people of color could not obtain credit to operate commercial enterprises. Throughout the eighteenth century, they could not sit as jurors or prosecute or give evidence against whites (Goveia 1965:218–19). Slave ownership provided one of few opportunities for them to earn a living and to improve their social standing. Nevertheless, free persons of color in Antigua were permitted to own land and they voted in elections if they succeeded in attaining the necessary qualifications—even though no statute specifically gave them that right until 1822 (ibid.:218).

Relatively few slaves were freed in Antigua: there were only 18 such persons in 1707 (12,892 slaves and 2,892 whites), 1,230 in 1787 (37,808 "Negroes" and 2,590 "whites"), and 3,895 in 1821 (30,985 "Negroes," 4,066 "coloured," and 1,980 "whites") (based on Gaspar 1985a:162; Flannagan 1967:vol. 2, 284). Freed blacks were forbidden to hold more than eight acres in property—a provision that prevented them from becoming freeholders and their children from inheriting significant property. Client-patron relations between free persons of color and freedmen evolved partly as a result of special legislation that supported such relationships and partly as a result of societywide consciousness of racial identity that linked people of color to slaves (Gaspar 1985a:49). The Antiguan custom of differentiating free Negroes from freedmen of mixed ancestry, however, "may have contributed to a lack of cohesiveness among freedmen and greater effectiveness of the forces of control" (Gaspar 1985b:141).

At the end of the eighteenth century, then, free Antiguans were a numerically small but diverse group. Free people differed in their country of origin, religious preference, ethnic affiliation, color, occupation, kind and amount of property, and the composition of their households. And most of these ascribed and achieved characteristics not only mediated and structured everyday interactions in the common order but also were reified in law and imbued with legal meaning and consequences.

Bondage and the Rule of Law

Historians do not agree on the sources for the first slave codes in the English-speaking Caribbean: Dunn believes they were developed in piecemeal fashion as slaves behaved objectionably (1972:228), whereas Long (1970: vol. 2, 493–96), Bridges (in E. Brathwaite 1971:119), and Mintz (1974:70–72) suggest sixteenth-century villeinage laws against vagabonds served as a template.[28] The English would have been aware of an already operative Spanish model, but there were crucial differences between the Spanish and English conceptions of slavery and their corresponding notions of how a slave colony was to be governed.[29] Acceptance of slavery in England was based on opinion—not law. Lord Mansfield's decision in 1722 to free the slave Somersett, who had accompanied his master to England and then subsequently refused to serve him, verified that there were no laws in England upholding slavery. The case of the Antiguan slave Grace, tried in 1827, confirmed the Somersett decision but also provided that if a former slave living as a free person in England voluntarily returned to the place where he or she had formerly been enslaved, the individual automatically reassumed slave status (Goveia 1965:155 n. 1).

The first evidence of the legality of slavery in the British West Indies appears in a 1636 bill from Barbados that ordered: "Negroes and Indians, that came here to be sold, should serve for Life, unless a Contract was before made to the contrary" (Sheridan 1973:236; Dunn 1972:228). By 1661, Barbadians had fashioned the Comprehensive Slave Code in which slaves were described as "heathenish," "brutish," and a "dangerous kinde of people" whose wicked instincts had to be suppressed (Dunn 1972:239; Beckles 1984:21). This Barbadian code seems to have served as the model for the slave codes of other colonies, although each of the British-settled islands and colonies on the mainland devised its own set of laws to enforce slavery.[30]

Slaves were property, albeit a special kind of property requiring a specialized set of rules. When they arrived in Antigua they were treated as merchandise. After their sale, they were reclassified legally as freehold property that could not be parted from an estate (Microfilm No. 1). Except in Nevis, Leeward Island slaves were chattels only in cases of debt and when other assets were unavailable (Goveia 1965:152–53).[31]

Gaspar estimates that 60,820 slaves were imported to Antigua between 1671 and 1763 (1985a:75). Slaves accounted for 41.6 percent of the population in 1672, 80.5 percent in 1711, and 93.5 in 1774 (ibid.:83). Dunn's study of records from St. Mary's parish points to the dramatic increase of slave holdings by large planters by the third quarter of the eighteenth century:

> In 1688 the biggest planter in St. Mary owned 73 slaves; eighteen years later, four planters held over 100 slaves. . . . By 1767 every taxpayer in St. Mary was a slave owner; a third of the taxpayers were very large sugar planters; the planters held an average of 86 Negroes each and one slave for every two acres—the Barbados ratio of 1680. (1972:142–143)

Of Britain's mainland American colonies, only South Carolina would approach such unusually high ratios of slaves to free persons.[32]

How was this multitude of living property to be governed? As Jordan suggests, the slave codes were directed first at the obligations of whites to maintain slavery and only secondarily at the activities of the slaves themselves (1968:108–9).[33] Nevertheless, the laws systematized a regime of organized violence and oppression that engaged masters and slaves in ongoing political, ideological, and oftentimes physical struggles over rights, responsibilities, and access to the predominant values and institutions of colonial society. Masters' strategies for disempowering slaves included controlling them: (1) temporally—by day and night, according to the seasons, by the time allotted to different tasks, by making Sunday a day for labor outside the sugar fields, by granting certain hours for the Negro market; (2) spatially—by separating the slave quarters, overseeing the construction of slaves' houses, fencing or walling those quarters, demarcating land for subsistence gardens; (3) economically—according to function (field slave, house domestic, boiler, etc.); and (4) by forbidding some of the most ordinary practices of everyday life—coming and going, caring for children, chatting, defending oneself against aggression.[34]

The earliest slave laws, for example, made it illegal for slaves to leave their estates without permission and outlawed assemblages, drinking, theft, and possession of weapons. Other provisions set penalties for harboring slaves or refusing to return them to their masters. Over time, the assembly supplemented police measures with economic restrictions, some designed to protect the markets of white settlers with small holdings (Goveia 1965:152–202). For example, slaves could not sell sugar, cotton, rum, molasses, or ginger without written permission. Salt beef, bread, and biscuit were restricted to the Negro market (ibid.:161–62). The slave codes excluded bondsmen from accumulating more than a little property, effectively cutting off the primary route to social mobility beyond the slave quarters, although not necessarily, of course, within those quarters.

Few laws protected slaves in the Leeward Islands until the end of the eighteenth century. A 1723 bill made it illegal to willfully kill, mutilate, or dismember a slave. Manumitting old or disabled persons who could not care for themselves was outlawed after 1757 (Goveia 1965:191; Gaspar 1985a:160). The Amelioration Act of 1798 was the first comprehensive act to consolidate and reregulate the conditions of slaves' labor and their more general living conditions. The act limited working hours from 5:00 A.M. to 7:00 P.M. except in crop time or under special circumstances, and stipulated compulsory clothing allowances, minimum rations, medical care, and holidays (Goveia 1965:191–97). As we shall see in Chapter 3, the Amelioration Act was significant beyond its function to shield slaves from abuse, for it brought the state into the family lives of slaves in a fundamentally new way, "protecting" certain forms of familial organization, dissuading others, invading what were previously private matters, and more formally incorporating slaves into the wider discourse and practice of creole kinship.

Two major and obvious weaknesses of these protective measures were the difficulty of proving a case when slave evidence alone could not bring about a conviction and the problem of enforcing the laws (Goveia 1965:197). Slaves were often punished in the privacy of their masters' quarters, making checks on owners' behavior difficult. On the other hand, some masters preferred to make public spectacles of slaves who committed offenses. Mary Prince, a Bermudan slave who lived in Antigua around 1800 spent a night in "the cage" in St. John's and was then flogged by a civil official for quarreling with another slave about a pig (Ferguson 1987:13). What is important to our argument is that Prince's experience, however unhappy, is still a sign of the gradual incorporation of slaves into the island's broader system of criminal and civil justice.

Mary Prince's autobiography is a saga of an intelligent slave woman's travail in several West Indian islands, in salt mines and domestic posts (Ferguson 1987). Although Antiguan slaves worked as domestics, craftsmen, overseers, boilers, barrel makers, shopkeepers, distillers, hawkers, peddlers, sailors, and wet and dry nurses, the vast majority labored on sugar estates (*A Genuine Narrative* 1972:4–5; Goveia 1965:83). An inventory from Parham Plantation for the year 1737, for example, shows that its 202 slaves (76 men, 70 women, and 56 children) were mostly confined to working in the canes. Among the men, 3 slaves served as drivers, 1 as a doctor, 4 as coopers, 5 as carpenters, and 3 as masons. Only 7 women escaped field labor: 3 cooks, 2 domestics, 1 seamstress, and 1 nurse (Gaspar 1985a:105). Betty's Hope plantation, one of the largest estates in Antigua and now undergoing archaeological excavation,[35] included 277 slaves in 1751, "the core of which consisted of 98 slaves, 39 men and 59 women." Almost 53 percent of its total labor force toiled in the field gangs (ibid.:105–7). As was true in Jamaica and Barbados, slave men in Antigua were more likely than women to hold nonagricultural and less arduous positions within the plantation community (Higman 1984b:188–99; Reddock 1988).

Field slaves were organized into gangs to perform the laborious, yearlong tasks that comprised the routines of planting, harvesting, and converting raw cane into sugar, molasses, and rum.[36] The conditions of life were brutal, the mortality rate extremely high, and fertility low. Sheridan computed the annual percentage decline in the Leeward slave population at 4.4 percent for 1701–25 and 4.8 percent for 1716–50 (cited in Gaspar 1985a:75). The exceptionally high mortality rates of West Indian slaves were the result of poor diet, malnutrition, overwork, infertility, rampant infant death, disease, inept medical treatment, and age (Craton 1978:85–133; Higman 1984b:317–48).

Although their choices were conditioned by different constraints and practicalities, Antiguan slaves, like the free settlers, adopted alternative household arrangements. Masters, of course, differed in the degree of autonomy they granted to slaves with respect to household composition. Nevertheless, some slaves lived alone, some with a conjugal mate, others with children and a partner, and some with their children but no adult partner (e.g., Beckles 1989; Bush 1990; Craton 1978; Higman 1976, 1984b; Morrissey 1989; R. Smith 1987, 1988). Some Antiguan planters housed slave families in barracks (see Chapter 6).

Another consideration influencing household composition was the slaves' own mode of production. Antiguan planters relied heavily on imported food and diverted proportionately less land on their estates to provision grounds for the slaves than did their counterparts in Jamaica. Nevertheless, on a smaller scale, Antiguan slaves replicated the pattern common elsewhere in the Caribbean. Slaves provided the subsistence crops, utilitarian items, and services upon which the internal economy of the island depended. They fed the townsfolk and fashioned their own consumer market (Mintz 1974).[37] According to one report from Antigua, every slave, male or female, was from the age of fourteen or fifteen apportioned a plot (Luffman 1789:94, 95). Slaves worked for themselves on Sundays and carried their produce to market twice a week (Andrews and Andrews 1934:88; Gaspar 1985a:146). When some ambitious slaves began using rural lands that had been set aside for the poor, their masters tried to abort their enterprises by redistributing the property (Spooner in Goveia 1965:198–99).

Town slaves benefitted from less arduous labor, greater freedom in their personal lives, and more frequent opportunities to work for themselves. They were hired out by their masters as porters, jobbers, messengers, domestic helpers, and washerwomen (Goveia 1965:230; Higman 1984b:226–59). Town slaves had much less opportunity to establish coresidential unions than their rural counterparts (Higman 1984b:373). Sometimes they did manage to tuck away personal savings. One slave on trial for conspiracy in 1736, for example, had "much more Money than Slaves are usually Masters of," and another "was also very kindly used by his Master, being admitted for his own Advantage to take Negroe Apprentices, and to make all the Profits he could of his own, and their Labour, paying his Master only a monthly Sum, far short of his usual Earnings; so that he too was generally Master of Much Money" (*A Genuine Narrative* 1972:4). As we see in Chapter 2, these findings greatly upset those colonists who presided over a special court to try slaves who had planned to take over the island.

Conclusions

Strong economic and political ties between Antigua and Great Britain, as well as continuity between their legal cultures, grew out of the exigencies of colonization and mercantilism. The first settlers needed capital investments, labor, a defense force, and guidelines for constructing an administrative order in the wilderness. Britain responded with money, men, arms, and law. The British, however, cared chiefly about exploiting the land and its resources and less for rules for governing the day-to-day activities of life in the common order.

The decentralized structure of political institutions between the settlements comprising the Leeward Islands, and within Antigua, fostered an independence of mind and action and encouraged local variation in law (cf. Goveia 1965; D.

Hall 1971). Within the first hundred years, a hierarchy of governors, councils, assemblies, vestry boards, civil and criminal courts, and itinerant justices of the peace defined and protected systems of legalities across and within each of the Leewards. This hierarchy of offices, like the emerging social hierarchy, promulgated indigenous customs and practices. "Government" was increasingly creole in its content, processes, and institutions.

Antigua's social organization evolved in conjunction with legal rules that encouraged production, controlled property and labor, supported immigration, and defined and regulated different ranks of persons. This chapter demonstrated how early Antiguan legislators wielded law as an instrument of class relations. Statutes and historical accounts reveal the evolution and legitimation of a society in which individuals were divided into three broad ranks—free persons, servants, and slaves—corresponding to their positions in the division of labor.

Nevertheless, the eighteenth-century population was diverse for its size. There were planters and ten-acre men, officials of the Crown, self-employed artisans, well-to-do merchants, shopkeepers, managers and overseers of estates, indentured servants, respectable married women, prostitutes, troublesome soldiers, transient poor folk, and slaves from Africa who spoke various languages and understood vastly different ways of living. Property and position made the man, but nationality, religion, family connection, office, and color also counted towards one's standing in the common order. Many of these ascribed and achieved characteristics were reified in Antiguan law and laden with juridical implications and consequences.

The diversity that characterized the people of the common order was mirrored in their homes. The households of the colonists in St. John's (Antigua), Bridgetown (Barbados), and Port Royal (Jamaica) were similar in their small size and in the complexity of their membership (Dunn 1972:106–10; R. Smith 1988:152–53; Wells 1975:208–34). They did not correspond to the "nuclear" and "neolocal" households of sixteenth- and seventeenth-century England (Laslett 1965:1–21; Macfarlane 1986:96–102), nor did they duplicate the stable, extended family households of New England (Dunn 1972:301; Greven 1973:92–106). Moreover, although today many West Indians believe the high rate of female-headed households in the Caribbean is the consequence of the slaves' inability to maintain nuclear families, we know now that it was "normal" for free white women to head households long before the end of slavery. Today 32 percent of all West Indian households are female headed, (cf. Massiah 1982:70), a number that nearly replicates that found among the free settlers of eighteenth-century St. John's. Diversity in household headship and structure was also characteristic of Antiguan slaves, whose living places were shaped by such factors as their sale to estates or small farms, to life in the country or life in an urban place. Some masters granted slaves some autonomy in their place of abode; others were more controlling.

Much of the evolution of the social structure we have traced reflected the evolution of the island's mode of production. The local Antiguan elite effectively directed the transition from small farming to a routinized plantation economy. An oligarchy framed the law, controlled politics, and manipulated the formal economy of the island. Astute politicians, the planters passed laws to control the work force by instituting regulatory systems for surveillance, codifying "unacceptable" behavior, exercising extraordinary discipline, meting out brutal physical punishments, and designing a specially created architecture for production (cf. Foucault 1979:172–76) that turned fields into grids in which slaves worked the lines.

The whole of this social and economic architecture, nevertheless, was engineered by colonists who believed fundamentally that relations between men, and the actions they take with respect to their property, must conform to some legal order. In 1736, slaves tested and learned exactly how deep seated were those convictions.

2

Legal Sensibilities
in the Common Order:
Revolution and Rights at Court

"POLITICS," DARNTON reminds us, can not "take place without the pre-liminary mental ordering that goes into the common-sense notion of the real world" (1984:23). For the early Antiguan colonists, a social order rooted in law was natural, fundamental to real politik. The system of legalities in Antigua needed no rationale for the settlers; it was hegemonic, fundamental to life in the common order. As we have seen, a great deal of the colonists' time was devoted to writing law and calling courts into session. A good deal of land, and money too, was set aside to provide for the proper processing and functioning of legal matters. The prospering town of St. John's, for example, had two promi-nent and architecturally significant buildings in 1750: the cathedral and the courthouse.[1]

This chapter begins with the 1736 slave conspiracy that challenged the substance and procedures of Antigua's law and tested the colonists' commit-ment to legalities. I examine in some detail the events that preceded the plot, its planning and preparation, and the slaves' proposal for an alternative government. I then consider the colonists' reactions to this blatant defiance of their rule.

The conspiracy engaged Antiguans in a fresh round of legalities; it also exposed temporarily a hidden world of illegalities in which power and leader-ship were differently constituted. In section 2, therefore, we balance the discussion of the enabling and constraining power of colonial law with the might and limits of obeah, an illegal body of knowledge and set of rites used by slaves. Social scientists and historians most often describe obeah as African-derived magic or religion, the counterpart to Western-based Christianity.

I argue that such characterization is too limiting conceptually and present an alternative framework. Obeah defies neat categorization as "religion," "magic," "medicine," or "social control," even if it sometimes commands spirits, uses wondrous tricks, heals, or inculcates principles of justice that condition socio-political action. Historically, it shares with other practices, including slave "marriages," the fact that it is forbidden, punished, denied—and undeniably resistant to the status quo. To allow obeah the full range of its knowledge and practice while attending to its structural features and capacity to mediate social action, I include obeah within a broader system of Caribbean illegalities whose component parts, processes, and relations to legalities defy neat characterization. Obeah took on a "*whole new meaning* in the societies of the Caribbean, a meaning derived from the power structures, the social oppositions, in these societies" (Bolland 1992b:69).

In section 3, we return to consideration of the judicial system evolving in the Antiguan common order, and especially to the changing composition of the courts' litigants. Readers will by now anticipate the colonists' continuing commitment to legalities. Remarkably, however, by the early nineteenth century we find the most disenfranchised people in the Leeward Islands participating actively in the legal system and claiming in court whatever rights the law allowed them. This evidence upsets the conventional view that Caribbean courts were not only corrupt but also mostly irrelevant to free persons of color and slaves. It suggests a more important role for law in intra- and interclass politics than has previously been recognized.[2] In fact, in the century following the conspiracy of 1736, certain ideas about courts, laws, and justice spread slowly across the ranks of creole society until they were as natural as the idea that individuals should be ranked into social groups.

Attempting Revolution

Several factors immediately preceding the 1736 slave revolt, the most complicated, ambitious, and widely supported conspiracy in Antigua's history, explain its timing and near success. The plot, slave leaders' use of alternative sources of power, and the events that transpired afterward exemplify especially creole social construction and the evolution of legal sensibilities in the common order.

Drought, insect infestations, and a depression in the British sugar market in the early 1730s worsened living conditions for the slaves. Estate records show an increase in the number of runaways and in the incidence of crime committed along the highways.[3] Between 1730 and 1735, forty-six fugitives were killed in flight or later executed. Slaves openly defied codes designed to prevent their communication and mobility, and patrols failed to enforce those laws. Meanwhile, in St. John's effective slave leaders emerged who were able to fuse a coalition between Antiguan-born slaves, acquainted with the island and its inhabitants, and recently arrived slaves, many of whom were of "Coromantee"[4] background (Craton 1980:6–8, 1982:118–20; Gaspar 1985a:221–22, 237).

The slaves planned their attack for 11 October, the night of a ball at the home of Christopher Dunbar in St. John's to honor the anniversary of the king's coronation. Tomboy, a slave carpenter and leader, planned to hide gunpowder in the house while working there making chairs for the event. The gunpowder was to be fired at the height of the festivities, leaving the gentry wounded and confused and serving as the signal for battalions of waiting slaves to descend upon the town. The slaves also planned to capture St. John's Fort and the fort at Monk's Hill, and to dispatch men through the countryside (Gaspar 1985a:4–5).

Due to the sudden death of the governor's son, however, the ball was postponed until 30 October. The conspirators' scheme was discovered in the interim, "mainly owing to the curiosity and later investigations of Robert Arbuthnot, one of the justices of the peace for St. John's town" (ibid.:13). An acute observer of the slaves in his district, Arbuthnot became concerned about their growing insolence. He therefore began a private investigation that eventually uncovered the plans for the islandwide slave revolt.

Gaspar claims that the 1736 slave conspiracy originated among the Coromantee minority because of their status as elders in the slave community and that its near success can be explained by the solidarity of Antiguan-born and African-born slaves, many of whom shared Coromantee background (1985a:216–17, 234, 236–54).[5] He argues, in contrast to Craton (1980:8, 1982:124), that the coalition of Akan-speaking and Antiguan-born slaves should be seen as "the fusion of two social groups of different status within the slave communities" rather than as a "triumph over divisive ethnic differences" (1985a:237). To buttress these points, he posits the development of a "Coromantee culture" in Antigua that included African "survivals," such as respect for elders, the use of magic, dances, and several religious rites.

Neither the solidarity of certain slave groups nor African survivals, however, fully explains the events of 1736. The conspiracy demonstrates that by the early eighteenth century, Antiguan slaves possessed a creole political/legal sensibility capable of prosecuting a revolution. This awareness included practical knowledge about the extent to which the existing legal codes could be circumvented, a desire for freedom, a charter for a different social order (which, according to some slave informants, included slavery), and a plan that redirected individual acts of resistance into a united force. The rebels recruited their followers through friendship and kin ties. They ritually crowned a king, their leader "Court," (alias "Tackey"), and devised plans for a new government (Craton 1980:120; Gaspar 1985a:4, 216–18). Moreover, and the point is critical to our understanding of the process of creolization, the slave leaders appropriated power through knowledge and practice of obeah in forms that were sometimes invisible or unintelligible to the colonists.

For example, the rebel leaders' *Ikem* dance, a dance performed by an Ashanti king before he goes to war, was described by the unsuspecting colonists as picturesque entertainment (Craton 1980:7–8, 1982:123). The conspirators also ate and drank special potions and swore oaths without attracting special attention. And yet these oaths

> administered in at least seven different places in the island, were sealed with a draft of rum mixed with grave dirt and cocks' blood, and included pledges to kill all whites, to follow the leaders without question, to stand by fellow slaves, and to observe secrecy on pain of death. . . . In some cases the oath was made with the hand on a live cockerel, and in one case the leader Secundi "called to his Assistance, a Negro Obiaman, or Wizard, who acted his Part before a great number of slaves." (Craton 1980:7, 1982:122–23).

Obeah and its practitioners played a pivotal role in the design and near implementation of the Antiguan slave conspiracy, as it did in slave revolts in Barbados (e.g., Beckles 1984) and Jamaica (Craton 1982; Price 1973). We shall explore obeah in greater depth in the next section. For the moment, however, the point of central interest is that by 1736 life in the Antiguan common order, the order of day-to-day activities and commonsense knowledge, had generated a politics of resistance among slaves nurtured in the domain of illegalities and using illegal practices. Antiguan slaves found in obeah strength, charismatic leadership, and direction for revolution. Until the coup was discovered, however, the colonists misunderstood these activities and misinterpreted them as "superstition" and "magic." Let us examine how the colonists reacted to the news that their property intended to revolt.

Their reaction was distinctly creole: it combined a sense of the "just" with the practical exigencies required to maintain a slave society. The colonists did not simply round up and execute the slaves they believed were involved in the conspiracy—they held court. Evidence had to be produced to explain the subsequent execution of forty-seven slaves and the banishment of forty-three others (*A Genuine Narrative* 1972:5). The colonists took pains in their report to the governor to justify any departure from the substance or procedure of the law on the basis of the special conditions that obtained. They had had to try the criminals privately and exclude all white persons from the trials, they explained, because public trials were too time consuming, civilians asked too many questions, masters tended to excuse the machinations of their own slaves, and open testimony alerted possible conspirators. Members of the court justified the testimony of enslaved persons convicted of treason, another departure from English tradition, by the argument: "A Slave is not a Person known by the Law of England, and in the Eye of our Law, is the same Person after Conviction as before" (ibid.:19).

The colonists intended to restore order according to just procedure, although they were not above trying to alter procedure to effect order. In the aftermath of the conspiracy, they passed a bill to try black freedmen using the testimony of slaves—an act that greatly troubled the English Board of Trade. The board decided to disallow the statute. The freedmen escaped on a technical point of law because the English feared that allowing the testimony of slaves to convict free men would establish a dangerous precedent throughout the colonies (Gaspar 1985a:43–62, 1985b:142).[6] It was one of the few occasions in which the British directly interfered with local events in Antigua. Yet it was also one of a growing number of instances in which the law protected free persons of color.

The colonists' decision to bring the rebellious slaves to trial had compelling and long-term ideological and political consequences. More than two months of torture, trial, and execution (Gaspar 1985a:28) joined masters and slaves in the practical experience of law, revealing to both groups law's enabling and constraining force. Undoubtedly, slaves and masters emerged from this experience with some different conclusions. If the colonists, for example, could congratulate themselves on their civil approach to handling a potential disaster, they were also reminded of the power of the Crown to disallow their actions. Slaves, on the other hand, lost their kin and friends to law's violence but discovered masters consistently devoted to legalities and judges capable of great discretionary power. One result was that law sometimes protected or gave liberty to free people of color or slaves. In section 3 we shall find that members of both groups turned increasingly to the courts to resist injustice, especially after armed resistance seemed impossible. Caribbean slaves came to understand quite well the paradoxical character of law as power, order, justice, and punishment. But they also had recourse to obeah.

Obeah

Creolization entailed the creation of legalities through the historical transformation of law and judicial processes under the conditions of plantation slavery. Simultaneously, creolization encouraged opposition to law and the formation of a system of illegalities. The creole characterization of Caribbean legal sensibilities is found in its capacity to incorporate both formal law and obeah.

In Antigua, as elsewhere in the Caribbean, obeah was used by slaves to poison,[7] to prevent crops from growing, to inhibit conception, to cause abortion, to wage psychological warfare, and to effect retribution (Flannagan 1967; Bell 1889; Anon. 1903; J. Williams 1932). The earliest travelers and local historians declared it was "sorcery" and "mere" superstition, even though some authors expressed fears about its potential power to incite rebellion (e.g., Anon 1903; Bell 1889; Flannagan 1844; Williams 1932).

Throughout the islands, colonists tried repeatedly to suppress obeah. A slave convicted of feigning supernatural power with the intention of promoting rebellion, for example, faced death in the British West Indies in the eighteenth century (Goveia 1970:23). An Antiguan act of 1809 set penalties for "Persons pretending to exercise Witchcraft, Fortune-telling, or by Crafty Science to discover Stolen Goods." If convicted under this act, an offender faced a year in prison and a public appearance in the town pillory once every quarter (*Laws of Antigua* 1804–17). Attempts to eradicate obeah continued after emancipation.

What were the colonists condemning so vehemently? The great complexity of obeah's belief system and rites can be gleaned from descriptions by late-eighteenth-century observers:

> Obeahmen filled calabashes or gourds with items such as "bits of red rag, cats teeth, parrot feathers, eggshells, and fish bones." . . . and these "obi" were buried at the doors of houses to harm the inhabitants or hung on trees in provision grounds to prevent theft. They made potions and charms to influence an overseer or a loved one, and took people's shadows so they would waste and die. They administered herbs, retrieved lost shadows, and extracted objects such as glass bottles, snakes, and other reptiles from the skin to heal the sick. The obeah man was a powerful, feared, and respected figure in slave communities. (Long in Wedenoja 1988:98)

> The Obeah Man is constantly appealed to . . . not only "for the cure of disorders, obtaining revenge for injuries, the conciliation of favor," but also for "the discovery and punishment of the thief and adulterer and the prediction of future events." (Edwards in Beckwith 1929:125)

> Slaves were "addicted to witchcraft" and in great awe of their "necromancers and conjurers of both sexes." Such men and women were "very artful" and had "a great ascendancy over other negroes." (Atwood in Bush 1990:76)

> Obeah . . . was said to have enabled Tacky, the leader of a revolt in 1760, to "catch the bullets of the soldiers and throw them back." . . . Obeahmen rubbed the bodies of Tacky's followers with a powder to make them invulnerable, and they administered a sacred oath and had the rebels mix their blood with gunpowder and grave dirt and drink it to ensure their secrecy, commitment, and solidarity. (Gardner and Long in Wedenoja 1988:99)

Obeah is defined in Cassidy's modern *Dictionary of Jamaican English* as "the practice of malignant magic" (1980:326). Most social scientists, including two who have written on Antigua,[8] describe obeah as an African-based form of religiosity—the counterpart to European Christianity. Following Herskovits's early direction, anthropologists attempted to trace obeah to specific African tribes and to examine how its rites changed in the New World, a methodology still widely used (cf. Dobbin 1986; Goveia 1965; Henry 1985; Herskovits 1937, 1958, 1966; Morrish 1982; Simpson 1976, 1978; Wedenoja 1988). Other observers have investigated obeah as folklore (Beckwith 1929; Hedrick and Stephens 1977; Robinson 1893), as a set of rites bearing some resemblance to the scientific method (Hogg 1961), as a psychological phenomenon associated with maladjustment and status frustration (M. Smith 1965) or poverty and racial discrimination (Gussler 1980; Henriques 1953; Sereno 1948), and as a medical/curative complex (Higman 1984b:271–72; Morrissey 1989; Trotman 1986). Several historians have described obeah's pivotal role in master-slave relationships and in fomenting slave rebellions (e.g., Brathwaite 1971; Bush 1990; Gaspar 1985; Patterson 1973; Schuler 1979, 1980; Wedenoja 1988). Other scholars, including Fischer (1974a, 1974b), R. Smith (1976), and Austin-Broos (1987), have noted obeah's role in the formation and creolization of West Indian religion and in conjunction with evolving class relations.

My analysis refines earlier theoretical insights first elaborated by structural-functional anthropologists working in Africa (e.g., Evans-Pritchard 1976; Middleton and Winter 1963; Nadel 1952; Wilson 1951) and Caribbeanists who advanced the critical proposition that obeah serves as a technique of social control and as a mechanism for mediating claims to status (Fischer 1974a, 1974b; Foner 1973; Patterson 1967; Reisman 1964; R. Smith 1956, 1976). This perspective is adopted by Patterson, for example, in his sustained examination of obeah among Jamaican slaves (1967:183–95).

Aware that obeah had diverse functions in the slave quarters, Patterson nevertheless misses its importance as a shared ideology of justice, power, and government. He mentions, for example, that obeah was used "in preventing, detecting and punishing crimes among the slaves," but it is unclear why he regards these as the "individual" as opposed to the "social" functions of obeah (1967:190). In my estimation, each of these activities implies communal consensus about the nature of illicit behavior and effective retribution. Patterson did not heed the significance of the fact, recorded by several West Indian historians, that ordinary slaves, not just obeah specialists, regularly employed obeah ordeals to try cases (ibid.:191). His analysis also reduces women's participation in obeah to the mixing of love potions for purposes of seduction (ibid.:189–90).

Since Patterson's analysis, regional specialists have paid greater attention to the ways in which obeah functioned in resistance to slavery and also to its capacity to generate other forms of domination. Higman (1984) mentions obeah's role in conflicts within the slave community, as well as between slaves and masters, in the context of investigating slave kin terminology. Trotman (1986) develops the point in an adroit discussion of the legal oppression of obeah men in postemancipation Trinidad.[9] Bush finds obeah "associated with a wide spectrum of subversive practices" and observes: "Even after Christianity became a more important force ... 'obeah' persisted as a strong element of cultural resistance" (1990:77). Both Bush and Trotman follow conventional scholarship, however, by attributing Europeans' lack of comprehension of obeah to Africans' religiosity and by reducing obeah's practices to magic (Bush 1990:76–77; Trotman 1986:222–23, 227).

Dividing a society into two spheres, one European and another African, poses fundamental theoretical problems (cf. E. Brathwaite 1971; Robotham 1980; R. Smith 1966). Indeed, one can argue that the dichotomy between European/Christian and African/obeah arises as a consequence of "ideology" in the sense Marx defined it: a false consciousness born of Europeans' self-serving interest in contrasting "paganism" with "the one true faith" (cf. Marx 1975; Marx and Engels 1977). As Fischer states, we are dealing in the West Indies with a history of "Christianization as a facet of Creolization ... the process of creating a continuous status system out of the dichotomous slave-master system" (1974b:18). By this reasoning, obeah becomes another integral facet of the creolization process.

Still, this alternative framework does not fully resolve all the shortcomings of earlier analyses of obeah. Even scholars who recognize that obeah evolved as a distinctly creole practice that might include a political dimension tend to concentrate on the ways in which obeah and the Christian sects relieve psychological, socioeconomic, and political tensions. Fischer, for instance, treats obeah as a religious form. He erroneously equates obeah with balm-yard cults and pocomania and then argues that these are all alternatives to fundamentalist Christian sects. Historians and political scientists analyzing American slavery share with Caribbeanists this tendency to oppose Christianity to "African" religious practices (e.g., Genovese 1972; Jones 1990; Schwarz 1988; Scott 1990). I have encountered only one historian who grasped the significance of obeah as juridical practice, but he too characterizes obeah practitioners as "witchdoctors" (Mullin 1977:483).[10] This propensity to fit native practices within preconceived social science categories, however, brings with it a host of problematic ethnocentric assumptions (Schneider 1980; Schneider and Smith 1973).

Instead, we should investigate obeah as an indigenous ideology and practice of power and justice, part of a system of illegalities whose conceptual opposition is not Christianity per se but an entire system of legalities. Obeah united and empowered slaves against masters and made group resistance possible (e.g.,

Bush 1990; Craton 1980, 1982; Gaspar 1985). It also permeated relations in the slave quarters between men and women, and thieves and their victims. Although its first practitioners certainly came from Africa, obeah evolved within an entirely new mode of production, unique hierarchical social, economic, and political arrangements, and competing ideologies. It flourished outside the rule of law as an alternative system using different technologies of power and other modes of domination and resistance. If we confine obeah to the realm of African survivals, to the domain of magic and religion, or even to the political praxis of a disgruntled underclass, we miss the ways in which it exemplifies and manipulates the politics of inter- and intraclass relations, as well as gender hierarchy. Obeah's continuing significance lies partly in its persistence within a broader system of illegalities that confronts hegemony, and partly in its generative capacity to "work" law, enfolding obeah within a wider creole legal sensibility and practice.

In the eighteenth century, the legal sensibility and juridical institutions of Antiguan slaves were not those of the colonists: the masters and the masses used different forms of power and embraced different forms of knowledge. Trial by ordeal has disappeared in contemporary Antigua, but as we shall see in Chapter 6, belief in the efficacy of other obeah rites has not. Creolization did not eliminate obeah, it refracted its course and functions as it penetrated different strata in the common order. Nevertheless, in the century following the 1736 slave conspiracy, Leeward Island slaves increasingly made the formal legal system their own. The idea that the law was ultimately just, even if the incumbent of a judicial office was a scoundrel, penetrated the different ranks of society. The formal system of legalities was becoming hegemonic in the sense that it depended "for its hold not only on its expression of the interests of a ruling class but also on its acceptance as 'normal reality' or 'common sense' by those in practice subordinated to it" (R. Williams 1983:45).

Rights at Court

Creolization involved a dialectical interplay of legalities and illegalities that forged West Indian legal sensibilities. For slaves and free people of color, this eventually entailed broadening the arenas and methods from which and with which one could vie for justice. Over time, slaves and free nonwhites expanded their search for justice beyond obeah and increasingly visited the courts. By emancipation, Leeward Island slaves had recourse to obeah, going to court, or some mixture of both. Caribbean scholars have correctly identified Caribbean courts as corrupt and oppressive, but they have missed the capacity of courts to serve as forums of and for resistance to domination.

In fact, academic wisdom holds a dim view of West Indian courts in the slave era. Historians suggest that the courts served the elite but not the slave (Bush 1990:30; Hall 1972:42; G. Lewis 1983:119; M. Smith 1965:97), courts were arbitrary and unpredictable (Goveia 1965:62), professional conduct and legal training were unsatisfactory (Brathwaite 1971:19; Dodd 1979:285–88; Goveia 1965:62–63; Great Britain, Commission of Inquiry, 1825–27 Series One, vol. 1:27–28, 29–30; Howard 1827:xiv–xv), judicial duties were regularly ignored (Brathwaite 1971:19–20), laws remained unpublished and documents fell into disarray (Long 1970:vol. 1, 70, 89, 90), courts failed to convene (Howard 1827:XVI), slave courts were "nothing more than a travesty" (Patterson 1967:89), and bar and bench were unabashedly corrupt (Pares 1950:28, 72). These characterizations are based on complaints from colonists and officials, on the findings of the British Commission of Inquiry sent in 1823 to examine law and judicial institutions in the Caribbean colonies (Great Britain, Commission of Inquiry, 1825–27), and on scholarly analyses of statutory law. From the seventeenth century to the twentieth, observers seem to have reached the same conclusion: West Indian courts made a mockery of justice.

This indictment, however, does not derive from published accounts of actual court cases or legal opinions from the British Caribbean in the slave era, both of which are extremely rare. Moreover, although a few academic studies (Goveia 1965:175–77; Higman 1984; Lazarus-Black 1990a) analyze excerpts of West Indian slave trials, there are almost no accounts from this era of cases involving free persons (Lazarus-Black 1990a). Later nineteenth-century trials are more readily available to scholars, but as was noted in the Introduction, few legal or criminal records have been analyzed by social scientists for the English-speaking Caribbean. As one historian remarks, Caribbean historians have "not given the whole complex of law and crime the attention it deserves" (Trotman 1986:8).[11]

Leeward Island colonists, especially in the early years, certainly did rule whimsically and according to their own interpretation of *stare decisis*. For example, Nathaniel Johnson, governor in 1688, complained:

> Some matters they will determine by the English law, in others, without any rational disparity, they reject English law; and in another island or even in another division of the same island, the reverse of these decisions will be the judgment given. As far as I have observed, the laws of England and the customs or pretended customs of the islands take place by turns, according to the fancy of the judge. (Pares 1950:28)

A similar state of affairs prevailed in 1786, when John Luffman visited Antigua (1789:17–18). Thus corruption in the Leewards may have been as widespread as it was in Barbados.[12]

Even if Caribbean courts were corrupt and oppressive, however, they sometimes served subordinated people generally and women in particular. The legal records reveal that by the end of the eighteenth century, people of color and slaves in the Leeward Islands had learned to use courts to their advantage; they had incorporated the system of legalities.

Why, when, and how did this change in slaves' legal sensibilities and practices occur? In the first place, precedent for slaves' participation in the courts in Antigua began as early as 1702.[13] After 1784, slaves charged with criminal offenses were tried before a jury of six free men. The most important change with respect to the rights of slaves in the Leeward Islands, however, came in 1798 with the Amelioration Acts. These statutes curbed some white violence against slaves; offered other legal protections against abuses; concretized rules about the length of the work day, holidays, and minimum food allowances; and importantly, allowed slaves to take complaints to specially appointed authorities. Second, committed to order by and through law, Antiguan judges ruled in favor of the most oppressed members of society just often enough to inculcate a way of seeing the world, self, and others through legal lenses. If we examine the records closely, we find examples of cruel masters condemned to death by courts of law, freedmen safeguarded by legislators, and slaves who were fed because of judgments by itinerant justices of the peace.

Cases of "excessive" abuse by slave masters, for instance, were occasionally brought to trial in the Leeward Islands. Although one sensational suit involving Edward Huggins of Nevis resulted in the acquittal of a barbarous master (Pares 1950:150–58), three cases indicting men for ill treatment of their slaves were prosecuted in St. Kitts in the eighteenth century (Goveia 1965:186). The Virgin Islands council condemned and executed Arthur Hodge, one of its members, for the murder of a slave in 1811 (ibid.:201).

Free people of color also found protection through formal legal channels. In 1707 legislators ruled in favor of Phyliss, formerly the slave of Major Kean Osborne, who claimed she had been manumitted by her master but was accused of being a slave by another white man. They also freed Ardra, a mulatto man who had deserted the French during the invasion of Guadeloupe in 1703 and had later served in the English army (Gaspar 1985a:163). The murder of an innocent slave woman by a black man was decried by the entire Antiguan community in March 1788, and her assailant was executed. After 1816, an Antiguan statute specifically granted due process of law to persons who claimed free status but were accused of being slaves (*Laws of Antigua* 1804–17:352).

The official British Commission of Inquiry sent to examine the state of law and judicial institutions in the West Indian colonies in 1823 found the corruption, delays, and lack of professionalism for which the colonists had become infamous. The commissioners complained that the judges of the

Courts of Chancery and Common Pleas in Antigua were usually gentlemen without legal training. They reported "a very strong dissatisfaction with the existing institutions and judicial habits of the country." In addition to the "prejudices" that people had to contend with, "there were violent personal animosities prevailing at the bar and invading even the bench" (Great Britain, Commission of Inquiry, 1826:vol. 3, 6).

To appreciate the complexity of the creole legal sensibilities developing in the common order, however, we need to examine the types of complaints placed before the courts and the litigants who brought them. In the cases reported by the Commissioners, white men prosecuted white men, black women prosecuted white men, and black men prosecuted one another.[14] Men and women quarreled about money, appropriate behavior, and inheritances. In fact, we discover that the privileges associated with class, color, and gender in the community were openly challenged in these courtrooms.

For example, on 29 August 1823 the commissioners heard a family case. Mary Morris, a black woman, brought a suit against the executor of the will of her late master. Captain Morris, for whom Mary had had three children, had left Mary fourteen slaves whose labor was to pay for the support and education of their children. Despite her class, race, and gender, Mary charged that the executor, Mr. Buntin, had immediately sold two slaves to cover the Captain's debts and that later he had sold the other slaves without compensating her or the children. Mr. Buntin admitted to the court that some payment was due to the complainant, but he claimed his books had to be brought up to date. He had failed to sort out his records by 4 September, when he returned for a second hearing. At that time, the court granted one last continuance of the case and warned Buntin that he risked being sued at the Court of Chancery, where he could be charged for the costs of the suit in addition to the compensatory sum due to Mary. Unfortunately, the commissioners left Antigua before the case concluded. They mentioned, however, that dishonest executors gave rise to a great number of cases brought by persons from the lower ranks of society (Great Britain, Commission of Inquiry, 1826:vol. 3, 17–18, 24).

The commissioners witnessed other trials involving nonwhite litigants too. A free black man, William Darrell, complained that his wife, a free woman, had been unlawfully imprisoned for taxes that were the responsibility of her former mistress. He charged, too, that when he went to the jail to release her, he was beaten. The jail keeper and the turnkey, however, proved to the satisfaction of the court that Mrs. Darrell had been discharged ten minutes after the mistake was discovered. The case of alleged assault was dismissed for lack of evidence, but the jailer was admonished by the judge to exercise discretion when he handled irate visitors (ibid.:24–25). Another case involved a black man named Donowa who accused a storekeeper, Mr. Pitt, of assault and battery (ibid.:25).

In addition to observing the flow of formal justice in Antigua, the commissioners held public hearings and questioned numerous witnesses. They learned that justices of the peace regularly entertained complaints by slaves against their masters and that failure to do so would be considered "a great dereliction of duties." In addition, magistrates and vestry members from each parish had been appointed to serve on "Councils of Protection." Their task was to ensure that slaves received adequate food and clothing allowances and security from serious physical maltreatment.[15] The coroner reported that he knew of only one case in which a slave had been killed by a master in Antigua, which was "the case of a free black woman, named Penny, for killing her female slave, but never by any person acting under the authority of a master." A justice of the peace testified that many of his cases involved injuries by slaves against each other (ibid.:141, 131).

To my knowledge, records of trials of Antiguan slaves do not exist. However, cases from neighboring St. Kitts confirm that justices of the peace visited estates in the Leeward Islands. The "Return of Slave Complaints in Basseterre [St. Kitts] from August 1822, to 26 December 1823" includes summaries of nineteen cases brought by slaves. The slaves complained about "insufficiency of food and severe treatment," excessive punishment for minor infractions of duty, assignment of tasks they were physically incapable of performing, and of being forced to work on overseers' personal estates. The justices ruled in favor of the slaves in eight of these cases, most of which involved complaints about shortages of food. Some compromise between the disputing parties was reached in five cases, and in six others one or more slaves went home with a sound lashing for wasting the officers' time (ibid.:236–40).

The St. Kitts record shows that Leeward Island slaves utilized formal judicial procedures to protest the behavior of their masters. Courts, cases, and formal legal rhetoric were part of their developing legal sensibility. They knew their rights and were ready to argue for them. Yet just as the 1736 rebellion revealed differences in the ways in which free persons and slaves defined and exercised power, the St. Kitts' data reveals two differences in the ways that these groups used the courts.

First, most of the cases brought by slaves were brought by them in groups rather than as single complainants. Perhaps they sought safety in numbers, but in any case their decision to prosecute a master was often an act of consensus, not an isolated decision by a disgruntled individual. Slaves were not full legal individuals, but they were legally a class, and in this sense they were active as culturally constituted.[16] Moreover, slave court cases were like slave rebellions: they were instances of collective resistance.

Second, a large percentage of these slave complaints were voiced by women. This was not peculiar to St. Kitts because records from Trinidad, Jamaica, and Guyana reveal the same pattern. One governor of Trinidad complained bitterly about the litigious nature of slave women—they were "the most prone to give offense." Trinidad's court records from 1824 to 1826 support the Governor's observation: almost twice as many women as men appeared before magistrates (Ferguson 1987:xi). Slave women played only a slightly less active role in Jamaican courts. There, they accounted for almost half of the cases brought between 1819 and 1835 (ibid.:xi). To cite one last example, in 1826 the protector of slaves in British Guiana complained in his "Half-yearly Report" to the secretary of state for the colonies: "There is no question as far as has come within my reach of observation as to the difficulty of managing the women and they are irritating and insolent to a degree (often instigated by the men), take advantage of the exemption from stripes and in town do little or nothing" (in E. Williams 1952:76).[17]

How can one explain the high incidence of women in the courts? A number of anthropologists have argued that people who are relatively powerless in their relationships with others find courts to be powerful allies (cf. Hirsch 1990; Merry 1990; Nader and Todd 1978; Yngvesson 1985).[18] It is not hard to imagine that powerlessness was a dimension of slave women's use of courts, but in effect they also opposed white gender stereotypes that held women did not belong in politically charged arenas such as legislatures or courts. In making a complaint, slave women resisted the idea that women should be reticent, docile, subservient to men, and attentive to the conventions of class. They spoke out in their own interests and on behalf of male and female friends and kin. Sometimes, too, they used courts to testify to brutality and crime within the slave quarters (Higman 1984a:64–69). Hence gender also influenced the forms and sites of slaves' strategies of resistance.

Thus despite scandal and obvious corruption, free persons of color and slaves began using local courts to air their grievances and obtain their rights. Sometimes slaves utilized law in ways that may have seemed peculiar to masters—in groups and using women as spokespersons. Their behavior substantiates the point that people in different classes use formal law and courts in different ways, for different purposes, and with different results (cf. Jayawardena 1963). As we shall see in Chapters 7 and 8, differential court use is not only indicative of class behavior but also an index to the structure of gender and revealing of the norms that govern relationships between men and women. These class and gender differences notwithstanding, participation in legalities was becoming part of everyday politics. Women like Mary Morris made the court their arena for pressing claims about family.

Summary

The behavior of the colonists who tortured, tried, and condemned the slaves who attempted revolution in 1736 may have been motivated by fear and revenge, but their response to revolution shows them equally devoted to legalities. Men believed firmly in preserving the rights of men—even slave men—even after an attempted slave coup. This concern for legalities prevailed. In 1750 we find successful planter Colonel Samuel Martin, author of "An Essay upon Plantership" and whose own father had been murdered by slaves, giving the following philosophical advice to his peers:

> The subordination of man to each other in society is essentially necessary to the good of the whole: but yet the meanest individual has an equal right with the greatest to civil protection; and to a share of what the earth produces in proportion to his rank and situation . . . He must also treat them with justice and tenderness; not suffering the least injury to be done by any one to another: for tho a master may and ought to forgive small injuries to himself, it is not in his power consistently with justice, to forgive injuries done to another, without due compensation. (1750:6, 7)

By 1750 the creole legal sensibility of free Antiguans was mature. Its core features included a commitment to life by the rule of law, to "justice" and "judgment," to formal legal procedures and institutions, and to effecting social change by legal proclamation. Its symbol was the magnificent courthouse in the city of St. John's. Despite the coercive character of the slave era and the corruption and malfeasance of the courts, both white and black Antiguans brought their cases there. Courts were arenas in which challenges to the class, color, and gender hierarchies could be made. Men and women understood this and used law to protest a variety of forms of domination. Thus a generative, conciliatory, inclusive, and yet resistant, dimension to Antiguan law drew in the people of the common order and nurtured hegemony.[19]

Those who rule with authority emanating from law, however, are often oblivious to the bearers and sources of alternative forms of power. Such was the case in the fall of 1736, when slave masters witnessed slave dances and assemblages and defined those activities as pagan curiosities, setting "precedent" of another kind:

> This imputation of mystery and the demonic by the more powerful class to the lower—by men to women, by the civilized to the primitive, by Christian to pagan, is breathtaking—such an old notion, so persistent, so paradoxical and ubiquitous. In our day it exists not only as racism but also as a vigorous cult of the primitive, and it is as primitivism that it provides the vitality of modernism. (Taussig 1987:215)

The colonists "read" obeah as satanic mystery. The trials of the rebels, however, revealed another legal sensibility, one forged by slaves in the realm of illegalities and using the forbidden knowledge and rites of obeah. I have argued that obeah was neither simple magic nor uncivilized religion. It was and remains an empowering phenomenon, a discourse and practice concerning rights, crime and punishment, and varying forms of domination and resistance. Like law, obeah can generate violence or mitigate its consequences. Like law, it can "name," as one of my informants once put it, with far-reaching consequences for a person's reputation, status, and fate.[20] Yet obeah contrasts sharply with law in its assumptions about the locus for authority and the nature of command. It does not locate power in the control of commodities or ownership of human labor. Obeah reorders social status, power, and hierarchy through its capacity to change people's characters, to compel or restrain action, to alter health, to claim possessions, or to fix a person's fate. To allow the full range of its capacity to influence the course of human affairs, obeah is best conceptualized as part of a wider system of illegalities that counters hegemony. In the next chapters, I unravel the links between legalities and illegalities in the making of Antiguan kinship ideology and structure. Toward that end, we turn first to law's prescriptions for the most intimate of human endeavors: sex, reproduction, and marriage.

3

Constructing the Kinship Order: Antiguan Family Law, 1632–1834

COMMITMENT TO an orderly society governed by statute was a principal feature of the Antiguan colonists' creole sensibility in the pre-emancipation period. Of no less critical importance to them, this emerging ideology also differentiated individuals on the basis of their position within the divisions of labor, property, religious affiliation, gender, and race, and discouraged alliances between persons of different categories. These features were crucial to the construction and development of the creole social and economic hierarchy; each was instantiated in Antiguan kinship law.

In this chapter, I begin my investigation of the making of creole kinship. I consider first the basic principles underlying the idea of "family" in English statutory and common law, for those laws served as models for the men who drafted legislation in the colonies. I treat kinship law as a cultural text, examining the assumptions and presumptions it contains about the natures of men and women, the duties and obligations of husbands and wives, the relations between parents and children, and the crucial links between kinship and property.

In the remainder of the chapter, I describe how the kinship laws drafted in Antigua departed from those of Great Britain by focusing on the statutes designed to regulate the behavior of free persons and servants. Then I review the steps legislators took to order the family lives of slaves. Both discussions are concerned with how law structured class, kinship, and gender as it facilitated domination by the planters. Antiguan legislators repeatedly tried to regulate miscegenation, marriage, fornication, reproductive practices, inheritance, incest, and illegitimacy. The number and content of these statutes lend strong support to my argument that from the very beginning of colonization, class structure, family patterns, and gender organization in Antigua were interwoven with judicial forms and processes. The laws also reveal the colonial administrator's dilemma as he attempted to reconcile the ideal English family of canon and common law with the practices of the settlers. This chapter, then, specifically concerns kinship legalities. In Chapter 4, we shall investigate how and with what consequences this creole juridical blueprint was thwarted.

The Early Marriage and Kinship Laws of England

At the time of West Indian colonization, ecclesiastical courts regulated matrimonial relationships in England. Until Henry's decision to marry Anne Boleyn shifted forever the relation between church and state, there was one universal law of marriage for all Christians, the jus commune of the Western church codified in the Corpus Juris Canonici (Haw 1952:32). By this code, marriage was a sacrament freely consented to by both parties. A husband and wife were "one flesh," and their union was indissoluble. The marriage vow, incorporated into the Book of Common Prayer, sealed the contract between husband and wife (Hammick 1887:101–2). Originally, English common law did not require any form of religious ceremony to establish a marriage; a man and woman could contract to wed by their joint declaration. That rule was modified by the Council of Trent in 1536 to require the presence of a priest (Bromley 1981:28). The church had already reversed its position several times on the question of marital eligibility within certain degrees of consanguinity and affinity, but otherwise canon law regarding marriage had been relatively stable. Henry had capitalized on the only really controversial issue relevant to the kinship rules to achieve his political ends, thereby launching the English Reformation.[1]

The Anglican church incorporated two changes related to marital eligibility during the English Reformation: "First, the use of dispensations allowing marriage within the prohibited degrees was discontinued; and secondly, the number of relatives between whom marriage was forbidden was drastically reduced" (Wolfram 1955:2). Henry's statutes invalidated the church's impediments to marriage beyond those established by Levitical authority—as interpreted by Henry's advisors. Under Elizabeth's reign, Archbishop Parker's Table of Kindred and Affinity (1603) was incorporated into the Church of England's canon law. When Antigua and Barbuda were colonized, therefore, church law and the laws of the state were fused. Canon law administered all marriages. Civil marriages performed by secular authorities were not recognized in England until 1836.[2]

Nevertheless, Parliament began to increase its role in governing kinship affairs in the middle of the eighteenth century. Lord Hardwicke's Act of 1753 extended the state's influence over clandestine unions by requiring all marriages to be publicly solemnized in the couple's parish. Prospective couples were obligated to publicize their intent to marry by church banns on three consecutive Sundays or by obtaining a special license. Marriages not publicized were voidable.[3] Quakers and Jews were exempted from this edict and permitted to marry by their own rites, but the law posed a severe hardship for Catholics and dissenters, who were only permitted to marry in an Anglican ceremony. Parliament rescinded this provision in the Marriage Act of 1836 at the same time that it granted other churches licenses to perform weddings and permitted a civil rite as an alternative to a church service. Henceforth English law recognized the validity of a strictly civil marriage (Bromley 1981:38).

The first comprehensive text to codify English common law, Blackstone's *Commentaries on the Laws of England*, was published in the decade following Hardwicke's Act, between 1765 and 1769. An invaluable historical and anthropological source, it describes the nature of the British marriage contract, defines the rights and duties of husbands and wives, and discusses the concepts of consanguinity and affinity that prevailed in England as Antigua's planters began importing African slaves in unprecedented numbers, changing the social and economic organization of the island. The *Commentaries* enjoyed wide acclaim and circulation throughout Britain and the colonies; it served as a reminder and source of the cultural heritage upon which the Antiguan lawmakers drew to compose statutes for their settlement.

In the *Commentaries,* marriage was defined as a contract that, as in all other contracts, was valid as long as the parties were willing and able to contract and there was proof that they had actually done so. The impediments to forming a marriage included youthful age (without guardian consent), previous marriage, imbecility, venereal disease, or a relationship within the prohibited degrees of consanguinity or affinity. The marriage contract was dissolvable only by the death of a spouse. However, an ecclesiastical court could pronounce "separation of bed and board" or nullify a union if one or both parties had not met the conditions necessary to legitimize the contract.

Marriage entailed specific repercussions for husbands and wives, but its consequences for women were far more dramatic. In agreeing to marry, a woman agreed to become a legal non-entity and her "rights of person" ceased to exist:

> By marriage, the husband and wife are one person in law; that is, the very being or legal existence of the woman is suspended during the marriage, or at least is

incorporated and consolidated into that of her husband: under whose wing, protection, and cover, she performs everything; . . . and her condition during her marriage is called her coverture. (Blackstone 1765:430)

Husbands and wives had separate responsibilities as marriage partners. A wife's duty was to obey, respect, and submit to her husband's right to correct her behavior and speech within "reasonable bounds" (ibid.:432). A husband, on the other hand, was required to provide the necessities of sustenance for his wife and to maintain her in an "appropriate station of life"—an idea that took root and flourished in the new world of the Caribbean. The law also obliged him to pay her premarital debts, for "he has adopted her and her circumstances together" (ibid.:430–31). On the other hand, a man gained extensive control over his wife's assets. One legal authority summarized the legal consequences for men with respect to their wives' property as follows:

He acquired an absolute interest in her chattels, a similar interest in her choses in action [the right to bring an action or recover a debt] but only provided that they were reduced into possession, a power to dispose of her leasehold interests during his lifetime but no power to dispose of them by will, and no more than an interest for his life in her inheritable estates of freehold. (Bromley 1981:108)

Men not only presided over marital property, they were responsible for legitimate children. Following the teachings of the Anglican church, "the main end and design of marriage" was "to fix upon some person to whom the care, the protection, the maintenance and the education of the children should belong" (Blackstone 1765:443). In English law of the time, that person was the child's father.[4] Blackstone cited Montesquieu regarding the difference between mothers and fathers:

The establishment of marriage in all civilized states is built on this natural obligation of the father to provide for his children; for that ascertains and makes known the person who is bound to fulfill this obligation; whereas in promiscuous and illicit conjunctions, the father is unknown; and the mother finds a thousand obstacles in her way;—shame, remorse, the constraint of her sex, and the rigor of laws;—that stifle her inclinations to perform this duty; and besides, she generally wants ability. (IBID.:435)

Common law understood the father as best suited to provide the protection, maintenance, and education of children. Consequently, "a mother as such, is entitled to no power, but only to reverence and respect," whereas "the power of the father . . . over the persons of his children" continued until they reached maturity at age twenty-one (ibid.:441).

Marriage conferred explicit rights and duties between husbands and wives and parents and legitimate children; it also provided the fulcrum for the English system of consanguinity and affinity. English common law defined kinship as relations of contract and blood, depicting duties and relationships between affines and consanguines in terms of rights over persons and things. Those included were clearly marked by father's blood, symbolized and enacted in the transmission of land, monies, personal possessions, and such immaterial goods as names and titles. The family depicted in English common law was a unit separate and distinct from the outside world but represented to that world by its corporate head—the husband/father (cf. Schneider 1980; Lazarus-Black 1990a).[5]

For purposes of inheritance, the system of consanguinity and affinity measured relationships in "degrees" or generations from common ancestors. Consanguinity was defined as "the connexion or relation of persons descended from the same stock or common ancestor. This consanguinity is either lineal, or collateral" (Blackstone 1769:202). A distinction was drawn between persons who shared the same couple of ancestors (persons of the "whole blood") and those related through a single ancestor (persons of the "half blood"). Persons of the whole blood were always considered before persons of the half blood for inheritance, because whole bloods were theoretically closer to the "first purchaser" of property and rights to titles and names. Marriage also created kin relationship: a man was related to the same degree to his wife's kin as she was to her husband's kin.

Although the English theory of consanguinity and affinity defined a woman as being on equal footing with her husband as a procreator of "children of the whole blood," she was simultaneously the "bearer of less worthy blood" in issues of inheritance. Among the several rules in the *Commentaries* prescribing inheritance we find:

> The male issue shall be admitted before the female.
>
> Thus sons shall be admitted before daughters; or, as our lawgivers have somewhat uncomplaisantly expressed it, the worthiest of blood shall be preferred . . . where there are two or more males in equal degree, the eldest only shall inherit; but the females all together . . . in collateral inheritance the male stocks shall be preferred to the female . . . unless where lands have, in fact, descended from a female.
>
> Thus the relations on the father's side are admitted in infinitum before those on the mother's side are admitted at all. (IBID.:212, 213, 214, 234)

Sex and marital status were critical in distributing power, rights, and property in the common law. If a woman had a male sibling, she might receive no inheritance. If she had only female siblings, they divided the inheritance among them. A woman's control over property was usually limited to the period prior to her marriage. At that time, it passed under her husband's control, making her a link of transfer in a chain in which property was transmitted from male to male along legitimate blood lines. The chain could be broken only if special provisions were made, such as through a formal marriage settlement, by trust or special gift, or in a will.[6] Married women usually gained control over property only after their husbands died. For example, when a man died intestate, his widow took one-half or one-third of her husband's property, depending upon whether they had children.[7]

Special rules existed in English common law regarding illegitimate children. In the case of bastards, mother's blood was again distinguished from father's blood: "Bastards are incapable of being heirs . . . Such are held to be *nullius filii*, the sons of nobody. . . . Being thus the sons of nobody, they have no blood in them, at least no inheritable blood; consequently none of the blood of the first purchaser" (ibid.:247). A person who could claim only mother's blood was classified with two other groups of outcast persons in English society who also lacked "inheritable blood": aliens and felons. Under common law, neither mother nor father was held responsible for the maintenance of an illegitimate child. Early poor-law legislation subsequently made the mother liable for the child unless she had obtained a written contract for support from the father. A poor law of 1576 held both parents responsible for maintaining a bastard child if that child became dependent upon parish funds (Bromley 1981:595).[8] Neither Jamaica (Salmon n.d.:20) nor Antigua seems to have "received" that law.[9] Legislators throughout the British-speaking Caribbean, however, made the children of slave women nullius filii.

To summarize, Blackstone's *Commentaries* codifies and preserves basic features of a jural model of English kinship and inheritance. This jural model conceived of marriage as a contractual agreement bestowing specific rights and duties, placed married women under the coverture of their husbands, and made men responsible for the education and sustenance of their wives and legitimate offspring. English kinship began with a contractual agreement but was thereafter traced in blood. Law emphasized the father's line, legitimacy, and primogeniture. Kinship consisted of rights in persons and rights in things, distinguished the sexes according to those rights, considered the bearers of property (males) as superior, and equated bastard children with criminals and aliens. The crucial importance of the jural model is that power over persons and things was placed in the hands of legitimate men. Fathers and husbands were awarded power; mothers, wives, and bastards were not. The jural model of kinship validated and perpetuated a pragmatic set of political and economic relationships. Theoretically and practically, women's and bastard children's inferiority was related to and legitimized by their overall relation to property.

Founding Fathers, Unmarried Mothers, and Fatherless Children: Antigua's First Family Laws

The most striking similarity between the marriage and kinship laws of England and Antigua is that both assigned power over persons and things to legitimate males. The most striking difference between the two is that the West Indian laws that governed family were intentionally designed to create and maintain a hierarchical order based on the ruling elite's perceived requirements for the local division of labor. In the slave era, Antigua's family laws differed in detail, but not in overall design or rationale, from those of other islands governed by English-speaking colonists.[10]

Antigua's socioeconomic hierarchy was cut into three ranks: free persons, indentured servants, and slaves. Different marriage and kinship rules governed each of the three categories, and relationships between them were restricted. Initially, no statutes in Antigua specifically prohibited interracial marriages, nor was public permission required before an interracial couple could wed, as was true in Cuba between 1806 and 1881 (Martinez-Alier 1974).[11] Somewhat counterintuitively, then, "color" was not the central issue for the Antiguan lawmakers who fashioned the first marriage laws. They were primarily concerned with an individual's status as a worker and secondarily with gender and religion.

The first local Antiguan rule to regulate reproduction, for instance, was designed to contend with a consequence of the sudden proximity of Christians and "savages"—not all of whom found each other unattractive. An act of 1644, reissued in 1672, forbade miscegenation and imposed fines for "Carnall Coppulation between Christian and Heathen." The latter category included both Amerindians and Africans. The penalties for breaking the law were differentiated according to the offender's position in the division of labor: a free man or woman who slept with a heathen was made to pay a fine, an indentured servant had his or her contract extended, and an offending slave was branded and whipped. Henriques (1974:93–94) and Gaspar (1985a:167) claim the law was unique among the British sugar islands. We might add that it was a symbol and a harbinger of the developing creole kinship ideology in two respects: the Antiguan lawmakers felt compelled to adhere to a juridical ordering of kin, but they did not set rules for regulating relationships between the sexes without addressing the social rank of the parties. In short order, people's understanding of social rank was linked to their knowledge and use of juridical privileges.

The procedural compromise enacted to legitimate Antiguan marriages illustrates an early example of how creole kinship demanded legitimation, though in a form that necessarily departed from that of England. Antiguan Act No. 2 of 1672 confirmed all marriages solemnized by justices of the peace or magistrates. The preamble to the bill notes that "for want of orthodox ministers" on the island, "diverse marriages have been had and solemnized, by virtue or colour of certain orders of the Governor and Council in some other manner than hath been formerly used and accustomed." The statute made all such marriages and those later solemnized by any justice of the peace "taken to be and to have been of the same and no other force and effect, as if such marriage had been had and solemnized by an orthodox minister" (*Laws of Antigua* 1864:10). The legislators rationalized that these measures would not be necessary after the arrival of an orthodox ministry.[12] The law also provided for a jury of twelve men to decide cases of contested legitimacy. Acts similar to Antigua's were passed in Jamaica (Long 1970 2:238) and in Montserrat, where the islanders were also concerned "to prevent the manifold sins of incontinence which must inevitably ensue" without the clergy (Fergus 1978:37).[13]

Some earlier offense to public sensibilities must have moved the legislators in Antigua to make incest punishable by death in 1644 (Dunn 1972:228). Such regulation stands in contrast to England, which had no criminal law penalizing incest until 1908 (N. Anderson 1982; Wolfram 1983).[14] In Britain, incest was defined as sexual intercourse within certain prohibited degrees of consanguinity or affinity as described by Archbishop Parker's table and printed in the Book of Common Prayer. It was considered an ecclesiastical matter until the Matrimonial Causes Act (1857), when it became one of the grounds, coupled with adultery, for which women could sue for divorce (Bromley 1981:187). Yet the Antiguans brought incest under legal scrutiny before the end of the seventeenth century—further evidence of their willingness to depart from English kinship law of the same period.

Colonial legislators adjusted law to the lack of a local ministry, but they did not grant legal privileges to couples who neglected to formalize their relationships. In contrast to the North Americans, Antiguans did not bestow legal privileges to couples who failed to register their unions. Legal recognition of a couple's agreement to live as husband and wife, followed by cohabitation, the so-called common-law marriage that evolved on the North American frontier (Friedman 1973:179), did not emerge as a legitimate form of union in Antigua. Instead, in 1688, Act No. 2 of 1672 was repealed and there was an effort to bring matrimonial jurisdiction back under the auspices of the orthodox clergy. One of the clauses of An Act For Dividing The Island Into Parishes, And Maintenance Of Ministers, The Poor, And Erecting And Repairing Churches forbade any person not duly qualified by the Anglican church to perform marriage ceremonies: to do so carried a penalty of twenty pounds current money of the island (Microfilm No. 1). The Anglicans retained the exclusive right to wed couples in Antigua until 1844, eight years after the British Marriage Act allowed registered ministers of other denominations and civil authorities to celebrate marriages in England.

Antiguan marriages united men and women by Anglican authority and only with Anglican ministers' consent—and the clergy was instructed to keep separate free persons and slaves. In 1697, the assembly decreed that no minister was "to presume to marry a slave to any free person (either White, or of any other Colour)." The minister who disobeyed the law forfeited twenty pounds. For the crime of marrying a slave, a free person was fined the equivalent sum—or subjected to four years of servitude to the master of the slave he had married. Both statutory provisions to discourage nonendogamous unions were incorporated into the 1702 Act For The Better Government Of Slaves And Free Negroes. In that bill, the financial penalty imposed upon ministers who had the audacity to marry such couples was increased to fifty pounds. Any free person who proposed to marry a slave had to pay the owner twenty pounds or serve four years. In short, an individual who wished to marry a slave might sacrifice his or her own freedom.[15] The kinship order denied free fathers the right to transmit their social status to the children they had with slave women.

The Antiguan legislators were not content merely to discourage marriages between persons of different ranks in creole society; they also endeavored to control reproductive patterns within and between those ranks. A bill of 1698 for "encouraging the Settlement of this Island with White People and Promoting the Importation of Servants" is fascinating for its attempt to control intra- and interclass sexual relationships:

> If any servant shall get another with Childe, they shall each of them serve twelve months, or pay six pounds Money to the Master or Mistress of the woman servant, but any free person getting a servant with Childe, shall pay twenty pounds Money to the Master or Mistress of the Servant for her freedom, and keep harmless the parish. And also any free person intermarry with a servant without consent of his or her Master, or Mistress, shall pay twenty pounds current Money to the Owner of such Servant for his or her freedom, or serve two years time to the said Master or Mistress. And if the Servant married be a tradesman, then the penalty herein required to be double, or the time, and that at the election of the Master or Mistress of the Servant. (Microfilm No. 1)

In 1716, the Antiguan legislators reconfirmed their disapproval of marriages between indentured servants and free persons by re-enacting this bill and raising the penalty to one hundred pounds or, if the servant were a highly valued tradesman, two hundred pounds. (Once again, social rank changed the consequences of marriage.) The Antiguans tried to make sure the act would be widely publicized: captains were to read it to their militia troops four times a year (Microfilm No. 1).

These tactics to dissuade unions between free persons and servants were deployed in other English-speaking colonies in the Caribbean. In Jamaica, for example, the punishment for "getting a fellow-servant with child" was "a service of double the time the woman had to serve." For the crime of "marrying without the consent of their master or mistress," a servant faced "two years extra service." Penal clauses remained in effect in Jamaica for these crimes until the middle of the eighteenth century (Long 1970:vol. 2, 291, 292). The Barbadian indentured-servant codes were similarly hostile to sexual and marital relations between servants. A servant who married without his master's permission had his service extended four years. A freeman who impregnated a servant had to find her owner a replacement for his loss and pay his expenses in bringing up the child. If the father was himself a servant, he was to serve the woman's master for three years following the completion of his own contract (Beckles 1989:83).[16]

What was the consequence of the legal restriction on free-servant marriage in Antigua? As we shall see in Chapter 4, almost one out of five whites on the island (19.1 percent) was a servant in 1720 (Gaspar 1985:78). A fair number of the colonists, therefore, could not marry unless they could obtain permission from their employers, buy out their contracts, or pay heavy fines. Perhaps both servants and free persons were discouraged from marrying by the statute that only recognized nuptials performed by Anglican ministers. Legal separations and divorce were impossible to obtain locally. Given this combination of statutes, and the well-known fact that West Indian plantation owners preferred employing unmarried men because married men with families cost the estate more for support (cf. Brathwaite 1971:142), it is little wonder that concubinage and prostitution became common. In Antigua, as in Jamaica, there evolved a kinship system for men that "enjoined marriage with status equals and non-legal unions with women of lower status" (R. Smith 1982:121). In contrast, "respectable" women married and refrained from extramarital affairs.

Law contributed to the establishment of illicit arrangements among free settlers and indentured servants; it also delineated subordinate status for women and sometimes regardless of class. As they intervened in the family lives of persons of different ranks in diverse ways and by means of disparate rules, lawmakers also concretized a hierarchical arrangement between the sexes that crossed class lines.

Interestingly, Antiguan legislators rarely mentioned women explicitly; they were governed as a matter of course. The point is illustrated in an indentured servants' act of 1698, which gave female servants dresses rather than drawers and proportionately less food but did not otherwise distinguish the treatment of men and women (Microfilm No. 1). The exceptional situation, of course, was pregnancy. Employers regarded it as a nuisance, and lawmakers tried to discourage it legally by imposing fines.

As was true in Great Britain, women in the West Indies were barred from formal political participation, denied the vote, and hindered by law from developing an economic base that might allow them to gain power, a feat they sometimes accomplished when their husbands or fathers died. Usually, however, women's fathers and husbands acted on their behalf. Married women fell under the law of coverture. Their right to hold and transfer property in Antigua was further affected by the local assembly and the legislature of the Leeward Islands. In 1692, the assembly decided a man possessed of his wife's inheritance in land could convey that land—a right denied him in English common law. The Antiguan law only required that a local judge sign an affidavit to the effect that the wife consented to her husband's decision to sell her inheritance.

There were other contrasts with English law. If a man died intestate in Britain, his widow was granted one-half or one-third of her husband's property, depending upon whether they had children. In 1705, the General Legislature of the Leeward Islands protected widows by granting as part of their dower rights "all coppers, stills, and all cattle, horses, asses commonly used and exercised upon and about any plantation or plantations, and all other plantation utensils." A widow inherited these properties along with lands, slaves, and tenements if her husband died intestate, and she could sue to recover debts owed to him. This provided her with reasonable housing, slaves, and tools to work his estate, even if he had left large debts (*Laws of Antigua* 1864:4–5).[7]

Only well-to-do widows, however, benefitted from this rule. A different statute applied to the wives of the "ten-acre men," poor whites who had accepted the legislators' offer of free land in return for their services in defending the colony. The local Antiguan gentry found the division of the ten-acre plots troublesome, as there was not "a sufficient encouragement for new grantees to proceed in cultivating" those plots. Therefore, in 1747 they abolished dower rights in land for all future widows of men possessed of government grants and substituted instead a cash settlement of thirty pounds from the treasury—provided the widow submitted the proper forms within a designated period. If there were no heirs, the land reverted to the government (ibid.:49–51).

A free woman without a man or much property lived in a very precarious world in the eighteenth century. The poverty of such women became the subject of legislative concern in 1753. Lawmakers gave women a special dispensation exempting them from taxes if they owned fewer than ten slaves upon whom they depended for their livelihood (Microfilm No. 3). Other women faced hard times because they were mothers of illegitimate children.

By the evidence of the legal record, the "problem" of children born out of wedlock was serious by 1786—and it was not a problem confined to interracial unions. Antiguan Act No. 439 compels "reputed Fathers of illegitimate White Children to make a Competent Provision for them." Parish funds maintained them, "altho' their reputed Fathers have been in circumstances sufficiently competent to provide for such children" (*Laws of Antigua* 1690–1790:531–33; Goveia 1965:220). For several reasons, this law is important to both our investigation of the structure and ideology of creole kinship and our understanding of the plight of those in the lowest ranks of free society in the slave era.

First, both free or enslaved status and "color" were now issues in the legislating of relationships between parents and children. At the end of the eighteenth century, the state intervened only in the case of a destitute white bastard child.

Second, although precedent for charging parents to maintain their illegitimate children existed in English poor relief acts, the Antiguan law clearly reflects local reproductive practices. It suggests a diversity of kinship patterns obtained within the white population at least as early as the last quarter of the eighteenth century—a suggestion that, as we shall see shortly, is proved in narratives and numerical records from the period. Nonlegal unions were characteristic of intra- as well as interracial unions, and creole kinship law attempted to control them.

Third, the language of the law granted magistrates discretionary power to establish parentage and to enforce parental obligations. Whether the man and woman were married or not, a sexual union between two white persons that produced a child generated kinship ties carrying specific rights and duties. The bastardy law of 1786 gave justices of the peace the authority to investigate the circumstances surrounding the birth of an illegitimate white child, to "take-order as well for the Punishment of the Mother and reputed Father, as also for the better Relief of such Parish," and to arrange "for the keeping of every such Bastard Child, by charging such Mother or reputed Father, with the Payment of Money weekly, or other Sustenation for the Relief of such Child" (*Laws of Antigua* 1690–1790:531). Either parent could be sent to jail for their delinquent behavior. The law also allowed the justices to apprehend a man accused of having impregnated a woman whose child was likely to become a bastard and a burden upon the parish funds.[18] After investigating the case, they could send the man to jail unless he provided a surety to appear at the next Court of King's Bench and agreed to abide by the order of that court (ibid.:532).

Fourth, in this act local leaders institutionalized the convention of having justices of the peace mediate kinship disputes. Precedent was set for women to use the courts to manage crises in their familial relationships, to establish paternity, win child support, and act as advocates for their families in the courts. As will become clear, the function and meaning of resolving kinship disputes at court would change over the years; the central place of law and courts would not.

Finally, illegitimacy in the island's white population became an issue requiring special legislation toward the end of the eighteenth century either because there was deliberate neglect of children by their fathers or because of the genuine inability of some white men to support their offspring. A letter by John Luffman suggests the latter explanation. In February 1787 he wrote:

> This country is poor, most of the landholders being impoverished, from a series of bad crops, previous to the last three years. In fact, the greater part of the estates, in this island, are in trust, or under mortgage to the merchants of London, Liverpool, and Bristol. The resident merchants suffer considerable losses from bad debts, and are not in a small degree hurt by that bane of honorable commerce, smuggling. (1789:49)

Thus, although the end of the eighteenth century is usually considered a period of economic prosperity for West Indian whites, some Antiguans suffered serious financial setbacks, and this was reflected in the local kinship laws. The regulation of white reproduction was one consequence of the pervasiveness of intraracial, nonlegal unions.

To recapitulate, the first Antiguan laws regulating reproduction, marriage, sexual conduct, inheritance, and provision for illegitimate children were mainly devoted to controlling the behavior of free settlers and indentured servants. Legislators were anxious that sexual relationships, love, or marriage not threaten the boundaries between different categories of workers. The onus of protecting the hierarchy rested with the free settlers. After 1672, marriages were performed only by and with the consent of Anglican clergymen. Servants also needed their masters' permission to wed and were fined if they engaged in illicit unions resulting in pregnancy. Both free and servant women in Antigua fell under legal coverture at marriage. However, not all the white women in the colony legitimized their relationships. At the end of the eighteenth century, illegitimacy in the white population was sufficiently widespread to inspire lawmakers to legal action. The colonists preserved a jural model for kinship but reworked its features to reflect a creole consciousness about the crucial links between family and political economy.

The Matter of Marriage among Slaves

In sharp contrast to their regular efforts to legislate the form and content of settler and servant families, Antiguan lawmakers initially ignored conjugal and reproductive practices in the slave quarters. After all, slaves were not persons but freehold property (Microfilm No. 1).[19] As we have seen, the first slave codes in the English-speaking Caribbean were designed to promote labor and prevent resistance. Laws made it illegal for bondsmen to leave their estates without permission and outlawed assemblages, theft, possession of weapons, and insults or assaults to whites. Over time, legislators supplemented these police measures with economic restrictions to regulate slaves' participation in the economy and to prevent them from acquiring property (Goveia 1970:26).

It was the end of the eighteenth century before Antiguan legislators focused specifically on slave marriages.

The growing value of slaves and the profitability of the sugar crop, however, prompted local legislators to pass measures to increase the number of persons who could be counted as slaves and to discourage relationships between free persons, indentured servants, and bondsmen. In 1644, a mulatto child produced by a racially mixed union was enslaved until ages eighteen or twenty-one. After 1697, such a child was enslaved for life (Dunn 1972:228 n. 8). The law condemning a mulatto child to perpetual slavery coincided with the decree that no minister marry a slave to a free person.

Few laws protected slaves in the Leeward Islands until pressure from the antislavery movement in England forced local initiative to improve slave conditions. The 1798 Amelioration Acts were a West Indian response to the British cry to abolish the slave trade. Afraid that Parliament or the Colonial Office might authorize special legislation to significantly improve the environment in which slaves worked, Caribbean lawmakers drafted their own versions of "ameliorating" legislation (Goveia 1965:189–91). They fixed minimum food, housing, and clothing allotments for slaves and condemned "excessive punishments." Additionally, the final clauses of the act passed by the General Legislature included instructions to masters for promulgating steady, lifelong unions and increasing childbearing among slaves. One consequence for slaves was that masters suddenly began to play a more intrusive role in their family lives.

The kinship code proposed for the slaves in the Amelioration Acts derived from several sources. It came partially from the masters' own kinship ideology and from the planters' concern to protect their property and guarantee the convenience of transferring slaves as commodities. It also reflected the elite's assumptions about the mental and moral aptitude of Africans.

In the Amelioration Acts, slave owners were advised to induce their slaves to take one mate. Such encouragement of "monogamy" did not spring from Christian piety, because the planters believed licentious behavior inhibited reproduction, and the law held slave marriages by religious rites were "unnecessary and even improper" (Higman 1984:351). Lawmakers advocated a special kind of "marriage," which only partially resembled their own:

> And whereas the Marriage of Slaves cannot give any particular Right either to the contracting Parties or to their Children, and it being unnecessary and even improper to enforce the Celebration of any religious Rites among the Slaves in order to sanctify Contracts, the faithful Performance of which can be looked for only by a regular Improvement in Religion, Morality, and Civilization, should not be immediately enforced by any compulsory Methods, lest the Violation of sacred Vows be too often added to the Crime of Infidelity. (*Laws of Antigua* 1791–1804:31)

The lawmakers contended more time was needed to educate the slaves and to encourage their morality. They argued that the Africans were still too uncivilized to be capable of complying with a contract. Their plan for slave "marriages," therefore, preserved the idea of a faithful union between one man and one woman, but without the element of contract. (The Book of Common Prayer contract, of course, would have prevented these men from pulling asunder what God had joined.) As a result, the meaning of marriage had been changed. Nevertheless, these marriages without contracts were associated with gifts, increased status for women, the promise of an eventual end to harsh labor for mothers, a commemorative ritual, and its own method for assigning names and deploying inheritances. It was a complex system in its own right.

Relying on their own understanding about what motivated people, the Leeward Island lawmakers offered their slaves financial incentives to maintain steady unions. One dollar was awarded to each couple who remained together for one year. A woman in a stable union received four dollars from her master by law upon the birth of her first child and one dollar for each subsequent child (ibid.:31). Law relieved a mother with six children from heavy work when her youngest child reached the age of seven. Any master who failed to provide these rewards was subject to a penalty of fifty pounds.[20] Another clause fined white men one hundred pounds for raping "married" slave women (ibid.:31–32).

The local ruling elite also devised a ritual of acknowledgment for slaves who "wed" and found a way to shame those who did not. Within two months of the passage of the act, and every January thereafter, the owner or manager of every estate was to

> convene and assemble together the Slaves under his Direction, and inquire which of them have a Husband or Wife, or more than one; and if an Acknowledgement be Made in Consequence of such Inquiry of more than one Husband or Wife, then such Owner or Director shall compel such Slave making such Acknowledgement to elect some one Slave only as his or her Husband or Wife; and when such Election is made, such Owner or Director shall enter the same in a Book to be kept for that Purpose, and make the same as public as possible by convening once in every twelve months all the slaves upon such Plantation, and reading to them the same in a distinct and audible Voice, at the same time extolling the good Behavior of those who have been faithful to their Engagements, and reprobating the Misconduct of those Who have acted to the contrary. (Ibid.:31)

In addition, each owner was to do "his utmost to keep together in Harmony, the Parties who have made such Election" and to encourage each slave who reached the age of majority to choose publicly a spouse (ibid.:31).

In this proposed ritual, the planters drew upon their own religious creed, their faith in a book, and their self-conscious commitment to "the word" (cf. Comaroff and Comaroff 1986a:14). Reading these codes, one can not help but be struck by the irony of the symbolic gesture of recording slave marriages in plantation account books. Instead of preserving these marriages in the church register, the planters noted them in the ledgers in which transactions involving the estate's capital were recorded (cf. Weber 1958).

The system of kinship sanctioned in the law written for the slaves reversed the English common law prescription linking status and "title" (surname) with inheritance. The slave codes assumed the legality of the grant of absolute power over persons to other persons, a power legitimized by transfiguring slaves into commodities. By virtue of this power, the slave, as property, had to be inheritable. Slavery was transmitted to a child through its mother—but in English common law a person's status was determined by his father and property was inherited through males. The exception was the bastard child who was isolated from both his parents in common law and who, even though he was born of unfree parents, was free (Jacobs 1932:583). In compiling the slave codes, then, planters developed a kinship system for slaves that *reversed* their own kin behavior and its mechanism for the transfer of identity and property.[21] There was thus a second reason slave marriages could not be honored as true contracts: they were irrelevant to any integration of slave families with English common law because husband and wife roles were inverted. A child of a slave marriage was not allowed to take the surname of the father or inherit legally whatever property he might have accumulated.[22] Slave unions could be "broken" by planters with impunity. No cultural or legal conscience constrained them; only practical issues of slave morale, or a declining slave population might convince a planter to protect slave families.[23] Significantly, the locus for black identity did not change even after a planter granted manumission:

> The courts of law interpreted the act of manumission by the owner, as nothing more than an abandonment or release of his own proper authority over the person of the slave, which did not, and could not, convey to the object of his bounty, the civil and political rights of a natural-born subject. (Edwards in Goveia 1965:218)

Finally, in sharp contrast to the kinship expounded in English common law, but like the local regulations governing indentured servants, the Amelioration Acts barely differentiated the rights and responsibilities of slave men and women. This silence with respect to the ways in which gender mediates the conditions and activities of labor and kinship facilitated the organization of production on the estates and buttressed patriarchical authority. Antiguan law mostly denied the humanity and gender of the Antiguan labor force, even as it promoted a jural model for kinship.[24]

To what extent did slaves participate in the kinship system encoded in the Amelioration Acts? The answer must be tentative because the Antiguan record is so slim. Nevertheless, we know from one of the few available historical accounts that the acts did matter to some slaves, which prompts us to speculate why.

At the time of the acts, Antiguan slaves made up 94 percent of the population of the island. The majority worked under severe conditions on large sugar plantations. The marriage clauses of the Amelioration Acts gave these slaves a way to announce publicly, and force whites to acknowledge, that they were people living in families. Moreover, the public assembling of all the slaves on the estate, the announcing of marriages, the pressure to end relationships with more than one person, and the psychological effect of having one's union recorded for all posterity in the great book of the estate, could well have combined to exert some influence over slave conjugal and reproductive patterns—even if many slaves declined to accept the gifts, to give up mates, or to participate in the rites, and even if some masters refused to honor the law.[25] At least some slaves married according to these rites; historian Flannagan heard complaints after emancipation that some freed men "violated those [former] vows without compunction" and later "married" someone else! Flannagan also reported that as soon as possible, "it was their pride to be married at the established church" (1967:vol. 2, 96, 97).

Several points are evident from this discussion. After 1798, slaves began incorporating kinship legalities into their kinship practices. Despite the conventional view that law lacked significance in the family lives of slaves, the Amelioration Acts gave enslaved peoples another way to publicly acknowledge family ties. In addition, after 1798 the kinship system created in Antiguan law encompassed all of the island's people: settler, servant, and slave. Kinship legalities had penetrated every rank of society. At the same time, however, "marriage" in Antiguan law had different meanings and consequences depending on class, and within class, by gender. Similarly, depending on class and gender, "kinship" in Antiguan law used different methods for depicting social identity and deploying inheritance. Therefore, a comprehensive explanation of the emerging creole kinship system must take into account the inclusive character of Antiguan family laws, their exclusionary functions, and how commonsense knowledge and local practice bent, jarred, defied, and denied those laws.

Summary

The Antiguan laws governing reproduction, marriage, and inheritance in the seventeenth, eighteenth, and early nineteenth centuries were innovative in content and function. Only partially influenced by English common and statutory law, they were part of the design to build a commercially productive colony based first on the labor of indentured servants and then on that of slaves. Kinship law played a constructive role in shaping the character of this new social order and in formulating the meaning of marriage, legitimacy, and illegitimacy within it. Like the family laws of England, Antiguan kinship law placed power over persons and things in the hands of legitimate males. In contrast to the English case, local statutes established different kinship rules for people in different ranks and endeavored to keep them apart.

In the kinship order proposed for the free white settlers, marriage was a contractual union imposing specific rights and duties upon husbands and wives. After a brief period, marriages had to be celebrated by Anglican ministers, and common-law unions were legally invalid. After 1786, a proven blood tie between a man and a white child made a man financially responsible for the child—whether or not the child was legitimate—and despite the fact that in English common law a bastard child was *nullius filius*, the child of no one. The Antiguan bastardy law was unusual because it distinguished the color of the child. On this account, because it set precedent for the intervention of the state in the lives of free families, because it associated a blood relationship between a man and a child with the exchange of money and other commodities, and because it encouraged women to speak out in support of the rights of their children, the 1786 bastardy law had long-term ramifications for life in the common order even long after the statute itself was forgotten.

Indentured servants, that other class of settlers, were singled out for special attention by Antiguan lawmakers. Separate reproductive and marriage rules applied to servants. They could wed only with the permission of their masters, and they were subjected to special fines and servitude for unexpected pregnancy. In the early eighteenth century, almost 20 percent of Antigua's white population were subject to this rule. What little evidence exists suggests that a good many persons were dissuaded from marrying legally.

The Amelioration Acts brought yet another set of kinship rules into the common order. These codes created a different meaning for marriage, an alternative wedding ceremony, a financial gift, and a different method for dispensing names and inheritances. In a slave marriage, there was no contract, and no slave husband placed his wife under his coverture. Just how frequently slaves in Antigua and elsewhere in the Leeward Islands made use of these acts remains a question for further historical investigation. The historical evidence presented next shows that while the indentured servant population dwindled, and its marriage code became an anachronism, Antigua's slaves and free people of color grew in number and married formally with increasing frequency.

4

Legalities, Illegalities, and Creole Families in the Common Order, 1632–1834

WE HAVE been talking about legalities: codes for conduct, prescriptions for ideal behavior, rules to maintain order, and sanctions for those who depart from the law. We have examined kinship law wielded as an effective and innovative instrument to protect locally crafted social, economic, and gender hierarchies. We have observed several examples of the direct influence of local practices in shaping kinship codes and one case in which kinship rules—those contained in the Amelioration Acts—were instigated by pressure from Great Britain. Finally, we have noted that these acts encouraged new meanings and associations for old terms such as *marriage, kinship,* and *inheritance.* Like all locally crafted creole structures, Antiguan law used materials from several sources in new ways and invented new materials.

We have now to address again the relationship between codes and human behavior; in particular, the nature of Antigua's "system of illegalities." In this slave society, as in France under the Old Regime:

> Each of the different social strata had its margin of tolerated illegality: the non-application of the rule, the non-observance of the innumerable edicts or ordinances were a condition of the political and economic functioning of society . . . illegality was so deeply rooted and so necessary to the life of each social stratum, that it had in a sense its own coherence and economy. (Foucault 1979:82)

Like the serfs of the Continent, the lowest ranks of Antiguan society were granted few privileges but they too "benefited, within the margins of what was imposed on them by law and custom, from a space of tolerance, gained by force or obstinacy; and this space was for them so indispensable a condition of existence that they were often ready to rise up to defend it" (Foucault 1979:82). Perceived loss of rights, for example, was a factor in the slave rebellion in Antigua in 1736 and in their violent opposition to two attempts, in 1714 and in 1831, to make slave provision marketing illegal on Sundays. Passage of the latter acts caused "riots and disorders" in 1714 and a "near riot" a hundred years later (*Acts of Assembly* 1734:202; *Laws of Antigua* 1864:169–70; Horsford 1856:48).[1]

Lenient enforcement of some codes and neglect of others also diminished the effects of statutory provisions. In slave societies, masters relied upon stringent penalties during times of unrest, but otherwise they practiced tolerance. For example, in nearby Montserrat, where the council assumed jurisdiction over cases of serious crimes committed by slaves, court records indicate that capital punishment or mutilation were rarely used; the majority of cases were dismissed for want of prosecution or insufficient evidence (Goveia 1965:175–76).[2] To cite one last example, obeah, a critical component of Antigua's system of illegalities, waxed and waned in the consciousness of slave masters and in their prosecution of its practitioners. In short, a variety of forms of illegalities were a crucial part of the normative order, and their violation produced deprivation, indignation, and sometimes outright revolt.

The system of illegalities that evolved in the British West Indian colonies left its mark on various practices in the common order; it also penetrated relations between men and women within and across the different ranks of society. Its mark on the kinship order was threefold. First, throughout the British Caribbean and its history, marriage rates have remained low and illegitimacy rates at birth have averaged from 40 to 75 percent (Senior 1991:82). From the beginning, mating and the birth of children outside of legal unions were part of the behavioral repertoire of each rank. Second, in association with miscegenation, illicit relations created a stratum of racially mixed people—between black and white, between slavery and freedom—who then had to be legally constituted. Initially, the formal political and legal institutions of society excluded from membership the majority of inhabitants. Except for a few, they were all "outlaws."[3] Over time, however, the majority was incorporated in fits and starts through an evolutionary, legal process, rather than by revolution. Third, if the system of illegalities was an intricate component of class relations, it also transcended class to shape creole gender roles. The complex connotations of marriage, family name, and "outside" children, as well as what it means to be a "big man" or a "big woman" in Antigua today are linked historically to ideas reflecting the age-old tensions between legalities and illegalities. In practice, the local dichotomy between legal and illegal

TABLE 2   **Census of the White Population of Antigua, 1678**

	Men	*Women*	*Children*
English	800	400	400
Irish	360	130	120
Scottish	76	14	8
Total	1236	544	528

SOURCE: Oliver 1894–99:vol. 1, xlix, lxi.

relationships facilitated women's overall subordination to men and sometimes created divisiveness between women over men.

Creole family life in the pre-emancipation period, then, emerged in the play between law and lawlessness, justice and injustice, and crime and punishment. In the following pages, I continue to investigate the role of the law in the formation of creole kinship, but my perspective shifts. That is, I move from an analysis of legal codes, the cultural constructs of Antigua's elite, to the facts, figures, and historical accounts that describe marriage, concubinage, and miscegenation within and between the different ranks of Antiguan society. We shall consider first the conjugal patterns of free whites and servants, followed by those of free people of color and slaves. Finally, we shall analyze the record for the pervasiveness of miscegenation in Antigua and for its influence on kinship ideology. It will become clear that the possibilities and limitations of legal and illegal relationships were known and shared within and across social groups.

Mating and Marriage among Free Whites and Their Servants

In the seventeenth century, the white population was remarkably small and remarkable for the proportion of its members who were children. The 1678 census differentiated the colonists by sex, age, and nationality and is summarized here in Table 2. What were the principal features of their familial practices and how did these compare to colonists elsewhere?

Our study of local legislation indicated that both legal and nonlegal unions were a regular feature of the family life of free and indentured settlers in seventeenth-century Antigua. This was true elsewhere in the Caribbean and in other New World colonies.[4] The Puritans of Massachusetts Bay, for example, married more frequently and had larger families than West Indians. Yet they, too, faced the problem of children born out of wedlock. Puritan court records are filled with charges of wanton behavior, adultery, rape, and bastardy. Indeed, cases of illegitimacy became so frequent that the General Court of Massachusetts passed a law in 1668 requiring fathers to assist the mothers of their bastard children in child rearing and education (Morgan 1973:74–75). That act was passed more than a hundred years earlier than the white bastardy law in Antigua.

Morgan attributes the pervasiveness of illegitimacy among the Puritans to two factors: many men had left their wives at home, although they brought their sexual appetites with them and found partners, and others were indentured servants who could not marry without the consent of the master. Such permission, he explains, was unlikely to be granted unless the couple already lived in the same household (ibid.:72).

Although profoundly different social, economic, religious, and judicial differences conditioned reproduction and marriage in Massachusetts Bay and Antigua,[5] Morgan's explanation for the high rate of illegitimacy among the Puritans also partly explains that rate in Antigua. Recall that in 1720 almost one out of five whites (19.1 percent) in Antigua was a servant (Gaspar 1985a:78).[6] As we have seen, these people could not marry unless they could pay off their contracts or the heavy fines their masters might impose. By Antiguan law, two servants who married risked having their contracts extended, and a free person who married a servant owed his or her master years of labor or a cash equivalent. And, as noted earlier, West Indian plantation owners preferred employing unmarried bookkeepers, overseers, and attorneys because families cost the estate more for support than they contributed in productivity. This preference for employing unmarried men was a creole characteristic of West Indian planters; it was not characteristic of British landlords.[7]

Other factors also influenced the low marriage rate among Antiguan whites. Judging by the number of statutes restricting "aliens" from full participation in the political and military affairs of the community, non-Anglican foreigners, including Frenchmen, Jews, and Quakers, eventually found their way to the island.[8] Some of these people would have resisted marrying in the Anglican church. Finally, other emigrants might not have wed because they did not wish to or because they could not obtain a nullity of a previous marriage or a divorce.[9]

Legal, religious, and personal impediments notwithstanding, throughout the Caribbean, free whites used marriage and kin networks for purposes of economic aggrandizement.[10] The history of the Pinney family of Nevis, whose great wealth was amassed through a combination of skilled entrepreneurship and plantation management, good luck, and shrewd marriages, provides one example of a common West Indian pattern. The Pinneys created networks of familial ties that spanned both sides of the Atlantic. In its heyday, the family firm sent merchandise to Leeward Island planters, lent them money, arranged for shipping their sugar, and sold their produce through brokers in the Bristol market. The last of their Nevis estates was sold in 1808, but by then the family was solidly established as Bristol merchants and factors (Pares 1950).

The pattern whereby a man of relatively small means expanded his business affairs by combining merchandising, factoring, and plantation management, together with a judicious marriage was common in Antigua. The biographies of Dr. Walter Tullideph and Colonel Samuel Martin provide two examples. Dr. Tullideph, the son of a Scottish minister, arrived in the island in 1726. His friends and relatives immediately helped him develop connections with prominent people. Tullideph built his fortune on the basis of his medical practice, factoring for his brother, money lending, and plantation management. He acquired his first estate by marrying "an agreable young Widow" by whom, he wrote his brother, he was likely to have an heir (Sheridan 1973:198). In fact, he had three children, and although his son died young, his daughters married into "good" families (Sheridan 1971:111). As he moved up the ranks of society, Tullideph also moved up the ladder of political office: he was first a parish vestryman, then a justice of the peace, next an assemblyman, and finally a councilor to the governor (ibid.:199–200).

Tullideph's colleague, Samuel Martin, was the eldest son of Major Samuel Martin. The family was very well established in North America and Suriname by the time young Samuel was born in Antigua in 1693. After his father was killed by his slaves, Samuel went to live with relatives in Ireland. He was educated at Cambridge before he returned to Antigua to manage his inherited estates. Over the course of a very long life, Martin lost two wives and sixteen of his twenty-one children, but his plantations reaped fortunes (ibid.:202–4).[11]

Sheridan's study of sixty-five leading Antiguan families in the eighteenth century also clearly illustrates the importance of kin ties in consolidating the planters' fortunes. He finds: "Except for the Irish-Catholic group, national origin was apparently no barrier to intermarriage for all but eight families were intermarried with at least one other gentry family" (1961:345). Moreover, these alliances spanned both sides of the Atlantic: "It was customary for younger sons to take up residence in London to market the family's sugar, purchase plantation supplies, and perform numerous services connected with trade, shipping, and finance" (ibid.:348).

Kinship and marriage patterns among Antiguan whites were affected by the island's changing economy, which increasingly encouraged the importation of slaves and discouraged small landholders and free artisans, and by the characteristics and numbers of free colonists who settled in the island. Antigua's earliest plantocracy included some wealthy families who arrived from Suriname after that colony was ceded to Holland in 1667. Others were recruited among government officials, merchants, lawyers, doctors, and the armed services (Sheridan 1973:191–92). Then two events, the Act of Union (1707), which allowed the Scots to travel to the British colonies, and the Treaty of Utrecht (1713), which ushered in years of peace and economic prosperity, brought new elements into Antiguan society (ibid.:197). Men initially outnumbered women, but the imbalance in the white sex ratio gradually improved.[12] The total number of white inhabitants in 1753 included 1433 men and 1123 women, but only 705 children (Oliver 1894:vol. 1, cxv).

Over the course of the eighteenth century, then, the white sex ratio improved, and white women were more readily available as marriage partners (Wells 1975:218–19). There were important changes, too, in the educational backgrounds, occupations, and religious and national affiliations of the later free immigrants and indentured servants. These men and women carved new places for themselves in the expanding town and commercial life of the island, and they contributed strongly to the persistence of a legalistic kinship order:

> By the third quarter of the eighteenth century the West Indies no longer served as dumping grounds for English prisoners of war, dissenters, convicts, prostitutes, orphans, and vagrants.... During Janet Schaw's lifetime all but a few of the Scotsmen who went to the West Indies emigrated voluntarily and with a view to mend or make their fortunes. Richard Pares has observed that Scotland was a country poor in natural resources but possessed of an educational system several sizes too large for it. Not only did middle-class Scots leave home because all the professions were overcrowded, but yeomen farmers and craftsmen also sought opportunities in the colonies. (Sheridan 1977:95, 97)

Janet Schaw, to whom Sheridan refers, wrote *The Journal of a Lady of Quality* (Andrews and Andrews 1934). A genteel, intelligent Scottish woman, she accompanied her brother on a trip to Antigua, St. Christopher, and North Carolina in 1774–76. Her journal begins with a description of the "Jamaica Packet," the small ship that carried her party, and, as she discovered two days later at sea, several Scottish families secretly concealed "under the hatches." A few had paid their fares; others were to be indentured in the colonies in return for their passage (ibid.:35–38, 54–55). They were among thousands of

Scots who left for the colonies between 1763 and 1776 due to sharp increases in rents and unemployment.

The majority of Scottish men in Antigua probably began their careers as overseers and bookkeepers (Sheridan 1977:97), but they moved quickly into more lucrative professions as plantation attorneys, shopkeepers, and merchants.[13] When Janet Schaw visited, she found "a whole company of Scotch people, our language, our manners, our circle of friends and connections, all the same" (Andrews and Andrews 1934:81). Her ship's emigrants were soon "disposed of to their hearts contentment, except two families, who, steady to their first idea, persist on going forward to America" (ibid.:116).

Some of the children of the indentured servants of this period joined the ranks of high society in the colony. By 1844, Flannagan observes:

> The Scotchmen of the present day scorn the lowly ideas of their predecessors. They ape the men of fashion, call their haberdashery store a merchant's warehouse, and foregoing the vulgar title of draper, take to themselves the loftier name of *merchant*. Nor is this all. They attend the governor's *levees*, play the amiable at a quadrille party, frequent the billiard table, or perchance take wine with his excellency, and grin and bow with approved precision. Their shops prove an agreeable morning lounge for the superiors of the island. . . . The difference of grade between the entertainer and entertained is overlooked. (1967:vol. 1, 212)

It was not only differences in grades that were overlooked: changes were occurring in the local definition of a "suitable spouse." By the time Flannagan penned her history, the choice of a marriage partner for Caribbean whites was only partly governed by the same considerations that influenced those decisions in Great Britain. The laws of Antigua included provisions to encourage class endogamy; the colonists acknowledged these and created other, nonwritten rules.

A successful Antiguan planter or merchant certainly considered the property and political connections of his intended—just as he would have in England. If he married, he did so with the hope of eventually taking his wife and children back "home." In choosing marriage partners, however, Antiguan whites ignored other features of biography that the English in England would never have ignored. The small size of the white population and their fear and disdain of people of color contributed to the rise of a marriage creed intolerant of racial differences but accepting of other attributes of low status that hurt marital eligibility in England. If a man was financially successful, West Indian whites were disposed to overlook his pedigree, his religion, the means through which he had acquired his estate, and the size of his illegitimate brown family. Over time, a system evolved for men that "enjoined marriage with status equals and nonlegal unions with women of lower status" (R. Smith 1982a:121).

These liaisons, legal and illegal, occurred serially in some cases, simultaneously in others.

Marriage across radically different class or color lines was rare throughout the English-speaking Caribbean. The Antiguan data, for example, are compatible with data from Jamaica, where there were only fourteen mixed marriages between 1780 and 1815 in the parish of St. Elizabeth (E. Brathwaite 1971:188). Heavy sanctions were imposed upon those who rejected either the code or the custom. In 1798, for example, when John Gilbert, an Antiguan of European extraction and an officer in the militia, chose to marry Anne Hart, the daughter of "a gentleman in mind and manners, a landed proprietor, but a coloured man," the white community went up in arms. The governor refused to grant the couple a license, and Gilbert finally resorted to the banns "as though he had been one of the commonest persons in the community." Meanwhile, one of his relatives wrote to all the ministers in Antigua requesting that they not marry the couple. The day after they wed, someone painted Gilbert's front door half-white and half-yellow. He found it necessary to resign his post in the militia (Flannagan 1967:vol. 2, 178–79; Horsford 1856:65–68).

Gilbert and Hart confounded the norms of the system of illegalities that permeated the creole kinship system. Hart was brown and therefore not a suitable marriage partner for a white man. Still, the marriage was celebrated because there was no legal impediment to prevent it. Gilbert's willingness to marry Hart suggests a change was taking place in the class structure of the island. Hart's father, though nonwhite, had acquired an estate of sufficient proportions to have gained his daughter at least partial entry into white society.

The case is also a sign that the institution of marriage was acquiring an unorthodox connotation among the free settlers, regardless of color, and quite unlike its meaning in England. In 1818, visitor James Walker reported "rank and privilege, which are strongly marked in everything, seem to turn marriage into a distinction somewhat of the nature of nobility, and to reserve it in general for the proprietors and leading men of the colony" (in Goveia 1965:215). Walker wrote about what he perceived to be an unusual correlation between upper-class status and marriage. We shall see shortly that the association between social class and marriage developed concomitantly with an association between marriage and salvation, but the latter was especially emphasized in the creole family ideology evolving in the slave quarters.

Long-term concubinage existed as an alternative to marriage. Like matrimony, it was rule governed with respect to class and gender. A different code of conduct, for example, was expected of men and women. Both Janet Schaw and John Luffman, who lived in Antigua twelve years after Schaw visited there, describe the island's white "society" women as amiable and virtuous. Luffman gives this account of them:

> As mistresses of families, they are unimportant, almost every domestic concern being left to the management of their negroes and mulattoes. ... The virtue of our fair [sex] is said to be superior to the arts of seduction, infidelity to the marriage bed being very rarely known on their parts. I wish I could say as much for the men. (1789:36–37)

Luffman hints that all Antiguan men took their marriage vows rather lightly, but in another letter he writes that it was mainly Antiguan estate managers and overseers, not the plantation owners, who were likely to develop illicit liaisons:

> To be the manager of an estate of an absentee, in this isle, I am well satisfied is one of the best situations in it, altho' their stipends amount to no more than from eighty to one hundred pounds sterling per ann., and not withstanding the necessaries and the superfluities of life are considerably dearer than at London; yet, however paradoxical it may appear, when I tell you this description of men sport several dishes at their tables, drink claret, keep mulatto mistresses, and indulge in every foolish extravagance of this western region, it is nevertheless strictly true. ... But here I must observe that many of these gentlemen managers, as well as the overseers under them, contribute, in a great degree, to stock the plantation with mulatto and mestee slaves; it is impossible to say in what numbers they have such children, but the following fact is too often verified, "that, as soon as born, they are despised, not only by the very authors, under God, of their being, but by every white, destitute of humane and liberal principles," such is the regard paid to the hue of complexion in preference to the more permanent beauties of the mind. (Ibid.:43–44, 45–46)[14]

This commentary suggests that in Antigua miscegenetic concubinage was normative for white men, but not white women, and was more commonly practiced by middle- and lower-ranking free men, such as overseers and estate attorneys, than by the elite. How accurate was Luffman's observation? We shall return to the issue of miscegenation to investigate its pervasiveness and relevance to family ideology and structure in the final section of this chapter. First we will continue our investigation of the conjugal practices of people in different social ranks.

Concubinage and Marriage among Free People of Color

The central point to understand about the family ideology that evolved among free people of color in Antigua and describes modern creole family ideology is that it was characterized by a strong regard for legalities. Because other scholars' discussions of the conjugal practices of the free nonwhite sector in the Leeward Islands concentrated on the seventeenth and eighteenth centuries (e.g., Dunn 1973; Goveia 1965), they missed the evolution of this allegiance to the principle of legally constituted unions. The significant characteristics of modern family organization, however, emerged in the period just before emancipation.

In the first hundred years after settlement, the free nonwhite population of Antigua included relatively few persons. A list of the inhabitants from 1707 shows 1,001 "able" men, 805 white women, 1,038 white children, 48 "superannuated" men, 8 free negro and mulatto men, 4 free negro and mulatto women, 5 free children, and 12,943 slaves (Oliver 1894:vol. 1, lxxviii). Two decades later, however, there were 1,337 white men, 1,096 white women, 1,124 white children, and 531 other "free persons" on the island (ibid.:xciii). The number of nonwhite free persons increased to 1,230 in 1787, to 1,300 in 1805, and to 3,895 in 1821 (based on Coleridge 1826:253 and Gaspar 1985b:135).[5] Most resided in St. John's. They were employed as domestics, servants, messengers, artisans, and boatmen. Despite laws restricting their employment opportunities, the amount of property they could hold, and their political rights, some achieved economic security. By the nineteenth century, their socioeconomic status had greatly improved. Lowes finds that contrary to the "commonly held pyramidal view of West Indian social structure [which] places the free colored in the middle in terms of wealth as well as phenotypic skin color . . . by the 1820s there was a very wide range of both wealth and color, as well as education and social status, within the free colored category" (1992:13). Coleridge, who visited Antigua in 1825, found this class owned considerable personal property; indeed, the principal newspaper of the island at the time was owned by a man of color (1826:253).

Goveia argues that free women of color in Antigua preferred liaisons with whites to marriages with men of their own class because of the status and economic advantages the former unions could bring. Given this situation, free men of color had little choice but to choose slave women for mates, and their children, inheriting the status of their mother, became slaves (Goveia 1965:316–17).[6] Cousins penned a different explanation for why a woman might choose not to marry:

> In the year 1830 a married woman was more truly a slave than her own black servant. The mulatto woman who, being free, contracted an irregular union, escaped both servitudes. Legacies from her father, and gifts from her man, became her own property, and thus coloured women often built up substantial little fortunes, which they bequeathed to their children. A father often left part, at least, of his property to his irregular family; and in cases of escheat (which, where most people were born out of wedlock, was a common occurrence), the Crown conceded them a limited right of inheritance. (1935:45–46)

Thus marriage and inheritance laws may have been partly responsible for encouraging concubinage, especially for women who chose to build independently a legacy for their children. Other local laws, as we have seen, discouraged whites and free persons of color from marrying servants or slaves, prohibited

TABLE 3   White and Colored Population by Parish, 1821

Parish	White Men	Women	Colored Men	Women
St. John's	644	563	1210	1623
St. Philip's	116	46	62	99
St. George's	56	35	24	44
St. Mary's	81	43	65	94
St. Peter's	100	37	53	65
St. Paul's	142	117	292	435
Total	1139	841	1706	2360

SOURCE: Adapted from Flannagan (1967:vol. 2, 284). These totals vary slightly from those in Oliver (1894–99:vol. 1, cli).

marriages except those celebrated by an Anglican minister, and made common-law unions illegitimate.

The persistence of concubinage in the free colored population in Antigua, like its incidence in the white community, must therefore be attributed to several factors. Kinship codes discouraged legal unions between persons of different ranks and white settlers were reluctant to break the color barrier. At times imbalanced sex ratios in the free community also perpetuated nonlegal unions. Because the sex ratio of free people of color mostly favored women, there were too few men available to them as marriage partners.[17] Moreover, in the early nineteenth century, the white population once again experienced a decline in the number of women. The 1821 census, partially summarized in Table 3, lists many more white men than white women, and many more free colored women than colored men in every parish. Given these ratios, some free women of color who chose not to remain celibate, or who wanted children, may have accepted unions with white men.

Concubinage persisted as a viable mating form in the free black and colored sector: social, economic, demographic, legal, and ideological forces ensured its continuity. Nevertheless, by the first quarter of the nineteenth century, free

TABLE 4 **Marriages at St. John's Anglican Church, 1814–1826**

Year	Total Number of Marriages	Marriages of Free People of Color	As a Percentage of All Marriages
1814	5[a]	2	40
1815	22	6	27
1816	7	1	14
1817	10	2	20
1818	18	6	33
1819	12	5[b]	42
1820	13	0	0
1821	6	4	67
1822	12	2	17
1823	11	6[c]	55
1824	13	7	54
1825	11	4	36
1826	10[a]	0	0

SOURCE: Adapted from Anglican Church records, *Baptism June* 29th, 1814 to December 31st, 1826, Marriages June 24th, 1814 to November 13th, 1826, Burials June 9th, 1814 to December 21st, 1826, National Archives, St. John's, Antigua.
[a] Records are available for only part of the year.
[b] Includes two couples listed as "free Negroes."
[c] Includes one couple in which the man is listed as a "free Negro" and the woman is described as a "free Mongrel."

people of color in St. John's embraced the institution of marriage. Records from St. John's Anglican Church, shown in Table 4, indicate that marriages of free nonwhites constituted a surprisingly high percentage of all marriages in that church between 1814 and 1826. These records are especially important because according to the law of the period, Antiguans could only be married by an Anglican minister.[18]

Clearly the popular impression that in Antiguan slave society marriage was reserved for free whites overstates the case. Between 1814 and 1826, the free nonwhite population married at a rate approaching that of their white neighbors. They adopted legal, Christian unions—unions that protected certain relations of power over persons and things. Free people of color adopted the legalistic kinship order developing in situ as their own. Legal marriage was a sign of status, a practical way to protect property, and a symbol of one's acceptance of Christianity.

Just as they accepted the local marriage code, free people of color regularly used other laws to order kinship relationships. They wrote wills to distribute their property to their children, a right formally granted in 1824 (Microfilm No. 5). In 1830, they petitioned the British Parliament directly for a redress of several political grievances, including the right to participate in the system of parochial aid, which, as we have seen, included provision only for illegitimate white children (Oliver 1894:vol. 1, clii).[19]

Moreover, in 1816, when many free colored women were becoming respectable married ladies, and, one assumes, members of the Anglican church, they founded a formal association specifically devoted to combating the consequences of family illegalities in the common order. The Destitute Females' Friend Society, later renamed the Female Orphan Society, was organized by "a few subscribers, chiefly respectable coloured persons" (Flannagan 1967:vol. 1, 259). The name of their charity was misleading; it was actually an association to care for destitute young women who were the children of illicit unions:

> Few of the inmates are orphans in the true sense of the word, they being, but with few exceptions, the illegitimate children of black or coloured women, (by white or coloured persons,) whose parents, still alive are, from penury, incompetent to maintain them, or are living in a state of concubinage, and consequently not proper guides to youth. (Ibid.:258)

The women who organized and supervised the society realized that there was an "indigent class of coloured children of their own sex, (for whom there was no parochial relief)" (ibid.:258). The girls received shelter, food, clothing, and religious and vocational instruction. They made straw bonnets for sale and worked as seamstresses and domestics. In 1843, they earned just over 107 pounds from their labors (ibid.:260). The society was proud of its achievements:

> The success, though not in every instance unfailing, has been considerable. A few, there is reason to hope, are where sin and sorrow cannot enter. Others, as useful domestics, or conductors of their own households, testify to the truth of the fact.

Three of the elder girls have been sent into creditable situations, with a prospect of comfort to themselves and usefulness to their employers. Four more have been admitted to fill their places. Seventeen are now in the house. . . .

That it is an invaluable charity none can deny, for it strikes to the root of all West Indian misery—*illicit love;* and what can be more acceptable to "the community at large" than the endeavouring to inculcate into the minds of its youthful members the doctrine of chastity and diligence in well-doing? (Ibid.:259)

Thus, well before abolition, free women of color in Antigua embraced legitimate unions as desirable and organized a charitable association to contend with undesirable mating illegalities. Their association is evidence of an indigenous, female-headed, and female-directed political approach to an indigenously defined kinship "problem."[20] After a time, they received financial assistance from other members of the community as well as from "benevolent individuals in England and Scotland" who believed in their cause (ibid.:259). Together, these women were working out a pattern, evident in this century, in which law, order, and formal institutions are basic to conceptualizing and managing family.

Free persons of color thus participated in and perpetuated a family system composed of both legalities and illegalities. As people do today, men and women married, remained in, or terminated illicit relationships after considering the benefits and pitfalls of choosing one kind of union over another. By the time slavery was abolished, marriage was associated with high status and the civilizing precepts of Christianity; it was also a route for social mobility and offered certain property advantages to one's children. Concubinage, on the other hand, was a choice for those who loved but who could not wed because of law or other structural constraints, creole norms regarding color, or personal considerations. Visiting relationships, a third option, gave free men and women more time, fewer responsibilities, greater control over the operation and economy of their own households, and freedom to keep the company they chose.

Love and Marriage among Slaves

In contrast to some of the larger sugar islands, little information exists about the social and kinship organization of Antiguan and Barbudan slaves (Gaspar 1985a:97). Few records describing individual estates have been published (Phillips 1926:439), and the early Antiguan censuses record only absolute numbers of slaves or, more rarely, distinguish them by sex or as adults and children (Wells 1975:214–20). We do have surviving notes of Antiguan planters, missionaries, and visitors.

Antiguan slaves established family networks consistent with those described for other Commonwealth Caribbean societies. Some of the slaves involved in the 1736 conspiracy, for example, confessed that they had been recruited by their kin (Gaspar 1985a:249). Dr. Tullideph, manager of the Winthrop estate for absentee owner George Thomas,[21] recognized the usefulness of encouraging slave family life. On 19 June 1749, he wrote to Thomas for approval for his plan to find wives for the laborers:

> I have recd. the £.100 nearly from Mr. Malloon for the Cattle Mill, which with the rent of the house at five Islands, and the Surplus for the Rum at Winthropes this Crop I think could purchase 5 or 6 young People for that Estate. You really want them, indeed the negroe Men are craving for wifes and therefore would advise Girls to be bought for that Estate and boys for No. Sd. (Cited in Sheridan 1957:19)

Forty years later, Christopher Bethell Codrington of Antigua commented on the strong familial ties that had evolved among slaves within and between different estates. Sent to Antigua by William Codrington in 1789 to learn "plantonship," young Christopher advised his uncle to purchase new female slaves rather than "seasoned" males

> because they will bear as much work and do it well as men, and it is better that the ladies should seek company at Brooms than that the gentlemen of Brooms should be obliged to seek the company of the ladies elsewhere: the child becoming the property of the proprietor of the female. (Codrington Family Archives, letter dated 12 May 1790)

Codrington observed that women worked as hard as men and also increased the labor force by bearing children. Conversations with other planters also convinced him that "seasoned" slaves frequently ran away—"their having formed attachments elsewhere on the island."

The historical record indicates that in Antigua, as elsewhere in the Caribbean, there was never a singular type of slave family. There were long-lasting unions between men and women and short-term, serial relationships. Single and multiple unions coexisted with different proportions in different places and in different times because the social, economic, and ideological contexts in which slaves labored influenced both the number and types of their conjugal relationships and patterns of reproduction. Those who spent all of their lives in the fields differed in their mating and reproductive patterns from those who lived in towns or belonged to masters with small estates. Slaves on large and profitable estates, for example, might experience relative stability in their day-to-day lives and had access to a pool of potential conjugal partners on their own and nearby estates. "Elaborated families," explains B. Higman, "were . . . most common on large-scale plantations" (1984:366). The record suggests a pattern in which slaves experimented initially with a number of partners and later settled into more permanent and long-term unions with single partners.

Historians have also traced some differences in the conjugal practices of field workers, domestics, and skilled artisans. Men recognized as leaders within the slave community maintained multiple unions that were accepted as "legitimate" relationships within the community (e.g., Brathwaite 1971; Bush 1990; Craton 1978; Goveia 1965; Higman 1976, 1984; Morrissey 1989; R. Smith 1987). Slave women living on very large estates were more likely to become involved in miscegenistic relationships (Higman 1976:148). Sexual unions and blood ties with whites in different ranks of society changed the daily lives of some slaves and the course of their future relationships. Slave household sizes and the demographic characteristics of household members were functions of alternative mating choices, personal preferences, beliefs about the relations of women and men to their children, and, in all likelihood, pragmatic decisions about how best to organize the sexual division of labor in the home and beyond its walls. Sometimes, too, household membership was affected by law. For example, the Leeward Island Amelioration Acts urged masters to provide a pregnant female slave with her own two-room house (Flannagan 1967:vol. 1, 129).

Slaves who labored in towns where the demographics and daily life were decidedly different manifested a different conjugal pattern. A large percentage of town slaves were domestics and laundresses, tasks assigned to women. Although slave men worked as messengers, on public works, on docks and in a variety of other pursuits (Goveia 1965:230), their masters were unlikely to allow them to establish independent households (Higman 1984:373). Subjected to constant supervision, domestics were also more likely to live in mother-children households than were field laborers (ibid.:371).

Importantly, town slaves were also much more likely to come under the influence of missionaries, who introduced to their converts the notion that marriage was a critical component of one's religious salvation. Fornication, an offense in law, then acquired an entirely new connotation. As the churches evolved into institutions designed to educate slaves and to save their souls, Christianity came to play a decisive role among the structural and personal variables influencing the conjugal and reproductive practices of slaves—not to mention the structure and ideology of gender relationships. At the end of the eighteenth century, a discourse about kinship that incorporated the language, some of the rituals, and the symbols of "Christian" marriage began spreading across the different social ranks (Lazarus-Black 1992:872–74).

The extraordinary rapidity with which Christianity was accepted by Leeward Island slaves argues for its decisive role among factors influencing reproduction and marriage. By the end of the slave trade in 1807, the missions had converted approximately 28 percent of the black and colored population in Antigua, St. Kitts, Montserrat, Nevis, and the British Virgin Islands (based on Goveia 1965:307). The three most influential denominations in Antigua were Anglicanism, Moravianism, and Methodism. A few Catholics also resided there, but the first Catholic church in the island was not established until Bishop Porrier arrived from the diocese in Dominica in 1868. Some Catholics living in Antigua were married by Anglican ministers and then remarried in their own faith when a priest visited their island (Catholic Church Marriage Registers, St. John's, Antigua).[22]

Antigua had the largest proportion of Anglican ministers in the Leeward Islands—one for each parish at the end of the eighteenth century. Some of the early Anglican ministers, however, were not of an admirable sort, as the following example shows:

> Sep. 23. (1707) The Rev. Simon Smith is accused of Bigamy & Forgery. It has been proved that he forged the Bishop's seal. The Bishop of Bath & Wales having written to say that he did not ordain him on Trinity Sunday 1692. Mrs. Smith lives in town (his primitive wife). He was married to Mrs. Elliot the wife he now lives with in the Governor's House, & Mrs. Yeamans gave Mrs. Elliot away. He married Mrs. fflower (sic.) (who is now living in St Johns Town) at New York & had previously cohabited with her for some years. (Oliver 1894:vol. 1, lxxix)

At first the Anglican ministers tended mainly to the white colonists, making little effort to convert the slaves. When the Bishop of London inquired in 1723 about the means used to redeem the infidels, for example, Reverend Smith of Falmouth parish replied there were two thousand Negroes in his parish, but no care was taken for their conversion. Rev. Knox of St. John's parish, one of Smith's colleagues, voiced concern that the slaves were likely to remain heathen. Yet at least some Antiguan slaves had been converted by 1736, because judges at the conspiracy trials reported that some of the ringleaders had been baptized (Gaspar 1985a:133, 232). Moreover, by 1774, when Janet Schaw attended services at the St. John's Anglican cathedral, she wrote to her friend: "What pleased me more than all I saw, was a great number of Negroes who occupied the Area, and went thro' the Service with seriousness and devotion" (Andrews and Andrews 1934:94). At least some of these persons, we can assume, were free men and women, but others must have been slaves.[23] Still, the Anglican church remained associated with the "establishment" long after its "disestablishment" by legal proclamation in 1873.[24]

In contrast to the Anglicans, Moravian missionaries arrived in St. John's in 1756 with the deliberate intention of proselytizing to the slaves. They had already established successful missions in the Danish islands of St. Thomas, St. Croix, and St. John,[25] although their first church in Jamaica failed.[26] The history of this church in Antigua and St. Kitts is a remarkable success story. In 1788, only 32 years after their arrival, the Antiguan Brethren claimed 6,038 nonwhite converts, not including catechumens and children. By 1798, the membership had increased to 9,609 adults and 2,178 children. Churches were erected in St. John's, in Gracehill near English Harbour, and in Grace Bay at

Old Road Town (Goveia 1965:271–72, 280–81). The Moravians numbered an estimated 11,000 in 1842 (Flannagan 1967:vol. 1, 250).

The Methodists, too, garnered a large following. Their first spiritual leaders were Nathaniel Gilbert, a lawyer and planter, and John Baxter, a local Antiguan shipwright. Later they were assisted by Dr. Thomas Coke, the "Father of Methodist Missions in the West Indies," who arrived in Antigua after a storm set his ship ashore. By 1793, there were said to be 6,570 Methodists in the West Indies—most of them black. The congregation in Antigua included 2 ministers, 36 whites, 105 mulattoes, and 2,279 blacks (J. Brathwaite 1973:57; Goveia 1965:288, 293–94). In 1830, the Incorporated Society for the Conversion and Religious Instruction of the Negro Population reported that in Barbuda, 56 couples, most of them "married" by the Wesleyans, were living together faithfully as husband and wife (cited in Higman 1984b:368).

Opportunities to assemble, to learn to read, to assume positions of leadership, and to learn "the Christian idiom," a status marker that enhanced the black man's "believability" in a world controlled by white men (Monk in Fischer 1974a:29), as well as religious conversion, account for the rapid acceptance of Christianity among Antiguan slaves. By 1823, British commissioners reported "several Sunday schools are formed in different parts of the island and religious establishments abound in every quarter." They found "a very decided superiority in the mulatto and negro character in this island." The commissioners believed "the treatment of slaves to be nowhere so generally humane and so laudably attentive to their religious instruction and intellectual and moral improvement (1826:vol. 3, 15, 28).

Christian ministers and their assistants depended upon the generosity of followers in England and Europe to finance their Caribbean programs; they depended upon the good graces of the white population in the islands to make them operable. The missionaries were therefore unwilling to tamper overtly with the political, social, or economic organization of the West Indian societies in which they worked (cf. Goveia 1965:271–73). The Baptists, for example, cautioned ministers "against engaging in any of the merely civil disputes or local politics of the Colony to which you may be appointed, either verbally or by correspondence." They also admonished: "The whole period of your residence in the West Indies is to be filled up with the proper work of your Mission" (Horsford 1856:34).

A long history of noninterference in the politics of state by churchmen in the Leeward Islands thus began in the eighteenth century. Here, the potentially revolutionary implications of the idea that there was only one true religion for black men as well as for white was mitigated; the missionaries preached submission to secular authority and obedience to the masters (Goveia 1965:271–73). Antiguan planters initially feared the ramifications of making slaves into

Christians, but eventually they supported the work of the missionaries from their own pockets. In 1817, for example, they passed a law to pay the head of the United Brethren "the sum of 1,000 pounds current gold and silver to allow them to erect a chapel and other buildings on Pigott's Land." The bill also provided three hundred pounds per year to maintain the facilities. The legislators explained that "by long experience the inhabitants of this Island have found the beneficial effects of the religious principles instilled in the minds of the negro population by the church of the United Brethren" (*Laws of Antigua* 1864:152–53). The law remained in force until 1892 (*Laws of Antigua* 1920:xiv).

Although Antiguan ministers had almost no effect upon overt political transformation in the Leeward Islands, their influence on family ideology was enormous. Their power and their greatest success lay in their apolitical role, "in the domain of implicit signs and practices, of the diffuse control over everyday meaning" (Comaroff and Comaroff 1986a:1). The missionaries' presence accelerated the acceptance of European forms and practices in the common order. They demanded a change of heart, of principles, and of life-style from their converts. Deploring the "savage" and "heathenist" courting and mating practices that they alleged most slaves practiced, they beseeched their followers to live in a "Christian manner."[27]

The missionaries' charter for what constituted Christian behavior, of course, underwent a subtle transformation of meaning in the West Indian context. For example, the Moravian Brethren found themselves confronted with slaves who wished to be baptized but were obviously involved in multiple partnerships. They decided that although they would not condone such behavior, they could not compel a convert to leave a partner without consent. They were realists, too, when it came to the question of the planters disrupting slave marriages: should wives be torn from their husbands, or husbands from wives, and carried off to distant lands, the missionaries would not prevent a second marriage, especially if young children were involved (Edwards 1819:493–95; Goveia 1965:279–80).

The experiences of other Christian mission groups in Antigua were similar: doctrines, practices, and institutions underwent creolization. The Wesleyans, for example, instructed that no woman of color "be allowed to belong to our Society in the West Indies who cohabits with any man to whom she has not been married: only, when the slaves are not allowed to marry according to law, a solemn agreement before witnesses must be deemed sufficient" (Horsford 1856:131). Similarly, Mr. and Mrs. Thwaites, who opened the first Methodist school for slaves in Antigua in 1813, taught only "moral" persons (ibid.:208). Very few of the missionaries were like Daniel Gateward David, Rector of Charlestown, Nevis, who, "in defiance of law and usage," united slaves in matrimony (ibid.:18).

As their churches filled, West Indian missionaries placed more and more of the work of the civilizing mission in the hands of women—a fact important in the evolution of both family and gender ideology and structure. Free and slave women were devoted converts who tended to a host of church functions. They spread the word, brought their children to be baptized, and labored to make the mission a success. In 1803 Thomas Richardson, a Methodist missionary, reported there were "6 or 8 local preachers, besides several coloured women, who are very useful & possess considerable abilities for prayer & exhortation. The women in St. Johns hold public meetings every week" (in Oliver 1894:vol. 1, cxliv). Yet the missionaries' position with respect to women was not significantly different from the stance they took with regard to slaves. Their teachings buttressed the status quo and re-enforced gender hierarchy. Because it saw women as "the chief source of sin Christianity tended to degrade motherhood, to accentuate masculine supremacy and to maintain a double standard of morality" (Jacobs 1932:579). Women who refused to marry were often excluded from congregations and sometimes from church schools. Their illegitimate children could only be baptized on special days.

The churches were unsuccessful in destroying the slaves' willingness to accept a variety of relationships between men and women. The ministers were successful, however, in convincing people that Christian marriage was the most ideal form of union. Their influence in transforming the world view of the slaves, in introducing a way of talking about the union of man and woman that incorporated the hierarchical symbols and language of the canon and common law, helps to account for the origin and persistence of the high status of legal, Christian marriages (cf. Roberts and Sinclair 1978).[28] The missionaries implanted the belief, still widely held today, that salvation and marriage were intertwined. The sudden increase in marriages in Barbuda in the early 1970s, for example, may be attributed to the clergy's interpretation of hurricanes and earthquakes as signs that judgment day was near.[29]

At the end of the eighteenth century, then, the Amelioration Act and Christian marriage offered to slaves opportunities to acknowledge formally familial ties. Slave marriages differed from those of free persons: they were never contracts in the same sense of the term; they did not allow men to legally pass their name, status, or property to their children; and they did not provide a route for social mobility. Not surprisingly, then, the meaning and purpose of marriage differed for slaves and free persons: they shared some, but not all, of the assumptions and principles about marriage that were held by their owners. Nevertheless, because a very large number of Antiguan slaves embraced Christianity, Christian marriage became associated with the salvation of a cohabiting couple, and the church wedding became fixed as a cultural ideal. Thus by the end of slavery in 1834, marriage had acquired special connotations within and across the ranks of this society. Socially, it was a mark of civility, education, financial stability, enduring love, and religious salvation. Pragmatically, it ensured certain legal protections for men, women, and their children (Lazarus-Black 1992:874). In contrast, concubinage was relegated to the system of illegalities. So was miscegenation.

The Role of Miscegenation in the Development of Antiguan Kinship Ideology and Structure

Miscegenation rattled West Indian whites because it jostled legally constituted familial rights and duties and also threatened the color-coded division of labor. It was prohibited by law in most of the sugar colonies, but everywhere it assumed a regular place in family life in the common order. Even so, miscegenation did not occur with the same frequency throughout the West Indies and, as a result, there are noticeable differences between the islands in ideologies of kinship, class, and race.[30]

In the next few pages, I summarize how historians have accounted for miscegenation, consider the evidence for interracial unions in Antigua, and compare this data with previous research from Jamaica, where rates of miscegenation have been systematically investigated. These inquires lead me to three conclusions. First, Higman's important contribution to our understanding of the role of miscegenation in the evolution of family life in the West Indies can be further elaborated so that it is more sensitive to the cultural construction of gender, race, and class in different locales. Second, in Antigua intraracial concubinage and marriage were more usual and of greater significance than miscegenation in shaping creole family structure and ideology over the *longue durée* (Braudel 1980:27). Third, varying incidences of miscegenation help explain differences in beliefs about color with respect to both family and social mobility in different islands. Therefore, although there are general similarities in patterns throughout the region, we must be aware of important differences between islands. The Antiguan kinship system is no more a replica of the Jamaican kinship system than it is of the English system.

The proslavery debates of the mid-eighteenth century labeled concubinage and miscegenation morally deviant and advocated strengthening the institution of marriage to discourage both practices. Writing in 1774, Jamaican Edward Long also placed part of the blame for concubinage on white, island-born women, suggesting improvements in their education might make them more agreeable as wives (1970:vol. 2, 330). Later historians have explained the illicit interracial unions of the slave era by demographic imbalances in the sex ratios of whites, abuse on the part of planters and their hired hands, and the preference

93

of free colored and slave women for white men because the association with whites brought increased privileges and opportunities (e.g., Goveia 1965:217; Heuman 1981:52; M. Smith 1965b:99).

It is fair to say that each of these factors was responsible for miscegenetic encounters in Antigua. Some evidence, for example, indicates that slave women were forced into relations of concubinage with white men:

> There are persons in this island who let out their female slaves for the particular purpose of fornication, and that, as well as publickly cohabiting with them, is considered here merely as a venial error. These women are much more subservient to the will of their enamoratos, from a dread of punishment than a white would be, or even the laws of the country suffer, for it is not uncommon for some men to beat, and otherwise severely correct their colored mistresses. This connexion strikes at the root of honorable engagements with the fair, prevents marriage, and is, thereby, detrimental to the increase of legitimate population. (Luffman 1789:115–16)

According to another source, women of color sometimes sold their own daughters to white and colored men for personal gain (Thome and Kimball 1839:82).

Miscegenation was often the result of brute force; the physical domination of men and women over other women. Yet on the whole it was not a disorderly practice. Using a Jamaican sample, Higman demonstrates that miscegenation evolved its own regularities and normative principles. He found that it followed a pattern of increasing "whiteness" through slave women and increasing "blackness" through slave men. Light-complexioned women tended to bear fair-skinned children and were likely to have darker-skinned children, if any, only later in their lives. In contrast, light-skinned males were unlikely to father light-complexioned children (1976:152). Thus planters did not regularly tear slave women from their mates: miscegenation was rule governed, and the rules were "known and obeyed by the whites as well as the slaves" (ibid.:153).

Miscegenation was rule-governed not only with respect to color but also with respect to gender and class (Douglass 1992; Lazarus-Black 1990a; M. Smith 1965d; R. Smith 1988, 1992). As we have seen, free West Indians transformed the English notion of a "suitable husband" in a way that allowed even the most respectable men to participate in the system of illegalities that included concubinage and miscegenation. On the other hand, white women who overstepped the boundaries of "proper" and legally constituted relationships faced strong sanctions. Not one case of the union of a white woman with a black man appears in any of the historical records from Antigua.

In addition, the class standing of a white individual with whom a slave became involved played a decisive role in determining his or her future. The point can be illustrated with an example from Jamaica. Rose Price, the proprietor of Worthy Park plantation between 1797 and 1835 (Craton 1978), followed the norm, if not the law. Like his white hirelings, Price fathered illegitimate children during his stay in Jamaica. When he left permanently for England, he privately arranged for their future education and financial welfare. Alternative provisions for illegitimate progeny—appropriate to their class situation—were made by two white craftsmen hired at the Price estate:

> In 1816 Thomas James, aged 5, was manumitted by his father in return for another slave, Martin, aged 10, and carried away from Worthy Park when Charles James moved on in the following year. By doing this Charles James was following a pattern already established by Robert Richard, Sally's millwright father, who had manumitted two of his other colored children in 1795. Perhaps "passing white" craftsmen were more likely than overseers to acknowledge their bastards, who were valued greatly as potential helpers and successors in their craft. (Ibid.:238)

As the fates of these descendants show, the relation between slaves and free members of the society cannot be analyzed without reference to West Indian precepts of hierarchy and class. A craftsman might free his slave child to work at his side; plantation elites would never consider such an arrangement, although they might free the children as a matter of grace.

Miscegenation was rule-governed with respect to color, gender, and class; it was also most likely to happen under specific economic, social, demographic, and legal conditions. Higman finds that in pre-emancipation Jamaica, interracial relationships occurred most frequently in towns and on large sugar plantations; less often on smaller coffee and pimento estates and on those with resident proprietors. Miscegenation was at a minimum on holdings of between 21 and 100 slaves (1976:147–48), whereas the proportion of colored births was highest in units containing 301 to 400 slaves, the large plantations with transient white managers who fathered slave children (Higman 1984b:150). Further comparison between Antigua and Jamaica, presented below, highlights critical differences between the two islands that affected their respective rates of miscegenation, the compositions of their middle classes, and, ultimately, the different emphasis upon color in their respective family and class ideologies.

To begin with, the overall number and size of the sugar estates in Jamaica and Antigua probably influenced their different rates of miscegenation. Sheridan estimates that a medium-sized sugar plantation in Jamaica in 1774 included 600 acres (266 in cane) and 200 slaves (1973:231). Bryan Edwards counted 710 sugar estates there in 1789, with an average of 181.4 slaves per estate (Craton 1978:17). In the period just before abolition, almost 50 percent of Jamaican slaves lived in units of more than 150, and another 25 percent lived in units of more than 250 (Higman 1976:69). The vast majority, in other words, lived under conditions in which miscegenation occurred regularly.

Antiguan estates eventually grew as large as their Jamaican counterparts—but not until the nineteenth century. After the French invasion in 1666–67, the assembly passed measures limiting the size of future land grants

TABLE 5   **Antiguan Estates and Slave Holdings, 1829**

Parish	Estates in the Sample	Average Acreage	Average Number of Slaves
St. John's	38	356	171
St. Peter's	17	426	247
St. George's	14	326	200
St. Paul's	12	556	142
St. Philip's	23	286	168
St. Mary's	21	438	167
	Total estates: 125	Average acreage: 398	Average number of slaves: 182

SOURCE: Adapted from Oliver 1894–99:vol. 3, 355–57, 379, 382, 384, 389–90, 392–93. These figures are based on my calculations for 125 estates reporting both size and slave holdings.

or sales to 600 acres and forfeiting unsettled lands. These measures were designed to discourage owner absenteeism and to promote internal development (Sheridan 1973:190), but they also impeded the growth of very large holdings. In 1678, only 258 of 563 householders held slaves, and the vast majority of these (199) owned between 1 and 9 slaves. Only 7 householders owned 40 or more slaves (Sheridan 1973:189). In 1734, only a handful of Antiguans owned 300 acres of land. About 30 years later, the average number of slaves on each estate in St. Mary's parish was 86 (Dunn 1972:142).

Only after the end of the slave trade, years of drought and soil erosion, falling sugar prices, and the subsequent consolidation of several estates did Antiguan sugar plantations rival Jamaica's in size and slave holdings. A sample of 125 Antiguan estates in 1829 shows that the overall average number of slaves on each (182) was almost the same as the average Jamaican estate 30 years earlier (181). On the other hand, the Antiguan estates, documented in Table 5, were still significantly smaller in acreage than those in Jamaica.

Of 125 Antiguan estates for which size and slave holdings are reported in 1829, only 24 (19 percent) held 250 or more slaves, whereas 46 (37 percent) included 150 or more slaves. Another 34 (27 percent) of the estates were composed of between 100 and 150 slaves, and 21 (17 percent) consisted of fewer than 100 slaves. In other words, in 1829, 56 percent of the Antiguan slaves on these estates lived under conditions in which miscegenation might be expected, but the other 44 percent did not. In contrast, almost 75 percent of the slaves in the Jamaican sample of the same period lived exposed to the likelihood of interracial unions.

These figures are suggestive rather than definitive: they allude to a demographic profile less likely than that of Jamaica's estates to promote interracial unions.[31] In addition, there were other demographic factors that deterred miscegenetic relationships in Antigua. Higman finds neither the white/slave ratio nor the white male/female ratio could fully explain variations in the size of the colored slave population. There was a positive correlation, on the other hand, between an excess of female slaves and a large colored population (1976:145–46; 1984b:149). The male/female ratios of slaves in Antigua probably varied in different parishes, as they did in Jamaica, but the overall sex ratio for the slaves in Antigua was not terribly imbalanced in 1678 (Wells 1975:219), in 1821, when there were 14,531 males and 16,533 females (Oliver 1894:vol. 1, cli), or in 1832, when the total number of slaves included 13,483 males and 14,971 females (Higman 1984b:420). It seems safe to surmise that by itself the slave sex ratio did not compel slave women to choose white mates. Moreover, in the period right after abolition, miscegenetic relationships were less and less commonplace because both whites and mulattoes emigrated in large numbers.[32]

The high rate of resident Antiguan planters, perhaps with resident wives, further hampered the incidence of black-white unions. Slaveholding patterns in St. Philip's parish in 1720, for example, show "most proprietors were probably resident and knew their slaves personally" (Gaspar 1985a:97–99). This claim is consistent with Wells's analyses of Leeward Island censuses before 1776 in which he reports that there is no basis for concluding that "an overseer living with a gang of slaves was a common pattern" (1975:235). Janet Schaw wrote in 1774 that Antigua had more proprietors on it than any of the other islands. In her opinion, that fact was responsible for its "great Superiority" (Andrews and Andrews 1934:92). Just after abolition, another visitor commented: "Although the Island suffers from absenteeism, it has proportionately a more numerous resident proprietary than any other Colony except Barbados" (Sturge cited in Horsford 1856:90). Similarly, Thome and Kimball found "an accumulation of talent, intelligence and refinement" in Antigua in 1837 due to the greater numbers of resident proprietors there (1839:21). A hundred years later, historian Ragatz also concluded Antigua was the notable exception to prevailing conditions of backwardness in the island societies of the Caribbean. He attributed the quality of its public institutions, the advances in its agricultural techniques, and the higher birthrates of its slaves in the eighteenth century to the fact that a far greater number of proprietors were permanent residents (Ragatz 1931:22–24).[33]

Finally, voluntary participation by slave women in interracial unions with free white men was probably less widespread in the Leeward Islands because the offspring of such unions were unlikely to be freed legally. Colonial Office records show that except in 1831–32, less than 1 percent of Antiguan slaves were manumitted in selected years for which data is available (Handler 1974:50, 52).[34] In contrast to the situation in Jamaica, few Antiguan slaves received their freedom by private acts of the local legislature. Legislators freed a few slave men who had displayed exceptional courage in battles against the French, and some men and women who informed on other slaves involved in the conspiracy of 1736 (Microfilm No. 2), but I found less than a handful of other manumissions in my examination of Antiguan statutes. Moreover, judging from a survey of wills, few masters freed their slaves by will before the nineteenth century (Gaspar citing Oliver 1985b:135). Wills from Antigua show slaves bequeathed to the testator's widow, legitimate children, or other relatives of the whole blood. James Brown, Esq., who drew up his will on 27 September 1797 as he was about to embark upon a voyage to North America to improve his health, was typical in this respect. Brown left all his property, including his three mestee children, to the care of his widowed sister, Elizabeth White (Oliver 1894:vol. 1, 75).[35]

There is other evidence, too, of the reluctance of masters in the Leeward Islands to manumit their slaves. In 1826, when representatives from these islands were asked by British commissioners if descendants of slaves ever became free "by conmixture with whites," the responses were all negative. The delegate representing St. Christopher and Nevis explained that "the child follows the condition of the mother." The authority from Tortola stated: "Descendants of slaves never become free, by reason of a conmixture with whites." The Antiguan representative was very succinct. He simply said: "Never." It was the same in Dominica and St. Vincent.[36] Thus although each of these small island governments wrote and enforced their kinship codes independently, they shared a common disdain for the notion of legally freeing a mulatto child from slavery by virtue of changing complexion. Clearly it was uncommon for Leeward Island slaves to achieve free legal status by reason of increasing "whiteness" or because of marriage.

To summarize, the Antiguan case suggests that miscegenation did not occur with the same frequency in each West Indian colony. Nor did it everywhere receive the same treatment in law or the same response in practice. Although miscegenation was certainly a feature of the developing creole ideology and structure in Antigua, it was not as pervasive as in Jamaica. Different social,

economic, and demographic conditions, different conjugal norms with respect
to gender and class, and different legal precedents affected voluntary interracial
mating in various islands. In contrast to Jamaica, Antigua had only one sizable
urban place,[37] fewer sugar estates with more than 250 slaves, a greater percentage
of resident proprietors, a smaller number of slaves freed because they were
kin to their masters, and none who were freed because they had become
"white." Not surprisingly, then, Antiguans never developed a large "brown"
middle class or a complex vocabulary of colors that was then used to legally
distinguish the rights of persons of different hues.[38]

If, over time, the white planting elite deliberately managed to quell most
opportunities before emancipation for miscegenation—recall the statutes preventing marriages between slaves, indentured servants, and free persons—then
we are less surprised to find that "color" has become less of an issue in
Antigua than in Jamaica. That is not to say that color was not an issue in
postemancipation Antigua. Researching the character and composition of the
Antiguan middle class between 1834 and 1940, Lowes found respondents who
claimed a white ancestor, though very few people included in their genealogy
free people of color (1993:157–60). In sharp contrast to Lowes's subjects, and
to middle-class Jamaicans (Alexander 1977a:431; Austin 1979:500), but consistent with the history recounted here and in the following chapters,[39] Antiguans
I interviewed in 1985–87 did not explain the origin of today's middle class in
a kinship myth about the union between a black slave woman and a free
white man. In fact, few people I interviewed claimed a white relative at all.
Apparently, these people did not find such a lineage especially prestigious, as
is the case in Jamaica. Alexander found that Jamaicans expressed a "bias toward
marrying someone of the same color": and that "the notion of union between
persons of different races has an air of illegitimacy around it" (1984:167).
Antiguan subjects, in contrast, rarely noted color as figuring in their choice
of a lifelong partner. Of far greater importance were an individual's personal
traits (warmheartedness, generosity, wit, intelligence, etc.), his or her class
standing (associated with ability to contribute to the needs of the household
and its members), and the fact that he or she was at least a nominal Christian.
Antiguans with Syrian and Lebanese backgrounds stressed, in addition, the
importance of finding a spouse who understood the structure of dominance
and the division of labor between the sexes in an "Arabic family." The lack
of emphasis on color was even more noticeable in Barbuda than in Antigua.
A woman from Codrington village, for example, told me, "Well, just one color
here, black people."

The small size of Antigua's white population, together with a variety of
social, economic, and cultural variables that have mitigated against interracial
unions, have meant that these do not hold the same symbolic significance as

99

they do for Jamaicans. Intraracial concubinage and marriage have been far more usual and of far greater significance than miscegenation to the evolution of Antiguan family ideology and structure. Leaving aside aesthetic preferences, color is a dominant issue in marriage only among the local white elite who conflate skin color and social class (Lowes 1982). For all other groups of the mid-1980s, class, law, religion, and gender were, and remain, determinant variables shaping familial patterns in the common order.

Summary

In the seventeenth, eighteenth, and early nineteenth centuries, diversity, but not chaos, characterized the familial patterns of the different ranks of Antiguan society. Creole kinship laws, like their English counterparts, distinguished between legitimate and nonlegitimate unions, privileged the institution of marriage, and guarded the devolution of property among legitimate males. The development of the creole kinship system in Antigua was partly the consequence of its legislators' deliberate decisions not to grant legal privileges to couples who failed to register with the governor, to enact, but then to rescind, a civil form of marriage, and to punish those who attempted to breach the boundaries of socially acceptable alliances through fines and forced servitude. Missionaries later reinforced the conception of marriage and family idealized in the codes and associated religious nuptials with the salvation of a cohabiting couple.

Yet a system of mating illegalities meshed with this system of conjugal legalities; the two together fashioned a distinctive creole family ideology and structure. Though they were themselves rule-governed with respect to gender and class, concubinage and miscegenation created intercategorical persons whose very existence altered forever expectations and assumptions about family as it was understood in English law. The children of such unions shared the blood of their parents, but they were denied the property and protection that a marriage contract provided. Custom, sentiment, and honor persuaded men in every rank of society to attend to their illegitimate families, but they cared for them differently, depending upon their means and their class. Therefore, some variations in the meaning of marriage, in expectations between husbands and wives, and in the relationships between parents and children arose within the different ranks of creole society. On the other hand, these variations were tempered by the homogenizing effect of religious and secular educations—which reinforced the kinship ideology and gender hierarchy of the dominating socioeconomic class.

As we see next, some of the most important influences upon Antiguan kinship law after abolition came not from any sudden restructuring of the class system but from the loss of local autonomy that resulted when the legislature partially adopted the Crown colony system of government in 1868 and joined the Leeward Island Federation in 1871. After these dates, events and trends within the empire more directly affected the organization of social reproduction in Antigua. The governing of familial relations was tied increasingly to the management of the society's poor laws. The legal discourse concerned with managing families in Antigua, however, was distinctly creole in its approach to class, race, and gender.

5

The Postemancipation Period, 1834–1986: The Era of Free Individuals and Governable Families

EMANCIPATION ALTERED the class structure and the organization of power in Antigua; it also stimulated changes in lawmakers' ideas about the relationship between individuals and the state and about managing families. Because people were no longer commodities and the earlier marriage laws governing slaves, servants, and free persons had expired, the local elite were forced to reconsider the rights of individuals, the conditions of labor, and the functions of kinship. Once slavery was abolished, lawmakers placed increasing emphasis on individuals' rights to enter into contracts and concomitantly developed a new relationship between individuals, families, and the state (Lazarus-Black 1992:877).

This chapter focuses on the content of the postslavery statutes and government strategies (cf. de Certeau 1984) to control labor, leaving aside momentarily the questions of what response these drew from the people of the common order and how ordinary men and women altered the meaning and practice of these state directives. I argue first that local law constitutive of class, kinship, and gender relations developed in three general directions in Antigua between 1834 and 1986. I also find the Antiguan case exemplifies broader political and legal trends underway elsewhere in the English-speaking Caribbean and beyond. These involved new forms of government interventions in peoples' everyday lives (cf. B. Anderson 1983; Cohn 1983, 1985, 1989; Cohn and Dirks 1988; J. Comaroff 1985; Comaroff and Comaroff 1991; Cooper and Stoler 1989; Corrigan and Sayer 1985; Donzelot 1979; Foucault 1979, 1980; Hobsbawm and Ranger 1983; McGlynn and Drescher 1992; Moore 1986; Starr and Collier 1989; Stoler 1985, 1989a, 1989b) and dramatic shifts in the definitions of legal, illegal, and extralegal behaviors.

The first important change affecting the system of kinship legalities in Antigua was lawmakers' increasing emphasis on individualism and, concomitantly, the new relationship between individuals and the state. We find evidence for this in diverse places: in bills to regulate sugar workers and indentured servants, in acts to ensure the "tranquility" of the countryside, and in statutes ostensibly saving children from the ignorance and superstition of their parents. The language of these laws cut class and gender hierarchies in new ways, differentiating the sexes but placing both in new legal categories such as "general hire," "special hire," "rogue," and "juvenile delinquent." Women were distinguished from men in labor contracts, for instance, and special provisions were made for the care, sustenance, and employment of children. Moreover, at the same time that freed slaves became individualized workers, "estate laborers" emerged as a legally constituted lower class bound to special rules and regulations. Although today we can find little evidence to support their excessive fears,[1] planters and lawmakers throughout the Caribbean worried about their own safety after emancipation and during later periods of economic recession. They believed the freedom of this class of laborers threatened to unleash a restless criminality; therefore, they also rewrote laws to outlaw formerly legal or extralegal behaviors.

A second development, however, tempered the emphasis on individualism. A new system of "government through the family" (Donzelot 1979:92) entailed changes in the state's goals for promoting a viable colony and in its methods for ensuring order. As was true in England, the Continent, and colonial Sumatra, nineteenth-century Antiguan welfare and kinship legislation governed poor families and the bourgeoisie by employing different techniques and standards (cf. Donzelot 1979, 1991; Foucault 1979, 1980, 1991; Procacci 1991; Stoler 1985, 1989a, 1989b). Western legal discourse about women and children, for example, was frequently a discourse about women and children of certain classes. Poor laws were drafted to shift the burden of caring for the underprivileged from the state to the family. Statutory law stipulated exactly who constituted an individual's "family" and who was, therefore, legally responsible.[2] The Antiguan case strongly supports Fox-Piven and Cloward's (1971) argument that welfare legislation is designed to regulate the poor while accommodating shifts in capital's need for labor.

The third change resulted from alterations in the relationship between Antigua and Great Britain and among the Leeward Islands. External forms and forces impinged upon local kinship law in this period to a degree hitherto unknown because the political organization of the island was restructured. In 1868, the local assembly dissolved itself and the island became a Crown colony. A single chamber called the Legislative Council replaced the former House and council.[3] As a result, "the power of the Crown, exercised through the Governor, was now sufficient to overcome any resistance to it by elected legislators" (D. Hall 1971:177).

With local autonomy consciously surrendered, English advisors and appointees exerted a more direct role in the island's internal affairs.[4] For the first time, a few British statutes affecting family organization were adopted virtually unchanged into Antiguan law. Importantly, this occurred when the English were making dramatic changes in their laws, including their kinship laws. Then, in 1871, Antigua became one of six "presidencies" within the Leeward Island Federation. The 1871 act gave the General Legislature of the Leeward Islands jurisdiction over matters between husband and wife and parent and child, over divorce, and over the guardianship of infants (*Federal Acts of the Leeward Islands* 1914:vol. 1, 2).[5] After this reorganization, inter- rather than intraisland concerns and events motivated many of the changes made in kinship legislation.[6] The years of the West Indian Federation (1958–62) and of Associated Statehood (1969–81) brought few developments in kinship law. Thus 150 years of postemancipation history began with a great flurry of kinship lawmaking; by 1981, few locally inspired kinship statutes drew any legislative attention.

Freedom by Contract: The Individualization of Labor

Just before the Emancipation Act passed, and no doubt in preparation for it, Mr. John Duncombe Taylor of Antigua declared himself out of credit with local merchants and incapable of supporting the slaves on his estate. His petition, supported by several of his fellow planters, forced the hand of the local council, which quickly passed An Act For The Immediate Relief And Support Of The Slave Population Of This Island. The law appointed seven commissioners to purchase food to be resold to estate owners at cost. As D. Hall points out:

> In other words, the colonial Legislature would underwrite the planters' credit, without charge.
>
> The speed with which Mr. Taylor had been heard and legislative measures taken, allows us the reasonable inference that a general hardship was indeed being felt by the planters and that he had been encouraged to speak out as he did in order to initiate action. (1971:18)

At the eve of emancipation, Antiguan planters and legislators stood convinced that slavery had become too costly and that they could run their estates more efficiently by accepting compensation from Britain and then paying wages to workers who, given the lack of available land, had no where else to go (D. Hall 1971:17–24).

D. Hall refers repeatedly to the "planter-dominated legislatures" of the Leeward Islands in the immediate postemancipation period, but I could uncover little other information about these lawmakers.[7] It is clear that the planters were experiencing downward social mobility, for Hall discovered many estates "too much burdened by the costs of settlements and annuities made in optimistic times and debts contracted in unprofitable times to be successfully transformed into competitive production" (ibid.:105). John Candler, a visitor to the island, found the white population experienced financial stress in this period (1965:54). Mrs. Flannagan relates in 1844:

> Some few years ago, about the smartest ladies in the Episcopal congregation were receiving parochial aid; but upon its being officially notified that the names of all paupers would be published, many of these dashing damsels became alarmed, and resolved rather to depend upon their own unaided exertions than let the world know how they procured their ribbons and laces. (1967:vol. 2, 222)

Flannagan distinguished two classes in Antiguan white society in the 1840s. The first consisted partly of "an aristocracy," "springing from a good old stock," and partly of persons who were "self-selected." The second class consisted of some industrious workers and poor but proud "bottom-foot buckras" (ibid.:191–92). As early as 1815, some "ladies of Antigua" had begun managing the Widows Fund for women who "were both penurious and forbidden by propriety to labour" (D. Hall 1971:168).

The repeal of the Sugar Duties Act in 1854 further contributed to the economic decline of the West Indian sugar interests: "The price of sugar fell by 30 percent between 1840 and 1850, and by a further 25 percent in the next two decades" (Mintz 1985:144, 70). By the late 1850s, Leeward Island planters could maintain their position in the market only by controlling labor through the Contract Act,[8] reducing wages paid to estate workers (D. Hall 1971:123), selling bankrupt estates to local merchant and foreign commercial firms "which completely undermined the family basis upon which the plantation system had been organized," and introducing technological changes (Henry 1985:48, 49).

Emancipation partially dismantled the hierarchical order an earlier plantocracy had designed, but the next generation of Antiguan lawmakers did not intend to witness a social and economic revolution. Those who governed Antigua in the three decades after 1834 had several concerns: they wanted assurance that workers would remain tied to the sugar estates; they wanted to attract immigrants and their families from abroad to cover any labor shortage, however unlikely; and they wanted peace and tranquility throughout the countryside. The Contract Act, which served as the Antiguan substitute for the apprenticeship period,[9] was one law that enabled the planters to accomplish their agenda and control the labor force without breaking from their own creole legal sensibility. Statutes encouraging the importation of indentured servants also display the legislators' intentions to control life in the lower ranks of creole society. As time passed, the range of permissible illegalities, including kinship illegalities, was deliberately narrowed.

The Contract Act divided estate workers into two broad categories, based on the type of their contract: "general hiring" or "special hiring." Most workers fell into the legal status described as "general hiring."[10] This contract provided a job, shelter, medical attention, and gardening rights to every former slave who continued to reside on his plantation. Those who worked under general hire could be employed on only one estate. Wages were set at six pence sterling per day for able-bodied men; women and children received a percentage of that pay. Contracts were entered into for a year but could be terminated earlier with a month's notice. In contrast, an individual who made personal arrangements with his employer did so under a "special hiring" contract recorded in the presence of a justice of the peace. Those working under special hire could offer their skills to more than one employer, but they rarely received estate benefits. Whatever the form of the contract, employers were automatically entitled to deduct wages for absence from work, extended illnesses, or damages to their property. Unresolvable disputes between employers and laborers were referred to justices of the peace (Microfilm No. 6; *Laws of Antigua* 1864:183–86).

The Contract Act fostered continuity between slavery and freedom by binding men and women to the lands and houses they had occupied during slavery and, in most cases, to similar work patterns. Nevertheless, the change involved granting former slaves the legal status necessary to enter a contract—a status that conferred the legal competence enjoyed by free persons. Although the old law aggregated slaves as commodities, the new law individuated free persons into contract laborers. In the language of the new statute, each laborer was capable of committing himself to a contract, expected to fulfill its terms, and subject to punishment for failure to do so.

Besides recreating many of the conditions of labor under slavery, the contract labor system had consequences for family life in the common order. The Contract Act, for example, gave statutory force to the old common-law tradition that held parents responsible for providing the necessities of life for their children. The act included provision of a sentence of "imprisonment and hard labour for any time not exceeding three months" for any parent who failed to provide "according to his or her ability, for his or her infant children" (Microfilm

No. 6). The clause was obviously intended to remove the onus of responsibility for children from the former masters; it also implied that another sort of contract existed between parents and offspring.

The individualization of labor left women in particularly precarious positions. Estate owners generally preferred to hire men for field labor, although they paid women less for the same tasks. In St. Vincent, the law allowed a legitimate wife to remain in the house of her husband, or to join him on another estate if they had belonged to different masters, but no other form of union was protected. By refusing to work for wages on the same estate as her man, a "reputed wife" might sacrifice her claim to residence (Marshall 1977:229–30). In Antigua, anybody residing in a house on an estate after 1865 was expected to labor on that estate:

> The entering into the occupation of a House or Tenement situate upon the estate of such a Master, Mistress or Employer in the character of a Servant in Husbandry, or Artificer, Handicraftsmen, or other Laborer to such Master, Mistress, or Employer, or the residence in such character as aforesaid . . . even where such last mentioned residence is in the house of any other laborer or person, shall be sufficient prima facie evidence of a retainer in service under a general hiring within the terms and provisions of this Act. (Microfilm No. 9)

In addition, this bill included examples of model contracts between the former slaves and their employers that protected the employer's right to the labor of his employee's "wife" and children:

> The said servant hereby agrees to enter into the service and employment of the said Master as a Servant in husbandry (on his Estate or Estates called _____ to serve the said master for one year (or other period) from the _____ day of _____ next at the weekly wages of _____ and a Cottage and Garden free of Rent and taxes.
>
> And he also agrees that his Wife shall likewise enter into the service and employment of the said master in a general capacity during the said period if required at the weekly wages of _____ and his son _____ (a minor) shall likewise enter into the service and employment of the said Master at the weekly wages of _____. (Microfilm No. 9)

In other amendments of 1865, contracts between employers and youths aged twelve to twenty-one were held valid as long as the parent or guardian of the child did not specifically object within four weeks. Any person who worked for five days on any estate was considered to have contracted to work on that estate for one month.

The planters found it convenient and profitable to make workers individualized contract laborers. Ironically, they also found that workers sometimes acted too individualistically. Too often, lamented the lawmakers, unscrupulous persons were "induced to desert their infirm relatives, wives and children of tender years, leaving them in an impoverished and destitute state, or are frequently otherwise under obligations of debt." To prevent this, any person who wanted to leave the colony was made to appear before a justice of the peace who would then determine

> whether such labourer, artificer, handicraftsman or domestic servant hath any aged or infirm grandfather, grandmother, father, mother, or wife, or infant child, legitimate or illegitimate, under fourteen years of age, who may, or ought to be dependent on him or her for support, and who on the departure of the said labourer . . . will become destitute of support. (Microfilm No. 6)

A magistrate granted permission to leave the island only when he was satisfied that a worker had "no such kindred or claims upon him or her, and is not bound by any existing contract for labour or service with any individual in this Island" (Microfilm No. 6).

The extent to which law pervaded every aspect of the lives of the freed estate workers recalls the penetration of law in the daily lives of slaves during the thirty years preceding abolition. Similarly coercive intervention characterized various schemes to attract new indentured labor to the island and to regulate their lives on the estates. The new indentured servant acts not only outlined rights and obligations of workers and employers but also addressed family life, education, religion, and housing (*Laws of Antigua* 1864:574–93). These agricultural servants found themselves pressed into a way of life that hardly differed from slavery.

A health officer physically inspected and then registered each arriving immigrant in one of five ledgers: "Africans," "Portuguese," "Chinese,"[11] from "Her Majesty's dominions in the East Indies," or "Other."[12] Only documented Indians could request a return passage at the expiration of their contracts. Officials noted the expenses incurred by the laborer, his or her age, name, sex, size, birthplace, distinguishing marks, and fitness for agricultural work. Employers' names and costs were also recorded. Immigrants were promised immediate work or sufficient food and lodging until a job could be found for them. Prospective employers showed proof that they could provide suitable lodging, a hospital, and medical attention for their employees. Initially contracts were for three years, but this was changed in 1851 to one year (Microfilm No. 8). An 1880 act prevented immigrants from securing passports until after they had resided in Antigua for five years or had repaid the cost of bringing them to the island (Microfilm No. 10).

Antigua's indentured-servant codes closely resembled those in other English-speaking Caribbean colonies.[13] In general, these acts commanded very rigorous working and living conditions. Like the former slaves, indentured servants labored under oral or written contracts. Every servant agreed to work nine hours each day except Sundays, Good Friday, Christmas, and New Year's Day. The law prescribed a daily roll call on each estate, with desertions to be reported within forty-eight hours. There were fines for being more than two miles from one's work place during working hours or for traveling without a ticket of leave from one's employer. Failure to report desertions and harboring runaways became crimes too—enabling lawmakers to control the kin and friends of estate laborers. Act No. 200 of 1863 made legal searching vessels "to prevent the absconding of indentured servants" (*Laws of Antigua* 1864:704–5).

As had been true in an earlier era, law gave some protection to indentured servants. Disputes between servants and employers were investigated by police magistrates. Servants' contracts could be canceled if a magistrate found an employer failed to provide enough work to allow the servant to earn a sufficient wage or consistently denied him lodging or medical attention (*Laws of Antigua* 1864:592). Although comparable data is unavailable for Antigua, Trotman found that in Trinidad some 20 to 30 percent of the indentured labor force went before the courts every year between 1838 and 1900 (1986:194). Certainly most of these cases would have been settled in favor of the planters. As we shall find, however, enough of them would satisfy workers to retain their general faith in law and their desire to participate in the state's hegemonic legal institutions.

In contrast to the indentured-servant codes of the seventeenth and eighteenth centuries, as well as to the situation encountered by the former slaves, the 1860 Indentured Servant Law prevented forced separation of family members. In bringing immigrants to Antigua, it was illegal for an immigration agent to separate husbands and wives or children under age fifteen "from their parents or natural protectors" (*Laws of Antigua* 1864:581). Employers were therefore expected to accept whole families. Instruction for the children of "liberated Africans" was mandated for at least one afternoon per week, and the law penalized employers who prevented youths from attending school or who tried to prohibit ministers from visiting families on the estates (ibid.:587).

The Contract Act and the indentured-servant codes made the former slaves and newly arriving agricultural laborers highly dependent "free" workers. Still, in the minds of their employers and the legislators, these estate workers, like the former slaves, were potential criminals. To protect themselves and their property, the lawmakers expanded the category of illegal behaviors and punished transgressors with a vengeance.

New vagrancy laws went into effect as soon as the slaves were emancipated. It became illegal to behave in a "disorderly" fashion, to wander about without specific direction, or to be idle. Any suspicious person could be charged as a "rogue" for "not having any visible means of subsistence, and not giving any good account of himself or herself." By law, "any person whatsoever" might capture a rogue and bring him before a magistrate (*Laws of Antigua* 1864:178–83).[14]

New legislation outlawing obeah appeared in 1834, 1851, and 1857, reflecting the legislators' fear of obeah practitioners. The 1834 statute made obeah practitioners "rogues" and "vagabonds" who could be sentenced up to three months in prison with hard labor (Microfilm No. 6). In 1851, the prison term was extended to one year, and public whipping for men and solitary confinement for women were reinstated (Microfilm No. 8). Another law against "certain vulgar frauds, commonly known as Obeah" passed in 1904 (Smith and Smith 1986:171). Legislators in Trinidad also banned obeah at regular intervals (Brereton 1979:155–56; Trotman 1986:208–9).

To enforce these new laws, and to further discourage wanton criminality, the size of the police force was steadily increased, rural constables and magistrates were appointed, and new regulations went into effect at the House of Corrections.[15] The police force consisted initially of twenty-five armed men assigned to stations around the island. At the request of any plantation owner, magistrates could appoint two additional rural constables to any estate of more than one hundred laborers or one constable for estates employing fifty to one hundred persons. The police force was expanded and its men redistributed to key locations on the island in 1836, 1845, and 1854.[16] After 1854, any two justices of the peace could appoint additional constables whenever they saw the need to do so (*Laws of Antigua* 1864:322). The police prevented "Tumulth and riotous Assemblies" by enforcing an act outlawing "unruly" groups of more than twelve persons. For failing to separate on command, those so assembled could be charged with a felony carrying the death penalty (Microfilm No. 6).[17]

Not surprisingly, the working people in Antigua were law abiding. A police report from 1835 lists only a few criminal offenses, most of which involved very petty crimes. Minor thefts and breaking of sugarcanes to eat were common; "heinous" crimes rare. Superintendent of Police Richard Wickham concluded in 1837: "A due fear of, and a prompt obedience to, the authority of the magistrates, is a prominent feature of the lower orders, and to this I mainly attribute the successful maintenance of rural tranquility" (Thome and Kimball 1839:143). The same pattern prevailed in the early twentieth century. Samuel Smith, an Antiguan working man born in 1877 whom we shall encounter again in the next chapter recalled:

Back then there was two magistrates courts in that part of the island, one at English harbour and the other at Parham. The magistrates also use to go around the estates on every other Tuesday and settle cases. Now when you see the magistrate come, who have case would straighten up. Them frighten. A lot of them magistrates was planters or in the family of planters.

In them days a good portion of the people would go to jail for all kinds of simple things. The cat-o-nine was the worse that could happen to you in the jailhouse. And if you be unruly, you would also get a 75 lb. ball locked to your waist or ankle by a chain and you would have to try and move around with it.

Back then, the jail-houses was built on wheels and they was pulled all over the island by the prisoners. Most of the people that was sent to jail from the district use to end up in them jails on wheels. They were moving prisoners: where night meet them, them sleep. Them prisoners was forced to shoot hard labour for the planters and that happen to be one of the main reasons that people get put in jail. (Smith and Smith 1986:79–80)

Both in theory and in practice, laws, police, and courts exercised considerable power in Antigua after 1834. Yet because scholars investigating the postslavery era in the West Indies have focused most of their attention on the apprenticeship and indentured-servant codes, they have missed seeing that the local legislators' use of statutes to sustain their hegemonic power went far beyond labor and police codes. Policing the masses involved more pervasive and myriad strategies (cf. de Certeau 1984).

Government through Antiguan Families

Changes in Antiguan statutes after emancipation individualized labor, created well-regulated work crews, and made people dependent on the plantations. In addition, the state greatly expanded the domain of legalities by generating a system of "government through the family" (Donzelot 1979:92). As was true in France beginning in the 1840s, the movement to "take care of children" in Antigua precipitated a new relationship between the state and the families under its domain. As Donzelot explains, in government through families, the object of the state's programs is "hygienic and political in nature, the two facets being indissociable" (ibid.:78). In the name of improving standards of living, the state altered the relationship between parents and children and reduced "the sociopolitical capacity of these strata by breaking the initiatory ties that existed between children and adults, the autarchic transmission of skills, the freedom of movement and of agitation that resulted from the loosening of ancient communal constraints" (ibid.:79). Over the course of the nineteenth and early twentieth centuries, the state infiltrated the families of the common order, and the Antiguan family, like the French, changed

from the inside, as it were, resulting from the propagation within it of medical, educative, and relational norms whose over-all aim was to preserve children from the old customs, which were considered deadly . . . [and] in its exterior status by the modification of family law. (Ibid.:1979, xx, xxi)

In Antigua, the history of government through families begins with the lawmakers' postemancipation obsession with counting. Although formerly masters had been loath to register their slaves (they were taxed on the number of slaves they owned), after emancipation property owners needed to count heads to collect compensation for freed slaves, to qualify for loans, and to buttress their arguments about why they had to import indentured servants. Therefore, they conducted censuses and accumulated information about births, deaths, marriages, and emigration.[18]

Having granted themselves the authority to count, however, the legislators were compelled to contend with the startling reality, especially the appalling mortality statistics. In 1856, the registrar general reported infant mortality approached 21 percent. His committee attributed the high death rate to ignorance and the general unfitness of midwives (Watkins 1924:42). The legislators then ratified An Act To Provide Medical Attendance For The Infant Children Of The Laboring Population, And For The Poor And Destitute, And To Render Such Medical Attendance Accessible To The Labouring Population At Large. Doctors were appointed to each of several districts (Microfilm No. 9). Still, the situation did not rapidly improve, and in 1863 the legislators determined that "an undue mortality, ascribed in a great measure to the want of proper medical attendance, prevails among the infant children, more especially of the labouring population" (*Laws of Antigua* 1864:604–5). Something had to be done quickly—or there would soon cease to be a work force.

The technique adopted was "tutelage": effective rights within the family were changed and families were brought into a relation of dependence on welfare and educative agents (Donzelot 1979:xxi). The revised Contract Act of 1865, for example, mandated that each proprietor of estates of fifty acres or more retain the services of a medical practitioner. Other programs, more extensive and expensive, were also initiated. In 1868, the people of the free villages—"those agricultural laborers, not provided for by the Contract Act, porters, boatmen, and menial and praedial servants"—became eligible to receive free medical assistance. As they do today, doctors traveled the island to provide care and surgical aid to the destitute, to furnish medicines to children younger than ten and adults older than sixty, to vaccinate infants, and to tend to women in childbirth. Those who could afford to pay for the doctors' services were asked to do so at fixed rates. Medical officers also admitted patients to the hospital and inspected the villages for sanitary conditions (Microfilm No. 9; Microfilm No. 10; *Laws of Antigua* 1864:604–7).

The system of government through families sent various other "experts" onto the estates and into village households. Their duties were to observe and advise the people of the common order and to enforce the contents of the new codes among them. In 1880, for example, the governor appointed midwives to designated health stations. The midwives acted as sick nurses, tended to pregnant women, "supervised" (or kept an eye on) the children in their districts, and reported their findings to the medical officers (Microfilm No. 10; *Laws of Antigua* 1920:xxxix, xlix; *Laws of Antigua* 1962:vol. 3, 1923–34).[19] The assembly also passed laws to try to prevent the spread of contagious diseases, established a Board of Health, and arranged for rubbish to be removed from the streets (Microfilm No. 9; *Laws of Antigua* 1864:596, 673–79).[20] The public charity known as the Daily Meal Society was expanded to create Holberton Hospital. The same act authorized the creation of a soup kitchen and workhouse to employ the destitute "if deemed necessary by the Governor" (*Laws of Antigua* 1864:340–44). Finally, along with the medical officers, midwives, and health inspectors, came the coroners. They performed inquests on the bodies of children who died before their first birthday because "the rate of Infant Mortality has for many years past been excessive and it is expedient to ascertain better the causes of death amongst infants" (Microfilm No. 10).

Children's behavior also concerned government through families. The law gave parents a hand in dealing with disrespectful, unruly, and idle youngsters. We find a plethora of rules around midcentury, for example, pertaining to "juvenile offenders." An act of 1840 proposed that an "Asylum" be established:

> And whereas at the breaking up of the old system of slavery, great numbers of the rising generation of both sexes, deserted the Estates and congregated in the several Towns of this Island, many in direct opposition to the wishes of their parents, relatives and friends, and have continued to live without any permanent or regular employment, but on the casual work which may be obtained at the moment, or by more irregular practices destructive to their own morals, as to the peace and good order of society. And whereas from the almost total absence of all check and control, some children desert their parents and guardians [and others] their Masters or Mistresses . . . it has become absolutely necessary to provide an adequate remedy for such crying grievances. (Microfilm No. 7)

After investigating complaints from parents, guardians, or employers, justices could send offending children to the asylum for up to three months. A law passed the following year empowered parents, guardians, churchwardens, and "others" to bind children under the age of twenty-one as apprentices in any trade or occupation "save that of agriculture or the manufacture of colonial produce . . . in like manner as apprentices in England for a term not exceeding five years" (*Laws of Antigua* 1864:212–14).[21] Two justices of the peace heard complaints against masters and mistresses for maltreatment, incompetence in their craft, or failure to conform to the terms of the apprenticeship. Masters and mistresses displeased with their apprentices had recourse to justices of the peace or the Court of Sessions (ibid.:213).

Delinquent children faced forced apprenticeships, corporal punishment, or confinement. Youths convicted of stealing fruits, vegetables, or livestock, of destroying property, or of "leading an idle and vagrant life, not attending any school or being sufficiently under the care and control of the parent" might be apprenticed for up to three years for their first offense with parental consent

(Microfilm No. 10). Alternatively, a magistrate could order a delinquent to be whipped. Skerretts Reformatory School for Boys and the Scotts Hill Reformatory for Girls opened in Antigua in 1895. Profits from the farms on which these youths worked paid for their maintenance (*Laws of Antigua* 1920:240–43).

The state also intervened when working parents had no one to care for their children. An act of 1883 granted the governor authority to open public nurseries throughout the island. Initially, the managers of the nurseries were required to take in any children who were brought to them. A year later, a child was admitted to a nursery only if the staff determined that no one else could provide for that child (Microfilm No. 10; *Laws of Antigua* 1920:vol. 40, 159–61).[22] A few years later, the Leeward Islands Legislative Council made it a criminal offense for a parent to willfully neglect to provide an infant under fourteen with adequate food, clothing, medical attention, or lodging. *Parent* included the "mother of a bastard child and any person adjudged to be the putative father of a bastard child." Conviction carried a penalty of imprisonment for up to six months with or without hard labor (*Federal Acts of the Leeward Islands* 1889:No. 4).[23]

Finally, schools provided another arena for the propagation of government through families.[24] An Act For The More Effectual Support And Education Of The Poor Children Of The Several Parishes Of This Island ... (1831) explained that the system of educating the poor was "very ineffective" because the schools were "so unduly separated in small numbers in the respective parishes."[25] To remedy this, the legislators created the Antigua Central School in St. John's. The school's mission was to "benefit not only these students, but the community at large and to instill in the youths industrious and useful habits." It enrolled boarding students—applicants for parish relief—as well as day students. A broad education was envisioned: reading, writing, arithmetic, English grammar, history, geography, Greek and Latin, as well as modern languages (Microfilm No. 6). A short time later, the Antigua Grammar School opened its doors in which "boys could receive, on moderate terms, a good commercial and classical education, and girls be afforded as good instruction as may be obtained in all the ordinary branches of female education, combined in both cases with a due inculcation of Christian principles of religion and morals" (Microfilm No. 7). An act of 1848 authorized the vestries of each parish to send up to three children per year, and ten per year from the parish of St. John's, for education at the Grammar School (Microfilm No. 8). The Technical Instruction Act established an Agricultural College in 1895 (Microfilm No. 10), four years before the imperial government's comprehensive scheme for agricultural education reached the islands (Augier and Gordon 1962:193).

Law shaped the content of the curricula in these schools to espouse a Christian orientation. As Henry explains: "The aim of these schools was . . . not to educate but to mould through socialization and instruction" (1985:63).[26] The lawmakers intended that laborers be physically and mentally fit for their tasks. An act of 1857 appointed commissioners of education to review applications for aid to schools with twenty pupils that could show that their students were "educated in the Christian religion" (*Laws of Antigua* 1864:357–58; *Laws of Antigua* 1920:xxvii). Compulsory education for children between five and twelve years of age was established in 1890, the same year that a bill restricting the employment of children under nine years of age became law.[27]

The right of government officials to monitor children's education increased markedly over time. In the Elementary Education Consolidation Act, for example, the Legislative Council of the Leeward Islands created educational district officers with authority "to enter any yard, house, building or place, between the hours of six of the clock in the morning and five of the clock in the evening of any day in the week except Sunday, and there make enquiries as to any child who may there reside or employed." Parents who kept their children out of school could be fined five shillings (*Federal Acts of the Leeward Islands* 1925:No. 8).

Finally, government through families in Antigua provided for the separate educations of the lower and middle classes. As Lowes cogently argues, the purpose of education in Antigua, as in other British colonies, was "to select, not serve" (1993:240, 253). An act of 1882 specifically denied financial aid to institutions whose purpose was to educate the lower classes.[28] The law granted two hundred pounds per year for ten years to educate children of the upper classes. The preamble explained this was necessary because Act No. 2 of 1874 of the Leeward Islands Federation "granted aid to the education of the labouring population of the colony of the Leeward Islands" (Microfilm No. 10; *Laws of Antigua* 1920:xiv, xl, xlvii). When formal secondary education for men became available at the Antigua Grammar School in 1884 and at the Girls High School in 1886, both schools were too expensive for the vast majority of the population and the school boards always rejected applications from illegitimate children (Lowes 1987:9). As the nineteenth century progressed,

> the distinction between being legitimate and being illegitimate became central to the way in which the white population was able to control the growth of the nonwhite middle class. The crucial arena for affecting this connection was education: by opening education to nonwhites but tying access to legitimacy, and then by controlling occupational opportunities by tying them to education, the white population had a powerful means of limiting the growth of a competing class. (Lowes 1993:276)

Education remained mostly unavailable in the countryside in the 1880s because, as Samuel Smith explained, "Bakkra have no interest to see negra people learn to read" (Smith and Smith 1986:37). Support for building local public schools in the villages and teacher training did not begin in earnest until the 1950s, when trade-union and political leaders became actively involved in promoting education.[29]

After slavery ended, the working people of Antigua were the recipients of "philanthropy" (Donzelot 1979:64–66), a social inquiry into the conditions of their existence, directed and financed by the state, which gave them free advice and free vaccinations. As Donzelot remarks, the philanthropic strategy was successful because it provided a new synthesis from which to solve the problems of political order: the state would take account of the complaints of the poor, but the price to be paid was acceptance of the state's norms (ibid.:58). At the same time, government through families "normalized" law in the common order and in the public record of that life. Giving birth, inoculation, cleanliness, disease, day care, education, and troublesome children all fell under the jurisdiction of the expanding system of legalities. Yet as it had in the past, law continued to differentiate the social classes and subordinate women to men. In the poor laws, to which we turn next, the Antiguan legislators not only resolved the fiscal problem of how to pay for the destitute but also redefined the rights and duties of kin and extended those obligations beyond the nuclear family.

Poor Laws and Poor Bastards

Antiguan legislators thought of workers as individuals when they detailed the law of contract; they placed those same laborers within responsible kin groups when they rewrote statutes for the needy. Just before abolition, and in preparation for it, the state started shifting the responsibility for tending to the poor, and poor bastards, from the state to legally defined extended families.

Antiguan poor-law reform took a very different course than that pursued in Great Britain in the same periods.[30] England's infamous Poor Law Reform Bill of 1834, for example, dramatically altered the government's policy for handling the "able-bodied" poor and others too sick, old, or young to fend for themselves. It set a uniform policy for administering to the poor, discouraging "out door relief" granted to people in their homes and opting instead for "workhouses" in which the destitute were housed and forced to labor at the most menial tasks. Poor-law authorities in England sometimes discussed the feasibility of putting pressure on paupers' relatives to keep them from the workhouses (Webb and Webb 1963:126b), but the 1834 Poor Law did not explicitly force peoples' blood relatives to feed, clothe, and work for their maintenance (Lazarus-Black 1992:878–79).[31]

The change in managing the destitute in Antigua occurred more gradually, by way of several different statutes. For example, the British act abolishing slavery in the colonies contained a clause stating that the manumitted slaves would be eligible for parochial relief "in the same footing as all His Majesty's other subjects in the Colony." It also made it illegal for plantation owners to expel slaves who wished to continue working on the estates, the elderly, or the infirm "until proper measures can be taken to provide for them through parish relief" (Microfilm No. 6).

The locally inspired Act For The Punishment Of Idle And Disorderly Persons, Rogues And Vagabonds, Incorrigible Rogues, And Other Vagrants In This Island (1834), however, made it unlawful to refuse to work to maintain one's family. The Antiguan lawmakers considered this crime on par with prostitution and riotous behavior:

> Every person being able wholly or in part to maintain himself or herself, or his or her family, by work or by other means, and willfully refusing to and neglecting so to do, every common Prostitute wandering in the public streets or public highways or in any place of public resort and behaving in a riotous and indecent manner and every person wandering about or placing himself or herself in any public place . . . to beg or gather alms or causing or procuring or encouraging any child or children so to do shall be deemed an idle and disorderly person. (Microfilm No. 6)[32]

Thus Antiguan freedmen were eligible for parish relief only if they had no one whom they could claim as family and were also well behaved! Furthermore, justices of the peace could incarcerate persons who refused to care for family members for a month with hard labor. Perhaps the specific reference to women in this act was indicative of their inability to maintain themselves or their children. Unfortunately, after 1860 "words importing the masculine gender include females" in local Antiguan statutes and we lose track of the legislators' attempts to control crimes that were perpetrated by women as opposed to men (*Laws of Antigua* 1864:439).

The 1834 statute proved problematic because it left vague who constituted a person's family. By 1855, this defect was remedied and specific persons were charged with keeping each other out of the newly constructed poor house:

> Every husband shall be liable to maintain his wife and every child under the age of fourteen, whether legitimate or illegitimate, she may have at the time of marriage with such husband, every father to maintain his child, every grandparent his grandchild, every widow her child, and the father and mother of every bastard child their bastard child until such child respectively shall attain the age of fourteen years; and when any poor person shall through old age, infirmity, or other defect be unable to support himself, every child and grandchild of such person shall be liable, according to his ability, to maintain such poor person. (*Laws of Antigua* 1864:326)[33]

In other words, kinship was "extended" in the poor laws so that depending on the situation, the persons legally responsible for any child might include his biological mother or father, someone living with his mother, female care-taker, or father,[34] anyone marrying his mother while he was still a minor, his maternal or paternal grandparents, or any other person known to be related to him by blood or law. Similarly, the problem of the destitute elderly was resolved by making all children and grandchildren responsible for their parents and grandparents.

Antiguan lawmakers may have extended kinship to prevent a possible fiscal nightmare: they were avoiding the possibility that an impoverished working class with an extremely low marriage rate might leave the sugar estates or apply for parish relief for illegitimate children. The legislators accomplished much more than this, however. Passage of the poor laws effected a major adjustment in the relationship between kinship legalities and illegalities. Relationships between men, women, and children suddenly were imbued with different meanings because law now infiltrated what had previously been conceived as personal matters, as part of a realm of practice that had always been extralegal, if not necessarily illegal (Lazarus-Black 1992:879–80). The poor laws were significant in another way too. For the first time, formal rules applying to kinship organization and responsibilities resembled the actual practices of families in the common order.[35] I examine those practices in the next chapter.

In addition to restructuring the realm of kinship legalities, postemancipation legislators reorganized the processes through which poor bastards and the poor at large might obtain relief. In 1849, the assembly admitted that the 1786 statute providing a weekly stipend to illegitimate white children "has been found not only inefficient, but altogether inapplicable" (Microfilm No. 8). The replacement measure no longer specified the race of the child, but it assigned the unpleasant responsibility of searching for wayward fathers to churchwardens. After their "diligent inquiry as to the father of the child," the churchwardens could apply to two justices of the peace to bring charges against the man whose child "had become chargeable to any Parish in this island" (Microfilm No. 8). One can imagine the churchwardens' ire over their new assignment: this act made lowly constables of respectable church administrators.

Not surprisingly, this method for providing relief for illegitimate children became obsolete a short time later. In 1852 the legislature passed An Act To Establish A General Poor House For This Island and repealed the 1692 statute that made vestry boards responsible for collecting taxes to pay for the poor in separate parishes. A building "to the east of the prison" was dedicated to the "impotent and disabled Poor of this Island." Entrance to the poor house was by ticket provided by a vestry member or one of the newly appointed "Guardians of the Poor" who supervised conditions at the home. A "destitute person," that is, one who qualified for shelter at the poor house, included anyone "who from infancy, old age, disease, bodily infirmity, or mental incapacity is unable to labour for his support," for whom no persons could be found who were obliged by law to care for them, and who had resided on the island at least three months (*Laws of Antigua* 1864:325). Any person legally responsible for caring for a destitute person and refusing to do so could be taken before a magistrate and forced to pay a weekly support stipend. Three years later, the powers of the guardians were increased: they could appoint a teacher for juveniles at the poor house "if found necessary," apprentice young persons in their care, assign adults "any light work or occupation about the house or grounds," and distribute poor relief to persons not residing inside the home (Microfilm No. 9).

Extending the strategy of government through families, the state adopted the list of kin who could be made fiscally responsible for needy persons from the 1855 poor law into several later acts. The statute of 1870, which brought Holberton Hospital, the poor house, the lunatic asylum, and the lazaretto under one jurisdiction as Holberton Institution, for example, contained a "General Liability to Support Relatives" clause identical to that in the poor law (Microfilm No. 10). Similarly, in the 1880 medical-relief act, a "poor and destitute person" included only "any person who is possessed of no property, and who from age, infancy, disease, or other bodily infirmary or mental incapacity is unable to labour for his own support, or who has no relative bound by law to support him" (Microfilm No. 10).[36]

The Antiguans managed to confine the utterly destitute in a single place by the middle of the nineteenth century; they were much less successful in managing the problem of poor and illegitimate children. In 1875, however, the Legislative Council of the Leeward Islands passed An Act For The Better Support Of Natural Children, And To Afford Facilities For Obliging The Putative Father To Assist In The Maintenance Of Such Children. A product of the new Leeward Islands Federation, rather than of the local legislature of Antigua, the statute conformed to British standards of the period.[37] With slight modifications, the procedures for obtaining an affiliation order, the powers bestowed upon magistrates to regulate relationships between illegitimate children and their fathers, and the financial arrangements to protect such youth outlined in this act still obtain in Antigua.[38]

The 1875 statute permitted any woman delivering an illegitimate child to apply to a magistrate for an order for affiliation and support from the child's father. The act encouraged women to use the courts to establish paternity and to collect maintenance by making them easily accessible at minimal cost. Requests had to be made within a year after the baby's birth unless the mother could prove that previously the man had cared for the child. At the hearing, the evidence of the mother needed to be "corroborated in some material particulars by other testimony." Both parties could bring witnesses and had the right to counsel. Support payments were limited to five shillings per week for the first six weeks and to two shillings and six pence per week thereafter until the child attained the age of twelve or until the mother married.[39] A putative father could appeal his case to the High Court, but the magistrate had power to send him to jail and sell his property for failure to comply with the bastardy order.

The Leeward Islands Maintenance Act predates similar laws elsewhere in the Caribbean. By the 1880s, the number of illegitimate children in the region mustered several attempts to regulate the kinship order by legal proclamation. Trinidad and Jamaica, for example, passed bastardy ordinances in 1881–82 (Braithwaite 1953:91; Brereton 1979:60–61; Roberts 1979:252–53; Salmon n.d.; Trotman 1986:240–47). Both governments treated bastardy and poverty in remarkably similar ways. Writing about the Jamaican bastardy laws of 1881 and 1886, Salmon noted:

> The argument can be made that the principal motive behind this legislation was to relieve the state of the expense of maintaining destitute children, despite the noble sounding recital in the Preamble. This view would seem to be substantiated by Section 8 which provided for the punishment "as a rogue and a vagabond" of a mother who neglected to maintain her bastard child "whereby such a child became a charge on the funds applicable to the relief of the poor." It does not seem coincidental that a Poor Relief Law was passed in the same year. A procedure amendment in 1886 enabled the Inspector of Poor to enforce the Maintenance and bastardy law. (Salmon n.d.:20)[40]

Trinidad's version of the bastardy law included a clause disallowing "common or reputed prostitutes or women of known immoral character" from using the act, allegedly to prevent such women from blackmailing innocent men (Trotman 1986:243). Women who used the courts, therefore, had to be prepared to defend their character—a denigrating experience perpetrated by white and nonwhite men on mostly black women (ibid.:247). In short, efforts to reduce the public deficits sparked a restructuring of kinship legalities in several Caribbean colonies.

Creole bastardy and poor laws illuminate new uses for kinship in postemancipation Caribbean societies. Through a series of strategic measures, financial responsibility for the needy was transferred from the public purse to the private pockets of those who could be legally designated as relatives. Both near and remote affinal and consanguineous kin were implicated in the move: virtually every person could be assigned to a family. The idea that all persons belonged to responsible familial collectivities contradicted, of course, the dominant image of the person in the labor codes—that autonomous individual who was free to enter into or reject relationships of his own choosing. Nevertheless, both themes of local law—the stress upon individualism and the countervailing collectivity of kin—were critical in formulating a creole family system.

The Influence from Abroad

Over the course of the nineteenth century, the British reconstituted the fundamental legal rights of men and women in their society: they rewrote the poor laws, passed mandatory health and education codes, changed voting rights and property qualifications for office, and altered representation in the House of Commons. The 1832 English Reform Act, for example, reflected the economic and social changes that had begun with the antislavery movement in the 1780s. It destroyed the rotten boroughs, the basis of the West Indians' parliamentary influence, enfranchised the manufacturing towns, and gave the abolitionist movement unprecedented support (Turner 1982:190). Slavery in the colonies was abolished in 1834. Shortly thereafter, the British gave dissenters the right to wed in their own churches, allowed couples to divorce, altered custody and maintenance laws, and provided married women rights in property.

Given Antigua's greater political dependency on England after 1868, and changed political relationship to the other Leeward Islands with the establishment of the Leeward Islands Federation in 1871, it is hardly surprising to discover local kinship laws from this period adopting whole parts of or simply replicating British statutes. For Antiguans, three of the most important of these British imports were acts permitting non-Anglicans to wed according to their own rites, the divorce bill, and the codes affecting married women's property rights.[41] In the remainder of this chapter, I review these three statutes, explain their incorporation into the Antiguan legal order, and suggest their significance for the evolving kinship system.

These transformations began with British laws of 1836 that not only allowed Catholic priests and Protestant ministers to perform marriage rites but also made civil ceremonies available as alternatives to church services for the first time since the Middle Ages. They also created the Office of Registrar of Births, Deaths, and Marriages (Bromley 1981:37–38). The growth of religious toleration in England certainly precipitated passage of these acts, but they also displayed the state's growing interest in keeping an eye on kinship. A few years later, in 1844, Antiguan legislators followed the British example and repealed their 1692 statute prohibiting anyone other than an Anglican minister from marrying couples. As in England, the decision to allow dissenters to perform marriages was coupled with a plan to keep records of these events (Microfilm No. 7). The Antiguans, however, passed a less compassionate "toleration bill": initially only clergymen of the Church of the United Brethren, Wesleyan Methodists, and Presbyterians could perform marriages in Antigua. Perhaps the lawmakers restricted their act to curtail the authority of Baptist preachers who were proving themselves instigators of political unrest and discontent among the lower classes in Jamaica (Curtin 1955; Turner 1982). In later years, the presiding head of each new religious group in Antigua applied separately to the registrar general for permission to wed members of his congregation (*Laws of Antigua* 1962: vol. 5, 3037–66). Today, a minister's request to serve as a marriage officer must be accompanied by a "letter recommending that he be so appointed signed by the head, superintendent, superior, or other senior church officer of his denomination within Antigua and Barbuda" (*Laws of Antigua and Barbuda* 1984:No. 6). Thus although religious toleration is protected, the state continues to supervise carefully its marriage officers and remains reluctant to grant non-established ministries power to preside over marriage contracts.

Great Britain had refused resident Roman Catholics permission to marry by their own rites until 1836. Nevertheless, the Roman Catholic idea that made marriage a sacrament, a union not to be broken, had had a profound effect on the legal development of divorce in the United Kingdom. The first divorces in England were granted by the ecclesiastical courts *a mensa et thoro* (not permitting remarriage) on the grounds of cruelty or adultery. After 1700, Parliament heard requests for divorce, but the ecclesiastical decree remained a preliminary requirement. Parliament also mandated a "verdict at law," obtained by proving a civil suit against an adulterer for "criminal conversation" with a married person, though this could be waived if the offender was abroad or deceased.[42]

Parliament ended ecclesiastical authority over matrimonial relationships with the Matrimonial Causes Act of 1857. The newly created Divorce Court made legal separations and divorces easier to obtain, although the law still placed formidable obstacles in the paths of those who wished to leave their spouses. For example, a husband who wanted a divorce had to name his wife's paramour as co-respondent in the suit. If his case was successful, the court awarded him monetary compensation from his wife's lover—an interesting footnote in the history of British chivalry. A man's "indiscretion" was not considered nearly as serious, and a wife had to prove at least two suits against her husband to obtain a divorce.[43] She could request the court to compel her husband to pay for the suit and to provide her with alimony. If she was guilty of any objectionable behavior, the court deprived her of the company of her children.[44]

Since 1857, England has many times revised the procedures for divorce, the jurisdiction of divorce courts,[45] the rights of married persons who separate,[46] and the grounds for which one may apply for divorce. One of the most radical changes occurred in 1937, when the legal offenses leading to divorce were expanded to include mental or physical cruelty, desertion for three years, and incurable insanity (Bromley 1981:187–88). With one or two minor variations,[47] the present Antiguan divorce law is almost an exact replica of the British statute of 1937 (*Federal Acts of the Leeward Islands* 1948:No. 1; *Laws of Antigua* 1962:vol. 1, 489–500). The great movement for the reform of the divorce law that occurred in Britain after the second World War never reached the island.[48]

Antiguans first expressed their dissatisfaction over the lack of a competent local authority to settle matrimonial grievances when they were visited by the Royal Commission from England in 1826 (Great Britain, Commission of Inquiry, 1826:vol. 2, 80; Patchett 1973:34). Neither Antigua's elected assembly nor its subsequent Crown colony council, however, initiated any efforts to bring the English divorce law to the island. The Leeward Islands Federation Legislative Council proved remarkably unwilling to deal with matrimonial breakdown: it failed to enact a local divorce act until 1948![49]

The Leeward Islands Federation disbanded in 1956, but the islands continued to share an itinerant Supreme Court. When Antigua assumed Associated Statehood in 1969, its own High Court assumed jurisdiction over divorce and other matrimonial causes (*Laws of Antigua* 1969:No. 26). Yet the 1948 divorce statute, updated in 1957, continues in force. A person can apply for divorce only after he or she has been married for three years.[50] The grounds for divorce are adultery, desertion without cause for at least three years, cruelty, or that the defendant is of unsound mind and has not responded to treatment for at least five years. A wife may also apply for a divorce on the grounds that her husband has been guilty of rape, sodomy, or bestiality.

There were no successful efforts to revise Antigua's divorce law during the period of Associated Statehood or in the first decade after independence in 1981. By an act of 1975, however, the government recognized divorces and legal separations obtained in other nations without making any effort to redraft its own code (*Laws of Antigua* 1975:No. 25).[51] The idea that divorce should be available when a marriage fails, as opposed to only when a matrimonial offense is committed, has not yet taken root in Antigua, even though it gained popularity in England in the 1960s and culminated in the Divorce Reform Act of 1969. That law abolished the old grounds for divorce, replacing them with the singular cause that the marriage is irretrievably broken. Lawyers who met to remedy the divorce law in Antigua in the 1970s and 1980s found their efforts thwarted by government officials who believed that Antiguans would not welcome a bill that "destroyed" the family.

The general unavailability of divorce in Antigua until the relatively recent past helps explain not only the very low divorce rate in the island but also the custom whereby married couples simply live apart when they cannot live together. Indeed, "living in sin" and having children out of wedlock reflected not so much a failed morality as the near impossibility of canceling a marriage contract in the nineteenth century and for most of the twentieth century.[52] Thus although the divorce law did not originate in an attempt to regulate the nonlegal Antiguan family, it contributed to their numbers by making it extremely difficult to change marriage partners (Lazarus-Black 1992:883). Today divorce is more readily available, but, as we will see in Chapter 7, the difficulty of proving a case, the expense, the public exposure that court requires, and the religious sanctions against it continue to dissuade people from legally severing their relationships. By the end of the second phase of Antigua's kinship history, then, divorce had been incorporated as a way to break an alliance, but, because it carried such negative connotations in the common order, it was hardly an option for the faint of heart.

The distribution of matrimonial property between husbands and wives also obstructed acceptance of divorce in nineteenth-century England and Antigua. The 1857 Divorce Act allowed English couples to sever their matrimonial contracts, but it failed to alter the respective statuses of husbands and wives because the law continued to differentiate male and female relationships to property. Since Blackstone's day, very little had changed with respect to the position of married women. Wives remained under the coverture of their husbands, and unless a prenuptial marriage settlement specified other arrangements, all of a woman's resources, including wages, inheritances, estates, and rents became the absolute property of her husband.[53] A wife could not enter into contracts, sue, or be sued, and if she committed a criminal act with her spouse, she was assumed to have acted under his direction and at his will.

A dramatic change in the status of married women occurred in 1870, when England passed the first of three Married Women's Property Acts. The 1870 statute entitled a woman to control her own wages, stocks, and inheritances from next-of-kin who died intestate, to purchase life insurance, to place funds in a bank or the post office, and to sue and be sued with respect to her separate property. In 1874, a defect in the earlier bill that prevented creditors from charging husbands with their wives' premarital debts was eliminated. The Married Women's Property Act of 1882, the most significant challenge to the subordinate status of married women, consolidated these two earlier statutes and extended to all women married after 1 January 1883 the right to control separately all assets brought to her marriage or acquired in her own name after her nuptials. Her inheritance was her own, she could enter into contracts, dispose of property, be sued or charged with bankruptcy, and ordered to maintain her spouse and children. The last legal impediments against married women in England with respect to property were removed in 1935, when they gained the right to dispose of all forms of property and to contract with both strangers and their own husbands (Bromley 1981:151).

Throughout the whole of the Married Women's Property Acts debates in Parliament, neither side questioned the possible limitations of a system in which kinship was a relation of power over persons and property (Lazarus-Black 1982).[54] Nevertheless, because marriage provided the fulcrum upon which the English kinship system balanced, redefining the rights and duties of spouses implied reordering issues of kinship. The 1882 Married Women's Property Act was a landmark bill because it changed the jural status marking women's "place" in the kinship system. Women were no longer insignificant kin: they could control real and personal property, inheritances, and businesses (ibid.:51–52).

In contrast to their reaction to the British Divorce Act, the Legislative Council of the Leeward Islands Federation acted quickly to adopt the provisions of the 1882 Married Women's Property Act. In fact, they had produced an exact replica of the British statute by 1887, which remains part of the present Laws of Antigua (*Federal Acts of the Leeward Islands* 1914:vol. 2, 197–202; *Laws of Antigua* 1962:vol. 5, 3075–84). Unfortunately, there is no record of the extent to which Antiguan women used these laws in the early years after their passage. Although I located some nineteenth-century High Court records at the Antigua National Archives, these contained no cases involving either divorce or the Married Women's Property Act.[55]

It is probably safe to surmise that the three Antiguan laws that most closely replicated English family law of the same time period were also the least likely to have wielded much immediate or widespread influence in the common order. After all, Antigua was composed mainly of unmarried people without property. If anything, the law giving non-Anglican ministers the right to marry couples, the divorce law, and the Married Women's Property Act are mostly evidence of an elite's capacity to frame legislation on its own behalf. But even elites cannot control or predict the future. No one could have foreseen how important these acts would become to family life in the common order in the latter part of the twentieth century, when the island's political economy moved in a different direction.

Summary and Conclusions

As Bolland correctly points out:

> It would be inaccurate, of course, to suggest that all the colonies experienced the same situation after 1838, and erroneous to imply an evolutionary development in labor systems, but it is essential to examine, critically and comparatively, the shift from slave to wage labor as a transition from one system of labor control to another, each system characterized by its own mode of struggle. (1981:592; see also 1992a:115)

In Antigua in the years between 1834 and 1986, law directed, as much as it reflected, the making of a creole labor force and family ideology and structure. Early in this period, locally drafted statutes demanded of Antiguans both an increased emphasis on individualism and a countervailing stress upon the family whose broadened and codified membership became responsible for mitigating adversity. In later years, British statutes such as those permitting marriages to be performed by non-Anglicans, divorce, and married women's rights to property forced some liberalization of the old kinship order by redefining the nature of marriage and the status of married women. In combination, these laws help explain both the continuity of creole family ideology from slavery to modern times and its movement in new directions.

The increased emphasis on individualism after 1834 is most evident in the labor codes. In contrast to the situation in São Paulo, Brazil, where coffee estate owners directly encouraged familial labor (Stolcke 1984), Antiguan employers expected every man, woman, and child to sign separate contracts. We shall see in the next chapter that these laws helped frame the character of working-class life, including the form and content of familial relationships, because they determined who worked together during the day and who slept and ate together at night. The clause in the Contract Act stipulating that an estate laborer's "wife" and children agreed to work for the same employer as the husband/father was a means to force women and children to the fields and was hardly an expression of a concern for familial solidarity.

The individualization of labor was accompanied by a program of government through families that redefined the state's role in managing formerly private affairs of kin. As we have seen, quite a lot of the legislation of this era displayed a concern for the welfare and condition of children: their labor was carefully regulated, their health was preserved, their education was made suitable to their station in life, and they were disciplined when they were disorderly. The state declared that children had to be maintained—and when their mothers were not able, their fathers were made to provide for them. Moreover, Antigua's nineteenth-century poor laws specified that persons related by blood or contract for three generations were legally responsible for each other's welfare. By law, kin constituted the safeguard against all of the trials and tribulations of life in the common order. To refuse to house, clothe, or feed a son or a grandmother was no longer simply reproachable behavior, it was a criminal act. An expanding police force, additional magistrates, and the poor-law guardians enforced these statutes and kept vagabonds, rogues, and other idle and kinless persons off the streets. Thus some of the techniques of power that ensured a dependent work force were also critical in creating governable families. Ironically, as we see next, the poor laws envisioned a "family" that was in fact similar to that which had long existed among the working people.

The British kinship statutes adopted by the Leeward Islands Federation initially exerted less-dramatic influence on family life. For among the Toleration Act, the Divorce Act, and the Married Women's Property Act, the Toleration Act, which allowed non-Anglicans to marry couples, was probably most used. This is because non-Anglican sects steadily gained followers in the postslavery era and their members were no longer confined to Anglican marriage ceremonies. In contrast, divorces have been rare in Antigua until recently. The federation long avoided bringing divorce to the Leeward Islands, and those who have governed since independence have displayed a similar reluctance to ease the plight of people who want to sever their matrimonial ties. The Married Women's Property Act falls somewhere in between the two. It was readily adopted in the colony in 1887, but given the limited number of women at the time who were both married and able to afford court proceedings to sue for their property, the law must have been of practical value for only a privileged few. Nevertheless, I have argued that what was most significant about the Married Women's Property Acts was not their immediate practical economic consequences but their ideological impact on a kinship system that organized power over persons and property. The Married Women's Property Acts elevated the position of the wife. Indeed, law now fully supported what the ministers in the common order preached in church: it was better to be married than unmarried.

In the years between 1834 and 1986, then, law pointed family ideology and practice toward individualism for both sexes, commitment to familial solidarity in times of adversity, a respect for marriage, a disdain for divorce, and an increased status for married women. It is true to say, too, that the statutes of this period cut the class and gender hierarchies in new places. Nineteenth-century legislation first made estate laborers and indentured servants into a distinct group in Antiguan creole society. Today, these rural peoples remain a much-disparaged social entity, which, people explain, is due entirely to their poverty and ignorance. Similarly, women's longstanding subordinate "place" in Antiguan society, as well as the inferior status of unmarried women and their children, are explained by reference to men's and women's different "natures," even though these were long ago cemented in the kinship codes. Like the effects of the labor and welfare codes upon family life in the common order, these consequences of law have been naturalized over time as "the way things are in Antigua," and their relation with the legal order has been forgotten. To see these points more clearly, we must examine life in the common order between 1834 and 1986.

6

Family Life in the Common Order after Slavery

MUCH REMAINED the same in Antigua immediately after emancipation: the economy still depended upon sugar, local political institutions lost some of their earlier autonomy but continued to pass repressive statutes, and the working people labored under profoundly difficult conditions.[1] Family life in the common order, however, witnessed several important changes. Law gave new meanings, functions, and consequences to kinship, class, and gender relations, and government through families shifted the content and measure of state intervention in peoples' everyday lives. In addition, two developments shaped creole kinship ideology and structure after 1834: the internal composition of Antigua's class structure changed and ministers spread Christianity across the island.

Immigration schemes brought Portuguese, African, American, East Indian, and Chinese laborers to Antigua immediately after slavery ended and throughout the nineteenth century. Syrian and Lebanese traders arrived early in the twentieth century and stayed to raise their families. These new Antiguans, together with some of the children of the working class, eventually toiled their way into the middle class. They widened the basis of the economy, built retail trades, diversified the service sector, promoted construction, reorganized landholdings, and encouraged tourism. Still, if the composition of the class structure had changed, much of the earlier rhetoric about the ideal nuclear family had not. In section 1 we find the new middle class resembled its predecessor by vocalizing an ideology of kinship that disdained unlawful unions and unlawful children. When the players changed again in the later nineteenth century (Lowes 1993), the same middle-class ideology prevailed. In contrast, estate laborers and other working-class Antiguans described in section 2, retained their kinship patterns of an earlier era, in part because the Contract Act bound the majority to the sugar estates well into the twentieth century.

As the composition of the middle class changed, Antigua experienced two great waves of missionary activity separated by nearly a century. The first wave began just before abolition, when the long-established churches expanded their memberships and built schools for their congregations. These ministers envisioned themselves as the guardians of the civilized tradition, although they had no intention of interfering with Antigua's political economy. For that reason, and perhaps because of the poor conditions of the roads, they confined most of their preaching to the towns, and their voices rarely carried to the rural estates. The second great wave of church activity coincided with the severe economic recession of the late 1930s and the outburst of labor unrest throughout the Caribbean (Austin-Broos 1991; Post 1978). By the 1950s, the established churches in Antigua had moved into the countryside, where they soon met competition from small fundamentalist groups whose leaders came from conservative missions in other islands and from the United States. Evangelical churches also began their proselytizing in St. John's, gaining a following among the town's poor, but they spread throughout the island and to Barbuda over the next thirty years. These fundamentalists accomplished what the established churches had failed to do and what only a war or a natural catastrophe could: they raised the marriage rate for a few years. Much to their chagrin, however, they were unable to reverse the order of reproduction and marriage in the lower class. Section 3 analyzes this growing influence of the men from the missions.

Myalism, the Convince Cult, Cumina, pocomania, balm-yard meetings, and the politically radical Baptist sects that provided idioms for expression in Jamaica failed to engage significant numbers of Antiguans.[2] As far as I can discover, only the conservative churches flourished in Antigua. And yet the men and women of the Antiguan common order continued to practice obeah. As we shall see in the last section of this chapter, obeah offered, among other things, a contrasting ideology of justice, including ideas about just relationships between men, women, and children. We turn first, however, to the subject of mating, marriage, and reproduction in the common order after slavery.

The Local Elite and Middle Classes

According to nineteenth-century observers, there were changes in the family practices of upper-class married men after slavery: participation in open concubinage and legal provision for children born outside of wedlock declined. It seemed to these witnesses that great improvements were being made in the quality and morality of family life in the island.

Two American antislavery advocates, Thome and Kimball, observed these changes in Antiguan society when they toured the West Indies in 1837. They found Antiguan planters very satisfied with the effects of the new free-labor system. Emancipation afforded them a more economical way to run their estates, and the former slaves proved hard working and well mannered. As for race relations, some progress had already been made. In the churches, for example, people of different races mixed freely. In fact, some Antiguans advised the travelers that what hostility existed was less on account of color than past illegal, and still potentially disruptive, family practices:

> As to prejudice against the black and colored people, all thought it was rapidly decreasing—indeed, they could scarcely say there was now any such thing. To be sure, there was an aversion among the higher classes of the whites, and especially among *females*, to associating in parties with colored people; but it was not on account of their *color*, but chiefly because of their illegitimacy. This was to us a new source of prejudice; but subsequent information fully explained its bearings. The whites of the West Indies are themselves the authors of that *illegitimacy*, out of which their aversion springs. It is not to be wondered that they should be unwilling to invite the colored people to their social parties, seeing that they might not infrequently be subjected to the embarrassment of introducing to their white wives a colored mistress or an *illegitimate* daughter. This also explains the special prejudice which the *ladies* of the higher classes feel towards those among whom are their guilty rivals in a husband's affections, and those whose every feature tells the story of a husband's unfaithfulness! (Thome and Kimball 1839:33)

Thome and Kimball found that despite the whites' participation in the island's system of kinship illegalities, they still proclaimed an ideology that disdained unlawful children:

> An unguarded statement of a public man revealed the conviction which exists among his class that concubinage must soon cease. He said that the present race of colored people could not be received into the society of the whites, *because of illegitimacy;* but the next generation would be fit associates for the whites, *because they would be chiefly born in wedlock.* (Ibid.:83–84)

However, another contemporary historian, Flannagan, held a different opinion about the causes for prejudice:

> It is said, that the white ladies are the strongest upholders of prejudice; but that their refusal to mix with this class of persons is not occasioned from any shade of colour, but on account of their general illegitimacy. This, however, is not the sole cause; for there are illegitimate white people, whom they are in constant habit of meeting without any aversion; while, at the same time, many of the people of colour, particularly the younger ones, are the offspring of parents who have been

legally united within the sacred walls of the temple of God, and whose intellectual attainments fit them for any society. (1967:vol. 2, 181)

It seems likely that both color and illegitimacy remained components of the system of stratification, but also that tolerance of unlawful unions by the white community and men's willingness to recognize publicly their outside children varied at different periods. As abolition approached, for example, illegitimate children were less a part of respectable family life and less frequently mentioned in their fathers' wills (Lowes 1982:12). Moreover, after 1830 "the governor noted that 'no white man of respectability dare now openly violate the laws of morality' " (ibid.:12). Thome and Kimball were assured by Dr. Ferguson, a physician they encountered, that "a general spirit of improvement was pervading the island" and that although formerly it had been customary for married men to keep mistresses, the practice was becoming "disreputable" (1839:34). Similarly, an "aged Christian" who superintended some of the day schools told these visitors "there was not one-third as much concubinage as formerly. . . . owing mainly to the greater frequency of marriages, and the cessation of late night work on the estates, and in the boiling-houses, by which the females were constantly exposed during slavery" (ibid.:82). Finally, Flannagan wrote in 1844 that "the unhallowed custom of concubinage has greatly decreased" (1967:vol. 2, 181).

Were these changes the result of a depressed economy, and the consequent redistribution of inheritances favoring legitimate children? Were they the outcome of differences in the social and ethnic composition of the elite and middle classes? Were they the result of more balanced sex ratios within each of the different ranks? Or were they the eventuality of a renewed morality, the product of the increasing effectiveness of the clergy in managing familial relations?

Each of these factors contributed in part to the structure and content of the relationships between men, women, and children in the elite and middle ranks of creole society after 1834. As we saw earlier, abolition was not accompanied by a transformation of Antigua's economy and it failed to revamp the class structure. Instead, wealthier sugar planters consolidated their holdings, buying up those estates whose owners could not afford to sustain operations under the conditions of competition sparked by Great Britain's "free" trade policy of the second half of the century.[3] Propertied whites returned to England at abolition, during the serious recessions of the 1870s and 1890s, and again in the midst of the Great Depression. Census data in Table 6 shows a steady decline in the number of whites and a drop in the overall population of the island. These trends continued over the next few decades. According to one historian, "The general economic contraction, plus the contraction of the sugar industry itself, led the white population to leave in large numbers: its numbers

TABLE 6 **Population of Antigua, 1861, 1871, and 1881**

Year	White	Black	Colored	Total
1861	2,560	27,603	6,882	37,045
1871	2,146	26,386	6,890	35,422
1881	1,795	27,219	5,950	34,964

SOURCE: Henry 1985:56.

declined by almost half between 1891 and 1911 (from 1830 to 1008)" (Lowes 1987:9). The white population dropped to 909 persons in 1921 and to a mere 694 persons in 1946 (Jamaica, Bureau of the Census, 1948:xvi).

After the first major white exodus about 1834, some middle-class positions were filled by the better-educated and increasingly well-to-do people of color.[4] They included merchants, clerks, teachers, doctors, and lawyers—some of whom now served in government posts. The rest, of more limited means and education, worked as artisans, sailors, messengers, and hucksters in the towns (Lowes 1987:4, 5; 1993:217). John Horsford, a Methodist missionary who described himself as "a man of colour," explained their class position and common kinship pattern in 1856: "A large proportion of the middle classes in the towns are people of colour, many of whom are persons of intelligence, education, and true respectability. . . . Respectable coloured gentlemen generally marry their equals in point of intellect and character" (1856:90, 56). In fact, the marriage pattern of the privileged nonwhite community at midcentury was not noticeably different from that which had obtained fifty years earlier: legal Christian marriages were highly valued and people wed their status equals. Few persons risked breaching the color line. Only two white artisans, a watchmaker and a coachmaker, married nonwhite women in Antigua in the period between 1830 and 1930. Both cases occurred in the late nineteenth century (Lowes 1982:19).

By the 1870s, the Antiguan economy had entered a period of sharp decline and the nonwhite middle class had begun to contract.[5] Many migrated in search of jobs and education. Part of the explanation for their decline, however, had to do with family ideology: "One of the reasons that this class did not reproduce itself was that its members refused to recruit from groups below it on the social scale." Thus when men migrated in search of work, they left behind "a host of elderly never-married women who had not been able to find 'suitable' marriage partners" (Lowes 1987:7).

At the end of the nineteenth century, a "suitable" marriage partner for a middle-class woman of color was financially established, church-going on Sundays, and respectable in his manners. He identified with high society, spoke refined English, rejected the art, song, dance, and philosophy of the African heritage, and, preferably, was light skinned. Henry claims "shadism . . . an elaborate construction that labelled and attributed social status to a large number of shades between black and white" (1985:66) tempered marital selection and was prolonged by those on their way up the social ladder. Lowes argues, in contrast, that the postemancipation middle class distinguished its members on the basis of class, not color; they married and socialized with families of a similar economic rank (1982:3; 1993:413–14). Both historians agree that the small white population continued to exclude nonwhites from preferred jobs in the private and public sectors and did not intermarry with them.

As the century progressed, an important sector of the nonwhite middle class came to include upwardly mobile children of working-class parents. Lowes's study shows they followed three patterns. Most were either:

> 1) the legitimate children of newly arrived (i.e., in the mid-1800s) white men who came as high-grade office clerks and married nonwhite Antiguan men and women, or 2) the legitimate children of illegitimate nonwhite arrived Antiguan men and women, themselves the children of newly arrived white plantation managers or overseers and nonwhite Antiguan women, or 3) in a very few cases, the legitimate offspring of outside [illegitimate] branches of free colored families. (1987:8–9)

These Antiguans were part of what Lowes calls the second middle class of the postemancipation period, one originating in the "artisanal former free colored and in the children of white men, most of whom were new immigrants, who came to work on the estates or, less frequently, in urban clerical occupations" (1993:228). As she also points out, legitimacy now became a key factor in the struggle for upward mobility in part because it was a prerequisite to admission to the two schools that provided educations necessary for entry into most middle-class occupations; namely, the Antigua Grammar School and the Antigua Girls High School. No illegitimate child entered the Grammar School until 1939. Thus admission standards based on birth status kept the size of the nonwhite middle class limited (Lowes 1987:9). It was a tactic deployed throughout the English-speaking Caribbean (Senior 1991:47) and a strategy that allowed the Antiguan elite a degree of choice about who would be allowed into the nonwhite middle class (Lowes 1993:444).

The children of indentured servants and itinerant traders took other routes to the middle class. Of these, the Portuguese, and later the Lebanese and

Syrians, were especially important because of their contribution to the economic and political life of the island and for the model for kinship and gender they espoused.

The first Portuguese immigrants came to Antigua as contract laborers, recruited in the immigration schemes described in the last chapter.[6] As we have seen, a combination of private and public funds paid for these workers and they labored under elaborate codes. Planters especially hoped to attract European peasant farmers and their families. One of the more successful schemes from their perspective, therefore, brought Portuguese workers from Madeira. A famine in Madeira in 1846–47 forced thousands of Portuguese to leave their homes. Laurence estimates approximately twenty-five hundred Portuguese arrived in Antigua between 1835 and 1882. After that date, the number dropped significantly. Not surprisingly, planters were slightly less enthusiastic about receiving Africans, American blacks, East Indians, and Chinese servants.[7]

It was the Portuguese who flourished. After fulfilling their indentured contracts, they found their own economic niche in small retail shops, bakeries, and liquor stores (Laurence 1971:18). As in Guyana, many of the Portuguese in Antigua abandoned working in the fields in favor of retail trade, and "those who overcame the initial period of acclimatization usually achieved swift economic success" (ibid.:18). By the 1870s, baking and liquor sales were firmly under their control (Lowes 1993:426). Yet they remained socially and religiously distinct and did not intermarry with either the white or nonwhite population (ibid.:428). The governors and the Colonial Office considered them a separate community and chose John J. Camacho to represent them on the Legislative Council when Antigua became a full Crown colony in 1898 (ibid.:429).

Almost all of the men and women named in the eighty marriages recorded in the Catholic church registers between 1862 and 1877 have Portuguese surnames. In the case of one couple who married in 1864, the priest specifically mentioned they were legitimate persons who had "come from Madeira eleven years ago." There were only seven cases (three in 1872) of marriage with a non-Catholic. In each instance, the priest noted that he had obtained a special dispensation to marry the couple after the non-Catholic partner had agreed to raise the children in the Catholic faith. There was one instance, in 1872, in which a special dispensation was needed from the bishop in Dominica because the couple shared a blood line.[8]

Antiguan Catholics believed strongly in lawful matrimony. Both parties in each of the eighty marriages, with just three exceptions, were identified as legitimate sons or daughters.[9] It was also important to these couples to be married in their own church. Between 1867 and 1868, for example, we find seventeen cases of remarriage by a priest of couples previously united in matrimony by a Protestant minister. Three additional remarriages, two in 1869 and one in 1878, are also recorded. Justifying his decision to remarry one husband and wife, Father Blake explained that the couple "have been long previously married by a Protestant clergyman—notwithstanding all church prohibitions, excuse alleged that there was then at their nominal marriage, no Catholic Priest at Antigua." In other words, rather than live in unlawful sin, these Antiguans chose to be married by a Protestant. There were only two exceptions to the norm of lawful wedlock in the sample. In one entry from 1865, the priest explained that he had not published the banns: "The party had been living for years toogether [sic], at the time of the marriage hee [sic] very sick." Seven years later, he married a couple "without proclamation, as they had been living long in sin."

After 1885, all the Catholic marriages were recorded on standard forms, which left no room for the clergy to inscribe personal notes about the status of the couples they wed. Nevertheless, these registers provide information about the parties' ages at the time of their marriages, their places of residence, occupations, whether permission to marry was obtained by publication of the banns or by special license, and, if minors were involved, who gave permission for the youths to wed. Consequently, a review of the Catholic church records for the years 1886–1920, when a new middle class was emerging, reveals several interesting points about life and family in the common order.

This second sample includes seventy-nine marriages. It shows that almost all of Antigua's Catholics lived in St. John's. With just three exceptions, they publicized their intention to wed by church banns.[10] Most men married only after they were well into their twenties and quite a few entered matrimony for the first time in their thirties. Women married at a slightly younger age; between twenty and twenty-eight was usual. Given the delay in the age of marriage, the couple usually responded "themselves" to the question on the certificate as to who gave permission for them to wed. However, one especially young pair (she being "about 18" and he "21") also gave "themselves" consent, even though she was clearly underage. Possibly the girl was pregnant, for her spouse could not have offered her much economic security; the priest had written "none at the time of their marriage" in the spot provided for their occupations. Given the poor laws, the couple must have been provided for by one or both of their families.

Between 1890 and 1920, the men who married at the Catholic church were most commonly "shopkeepers," but they also described themselves as "haircutter," "shop assistant," "carpenter," "baker," "printer," "manager," and, after 1900, as "travelling merchants" and "peddlers." In other words, they worked in trades that had once belonged almost exclusively to free people of color. Only five men gave job titles that allude to possible membership in the local elite: two were listed as "planter," two as "barrister," and one as an "official." These men had wives who worked at home, except for one bachelor planter, who, in 1918, at the age of forty-four, decided to marry a forty-five-year-old spinster and "storekeeper."

Judging from given occupations and the parties' places of residence, Catholic men overwhelmingly married women from their own social class: they chose working and nonworking middle-class women from town. In forty-one of the seventy-five cases in which information about occupation is recorded, brides were not employed at the time of their marriage. After 1898, some women who married shopkeepers and clerks held the job description "lady." More often, wives' occupations were simply left blank. An unexpected number of men, however, relied upon their wives to assist them at work. Twenty-five women, a third of this sample, worked alongside their husbands. This was especially common if they married shopkeepers. For example, in seven of the thirteen marriages celebrated between 1886 and 1888, the man and the woman are jointly identified as "shopkeepers." A smaller group of wives, nine in all, worked for wages as seamstresses and laborers. Only one gave her occupation as "house servant." Few people married when they were unemployed, although one unfortunate couple wed in 1902 were described as "paupers" and their occupation listed as "begging." Table 7 summarizes the employment patterns of Catholic husbands and wives in Antigua, 1886–1920.

The majority of people marrying at the Catholic church in Antigua before 1900 were of European descent. After the turn of the century, immigrants from Lebanon and Syria augmented membership in the church. Its total membership was 646 persons in 1921 (Watkins 1924:84). Little has been written of the history of these people in Antigua, perhaps because they are such a minority, but today they constitute a very important sector of the middle class in Antigua. What other Antiguans find so remarkable about them is their phenomenal success in the business community and their very strong preference for marital endogamy.

The Syrians and Lebanese first worked as itinerant merchants in Antigua. Today people recall that the fathers and grandfathers of St. John's present shopkeepers, many of whom have diversified their interests and become important figures in the economy, walked from village to village to sell their goods. A working-class woman explained to me that Syrian peddlers were the first people in Antigua to extend credit to poor laborers:

Beforetime we use to use grass bed. And then the Syrian come and then you get a bed to trust [on credit], table to trust, three-piece set to trust. Black people here have dat store and you couldn't go there and [get] a piece of cloth to trust. Syrian come here, walk around, sell trust with their client, and sometimes people tink hard to pay them. They will walk for how many miles—with de suitcase on de

TABLE 7   Employment Patterns of Antiguan Catholic Husbands and
Wives, 1886–1920

Year	Marriages	Couple Share Employment (type listed)	Different Jobs (both wage workers, wife's job listed)	Wife at Home
1886	4	3 shopkeepers	0	1
1887	3	3 shopkeepers	0	0
1888	6	4[a]	0	2
1889–97 (no records)				
1898	4	0	0	4
1899	2	0	1 laborer	1
1900	4	2 shoemakers, peddlers	0	2
1901	1	0	0	1
1902	3[b]	0	0	2
1903	3	0	1 workwoman	2
1904	2	0	1 seamstress	1
1905	5	1 peddler	2 seamstress	2
1906	3	1 shopkeeper	0	2
1907	4	1 shopkeeper	0	3
1908	6[c]	2 peddlers, laborers	0	3
1909	2	1 laborer	0	1
1910	1	0	0	1
1911	2	0	1 (illegible)	1
1912	1	0	0	1
1913	3[d]	1 laborer	1 servant	0
1914–15	0 (or none recorded)			
1916	5	3 laborers, shopkeepers	0	2
1917	4	0	1 seamstress	3

Continued on next page

TABLE 7 **Continued**

Year	Marriages	Couple Share Employment (type listed)	Different Jobs (both wage workers, wife's job listed)	Wife at Home
1918	2	1 laborer	1 storekeeper	0
1919	4	1 shopkeeper	0	3
1920	5ᵉ	1 laborer	0	3
Total	79	25	9	41

SOURCE: Catholic Church records, Antigua.
ᵃ Includes one couple listed as "paupers" and one couple described as "unemployed."
ᵇ One couple was listed as "widow" and "widower." Neither their ages nor their occupations were recorded. Perhaps they were elderly.
ᶜ The priest wrote "none" for the occupations of one couple. The groom was a widower, aged 44; the bride was a single woman, aged 28.
ᵈ Occupations for one couple were left blank.
ᵉ Includes a "death-bed" marriage; occupations unknown.

back, and trust in cloth and so. Cloth to make ladies' dress, cloth to make men's pants and so . . . Is only since them Syrians come here people could get stove, and credit, and bed and so. I know, when I was small, is ground I use to sleep on.

People of Middle Eastern background whose families came to the island at the turn of the century identify themselves as Antiguans, but they also cherish and preserve a separate cultural tradition. Both Lebanese and Syrian peoples contend that Arabic Antiguan family life differs from that of African Antiguans. For example, marriage with African Antiguans is almost unheard of. Indeed, when I asked about its frequency, both African Antiguans and Arabic Antiguans cited the same couple over and over and most knew of no other cases. (That marriage ended when an interested third party suffered a gunshot wound.) During my fieldwork, a Catholic priest I interviewed informed me that a young Syrian girl, who spoke almost no English, had just arrived to marry a local man. Moreover, in sharp contrast to other Antiguans, Syrians (but not Lebanese) prefer first-cousin marriage, especially with the father's brother's daughter. First-cousin marriage, of course, is illegal in Antigua. Consequently, if a man wishes to marry his cousin, he is likely to return to

Syria. I interviewed a man whose father had gone to Syria because a suitable spouse was unavailable locally:

> They have a very staunch attitude about marriage. The old race, the old breed of them, feel if they get married to a quote-unquote—the Arab translation for it is "foreigner"—(they are really the foreigners)—they're not, but within their [the Arabic] clan, or within their clique. . . . So they feel if they get married to a foreigner the person is not going to be willing to go along with their customs, won't speak their language, can't deal with their traditions. It is a very male-dominated society, very, well, not overly chauvinistic, but let's say very male dominant. And 90 percent of the people born West Indian, whether they are Arab or pure West Indian, can't deal with an Arab marriage. We are accustomed to a set family life, a patriarchical-type situation where the man rules, plain as day. Even now. Women nowadays can't deal with that and so a lot of the younger guys have been brought up that way, with the father as the head of the household—and the real head—can't find Arab women or western women, to deal with that. So a lot of them still end up going back to the Middle East and getting married, even though they may not speak the language very well, or they have never been there before.

Another difference between the Arabic Antiguan and African Antiguan communities is that in the former courtship and marriage are family matters in the following sense:

MLB: Are there any arranged marriages?

D: Not really arranged, they are more discussed, not arranged. If one person likes a certain girl in the family, the parents will communicate the information to the family. The parents will discuss it amongst themselves first, before the children even voice their opinions. A son would voice his feelings or his desires to his parents and then they would talk to the girl's parents. So it is not really arranged. And then the girl's parents in turn would ask her if she is willing. If she is, then they kinda begin a courtship phase. If she is not, then it's a no-go situation.

MLB: So it is up to the man to take the initiative and he goes first to his parents?

D: Generally speaking, yes. In modern day times it is changing. It is changing, slowly but surely. As a matter of fact, even back in Syria now it is changing.

There are further dissimilarities in family practices between African Antiguans and Arabic Antiguans. Arabic men and women do not live together until after they are married, and it is very rare for a child to be born out of wedlock. Marriage is, for them, the prelude to a new family. As one interviewee explained: "In my opinion, a husband and wife are two people, man and woman, who decide to get married to have offspring, children, to create a family." Divorce is very rare, both because most are Catholics and because there is a strong belief and emphasis on the solidarity of the nuclear family in business and in leisure activities. Women frequently work with their husbands, some of the children go into the family business, and social life consists mainly of family-focused visits and dinners, although men sometimes meet without their wives and children. Finally, respondents described Arabic Antiguan family structure as "patriarchical" in that a father's word is always final, he makes all decisions of any consequence, he resolves family disputes, all wealth and property is in his name, and he plays a dominant role in the education and marriages of his children. He is the "real head," as my interviewee put it. The term *patriarchical,* however, does not accurately describe the family practices or beliefs of West Indians of African Antiguan backgrounds.[11]

Despite these several differences between African Antiguans and Arabic Antiguans, there are shared norms about family that promote understanding and solidarity between these two communities. In both groups, children are highly valued and families are large. Youngsters are taught to respect their elders and strictly disciplined when they misbehave. Based on my experience, almost all Antiguans accept that they owe certain duties, responsibilities, and considerations to persons related to them by blood, although hardly anyone knows that these were once actually prescribed in the law. The preferred household arrangement is for a nuclear family to reside without extended kin, but relatives, godchildren, and family friends arrive and stay for months. Gender roles within the household are strongly demarcated in both communities: house work and child care are women's work, even if they work for wages. Finally, Antiguans of both African Caribbean and Middle Eastern descent told me marriage is the ideal relationship between a man and a woman because it is the relationship "sanctioned by God."

In short, the ethnic and racial composition of Antigua's middle class changed rather dramatically in the hundred years after slavery was abolished, but the ideal model for family did not. The immigrants whose descendants later became middle-class Antiguans, voters, and lawmakers, brought with them beliefs and practices congenial with the existing system of kinship legalities. Like their predecessors, the English, the Irish, the Scottish, and the free people of color, persons of Portuguese and Middle Eastern descent remained devoted to the family as envisioned by the churches and the state. They bequeathed to their children a strong emphasis on the sanctity of marriage and a disdain for divorce. Family solidarity in times of adversity was and remains the norm. For the most part, the children of the working class who have taken advantage of growing educational opportunities and entered the professions, politics, and government service also share these values.

As we shall see, the impetus for the radical revision of Antigua's kinship laws in 1986 came primarily from this last group. A reassessment of the legal implications of legitimacy, illegitimacy, marriage, and inheritance was impossible until a bourgeoisie emerged with strong identification and ties to the working class, with an agenda for social and economic change, and with the opportunity to put those plans into action. Antigua's kinship system changed significantly when the political power to rewrite kinship codes was transferred from the old elite to the new middle class. I return to this point in the penultimate chapter.

Estate Laborers and Other Working-Class Antiguans

Contrary to what some of the planters tried to imply, the immediate departure of masses of Antiguan slaves from the sugar estates on 1 August 1834 was not due to laziness or vindictiveness. Although some fled from unbearable working conditions in the cane fields, others were motivated by their desire to find loved ones and children from whom they had been separated.[12] One Antiguan planter told visitors Thome and Kimball in 1837 that of the slaves who left his estate at emancipation "nearly all had companions on other estates, and left for the purpose of being with them." Moreover, he believed that "the greater proportion of changes of residence among the emancipated which took place at that time, were owing to the same cause" (1839:82–83).

The vast majority of the former slaves lived, labored, and loved near to where they were born. Lacking alternatives, they submitted to the terms of the Contract Act and their daily lives were not measurably different from the way they had been during slavery. In the oral history *To Shoot Hard Labour* (Smith and Smith 1986), Samuel Smith, the great-grandson of an African slave named Rachel, described the plight of children on the Antiguan plantation where he was born in 1877:

> As far as bring up picknee [raising children] goes, it was that the mother drop out the child and as soon as that child was old enough, well the small gang was there waiting. Sometimes the parents would not even know the child's age, but providing that that child look big enough, the parents would tell massa that the child was twelve years old.
>
> Back then, people was hungry for them picknee to reach twelve years or even look like twelve years. They wanted the day to come to get them in the small gangs to help the family. That was the way to survive in them days, so some parents never thought of school. (Smith and Smith 1986:38)

As labor became individualized, parents found themselves dependent upon their offspring for survival. Children and their parents worked all day for meager wages. At night, they returned to cramped, communal quarters hardly conducive to promoting the kind of familial arrangements idealized by the elite. Instead, the estate workers' households demanded the same solidarity of kin as the poor laws:

> The conditions of the houses rapidly run down after the Emancipation even though they were strongly built. The normal size house was about sixty feet long by forty feet wide and almost all the houses would have cellars. . . . The cellars was the pillars of the houses and was made up of stones fastened together with white lime. The sill would be made of wood that was five inches by five inches or six by six. The window side would be covered by board and shingles. The other sides would be of board only. The roofs too was covered with shingles and sometimes felt would be used. The houses were also strengthen by several upright posts but there were no partitions.
>
> Most of the houses were leak. We use to put in old cloth or trash to cork the holes. . . .
>
> Neither were there screens in the houses. Nothing to separate one family from the other. We use to live together like a flock of cattle, like goats or sheep in a pen. The truth is, there was no difference to speak of between the life of the animals and ours. (Ibid.:38, 41)

These barracks differed greatly from the homes men built for themselves and their families in the free villages when they had the opportunity to move off the estates.[13]

After 1837, the government released for sale some of the lands it held under the old "ten-acre" legislation and a number of large estates sold land. These sales enabled workers to build villages in the countryside. By 1842, there were twenty-seven villages with approximately thirty-six hundred inhabitants. However, because the land made available to the freed slaves was generally of poor quality and unsuitable for full-time subsistence farming, most of the villagers continued to work at least part-time for the estates. Still, the existence of the villages made it possible for the workers to bargain for task work and wages without signing "general hire" contracts (D. Hall 1971:43–45; Henry 1985:50). In places like Freetown and Liberta, men constructed homes, especially, for their partners and children, but mothers, siblings, and other relatives were taken in. These modest houses consisted of two rooms, a "hall" and a "chamber." Women cooked outside (Flannagan 1967:vol. 2, 131). Privacy, so hard to come by on the estates, was highly valued.[14]

In addition to being so poorly housed on the estates, the cane cutters were almost always hungry and overworked. Insubordination was punishable by whippings, jail terms, and blackballing. As suggested in the previous chapter, the organization of justice had taken a new turn:

> Whenever there was a fight or quarrel among nega-house people, it would be massa that would decide who was to get punish and how the punishment would be. Some of the times the massa would punish everybody mixed up in it, and rightfully or wrongfully, them all get punish when them ready. [masters punished whom they

liked, at their own convenience.] But to be driven off the estate was the worst that could happen to you. People would settle for almost anything else—be whipped, be locked up in estate cellar for a time. The least punishment was to get suspended without pay for some time. . . .

A nega-house man could not live on another estate if he offend even one planter. If one planter tell him to leave, the others would usually refuse to let him work and live on their plantation, and that poor fellow wouldn't have a place to turn to for a long, long time. Dog better than he when that happen. . . .

The planters also use to use the militia to keep people in check and the militia would have the back up of the magistrates and the jail-house and the government. No way for us to fight back—it was like worm going against nest of ants—for the bakkra was the militia and the magistrates and the jail-house and the government. Whatever happen to us, we must grunt and bear it. If you didn't have manners, them give you the cat-o-nine and them hang you in jail. (Ibid.:38, 39, 46)

Workers were exploited in other ways too. Minister Horsford lamented in 1856 that some of the planters and their managers still had mistresses on their estates (1856:55). Not all of these relationships were voluntary unions. Smith reports: "The women were terribly subject to rape and other things of that kind from the massa and his sons" (Smith and Smith 1986:39). On the Jonas Estate, where Smith grew up in the 1880s, an English planter named Ted Cole raped Missy Byam and her thirteen-year-old daughter Kate. Kate drowned when Cole's dogs chased her into a pond. None of the workers had the courage to try to save her; she had refused Cole's orders to keep her pregnancy a secret and to leave her home on the plantation (ibid.:39–40).

Samuel Smith's experiences on the sugar estates and his own courting, reproductive, and marital history are in many ways representative of men of his class. He was the son of Margarette Edwards and Daniel Smith, her "common law husband," both sugarcane workers all of their lives (Smith and Smith 1986:appendix C). They named Samuel after the chief planter at Jonas's, just as Margarette had been named for a planter (Edwards) at Vernon's Estate. As his parents worked, young Samuel was cared for by Countis, his maternal grandmother. Samuel was Margarette's first male child and he was primarily responsible for her in her old age. She protested vehemently against his marrying, a stance he attributed to her desire to live with him and an unwillingness to share his attentions and his earnings (ibid.:116–17). Smith did marry eventually, however, at the constant prodding of his later employers, the Goodwins, who wanted Samuel to be the first young man in his village to marry. He had been visiting a number of women when, at age thirty-one, he finally decided to tie the knot. His decision was not met with unanimous approval. When he asked Lou, the mother of one of his children, to marry him, Clara, the mother of another, slammed the door in his face:

I was under pressure, for my mother was also mad with me. I asked Massa Affie to call her and talk to her. He did and that quieted her for a while. You see, in them days, man and woman married when them old, so nega man wedding was far and few between. In fact, I doubt the people of All Saints [village] ever saw a nega man wedding before I get married. . . . On the big day—the last Saturday in November in 1908—I walked the mile and half with my father-giver [best man] from Freeman's Ville to All Saints Anglican Church. Lou walked with hers from the bottom of All Saints, that was about one quarter of a mile, and we met at the church. . . .

Affie Goodwin give me a big cake and two bottles of wine for the wedding and told me after that I would go down in history as the youngest black man in the island to get married. (When black people start to get married at an early age, it was just about the time of World War I and they start to do so because of the religion coming from the churches around that time). (Ibid.:119–20)

Lou's first baby, born in February 1908, nine months before she married Samuel, was her husband's fifteenth child. He fathered forty-three children in all, but didn't consider that unusual: "That number isn't too much because I start to make children in 1894, when I was seventeen, and to have two a year would be normal" (ibid.:140, 134). Because he could not "resist temptation," he continued to have children "outside" after the marriage (ibid.:120). His matter-of-fact style in recalling these illicit unions suggests that sexual relations, concubinage, and cohabitation outside of wedlock continued as part of the family system of the working class on the estates and in the rural villages. Unfortunately, Smith neglects to tell us much about his relationships with his "inside" and "outside" children. He does mention that he lost contact with Clara and her child (ibid.:119).

Smith's comments with respect to the infrequency of marriage among estate workers and rural villagers and about the increasing influence of ministers deserve further consideration. I investigate the role of organized religion in shaping the structure and content of familial relations in the next section, but first I want to point out that if sugar laborers married infrequently and at an advanced age, that was not necessarily true of the working class as a whole. Part of an 1836 report from the Antigua Branch Association of the Society for Advancing the Christian Faith in the British West Indies discloses:

"The number of marriages in the six parishes of the island, in the year 1835, the first entire year of freedom, was 476—all of which, excepting about 50, were between persons formerly slaves. The total number of marriages between slaves solemnized in the church during the nine years ending December 31, 1832, was 157; in 1833, the last entire year of slavery, it was 61."

Thus it appears that the whole number of marriages during *ten years* previous to emancipation (by far the most favorable ten years that could have been selected) was but half as great as the number for a single year following emancipation! (Thome and Kimball 1839:81–82)

Reverend Horsford lends further support to the point that many freed Antiguan slaves legitimized their unions as soon as they were permitted to do so. He wrote that former slaves held marriage in the highest esteem, used the title "mistress" (married woman) as an insignia of increased status and respectability, rejoiced at lavish marriage celebrations, and invented a rite to end an unhappy union:

> During the reign of slavery, marriages were necessary to qualify individuals to become communicants; and in many cases they were entered upon for the sake of acquiring respectability. Those marriages were multiplied when the nuptial rite was legalized; but immediately after Emancipation especially, hundreds were rapidly united in the bonds of matrimony. . . . Old couples, young persons, many who had long been living faithfully with each other, though unmarried, approached the hymercal altar. On the wedding-day, gigs and phaetons, borrowed or hired, were in requisition, and vehicle after vehicle dashed up and down the streets at full speed, hastening from church or chapel to the dejeuner. These vehicles contained well-dressed persons, who properly understood the nature of the solemn compact into which they had just entered. The men and women who continued still to live in concubinage lost caste; whilst the married regarded themselves, and were recognized by others, as having been raised by marriage tenfold in civilization and respectability. In some instances, females of the lower orders have been heard to taunt their antagonists with "Me da married lady." The ring is considered the emblem of the conjugal state; and in cases of disputes between husbands and wives, it has been often destroyed, and the union temporarily annulled; and not unfrequently, when the parties have been reconciled, the same ring has been taken to a goldsmith to be repaired, and then carried to the Minister of religion, that he may again place it on the finger in the presence of the husband; or if the Minister happened, as is sometimes the case, to be of a mechanical genius, he would be solicited to perform the double task of mending the ring, and of re-uniting the couple, and exhorting them to love and fidelity for the future. (1856:54–55)

Horsford's description of gigs and phaetons rushing wildly up and down the streets makes it clear that he is describing the wedding celebrations of St. John's working-class population. They were distinguishable from the group who earned their livelihood in the sugar fields by both the forms of their labor and the emphasis on status and class in their marriage practices. The men worked in trades such as shoemaking, butchering, and ironmongering and passed these trades on to their children. They were "highly 'respectable' artisans, the kind who went to work in suits with high stiff collars" (Lowes 1987:8). A number of them voted and served on juries, though they were not members of the assembly. They practiced endogamy and remained separated from other formerly free colored families. This "upper crust" working class reproduced itself through recruitment from within and by marriage to women from other islands, including those who came to study at the Spring Gardens Teacher Training College (ibid.:8). What was different about marriage in the middle class and in the upper ranks of the working class was the insistence on preserving legalities. Not that these men did not engage in illicit relationships—they most certainly did. But over the course of the twentieth century, it became a norm for men to practice greater discretion and for married women to set limits to kinship illegalities. In Chapter 8, I shall introduce Theresa and Charles Davis, a couple whose biographies, courtship behavior, and marital histories exemplify these very patterns.

A number of anthropologists have argued that lower-class West Indians marry when they can afford to (e.g., E. Clarke 1966; Dirks and Kerns 1976; Herskovits 1937; Rodman 1971; Rubenstein 1976).[15] The following tables, which span a forty-year period, however, do not lend support to that argument. To the contrary, although the overall standard of living in Antigua has risen, the marriage rate has decreased slightly (until just recently). Accessible government records and my review of local marriage registers show the number of marriages in proportion to the general population was highest immediately after World War II. The marriage rate fluctuated only slightly during the 1950s and 1960s. A similarly stable pattern, albeit with a slightly lower marriage rate, characterized 1970–84, even though inflation declined, the rate of unemployment held steady, and the overall standard of living improved.[16] One exceptional year in that period, 1974, was the year of the great earthquake (see Tables 8 and 9). The marriage rate increased in 1985–87, but it is too soon to evaluate whether this is the beginning of a new trend.[17] The figures in Table 10 demonstrate a similarly long history of high rates of illegitimacy.

The tables confirm my impressions from the historical and ethnographic record: as has been true in Jamaica and Guyana (R. Smith 1987, 1988; Roberts and Sinclair 1978), the economy does not determine the frequency of marriage or change the illegitimacy rates in Antigua. The popularity of marriage in the working class has vacillated somewhat over time, just as the extent of open concubinage and recognition of illegitimate children has fluctuated in the middle class. Of greater significance than local economic conditions to the marriage rate and to family ideology and structure in the twentieth century was the effect of the second great wave of missionary activity.

As Ye Sow, So Shall Ye Reap: The Men from the Missions

In Jamaica, membership in the long-established churches declined after abolition, whereas obeah, myalism, balm-yard religions, and other cults flourished (e.g., Austin-Broos 1987, 1991; Fischer 1974a, 1974b; Schuler 1979, 1980; Turner 1982; Wedenoja 1988). This is not surprising, writes Fischer, because the end of slavery "removed the advantages of presenting one's self as a Christian except for an increasingly specific class: the upwardly mobile, for whom a preservation of respectability was a requirement of the achievement of mobility"

TABLE 8   Population and Marriage Rates in Antigua and Barbuda, 1947–1969

Year	Population Estimate	Marriages	Rate per thousand persons
1947	43,442	200	4.7
1948	43,504	134	3.1
1949	44,532	177	4.0
1950	45,611	177	3.9
1951	46,937	195	4.2
1952–53	N.A.	N.A.	N.A.
1954	N.A.	N.A.	4.0
1955	N.A.	N.A.	4.6
1956	N.A.	N.A.	4.0
1957	N.A.	N.A.	4.0
1958	N.A.	N.A.	4.2
1959	58,839	218	3.7
1960	N.A.	207	N.A.
1961	57,568	172	3.0
1962	59,291	191	3.2
1963	61,664	203	3.4
1964	56,834	244	4.1
1965	59,697	213	3.7
1966–67 not available		N.A.	N.A.
1968	N.A.	233	N.A.
1969 not available		N.A.	N.A.

SOURCES: High Court records, Antigua, *Reports of the Registrar General's Office* 1952, 1959, 1960, and 1968, and *An Abstract of Statistics of the Leeward Islands, Windward Islands and Barbados*, August 1971. A census of Antigua and Barbuda was taken in 1901, 1911, 1921, 1946, and 1970. During the 1950s and 1960s, yearly population estimates were determined by computing annual increases and decreases due to births, deaths, and migration.

TABLE 9   **Population and Marriage Rates in Antigua and Barbuda, 1970–1987**

Year	Population Estimate	Marriages	Rate per thousand persons
1970	N.A.	N.A.	N.A.
1971	66,860	N.A.	N.A.
1972	68,010	N.A.	N.A.
1973	68,960	N.A.	N.A.
1974	69,750	296	4.2
1975	70,520	260	3.7
1976	71,420	247	3.5
1977	72,355	236	3.3
1978	73,245	206	2.8
1979	74,260	215	2.9
1980	75,235	211	2.8
1981	76,224	204	2.7
1982	77,226	224	2.9
1983	78,241	188	2.7
1984	75,067	203	2.7
1985	75,630	262	3.5
1986	76,296	309	4.1
1987	77,093	343	4.5

SOURCES: High Court records and *Statistical Yearbook* 1982, 1983, 1985, 1987, adjusted to reflect 1987 corrections. The Statistical Division estimated an annual population increase of 1.3 percent between 1970 and 1987. I am unable to adjust the tables for numbers of people of marriageable age or life expectancy because these statistics are unavailable.

TABLE 10   Legitimate and Illegitimate Births in Antigua and Barbuda in Selected Years

Year	Population Estimates	Legitimate Births	Illegitimate Births
1891	36,699	476 (33%)	974 (67%)
1899	36,699[a]	786 (43%)	1046 (57%)
1900	36,699[a]	390 (30%)	898 (70%)
1905	34,953[b]	387 (29%)	939 (71%)
1909	34,953[b]	319 (27%)	858 (73%)
1914	32,265[c]	325 (26%)	944 (74%)
1939	35,500	374 (29%)	920 (71%)
1947			(68%)[d]
1948			(67%)[d]
1949			(68%)[d]
1950	45,611	524 (32%)	1130 (68%)
1951	46,937	558 (32%)	1175 (68%)
1952			(68%)[d]
1953	49,692	560 (33%)	1127 (67%)
1954	50,908	534 (32%)	1126 (68%)
1955	52,454	602 (32%)	1278 (68%)
1956	54,228		(67%)[d]
1957	55,967	884 (34%)	1162 (66%)
1958	56,777	912 (34%)	1211 (66%)
1959	58,839	669 (37%)	1162 (63%)
1961	57,568		(62%)[d]
1962	59,291		(63%)[d]
1963	61,664		(63%)[d]
1964	56,834		(65%)[d]
1965	59,697	624 (36%)	1118 (64%)
1970	64,794		
1974		289 (23%)	985 (77%)

Continued on next page

TABLE 10 **Continued**

Year	Population Estimates	Legitimate Births	Illegitimate Births
1975			1010 (76%)
1976		325 (22%)	1119 (78%)
1977		318 (23%)	1091 (77%)
1978		317 (24%)	1025 (76%)
1979		301 (25%)	1053 (75%)
1980	75,235	238 (22%)	963 (78%)[c]
1981	76,224	215 (19%)	950 (81%)[c]
1982	77,226	218 (19%)	935 (81%)
1983	78,241	220 (19%)	954 (81%)
1984	79,269	229 (21%)	897 (79%)
1985	80,311	204 (17%)	986 (83%)
1986	76,296	239 (21%)	891 (79%)
1987	77,093	223 (20%)	879 (80%)

SOURCES: Leeward Islands, *Blue Books* 1891, 1899, 1900, 1905–6, 1909; Antigua, *Registrar General's Reports* 1940:Table 2, 4; 1951:1–2; 1952:Table 4, 7; 1954:2; 1955:1; 1956:2, Table 4; 1958:1 1959:2, Table 4; 1960:1, Table 2; 1968:1, Table 4; and *Statistical Yearbook* 1982:10, 1983:1, 10, 1985:1, 10; 1987:14.
[a] Based on census of 1891.
[b] Based on census of 1901 (34,971).
[c] Based on census of 1911 (32,269).
[d] These percentages were mentioned in later reports without further elaboration.
[e] Recorded in the *Statistical Yearbook*, 1983 and 1985, as "provisional."

(1974a:30). In other words, in Jamaica, emancipation provided the opportunity for the expression and play of a host of innovative and syncretic rituals. Interestingly, Jamaicans also did not rush to legitimize their unions immediately after emancipation (R. Smith 1988:102).

Events took a very different turn in Antigua. Over time, the Anglican, Methodist, Moravian, and Catholic churches played an increasingly influential role in managing affairs of the heart, raising children, and resolving familial disputes. Accounts for the year 1839 already claim that almost two-thirds of

TABLE 11   **Church Membership in Antigua and Barbuda, 1921**

Anglican	16,883
Moravian	7,684
Wesleyans	3,310
Roman Catholics	646
Other	1,244

SOURCE: Watkins 1924:84.

the former slaves and three-fourths of all Antiguans regarded themselves as members of local Christian denominations (N. Hall 1983:57–58). Possibly the rapid rise in membership in the Anglican church after abolition was due to its monopoly on marriage nuptials. Few slaves had joined the Anglican church before 1834, yet by 1921 the Anglicans were boasting more members than all of the other churches combined (see Table 11). As we shall see, Antiguans also exhibited a stronger desire than Jamaicans to register their unions once they gained access to ministers and churches.[18]

According to observers Thome and Kimball, the inability of the Moravians and the Wesleyans to marry people was a grave inconvenience (1839:83). Clergymen of the Church of the United Brethren, the Wesleyan Methodists, and the Presbyterian church finally gained the right to marry couples in Antigua in 1844 (Microfilm No. 7). Ministers of local fundamentalist churches such as Seventh Day Adventists, Pilgrim Holiness, Salvation Army and Pentecostal Missions lacked approval from the state to celebrate marriages until much later. Still, as the following charts indicate, the number of these small "wayside" churches increased substantially in the period in which marriage rates were higher than usual. As is true in Jamaica (Roberts and Sinclair 1978:16), the fact that civil ceremonies account for a very minor proportion of all Antiguan marriages testifies to the religious significance of marriage in both countries. Tables 12, 13, and 14 record marriages registered by religious denomination or civil service.

It is important to our account of the evolution of class differences in familial behavior to understand that the ministers' efforts to bring the beliefs and practices of the people of the common order in line with the system of kinship legalities were not equally dispersed throughout the island. Initially, the clergy

TABLE 12 **Marriages Registered according to Religious Denomination or Civil Service, 1939, 1947–1952**

Denomination	1939	1947	1948	1949	1950	1951	1952
Church of England	72	80	49	67	64	68	107
Roman Catholic	12	24	18	16	16	15	17
Methodist	19	31	10	27	21	29	15
Moravian	56	46	34	39	43	45	36
Seventh Day Adventist	4	7	5	9	10	3	9
Pilgrim Holiness	10	7	12	8	14	13	16
Pentecostal Assembly			2	3	5	10	4
Zion Church of God				3	0	0	3
Salvation Army	1	1	1	2	3	6	4
Christian Mission					1	0	0
Advent Sabbath							1
Civil Registers		4	3	3	0	6	0
Total	174	200	134	177	177	195	212

SOURCES: Antigua, *Registrar General's Report* 1940:1; 1952:Table 7; 1954:Table 7, Table D.

concentrated their activities in St. John's, the surrounding parish, and the other towns. As a result, laborers in the rural parishes were neglected. Samuel Smith, for example, recalled that in his youth most estate workers lived "common-law ... the normal thing for the times, for it didn't have conflict with any religion since there wasn't any church that catered to slaves and ex-slaves" (Smith and Smith 1986:48). Smith was describing life in the countryside: he was twenty-one years old before he even visited St. John's (ibid.:92). As mentioned

TABLE 13   Marriages Registered according to Religious Denomination or Civil Service, 1953–1959

Denomination	1953	1954	1955	1956	1957	1958	1959
Church of England	94	78	97	83	86	94	85
Roman Catholic	11	20	20	26	27	20	27
Methodist	24	14	34	30	29	44	28
Moravian	47	55	61	40	50	40	36
Seventh Day Adventist	10	12	4	3	3	8	12
Pilgrim Holiness	16	15	10	13	10	15	15
Pentecostal Assembly	9	4	3	9	7	7	5
Zion Church of God		1	1	1	3	2	0
Salvation Army	1	0	3	3	3	6	2
Advent Sabbath	1	0	0	2	1	1	1
Shiloh Gospel Hall			3	0	0	0	0
Bethel					1	0	0
Kingdom Hall				1	0	0	3
United Sabbath-Day Adventists					1	0	0
Church of God of Prophecy							2
Civil Registers	3	1	4	3	1	4	2
Total	216	200	240	214	222	241	218

SOURCES: Antigua, *Registrar General's Report* 1954:3; 1955:1; 1956:1; 1958:1, Table 7; 1959:1; 1960:1.

TABLE 14   Marriages Registered according to Religious Denomination or Civil Service, 1961–1965

Denomination	1961	1962	1963	1964	1965
Church of England	61	74	80	103	87
Roman Catholic	21	20	23	36	26
Methodist	30	37	40	25	30
Moravian	22	36	30	44	38
Seventh Day Adventist	6	6	6	7	7
Pilgrim Holiness	19	8	9	6	10
Pentecostal Assembly	1	1	1	7	3
Zion Church of God	4	0	1	2	2
Salvation Army		2	1	2	2
Advent Sabbath			1	0	0
Bethel	1	0	0	0	0
Kingdom Hall	2	2	2	1	0
Church of God of Prophecy		1	2	0	1
Shiloh Gospel Hall		1	0	1	0
Private Dwelling		1	0	0	0
Ebenezer Gospel Hall			1	0	0
Christian Union Mission					1
Civil Registers	5	2	6	10	6
Total	172	191	203	244	213

SOURCE: Antigua, *Registrar General's Report* 1968:Table 10.

earlier, Smith dated the beginning of active church participation by estate and rural village workers to the time of the First World War:

> No longer them try to stop us from going to church. The priests and the parsons was in every home preaching the gospel to nega people. Them say we must go to church or we would be going to hell; if we would not harken to the voice of God, we would not see His face... Mind you, although religion didn't change the misery and the hardships, nega drink it in. The doctrine take hold early.
>
> The priests get to be very powerful, more powerful even than the planters. ... If them wanted even the slightest improvement in our living conditions, it would have happened. A nar two people soak in the doctrine. [in a very short time the people were swayed.]
>
> The people that was as old or older was less convinced about the thing. I went along living my life. I had too much experience about what the church was like for me to hear them. ... No hell could be hotter than what was going on in this land against nega people. ...
>
> It was around the time of the war that the churches start to christen black people picknee, but never would they do it at the same time with white people. The rule was wedlock christen on Sundays and bastards during the week. And all the bastards was for black people. The massas knew that. Up to 1914 most of the men was just living with the women. (Smith and Smith 1986:121, 122, 125)

Scattered government reports show that preachers from small fundamentalist churches also concentrated their efforts in urban areas. For example, the oldest report I discovered that lists marriages by churches and parishes (1939) shows 174 marriages performed by clergy from 7 separate institutions: the Church of England, Moravians, Roman Catholics, Wesleyans, Pilgrim Holiness church, Salvation Army, and Seventh Day Adventists. The latter 3 were responsible for 15 of these marriages, all of which, with one exception, took place in the city or in St. John's parish (Antigua, *Registrar General's Report for the Year 1939* 1940:Table I). The next report available to me, for 1951, shows 103 marriages in St. John's parish, of which 71 were celebrated by the long-established churches (Anglican, Catholic, Methodist, or Moravian), 10 by the Pentecostals, 9 by the Pilgrim Holiness church, 6 by the Salvation Army, 6 by the Registrar, and 1 by the Seventh Day Adventists. Ninety-two additional marriages were recorded in the island's 5 other parishes that year, but of these only 6 were performed by ministers of 2 fundamentalist churches (Antigua, *Registrar General's Report for the Year 1951* 1952:Table J). The data for 1957 are almost identical to that for 1951.[19] By 1965, however, we begin to see increased activity by the fundamentalist churches in the parish of St. Paul, which includes the towns of Falmouth and English Harbour, and in Barbuda.[20] Fundamentalism, with its strong condemnation of those who lived in sin, had penetrated throughout Antigua and Barbuda.

The role played by religion in the formation of Antiguan society is similar in several respects to that described for Guyana by R. Smith (1976:312–41). In both places, emancipation was followed by the establishment of free villages and a great expansion in the number of churches and church-organized schools. For the former slaves, these institutions symbolized progress and provided avenues for social mobility in an environment with a relatively undifferentiated social structure. In Antigua, as in Guyana, Christianization was highly controlled and authoritarian, and church services and schools adopted British models (ibid.:326–27). Attempts to formulate rival religions were "nipped in the bud" (ibid.:328). Importantly, in both places "African-like" religious expressions were classified as obeah and outlawed. Antiguan planters even suppressed the music of the contract laborers (Smith and Smith 1986:66). Not surprisingly, then, the explanation for why African-derived practices such as witchcraft, drumming, and dancing persisted in Guyana also partly explains obeah's tenacity in Antigua: "The reason for their preservation in relatively unmodified form is, paradoxically, that Christianity remained both strong and orthodox, so that instead of syncretism one got the parallel existence of two types of belief and practice" (R. Smith 1976:328).

In the mid-1980s, Antiguan churches continued to espouse a political conservatism. If there had been any ambivalence in the relationship between the state and the churches, it has derived "largely from disagreements among the religious elites as to what their response should be to development issues" (Henry 1985:194). On questions related to kinship, there had been no such discrepancy. The local minister marries men and women and he acts as a mediator if he is called to help resolve a familial dispute. For some, he is a comfortable alternative to judicial authorities who are unfamiliar with the parties and their family norms. In any case, the minister's message accords with the lawyer's.[21]

Henry judges the success of the small churches and the more recent arrival of Rastafarianism[22] as important recent events in the history of religion in Antigua. Yet he is uncertain as to why these sects have flourished: "It could be a further indication of marginalization or it could be the result of the more powerful sales pitch that the new churches make" (1985:197). I suggest, instead, that the success of fundamentalism is entirely in keeping with the character of creole legal sensibilities in the twentieth century. The appeal of these sects lies partly in their capacity to respond to gender-specific needs and concerns (Austin-Broos 1987, 1991), but also in their redefinition of what constitutes a just community and social hierarchy. Austin-Broos's insights about Pentecostalists in Jamaica fully accord with my experiences with fundamentalism in Antigua:

> Pentecostalism has been a religion with a mode of organization and a theology readily adaptable to the particular situation of [working-class] women. It does not simply allow but endorses the active participation of ordinary members in the

church; the acquisition by women of a superior status generally denied them in other areas. . . . The practical networks that the church supplies very often enable women to become or remain modestly viable members of the work force through work sharing in the countryside and employment networks in town. (1987:23)

Church activism also increases women's autonomy from their partners and spouses. Thus, it is not surprising that women and the poor are most moved by the messages of these churches. However, when prayers go unanswered, or the righteous suffer unjustly, there are other techniques for obtaining justice.

Power, Justice, and Gender in Obeah

Despite all attempts to eradicate it, obeah survived slavery. In 1844, for example, Flannagan warned obeah "raged to a great extent among the Negro population in these islands, and led many of them into the deepest crimes" (1967:vol. 1, 138). As the churches spread and the ministers became increasingly visible, local knowledge about obeah and other practices unacceptable to the planters, the priests, and the police were suppressed. In freedom as in slavery, obeah lived in the realm of illegalities that men and women kept invisible. It was safest in the hinterlands. Samuel Smith remembered:

> Every village would have its obeah man or woman. I remember there was the coffee [fortune teller] woman that people use to check out to know what was going on or what would happen in the future. It was not a joke. The people believed in the superstition and the rituals. (Smith and Smith 1986:69)

Smith also recalled that those who practiced obeah faced formidable punishment if they were caught:

> English bakkra was mortally afraid of witchcraft. You get caught doing witchcraft and you would never miss the jail-house and the cat-o-nine. You would be lucky to get out alive and if you do, you would be bruise all over. (Ibid.:53)

Smith claimed that the planters poisoned people who offended them, that workers sometimes used poison against each other, but that laborers did not harm their employers (Ibid.:77–78). A different picture is painted by an individual who visited in 1903:

> That the old Obeah, the worst feature of which is malicious poisoning, is still fully in vogue is testified to in all reliable sources and "Negroe spite" is a recognized factor of so serious a nature that employers of domestic servants liable to discharge them and officials in a position to inflict punishment would be wise seriously to consider their symptoms when anguishing under mysterious maladies which somehow will not yield to the Doctor's conventional remedies or to any remedy other than change of air, in plain language, absence from their cook. (Anon. 1903:41)

Just a year after this was written, the legislators passed another law to punish obeah practitioners (Smith and Smith 1986:171). The situation in Antigua was not unique: lawmakers in Trinidad also rigorously prosecuted obeah in the final decades of the nineteenth century.[23]

By the 1930s, however, the elite felt sufficiently secure in their war against obeah to make light of it. Antigua's colonial governor reported in 1936, for example, that rural women had recently discovered a new purpose for the brilliantly colored seeds that grew wild in the country:

> The Jumbi beads, very hard red and black seeds, are threaded into necklaces by the Antigua peasant women, and were formerly considered a safe protection against Jumbies, or evil spirits. Nowadays they are chiefly made to sell to tourists, though the belief in Jumbies very much remains. (St. Johnston 1936:220)

Obeah no longer represents a threat to the political elite,[24] but belief in the efficacy of certain of its rites remains in the common order. An Antiguan man, about forty years old, whose grandmother had spent some years in one of the French islands, told me this story:

> I can recall that once someone entered our house and stole some money from my grandmother. And they tried to find out who the person was by using a clear crystal tumbler filled with water, a gold ring, and a piece of thread. There was something said, either in French or patois, I don't know which. Of course we were asked to leave the house, as children. My grandmother and my mother, they stood there, and they said what they had to say. We stood around, we eavesdropped through some of the crevices in the house and we heard the rumblings and mumblings. And we heard distinctly that a name was called and the ring hit the side of the tumbler in the water. A few days later, my grandmother left. She said she was going to town. She came back home again and we were asked to leave the house. And I heard her telling my mother, yes, she went to this man, this man took up a mirror and they had named with the ring. And she was the person. Suffice it to say, after the accusations were made point blank to the woman—she denied them at first—and then some days later she came crying and confessed that this happened.

The woman returned the goods she had stolen; there was no need to call the police.

Antiguan author Jamaica Kincaid describes some of the signs of obeah and a method for deflecting its power in her 1983 autobiographical novel *Annie John*. In this case, Annie's mother suspects a woman, one of many whom her husband "had loved, had never married, but with whom he had had children" (1983:15) might be trying to cause her harm. Speaking through the character of Annie, Kincaid explains:

> It was a special bath in which the barks and flowers of many different trees, together with all sorts of oils, were boiled in the same large caldron. . . . As we sat in this bath, my mother would bathe different parts of my body; then she would do the same to herself. We took these baths after my mother had consulted with her obeah

woman, and with her mother and a trusted friend, and all three of them had confirmed that from the look of things around our house—the way a small scratch on my instep had turned into a small sore, then a large sore, . . . the way a dog she knew, and a friendly dog at that, suddenly turned and bit her; how a porcelain bowl she had carried from one eternity and hoped to carry into the next suddenly slipped out of her capable hands . . . how words she spoke in jest to a friend had been completely misunderstood. (1983:14–15)

Later in the novel, Ma Jolie, an old obeah woman, comes to visit the John household. Annie has been ill with an undiagnosed malady and Dr. Stephens, the medical doctor, has been of little assistance. Ma Jolie makes cross marks on Annie's body, burns incense, and places the names of all persons who might want to harm her in a basin with lighted candles. She also pins a sachet to Annie's nightgown and leaves fluids to be massaged into her body.

Annie's father deliberately left the house when Ma Jolie was due to visit. He had not tried to stop his wife from calling her obeah woman, but he was clearly worried about the impropriety of placing the signs and symbols of the realm of illegalities in public view:

> When my father came in to see me, he looked at all my medicines—Dr. Stephens's and Ma Jolie's—lined up side by side and screwed up his face, the way he did when he didn't like what he saw. He must have said something to my mother, for she arranged the shelf in a new way, with Dr. Stephens's prescriptions in the front and Ma Jolie's prescriptions in the back. (Ibid.:117–18)

Like the bottles on this shelf, the realm of the illegal and the realm of the legal provide alternatives for restoring well-being, order, and justice in Antiguan society. In addition to cases in which obeah was invoked to determine theft, my field notes include instances in which it aided fertility, protected a home, lifted the spirits of a depressed child, healed a woman suffering from an illness no doctor could diagnose, and killed a young mother. Some of the lawyers, too, have had recent clients and cases "worked" by obeah men or women to influence the search for justice. It is precisely this search that leads Antiguan women to use an obeah rite to "tie" their men.

"Tying" is used to bring back a boyfriend or husband who has begun seeing another woman or who has neglected the woman and their children. People in Antigua suspect that a man has been tied when he stops acting like a "real" man in his relationships with other people, especially the woman he is tied to. Observers say, "He acting foolie, foolie." They notice that he seems to lose his independence. He stops visiting his friends and family and he spends an unusual amount of time in his woman's house. If he is strongly tied, he turns a deaf ear to rumors of his girlfriend's misconduct and, even if he finds her with another man, he does not beat her. In other words, people know that a man is tied because he fails to behave in a way that is expected of Antiguan men at different stages in life or in various positions in the community.[25]

The Antiguan rite described here is similar to one used among the descendants of slaves in Colombia, South America. There too, obeah is aimed at "'tying' an unfaithful lover, who, as happens so often, was declining to provide for the upkeep of the children he had fathered" (Taussig 1980:100). But the act should not be interpreted as mere jealousy on the part of a woman. As Taussig explains, a woman who ties a man seeks to keep him "within the bounds of *oeconomia*," to prevent him from "embarking on a vastly different system of exchange" (ibid.:100–101). I would add that tying is about justice—about "just" relationships between men and women and parents and children—including a just distribution of resources.

Because justice may be served in different ways in Antigua, the decision to go to court or to an obeah specialist depends upon certain structural, legal, ideological, and personal factors. As we shall see in the next chapter, several reasons keep people away from the courts. For some, it is a question of time or money. Others are persuaded by their ministers to "turn the other cheek." The association of the magistrates' court with ruffians and rogues troubles others. Some people find kinship cases embarrassing. Thus, I found the formal legal process does not always offer a satisfactory way to right a wrong because the courts conflate peoples' sense of what is public and what is private.[26]

Those who chose obeah as a path to justice share certain commonalities beyond their dislike of public formal processes, their distrust of lawyers and judges, and the fact that they are the casualties of a law that fails to define certain transgressions as crimes. Participants engage in obeah as a way to right a wrong that has been committed against them. As far as I can determine, the disputants are likely to share a similar socioeconomic status. Their grievances most often entail intra- rather than interclass conflicts, although there are certainly situations in which obeah is wielded between people of different classes. Neither educational background nor religious affiliation prevents a person from consulting an obeah specialist.[27] However, obeah is more readily available and less expensive in some parts of Antigua than in others, and this undoubtedly influences its pervasiveness. Two locales, for example, were repeatedly cited to me as places where one might find obeah specialists: Greenbay and Parham. Greenbay is a rough and poverty-stricken section of St. John's, home to immigrants from other islands and rural Antiguans trying to find work in the city. Parham, in contrast, is a rather quiet agricultural village. Interestingly, whereas Greenbay has one of the highest crime rates on the island, Parham has one of the lowest. Informants suggested that today women are more likely than men to choose the power of obeah to bring them justice.

I believe this to be the case because, now, as in the past, obeah belongs to those who are most publicly oppressed. Antiguan women engage in obeah more frequently then men because all of the formal institutions in their society are controlled by men.[28] Moreover, gender ideology teaches women that their proper "place" is not only domestic, it is private. As Barrow (1976:110) understood, recourse to obeah reflects an indirectness and ambiguity that avoids direct confrontation. This does not imply that women have no power or that they never utilize public arenas to voice their opinions; they most certainly do. Indeed, in Chapter 8 I will argue that Antiguan women go to magistrates' court to shame men who treat them with "disrespect" or claim to be "big men" but fail to support their children. Like taking a man to the magistrates' court, "tying" reverses the usual structure of gender relations in Antigua. It is another way in which women manage the behavior of men who mistreat them or their children and is part of the process of making, maintaining, and breaking alliances. It is one of the ways that they influence relationships in order to preserve a sense of justice while remaining in the sphere of private illegalities.

Conclusions

In the 150 years following emancipation, Antiguan laws emphasized individualism in labor, familial solidarity in times of adversity, and a more liberal interpretation of the marriage contract that gave women control of property and allowed divorce. In addition, the state intervened in the lives of families in ways previously unimagined—through education, medicine, control of juveniles, and by regulating the conditions of labor. Two extralegal processes were also extremely important in shaping the character of family life in the common order after 1834. First, the internal composition of Antigua's class structure changed. The planters lost their former hegemony and gradually departed, and the middle class incorporated the children of Antiguan artisans, teachers, and clergymen, Portuguese shopkeepers, and Syrian and Lebanese traders. Second, Christian ministers built new churches across the island, particularly after the First World War.

The effect of these extralegal events upon family ideology and structure was mainly conservative; that is, the system of kinship legalities retained its prestigious status and grew ever more normative in the practices of the common order. The changing composition of the middle class, for example, did not produce immediately new ideas about kinship. The Portuguese, Syrians, Lebanese, and upwardly mobile children of the working class, like the planters and professionals before them, espoused legal marriage, made legitimacy an important ideological determinant of personal, social, and business relationships, and disparaged divorce. The middle class re-enforced lawmakers' earlier assumptions about the family and its place within the hierarchical social system.

In effect, the legalistic idiom of kinship provided continuity between the differently constituted former and new middle class.

Former slaves participated fully in the system of kinship legalities only after emancipation. How quickly did they move to incorporate that system as their own? The historical record suggests that both individualism and family solidarity were part and parcel of daily life on the estates. Almost everyone worked and collected a wage; almost everybody was part of a family. But what about marriage? My data suggests that neither the simple opportunity to marry nor fluctuations in economy altered lower-class marriage rates. What did?

Religion—principally that introduced by missionary activity—caused people to marry and quite independently of the economic situation of the times. Marriage was first popular among the working class in the towns, where missionary activity was most intense. In contrast, the rural areas felt much less proselytizing and marriage was accepted much more slowly. After World War II, the efforts of a particularly active evangelical clergy brought the Antiguan marriage rate to one of its highest levels.

The working class' incorporation of legal marriage did not, however, imply complete consensus between the middle and laboring classes with respect to the norms that governed family life. The meaning of marriage, for example, was not the same for all of these groups. The Antiguan middle class married as a matter of course; it was necessary to protect property and heirs. Laborer Samuel Smith, who loved many women and fathered many children before and after his nuptials, married at the urging of his employer and as a sign of privileged social status. The majority of working-class Antiguans, however, accepted legal marriage only as they accepted the teachings of the men of the missions. The record suggests that women were more readily moved by these messages and that they were more likely to conform to the rigorous personal code of conduct required of married persons. Moreover, whatever the motivation for marriage, the working class did not attribute great importance to legitimacy—unless it kept a promising student out of school. Some of the norms governing family life on the estates varied from those of working-class Antiguans in the towns, as well as from the middle class, because techniques for survival, including reliance on children's labor and household arrangements, differed on the estates.

Although there is no evidence from Antigua to support the proposition that marriage rates fluctuate sharply with economic conditions, I suspect that once slavery was abolished, the economy played a more influential role in determining when and how often the middle class (principally men) participated in the system of kinship illegalities. After all, mistresses and their offspring are expensive. Some evidence indicates that open concubinage practiced alongside of marriage declined for several decades after abolition and during that period of economic recession. Further support for this hypothesis should be found in a close examination of middle-class men's wills. As we will see in the next chapter, however, lower-class participation in kinship illegalities is determined less by simple economics than it is by community norms about the different natures of men and women and a hierarchical scheme that makes some men "big men."

The normalization of the legalistic kinship system after 1834 was partly the result of the spread of formal institutions such as churches, schools, and courts (Stinchcombe 1975). No one succeeded, however, in abolishing obeah. Obeah still expresses an indigenous ideology and vehicle of power and justice, including ideas about just familial relationships. It is concerned with local ideas about improper behavior, inequality, and gender hierarchy. Obeah's special quality is that it can be directed either at individuals who control formal political and economic structures or at men and women who defy local community norms about familial responsibility. Because its extraordinary effects can transcend social class, as well as the structure of gender relations, it offers power and resistance. It remains part of everyday politics of class, gender, and family relations in the common order.

To conclude, it is fair to say that for much of the second stage of the history of creole kinship, 1834–1986, new actors sustained old structures. However, it also must be recalled that the modern middle and working classes lacked political power until quite recently. Universal suffrage was not adopted until 1951, and the authority to legislate kinship law belonged to the colonial Council of the Federation of the Leeward Islands until 1969. Not surprisingly, then, when I conducted fieldwork in 1985–86, four years after Antigua and Barbuda's independence, kinship legalities faced caustic criticism from lawmakers, lawyers, and laymen.

7

Making and Breaking Alliances: Family Crises and Kinship Legalities in the 1980s

De young girls today they don't make no sport
As they slip beneath me they put you in court
And lord they won't leave you alone
Til the lunatic asylum becomes your home.

—Growler (Boucher 1987:26)

CONFLICTS AND their resolutions are as common and integral to family life as are the enterprises of reproduction, socialization, and the provision of food, clothing, and shelter. Familial disputes may involve such disparate issues as the end of a marriage, a contested will, a quarrel between two brothers over a cow, or an assault by a man upon his cousin. Most often people resolve these differences by persuasive argument, compromise, avoidance, termination of the relationship, physical coercion, or by transforming the dispute into another matter (e.g., Felstiner 1974, 1975; Felstiner, Abel, and Sarat 1981; Mather and Yngvesson 1980; Merry 1979, 1986, 1990). "Carrying" a family case to court may be an act of last resort,[1] but it is nonetheless another viable and frequently chosen option in Antigua. Antiguans participate in their judicial institutions heavily and rely on the courts to resolve a variety of familial crises.[2] The method and manner in which familial disputes are resolved at court has broad significance for the construction and maintenance of creole class, kinship, and gender organization.

In this chapter, I describe the present judicial organization of Antigua and Barbuda, characterize legal personnel and typical litigants, and present an overview of the role of law and the courts in contemporary family relations.[3] I explain how the existence of two legal channels, relevant to legal and illegal unions, shapes pragmatically and symbolically the character of Antiguan kinship organization. I introduce cases of affiliation and maintenance, divorce, adoption, and inheritance. These cases speak to the rights, duties, and obligations of kin defined in current statutory law. But law also guides how cases are filed, how litigants and attorneys formulate their suits, and the extent to which magistrates and judges are "free" to interpret evidence and sentence offenders. In practice, these legal directives are then molded and modified by the pragmatic concerns of litigants, lawyers, and court personnel, by the backlog of cases, by the success or failure of the bailiffs in locating parties, by litigants' and judges' styles, and sometimes by whether one has or hasn't a relative who can speed things up or slow things down.[4] Each of these legal and extralegal factors plays a role in determining the history and outcome of a case. Each has some bearing on peoples' ability to use law as a form of resistance to domination in the common order.

To understand how kinship is processed at court, I drew upon anthropological and sociological methods—the survey, statistical compilation, formal interviews, and participant observation in the courts. These techniques identified the legal, structural, economic, and ideological factors that give the processing of cases in Antigua a culturally specific character. They also documented certain patterns of stability and change. Research limited to courts and cases, however, could not fully account for the motives that bring Antiguans to court and for the meaning of kinship cases to familial organization in Antiguan society. Those questions, addressed in the next chapter, could only be resolved by living in the community, by interviewing men and women who had never been to court, and by gathering life histories.

The number and nature of kinship cases in a society reveal the values, concerns, and activities of the people; they also demonstrate "the tensions and conflicts underlying the accepted rules of social structure" (Richards 1971:5; cf. Jayawardena 1963). In Antigua, these cases allow us to probe the form and content of familial relations within and between the social classes and they reveal culturally-constructed gender differences. As we shall see, the drama of a kinship case exemplifies the economy and politics of households within different social classes at the same time that it represents a specific moment in the context and history of creole family ideology and structure. We turn first, however, to the settings in which these cases are heard, the legal personnel who process them, and the litigants who are searching for justice.

Courts, Lawyers, and Litigants

A four-tiered court system presently serves Antigua and Barbuda. Different types of cases are adjudicated at each level. The first tier consists of five magistrates' courts. Affiliation and maintenance cases, arrears, disputes between persons over small property claims, and personal grievances such as indecent language, traffic matters, and minor assaults are litigated in these courts. Magistrate's District A includes St. John's and its immediate environs. The court serving this district meets each weekday, alternating between "civil" and "criminal" days.[5] Kinship cases are heard on Fridays.

The magistrates' court in St. John's occupies the second and third floors of a new concrete building. The bulletin board of the courthouse posts the "Order in Bastardy, Maintenance, and Collecting Officer's Cases for Hearing" on Thursday afternoons. The list includes complainants, defendants, and attorneys involved in cases the following day. In the morning, some five or ten interested parties wait outside the court building for their witnesses or their lawyers and the arrival of the magistrates. Some pass the time by peering into the shoe salon that rents the first floor of the building. After a while, the litigants will find their way upstairs to the formal waiting place. The magistrates' clerks, the collecting officer, the bailiffs, and other staff of the courthouse work in an open office facing the waiting area. The phones ring often, and the staff tease each other as they set to their tasks. There are two courtrooms on this floor, one was used regularly by the magistrates in 1985–86 for kinship cases.

The courtroom is a clean, well-lighted place cooled by two overhead ceiling fans. It is rather starkly furnished with a few wooden pews, tables and chairs for attorneys, two witness stands—where the litigants do, in fact, stand to tell their stories—and the magistrate's desk. The courts are public, but in contrast to criminal trials, few persons come to observe kinship cases. (They would most certainly be accused of "minding other people's business" if they did.) Some Fridays two or three attorneys appear to represent litigants; at other times there are no lawyers at all. The hearings begin when the magistrate instructs the officer of the court to call the first name. Prosecution of the scheduled cases may continue for several hours or for as little as twenty minutes.

In addition to the St. John's magistrate's court, there are three "country courts" in Antigua that comprise Magistrate's District B. These courts serve the villages of Bolans, All Saints, and Parham. They meet one day each week, alternating between "civil" and "criminal" weeks. The courts convene at the village police stations—a practice that perpetuates the unfortunate historical association between the police and the magistrates. The layout and furnishings of each of these courtrooms is similar to that of the court in St. John's, though the facilities are not nearly as modern. The court at All Saints is decorated with the flag of independence. The most notable differences between the city and country courts are the presence of so many police constables in the latter and, because kinship cases are heard along with other criminal cases in the country, they are more likely to be resolved before spectators. The fifth court, Magistrate's District C, sits in Barbuda. By law, this court meets once in three months. During my fieldwork, however, damages in the police station where the magistrate usually conducted proceedings allowed the court to meet only three times. Spectators and police also fill the court in Barbuda.

The second tier of the formal judicial system, the High Court, settles major property and criminal cases as well as divorce, adoption, contested wills, and appeals. The High Court sits in a rather nondescript concrete building on High Street, which also houses the Registrar's Office, land records, and birth, marriage, and death certificates. Proceedings at the High Court are more formal than at the magistrates' courts; the attorneys and judges are robed, greater attention is paid to court etiquette, cases are more likely to begin on time, and litigants are more likely to be fashionably dressed. Like the magistrates' courts, these courtrooms are furnished with raised desks for the judges, tables for attorneys, stands for the disputants, and pews for the audience, but these rooms are much larger and contain high-backed red leather chairs for jurors. The walls are bare except for a clock and a picture of Queen Elizabeth II. All conversation comes to a halt when an especially noisy motor vehicle passes by outside. All cases proceed slowly because judges must record their own notes in longhand.

The courtrooms on High Street also serve the third tier of the judicial system, the Appellate Division of the Supreme Court of the Eastern Caribbean. It consists of three judges and meets intermittently in the different Leeward Islands. The court resolved one important kinship case during my field research, when it decided in favor of awarding the custody of an illegitimate child to the father. Ordinarily, however, the Court of Appeals rarely tries family cases. Finally, because Antigua and Barbuda belongs to the Commonwealth, cases decided by the Supreme Court may be appealed, as a last resort, to the Privy Council in England. No one I interviewed, however, had knowledge of an Antiguan kinship case that went to England, and I found no evidence of such a case in the legal record.

The attorneys, magistrates, and judges who are the constant participants in these courts represent a small proportion of the population of the Caribbean by virtue of their education, social and economic status in their communities, and breadth of personal and professional experiences.[6] In 1985, almost all of the legal professionals practicing in the country were trained in England. This fact had important ramifications for the general processing of cases because English statutes, procedures, and lawsuits were most commonly cited in Antiguan courts and were most influential as models for new laws.[7] Continued reliance upon the form and content of British law reduced the influence of community customs on statutory law and swayed how judges and magistrates interpreted written codes.[8]

The legal professionals I surveyed in 1985–86 were seasoned attorneys: fourteen of twenty-five had practiced for more than ten years. Attorneys litigate a diversity of criminal and civil cases. Of twenty-one persons in private practice whom I interviewed, twelve characterized their office as "nonspecialized." Some do prefer to concentrate on particular areas of law, but even those who are more specialized must handle some range of cases as a matter of sheer economics.

Forty percent of those interviewed had been engaged in public as well as private practice at some time in their professional careers. Native-born Antiguans tend to enter private practice, which is highly lucrative, whereas magistrates and judges usually come from other Caribbean nations. They are selected by a legal commission and hold office for a period designated by contract. By hiring "foreign" magistrates and judges, the government avoids unpleasant accusations about case "fixing." Public service is not as remunerative as an established private practice, but admission to the bar brings social and economic rewards.

Caribbean women long have been noted for their independence and active participation in the wage economy (Brodber 1982; Massiah 1982, 1984; Senior 1991), yet for a very long time law was not a profession for Antiguan women. The first female attorney to practice in Antigua, Florence Lake, joined the bar in 1960. Since that date, women increasingly have been involved in all aspects of the criminal justice system. Still, I observed only a few in court, and they comprised only 20 percent of the legal professionals I surveyed. I found no obvious differences between the responses of male and female legal professionals I interviewed.[9] In general, lawyers' everyday working lives make them acutely aware of the ways in which norms and laws intersect and of the factors influencing the dynamics of family life in the community.

Legal advice notwithstanding, kinship statutes instruct who shall use which Antiguan court to resolve family disputes.[10] In 1985–86, statutes distinguished persons on the basis of their marital status (single or married) and birth status (legitimate or illegitimate). The High Court is responsible for settling cases of divorce, custody of children, division of property between married persons, adoption, and contested inheritance. With respect to certain disputes, married persons have the option of applying either to the High Court or the magistrates' court for legal remedy. For example, a married person may apply to the magistrates' court for relief if his or her spouse has committed adultery, aggravated assault upon the applicant, desertion, is guilty of persistent cruelty, or is a habitual drunkard. In addition, a married woman whose husband compels her to submit to prostitution or forces her to engage in intercourse while he knowingly suffers from venereal disease may apply to the magistrate. The magistrate has authority to order that the complainant no longer be bound to cohabit with the defendant, to award legal custody of children to the applicant, and to direct the defendant to pay weekly support for the applicant and any "children of the family." These children include "every child (whether legitimate or illegitimate) whom the applicant or defendant is liable under any law to maintain and who has been living with them as part of the husband's family." Only a woman in a legal union can ask for support for herself (*Laws of Antigua* 1962:417–21). In sharp contrast, conflicts between unmarried couples over child care and maintenance can only be adjudicated in the magistrates' court.

The persistence of these two alternative legal channels preserves the hierarchical social structure. The system, in place since the nineteenth century, funnels women with illegitimate children through one set of processes and married women through another. The law also differentiates in practice between persons of different social classes since the two courts are widely acknowledged to have quite different consequences for individuals' family ties and the economies of their households. When I asked whether the magistrate's court could be characterized as a "poor peoples' court," eighteen of twenty-one attorneys concurred.[11]

Structural, economic, and ideological reasons beyond the factor of legal jurisdiction account for why that characterization holds. First, the magistrate's court is more readily accessible to the lower class. It is cheap to take a kinship case there: the cost of a $3.00 (Eastern Caribbean) stamp. One need not hire an attorney and, indeed, the majority of litigants with maintenance cases are not represented. Second, magistrates can award only up to $15.00 E.C. per week for child support (U.S. $5.67), and up to $25.00 E.C. (U.S. $9.36) for a married woman's support.[12] Such small sums are valuable only to the most indigent. High Court judges, on the other hand, have much greater discretion in awarding support for wives and children and can base their decisions on the income and property of both parties and the ages and educational needs of the children. Members of the middle class, therefore, divide their property and arrange for the welfare of their children at High Court. Finally, there are ideological reasons why the middle class avoids the magistrates' court. Members of this class, and many lower-class persons as well, consider kinship cases shameful. They are analogous to "hanging one's dirty laundry in public." In addition, the court's long association with persons of low status—with criminals, rogues, and vagabonds—dissuades Antiguans concerned about their reputation from bringing a case there (Lazarus-Black 1991).[13] For all these reasons, the magistrates primarily hear kinship disputes of working-class parties. Thus, as it has in the past, law continues to intervene in the lives of families of different classes in different ways and with different consequences.

At the Magistrate's Court

The plaintiff who comes to the magistrate's court with a new kinship case is most likely to be a lower-class woman. Finding herself at odds with the man,[14] and the children neglected, she files a complaint. The woman may or may not have other children at home to support. In a great many instances, she juggles child care and some form of part-time employment to pay for rent or the mortgage and food. Usually the union between the man and woman has not been a casual one; most frequently the couple have been seeing each other for more than a year and up to several years. Five of six attorneys questioned about the number of children named by plaintiffs responded that there is "one child usually, but two or three is not uncommon." Of twenty-two such trials I observed in St. John's, seven involved one child, nine involved two children, four involved three children, and two involved four children. The parties tend to be young, commonly eighteen to thirty-five years of age, but the vast majority were not pregnant teens. Antigua's minority racial and ethnic groups, which include persons of white, British, American, Canadian, European, and Middle Eastern descent, rarely appear in the courts with familial disputes. Many Antiguans of Portuguese descent are Catholics, and most Antiguans who are descendants of parents who belonged to the Greek Orthodox church in the Middle East have joined the Catholic church. Hence their religious affiliation may keep these groups from the courts. Members of fundamentalist Christian sects are also dissuaded by their beliefs, and sometimes directly by their ministers, from using the courts. Three pastors of fundamentalist churches I interviewed, for example, read to me a biblical quotation that instructs Christians not to take their brothers to court and to turn the other cheek against adversity. Fundamentalist sects teach their members to resolve quarrels among themselves or with the help of their minister.[15] The lawyers told me they have few clients from among these church groups, though occasionally they are approached to handle a bad debt or a disputed land claim. Rastafarians rarely seek redress for kinship grievances at the courts.[16] The men and women

TABLE 15   **Kinship Cases in St. John's, 1980–1987**

Year	Cases
1980	2,733
1981	2,909
1982	2,024
1983	1,841
1984	1,492
1985	1,237
1986	1,377
1987	1,369

SOURCE: Magistrate's Court records.

who come to the magistrate's court are at least nominal members of the established Anglican, Methodist, and Moravian churches. Generally, they are unrepresented by counsel. Most have never been to court before, and they are clearly uncertain about what is expected of them when they file a case.

There are, nevertheless, a great number of kinship cases recorded in the magistrates' books each year, particularly in St. John's, as Table 15 demonstrates. The large number of cases stems in part from men who, after having been adjudged the putative father of a child or children and ordered to pay weekly maintenance, fail to make support payments. When a man neglects to provide child support for five or six consecutive weeks, the collecting officer requests the magistrate to order the man to give reason why he has not paid. If a man chooses not to pay, he does not pay until the police track him down. Meanwhile, the number of cases against him continues to multiply on the books.[17] In 1987, the police incarcerated fifty-six men for "Bastardy Arrears" and four for "Maintenance Arrears" (*Statistical Yearbook* 1987:58, 59).

After cases of unpaid arrears, the most frequently heard kinship disputes are those in which a woman requests that a man be judged the father of her child and an order be made for the child's support. These petitions constituted about 70 percent of all new kinship cases brought before the magistrates between 1980 and 1987. Eight other types of cases, however, also fall under the magistrates' jurisdiction—almost all brought by women. As is true elsewhere in the Caribbean (e.g., Durant Gonzalez 1982; Jackson 1982; Senior 1991:135–39), Antiguan women rely on the courts to establish affiliation and maintenance, to increase support orders, to deny husbands the right to cohabitation, to request maintenance for themselves and their children, to protect the financial interests of a child if a father is about to leave the country, and to remove a child from the home of a negligent parent. Antiguan men, on the other hand, file most of the requests for discharge of orders. They have that option as soon as a minor reaches the age of sixteen, if the child comes to reside with them, or if the mother takes the child out of the country. Table 16 summarizes the frequency of different kinship cases heard by the St. John's magistrates over an eight year period. Requests for paternity affiliation and maintenance clearly dominate the magistrates' court docket. How are these cases adjudicated?

A suit begins when the magistrate[18] or the clerk reads the charge filed against the man. He is told that he is alleged to be the father of X, born of the body of the complainant on a specific day. The magistrate then asks the man if he is the child's father. Antiguan men rarely disavow paternity in court. Although a few attorneys told me they had handled cases in which paternity was denied, I observed only one such case in eight months. Usually, the man admits paternity and the magistrate inquires of the woman, "How much are you asking?" Alternatively, he may ask the man, "How much are you willing to pay to support your child?" Either way, the magistrate informs both of them, in the next breath, that fifteen dollars is the limit the court can impose. If the woman asks for a sum that the man finds reasonable, and he agrees to it, the magistrate issues a consent order in that amount. Thus because of the way the law is worded, and the general feeling that the amount to be awarded is so limited, the court may distribute a man's resources without reference to his income and financial circumstances, the history of the relationship, the needs of the child, or other ancillary factors. The dispute is resolved without trial, and the magistrate has temporarily turned conflict into consensus.

The processing of a case becomes more complicated if the parties cannot agree on the amount of support or if attorneys represent one or both litigants. If the couple cannot agree and no attorneys are present, the court may be converted briefly into a market and a higgling session ensues. The woman tells how much she wants, and the man gives evidence about how much he can afford. The magistrate encourages them to compromise. As is true in American courts (Conley and Barr 1978, 1990; Merry 1990, 1994; Yngvesson 1994), witnesses' demeanor, language, and oratorical skills influence their

TABLE 16 **Kinship Cases Filed at St. John's Magistrate's Court by Type of Request, 1980–1987**

Type of Request	1980	1981	1982	1983	1984	1985	1986	1987
	Number and Percentage of Total Cases							
Paternity and maintenance	108 (65%)	90 (73%)	93 (56%)	152 (58%)	131 (67%)	110 (72%)	90 (77%)	92 (76%)
Vary maintenance	18 (11%)	9 (7%)	25 (15%)	44 (17%)	26 (13%)	12 (8%)	11 (9%)	8 (7%)
Discharge of maintenance	8 (5%)	9 (7%)	27 (16%)	42 (16%)	22 (11%)	17 (11%)	6 (5%)	7 (6%)
Maintenance of wife and children	8 (5%)	4 (3%)	12 (7%)	8 (3%)	6 (3%)	11 (7%)	8 (7%)	9 (7%)
Parental emigration	10 (6%)	4 (3%)	3 (2%)	9 (3%)	1 (1%)	1 (1%)	2 (2%)	3 (2%)
Reinstate former order	0 (0%)	0 (0%)	3 (2%)	1 (0%)	7 (4%)	0 (0%)	0 (0%)	0 (0%)
Separation and no maintenance	4 (2%)	1 (1%)	2 (1%)	1 (0%)	0 (0%)	0 (0%)	0 (0%)	0 (0%)
Separation with maintenance	8 (5%)	5 (4%)	1 (1%)	2 (1%)	0 (0%)	0 (0%)	0 (0%)	0 (0%)
Neglected juvenile, transfer custody	3 (2%)	1 (1%)	0 (0%)	3 (1%)	3 (2%)	1 (1%)	0 (0%)	2* (2%)
Total	167 (101%)	123 (99%)	166 (100%)	262 (99%)	196 (101%)	152 (100%)	117 (100%)	121 (100%)

SOURCE: Magistrate Court records.
* Includes a case of "harboring a child," an offense not recorded earlier.

believability and impact. Particularly important to the outcome of the case is the use or omission of key phrases that indicate to the magistrate that an individual is an "upright fellow." For example, one petition to increase an order for child support from ten to fifteen dollars was denied after the defendant, a married family man who owned his own automotive body shop, presented an open and detailed account of his monthly expenses and also admitted to the magistrate that ten dollars could not support a child. In denying the order, the magistrate explained to the complainant:

> I have heard what you had to say madam and I heard what he had to say. I have to say that I believe the gentleman and that he cannot afford more at this time. I will leave the order as it is at this time. I find he is honest. He admitted that ten dollars is not enough to feed a child. If he had lied, I would have made him pay. I feel he is a respectable gentleman.

He then lectured the defendant: "It is your child. Surely you don't want your child to suffer. See if you can't give more when you can."

The presence of attorneys does not speed up the processing of a kinship case; indeed, there is an inverse relationship between their participation and the resolution of the dispute. If counsel is retained, the past and present circumstances of the parties are more likely to become factors in the case and the details of law may be quoted and debated. The presence of lawyers mitigates against the higgling about expenses that takes place when they are absent and almost always results in the highest award the law allows.

The court docket for September 1985 was typical with respect to both the types of cases that appeared before the magistrate and their resolution. In all, twenty-seven new cases were called. By the end of the month, seven cases were struck out "for want of prosecution," nine were adjudicated, and eleven remained adjourned. Of the nine suits resolved by the court, lawyers participated in three. Seven petitions involved requests for paternity affiliation and maintenance for illegitimate children. Men admitted paternity in every case, and five immediately agreed to pay the maximum support. One man quarreled about the amount of the payment, but the magistrate heard his evidence and ruled that he could afford fifteen dollars. In the seventh case, the man offered ten dollars a week for each of his two children and the woman agreed. In addition to these paternity suits, the magistrate discharged one support order and suspended another. In the first case, a mother requested the court to dismiss a support order because the defendant regularly took care of his son and there was no need to press him to pay at the courthouse. A father who wanted the magistrate to discharge maintenance orders because the complainant had emigrated with his two children brought the final case. The magistrate suspended rather than revoked these orders.

Seven cases were struck from the court's docket. A variety of reasons explain why these and others drop out of the system. According to experienced court personnel, the lawyers, and my interviewees, some men "come 'round" once a woman files a case. Several women told me they had threatened to file suits a couple of times before they actually appeared in court. Once the word spreads that a woman has filed papers, some men will plead with her not to follow through with the suit, apologize for their negligence or misbehavior, and offer immediate financial compensation. A case may also fall by the wayside because a litigant is unable or unwilling to appear in court on the day(s) his or her case is scheduled, because of a careless clerical error, and because a litigant becomes disenchanted with the system. For example, one woman was present when her petitions for support for two illegitimate children were first called, but the cases were adjourned because the father had not been properly served. She missed court next time because one of her children was ill. The defendant was served on that date, but he failed to appear anyway. On the third and final date, the plaintiff locked her two small children alone in the house and got to the courthouse on time. However, she failed to hear the court officer call her name because she was not seated in the proper location. The magistrate, thinking the complainant was no longer interested in prosecuting the case, struck it from the list. The plaintiff failed to file the cases again in 1987. She told me that she was managing with help from her mother and her boyfriend.[19] Another plaintiff, who went to the courthouse on several occasions to see if her case was scheduled, found it never made the list. She confided in me that she believed her case was never called because her attorney's secretary was a distant relative of her estranged husband. Finally, other litigants with whom I spoke decided to drop their suits because they became disgusted at the length of time required to get a hearing, because it seemed too embarrassing to appear in court, and because they were annoyed about the limited compensation the court can provide. Occasionally a woman is intimidated into dropping her suit.

If a plaintiff fails to appear for two or three consecutive weeks, the magistrate strikes the case out. Alternatively, a magistrate may hear a case but decide the evidence does not warrant making an order because the complainant's testimony has not been sufficiently corroborated.[20] In my experience, dismissal of cases on the basis of insufficient proof is rare. For example, I never witnessed a situation in which a woman was denied support for illegitimate children. If the defendant does not appear and the woman has not brought a witness, the magistrate usually adjourns the case for the following week and instructs the complainant to bring someone who can testify on her behalf. Taken together, these reasons explain why only one-third to one-half of newly filed kinship cases in St. John's are actually adjudicated (See Table 17).

To conclude, well over a thousand kinship cases of various kinds are processed by the magistrates in Antigua each year. Many of these involve men who have fallen into arrears in their child support payments, but the courts entertain a variety of new cases, including petitions for paternity affiliation and maintenance, requests to vary or discharge old orders, pleas to protect

TABLE 17 **Requests for Paternity Affiliation and Maintenance Filed at St. John's Magistrate Court, 1980–1987**

Year	Total	Number Granted	Number Dismissed or Not Prosecuted
1980	108	56 (52%)	52 (48%)
1981	90	41 (46%)	49 (54%)
1982	93	37 (40%)	56 (60%)
1983	152	73 (48%)	79 (52%)
1984	131	48 (37%)	83 (63%)
1985	110	40 (36%)	70 (64%)
1986	90	27 (30%)	63 (70%)
1987	92	43 (47%)	49 (53%)

SOURCE: St. John's Magistrate Court records.

children whose parents are leaving the country, and appeals for assistance from married women. If plaintiffs, most of whom are women, can withstand the stresses and strains accompanying the processing of a case, there is a good chance that the magistrate will rule in their favor. When Antiguan women decide that their family relations are in crisis, they call upon the courts to formalize the ties that bind children and fathers. The courts comply with these demands; they construct a legal alliance between fathers and illegitimate children. There is limited success, however, with respect to enforcement of support orders. In 1987, I reinterviewed nine women whose child support cases I had followed in 1985–86. Only two of those women received child support regularly, two obtained support every few months, and four had checks only two or three times a year. A review of the collecting officer's notebooks confirmed what these women told me.

My investigations affirm that the magistrates' courts serve as forums for Antigua's poor—particularly for its poor women. I have examined the legal, structural, and economic factors that account for the continued association between the lower class and the lower courts, as well as some of the ideological factors that dissuade Antiguans from bringing cases there. Poor women who do use the magistrate's court must ignore unpleasantness. In part, women use this court because their children are illegitimate and they are denied access to the High Court. In part, women use it because, even if they were married, they cannot afford to bring a case to the High Court. My analysis also shows that if women are persistent, they usually win their suits.[21] Even if the law restricts the amount of child support the magistrate can order, it formally establishes a parent-child relationship and assigns financial responsibilities to the putative father. As we will discover in the following chapter, however, these women take their cases to court for another reason, one more important than simply monetary support for their children.

At the High Court

Marriage is held to be a lifelong commitment throughout the West Indies; it is a contract not entered into lightly, and it is severed only with the greatest reluctance. As we saw earlier, the high regard for marriage is a consequence of several historical factors, including its sanction by the churches and its continued association with the life-style of the materially secure middle class. In Antigua, as elsewhere in the English-speaking Caribbean, marriage remains the preferred type of union among people in every social class (Jagdeo 1984; Lowes 1982; White 1986). This ideal notwithstanding, we have seen that the marriage rate has remained consistently low. In contrast, the number of divorce cases filed at the High Court has been increasing at a dramatic rate, rising from an average of fourteen per decade in the 1950s to fifty-three per decade in the 1980s (see Table 18). The figures show that the average number of divorces filed almost doubled between 1950 and 1960—and then doubled again between 1960 and 1970. The trend continues in the 1980s, although not as rapidly as in the previous decade.

In analyzing the frequency of divorce and its implications for familial organization, it is important to bear in mind that divorce is a relatively new and, until recently, a rather rare phenomenon. Although at least some Antiguans have had recourse to the magistrates' courts for resolving issues of paternity since 1786, divorce was not readily available in England until 1857, and Antigua did not have a local divorce law until 1948. By all accounts, it remained very unpopular until fairly recently. Indeed, its increasing frequency and acceptability causes considerable alarm among older persons and ministers. Plans to alter the divorce law have been shelved repeatedly by government

TABLE 18   **Number of Divorces Filed in Antigua and Barbuda, 1951–1987**

1950	N.A.	1960	18	1970	57	1980	40
1951	23	1961	16	1971	63	1981	72
1952	8	1962	27	1972	41	1982	72
1953	12	1963	19	1973	53	1983	48
1954	11	1964	20	1974	47	1984	43
1955	14	1965	19	1975	40	1985	44
1956	19	1966	32	1976	46	1986	54
1957	13	1967	24	1977	50	1987	53
1958	15	1968	45	1978	62		
1959	12	1969	46	1979	55		
Total	127		266		514		426
Average per decade	14		27		51		53

SOURCE: High Court records.

officials on the grounds that Antiguans do not vote favorably for persons who support measures that dissolve families.

As was true of the kinship cases processed in the magistrates' courts, legal, structural, economic, and ideological factors influence the cases filed at the High Court; they also account for courthouse records delineating the reasons for divorce. An antiquated statute places the first set of constraints upon who may or who may not file for divorce. Except in extreme circumstances, divorce proceedings will not be entertained unless the couple have been wed for three years. Moreover, a divorce requires proof that a matrimonial offense occurred. The three most commonly cited grounds for divorce are desertion, cruelty, and adultery.[22] Of the three, desertion consistently outnumbers cruelty and adultery. Indeed, the courthouse records give the impression that adultery

TABLE 19   **Grounds for Divorce as a Percentage of Total Divorces Granted,** 1960–1987

		Percentage of Total						
Year	*Total Number of Divorces*	*Adultery*	*Desertion*	*Cruelty*	*Unknown*	*A&C*	*D&C*	*A&D*[a]
1960–69	221	13	35	12	25	4	5	5
1970–79	337	11	48	26	9	1	4	1
1980–87	261	11	47	30	9[b]	2	2	0

SOURCE: High Court records.
[a] A&C, D&C, and A&D refer to divorces granted for two matrimonial offenses: adultery and cruelty, desertion and cruelty, and adultery and desertion.
[b] I included in this category one case adjudicated in 1987 for which the cause for the divorce was described in the court record as "consummate willful refusal." It was the only instance of its kind I encountered.

offenses are rare: only 11 percent of divorces since 1970 have been granted for adultery. Table 19 illustrates that a pattern has persisted.

The statistics convey that many Antiguans desert their spouses; desertion accounted for 48 percent of cases between 1970 and 1979 and for 47 percent of those between 1980 and 1987.[23] The attorneys' personal experiences concurred with this conclusion, and some suspected cruelty as a reason for divorce was on the rise. Several lawyers remarked that if an Antiguan woman files for divorce, she files on grounds of desertion or cruelty; if a man files, he files on the basis of adultery. My impression is that men are more likely to dissolve their marriages when their wives shame their manhood. Unfortunately, the government has only recently begun to differentiate the grounds for divorce by sex. These records, summarized in Table 20, reveal that if a divorce is granted for adultery, the petitioner is likely to be under thirty-five years of age.

Numbers tell only part of the story. When attorneys elaborated the causes for divorce and litigants described their case histories, a very different picture emerged to explain why people dissolve their marriages. In the first place, applications to the court are made only after several matrimonial offenses have occurred and a variety of other techniques for reconciliation have failed. Second, the reasons people divorce are far less cut and dried than the records would

TABLE 20 Divorces Granted by Sex, Age at Marriage, and Grounds for Divorce in Selected Years

| | 1980 | | | | | |
| | Cruelty | | Desertion | | Adultery | |
Age	Male	Female	Male	Female	Male	Female
Under 25	1	3	5	9	2	4
25–34	3	3	12	10	2	0
Over 35	2	0	3	1	0	0
Not stated	2	2	1	1	2	2
Total	8	8	21	21	6	6
	1985					
Under 25	1	5	3	5	0	4
25–34	6	3	4	3	5	1
Over 35	2	1	5	4	0	0
Not stated	2	2	6	6	1	1
Total	11	11	18	18	6	6
	1987					
Under 25	5	7	4	6	1	3
25–34	2	1	7	4	2	0
Over 35	1	0	0	1	0	0
Not stated	3	3	2	2	1	1
Total	11	11	13	13	4	4

SOURCES: Adapted from Antigua and Barbuda Statistical Yearbook (1982:13; 1985:15; 1987:20).

have us believe. I shall take up the questions of the motives of litigants and the meaning of divorce in Antiguan society in depth in the next chapter.

Whatever a complainant's "real" reasons for divorce, counsel must make a case before the court. That entails a process of a different sort; the ability to persuade a judge to decide on the client's behalf. Cases of "persistent cruelty," for example, require proof of the intention of the defendant, the nature and duration of the alleged actions, and whether the complainant could reasonably be expected to accept such behavior. Cases of alleged adultery are even tougher to prove: one must name the person with whom the adultery was committed, and testimony must be supported by other material evidence. It is far easier to prove a case of "simple" or "constructive" desertion. Simple desertion can be filed if one party has deserted the other for three years. It includes cases of physical absence or emotional or sexual desertion. Constructive desertion applies to situations in which the plaintiff left the matrimonial home because the behavior of the spouse was such that he or she could not reasonably be expected to stay. Attorneys and their clients generally find it "better," "neater," and "cleaner" to apply for divorce on the grounds of desertion. I found some litigants, including Trevor Roberts, whose case is described in the next chapter, would refuse to divorce if the grounds were either adultery or cruelty but would agree not to contest the suit if the case was filed for desertion. In short, the statistics proving that desertion is the chief cause of divorce in Antigua are a function of statutory rules of evidence, of legal procedures, and of the local norm that proscribes discussions about intimate relationships in public. As one woman explained to me: "If there is a disagreement in the house and you not living there, you shouldn't come in."

Another factor influencing the frequency of divorce is undoubtedly cost. In 1985–86, the bar association suggested a fee of $750 for a divorce not entailing contested property settlements or child custody. Some attorneys charged more. Due to the high cost of the suit, people commonly neglect to separate legally unless there is compelling reason for them to do so.

How do the attorneys and judges who work in the High Court describe the socioeconomic status of the litigants involved in typical divorce cases? Although the association between legal marriage and the middle class persists, an increasing number of attorneys find their clients are lower-class women. Seventy-five percent of the respondents polled said these women hold jobs such as "laborer," "domestic," and "clerk." My other sources confirm their findings: the important factor is not a woman's class origin but whether she is economically self-sufficient.[24] Data on the occupations of female litigants in fifteen divorce suits shows that only two women did not work outside the home, two had worked for years as schoolteachers and lived quite comfortably, one owned a boutique, and the rest were working-class maids, factory workers, saleswomen, and the like. When they are granted a divorce, Antiguan women do not want to retain emotional or financial ties to their former husbands. Unless they were married to very well-to-do men, women divorce "to finish and be done with it." They rarely ask for alimony. On the other hand, they are extremely insistent that men support their children and expect their attorneys to work out generous arrangements.

Though differences in class membership distinguish some litigants at the High Court from those who appear at the magistrates' courts, certain other sociological characteristics are shared. First, divorce litigants are most often younger and middle-aged persons. One of the parties may wish to remarry. Second, they have been involved in the relationship for a long time and have children. Of fifteen divorce cases I investigated at length, ten involved marriages of more than eight years' duration and eleven involved children. Third, Antigua's minority racial, ethnic, and religious groups are statistically underrepresented in divorce cases, just as they are in child-support cases.[25] Fourth, the litigants find the experience of going to court shameful. Most of those I interviewed mentioned shame as a factor that caused them to postpone filing divorce proceedings. They did not, however, experience the same embarrassment and fear that stems from the stigma associated with bringing a case before a magistrate. Finally, in both settings the majority of new cases are brought by women.

If some Antiguan laws discriminate against women (Cumper and Daly 1979; Forde 1981; Senior 1991), and if men dominate each domain of the formal legal system—from the police to the judiciary—women institute the procedures to create formally alliances between men and children and to break conjugal ties when these become untenable. Of the twenty-three attorneys I questioned about this, nineteen told me that women, not men, most often file for divorce. Women filed suit in the majority of divorce cases I observed in 1985–86. Thus women, not men, emerge as the dominant actors when the family is in crisis.[26]

The drama and trauma that mark the lives of the litigants about to be divorced are not apparent during the brief formal ritual that breaks the marriage contract. Indeed, the silence surrounding the breaking of a union at the High Court contrasts strikingly with the noisy speech events that surround declarations of affiliation and maintenance orders at the magistrate's court. But, then, one is a ritual for maintaining an alliance, the other for breaking one.

In a typical divorce case, the plaintiff responds to a series of prepared questions posed by counsel. The attorney must establish that the complainant resides in Antigua or Barbuda, that the couple married on a particular date, if and when any children were born, if there are previous or related cases to the suit, and proof of a matrimonial offense. Ideally, and in most cases, the litigant's responses are brief. After ten to fifteen minutes of testimony, the judge enters a "decree nisi." The petitioner's attorney must return to court six months later to obtain the formal "decree absolute."

Divorce has recently become more socially acceptable in Antigua for several reasons. Satellite communication brought increased awareness of its acceptance in economically developed countries, and the women's movement has undeniably influenced the thinking of the present generation. Perhaps even more important, expansion and changes in the economy that allow women to work to support themselves also enable them to divorce. Some Antiguans claim the clergy is less successful today than in the past in preventing divorce. Finally, women are now less afraid of the ramifications of their being divorced; before, men considered them especially easy marks for sexual and economic exploitation.

With greater toleration of divorce, judges are loath to keep a couple together even when evidence of a matrimonial offense is not apparent. Indeed, in one contested case described in the next chapter, the judge was hard pressed to rationalize his decision to grant the divorce. In at least two others I witnessed, the "evidence" proving the matrimonial offense was similarly unconvincing. One attorney explained:

> People come in and they say, "Look, my marriage can't continue. We need to divorce and get on with our lives." So we as lawyers have to impose a more modern viewpoint onto an archaic legislation. So, as lawyers, we press, stretch, and pull, if the marriage is irretrievably broken down, to find a way to pigeonhole it. And the judges, God bless them, they go along with this farce. The other day I had a case which, in strict definition of cruelty, there is no way if I were a judge I would have granted the divorce. But judges have accepted the view that the law has not kept pace. So, we have to bend a little there, stretch it there. And we do stretch it. We call a slap cruelty!

In most instances, attorneys skillfully present their clients' stories so that the case is proved—and that means making a "mere" slap into brutality.

To conclude, as is true of kinship cases at the magistrate's court, the processing of divorce cases is constrained by legal, structural, economic, and ideological factors. Furthermore, litigants in both types of cases share several sociological characteristics—the only notable exception being the absence of middle-class disputants at the magistrate's court. In both courts, women are more likely than men to use kinship legalities to manage conflict in their families. I explain why women take steps to formalize their own and their children's kinship statuses in the next two chapters by examining what litigation and law reform mean to the Antiguan men and women I interviewed.

Minding the Children: Informal and Formal Adoption

Children are loved and desired by men and women in Antigua, and, as in the region generally, informal adoption of a child's child, a sister's child, or even a neighbor's child, is not uncommon.[27] Indeed, informal adoption by a blood relation is the usual and preferred method for caring for children who cannot reside with their mothers. In particular, women trust their own mothers and their sisters to take good care of their offspring. They relinquish custody if they believe the adoption best serves the interests of the child. For example, parents know that there are superior educational opportunities abroad and they may agree to adoption so the child can be schooled in the United States, Canada, or England. Because Antiguans do not try to suppress the ties between an adopted child and his or her biological parents, no one fears that a child will forget them.

Like informally adopted children, legally adopted children are usually adopted by blood relatives. One attorney made the point that formal adoption is hardly ever a matter of creating fictive kinship ties: "There are so few *real* adoptions here. You know, like you have in America, where there is no relationship between the parents and the child." A search of the Adoption Register reveals that married couples (with the husband adopting his wife's child(ren) from an earlier relationship) and single female relatives most frequently legally adopt Antiguan children. Yet I also discovered that it was not uncommon for Antiguan men to adopt formally their own illegitimate children. Of twelve attorneys questioned about whether they had heard of such cases, nine responded positively, two replied negatively, and one could not recall if he had processed such a case. Six of these lawyers allowed me to examine files in which men adopted their illegitimate children, and another discussed a father-daughter adoption with me. I stress the significance of these cases because in the past, Caribbean ethnographers have emphasized women's roles and female networks in discussing adoption without due attention to men's participation.

In most of the thirteen cases in my sample, the men had fathered the illegitimate child(ren) in their youth. Two adopting fathers had remained bachelors, one was separated from his wife and planning to divorce, and the others were married. If an adopting parent is married, both the spouse and the mother of the illegitimate child must consent to the arrangement. In four cases, the spouses had children of their own—an indication of women's willingness to bear the burden of caring for other women's children. One wife consented to the adoption of a child born after she and her husband had wed. Five of the adopted children were girls; eight were boys. They were not youngsters: four were over sixteen years of age and six were between eleven and fifteen years old. At the time of the adoption, ten youths resided with their natural mothers, a paternal grandmother raised one, and two children were already in their fathers' custody. There was nothing particularly striking about the class affiliation of the adopting parents; with one exception (a very wealthy business man and landowner), they included both middle- and working-class Antiguans. The adopting fathers had occupations such as "heavy duty [equipment] operator," "airplane service man," "trade man," "business proprietor," and "fisherman and livestock owner." Five of the married men had working wives whose occupations included "seamstress," "accounts clerk," "machine operator," "civil servant" and "packer."

Why did these men decide to adopt? Confidential evidence in the files reveals six of the children were being adopted because their fathers planned to migrate. In two cases, men disapproved of the circumstances in which their children lived and wanted to provide for them more stable and financially secure environments. One bachelor adopted his illegitimate son after the death of the young boy's mother. Another had raised his boy from the time the child was a year old and the baby's mother had run away. He formally adopted him thirteen years later.

These adoption files confirm several characteristics of legal adoptions more generally. In 1985–86, the professionals knew that people formally adopted children for two main reasons: a desire to secure legal rights for them and to facilitate migration. Actually, the intention to migrate soon after adoption outweighed the other cause seven to one. As an attorney told me, "You find your Antiguan auntie—maybe someone who made good in the U.S.A.—has a sister at home struggling and she wants to adopt one of her sister's children to give them the benefit and the advantages that you can get overseas. It gives the children the benefits." Not surprisingly, one-fifth of the attorneys I interviewed expounded upon the need to amend the residency requirement of the present adoption law that restricts an adopting parent from taking the child out of the country.

Of the kinship cases we have examined thus far, legal adoptions are different on two accounts. First, only in adoptions are statutory regulations so blatantly ignored. Judges rationalize that parents must have the opportunity to provide what is best for their children, despite the fact that the law demands that adopted children remain in Antigua. In practice, then, they disregard any information that implies an adopting parent plans to take the child abroad. Second, these kinship cases illustrate most clearly the interdependence between nations and the manner in which such relations impinge upon a kinship order and familial norms. It is not only the Antiguan state that intervenes in the lives of families, it is also foreign states.

An ever-increasing number of Antiguans, for example, migrate to the United States. Yet American immigration law makes it extremely difficult, if not impossible, to bring into the country a dependent who is not legally a member of one's family. One attorney vocalized what others preferred to leave unsaid:

TABLE 21   **Number of Legal Adoptions in Antigua and Barbuda, 1960–1987**

1960	6	1970	8	1980	30
1961	1	1971	3	1981	48
1962	0	1972	13	1982	34
1963	5	1973	17	1983	26
1964	0	1974	24	1984	19
1965	2	1975	12	1985	11
1966	3	1976	19	1986	18
1967	6	1977	35	1987	19
1968	2	1978	20		
1969	6	1979	23		
Total	31		174		205
Average per decade	3		17		26

SOURCE: High Court records.

> You know what law plays the most significant role in family life here? It's the U.S. immigration laws. I'd say nine out of ten adoptions are the kids of extended families who want to take them to the U.S. . . . And so you know we all fib? We all fib. The court turns a blind eye.

This willingness to turn a blind eye—in combination with shifts in local social and economic conditions which permit more Antiguans to travel or to reside abroad—is responsible for the steady increase in the number of formal legal adoptions over the years (see Table 21).

Reviewing new developments in the anthropology of law since 1975, Merry argues "transnational processes are becoming increasingly important in theorizing about the nature of local legal phenomenon" (1992:357). The case of Antiguan adoption is a neat illustration of the power of transnational processes to reconstitute local kin relations. Antiguan norms are flexible when it comes to the question of who should raise a child if his or her mother can not. Informal adoption is prevalent, and many people grow up in several different households with several different families. American immigration law, however, forced the hand of those who would have ordinarily followed the Antiguan custom of informally caring for a child. That law demanded that a child's kinship status be fixed and that he or she be assigned to a singular nuclear family. Men and women carried their cases for adoption to the High Court to comply. As we shall see, after 1987 they used another legal remedy, the Births Act, to accommodate U.S. immigration law.[28]

Inheritance: "A Man's Will Is a Man's Will"

Antiguan law provides three methods for deploying property at death. If a person leaves a will, the named executor administers the estate according to the deceased's wishes. A will can be contested in court on the basis of certain technicalities, but by all accounts this is an arduous process to be avoided unless significant property is involved. If no will exists, a legitimate heir of the deceased, usually a spouse, parent, child, or sibling, applies to the registrar for letters of administration. Until 1987, a "legitimate heir" in Antigua was defined similarly to the way it had been in English common law: one had to be related legally by blood or contract. Illegitimate children, therefore, were not legally entitled to apply for letters of administration for their fathers' estates. A person seeking letters of administration usually contacts an attorney to obtain the proper forms and learns that all legitimate heirs have rights to the estate.[29] The third form of transferring property at death occurs if there are no legitimate heirs. Interested parties not related to the deceased, including illegitimate children, might gain control of an estate after a long process in which they applied to the prime minister's cabinet for permission to take part or all of the deceased's holdings. In a nutshell, inheritance law mostly protects those who protect themselves—legally—by making a will.

In a study of land-tenure and inheritance practices in Carriacou, M. Smith found that most people did not make wills unless a family feud was brewing: "The basic condition of will-making, and hence its function, is to record or to initiate departures from the folk system of land tenure, and especially from folk norms that govern transmission of rights at inheritance" (1965c:245).[30] Kinship disputes over inheritance in Antigua, as in Carriacou, generally do not arise because there are traditional patterns for deploying property among kin. People in Antigua do not like to make wills because a belief persists that tragedy befalls the testator. Even so, quite a lot of people made wills prior to 1987 to depart from the intestate laws.[31]

One of the norms governing inheritance in the Antiguan common order specifies that sons and daughters should inherit equally. Another rule recognizes that although theoretically each child holds a share in their parent(s)' home, siblings should defer use rights in the house to the child or children who remained with the parents to care for them in their final years. One woman explained: "People feel like whoever takes on the funeral expenses, who buries the person, is entitled."

Concessions to these normative rules also appear in wills. The attorneys find that boys and girls usually inherit equally, but one respondent said that he could differentiate between the kind of property left to boys and to girls. He had observed a tendency among testators to leave undeveloped land, jewelry, household items, and sometimes a car, if there was more than one, to daughters, and to bequeath developed land, houses, occupational tools, and herd animals to sons. In these gifts, parents reveal Antiguan conceptions about work and about what it means to be a man or woman in this society.

Although Antiguans dislike making wills, men make them more often than women. In part, this may be due to the simple fact that they hold more property. "Family property," obtained through the joint efforts of a married couple, for example, is likely to be held in the man's name. Men make wills more frequently, too, to provide for their illegitimate children, who, until 1987, could not otherwise inherit. Indeed, the desire to provide for illegitimate children was the main reason behind a lot of wills prior to that date, even though the testator rarely mentioned the consanguineous relationship in the document. Instead, the child was simply included among those receiving a gift from the estate.

As they have historically, Antiguan men use a variety of tactics to diffuse potential arguments after their death between legitimate and illegitimate offspring, wives, and the mother(s) of their illegitimate children. For example, a man might leave his legitimate children the family home and the land that surrounds it, whereas his illegitimate children might receive a less valuable plot, perhaps with a little house, elsewhere on the island. This plot is probably one in which the legitimate children have little interest. Other men leave cash settlements to their illegitimate offspring. Finally, if a man suspects his wife might dispute a will naming his illegitimate children, he might transfer property to them during his lifetime. The children are told the property is their inheritance—and the man weathers his wife's wrath if she learns about the gift. In keeping with the strong emphasis on blood relationship, a man's illegitimate children will almost always inherit if there is a will, but their mothers do not. Female friends appear only occasionally in wills; four of the six attorneys I questioned about this never recalled men naming the mothers of their illegitimate children in wills they had processed. Two persons said they had seen women friends named very occasionally. The lawyers' experiences accord with my impression after reading through probate records at the High Court. Not that wives fare that well in the wills of Antiguan men—the third most commonly cited reason for drawing up a will is the desire to disinherit one's wife.

Thus, when we turn to the issue of inheritance and the devolution of property through legal channels, men rather than women become the dominating actors in the kinship system. Their power is of a different sort than that of women: men transfer commodities along the family lines they specifically choose. The rule of law grants them the right to do so. Women, in contrast, manage relationships between kin. They rely on the law to construct, maintain, and destroy familial alliances.

Legal Codes, Forensic Processes, and Kinship: Some Concluding Remarks

As earlier "processual anthropologists" (e.g., Epstein 1967; Fitzpatrick 1984; Gluckman 1967; Moore 1978; Nader and Todd 1978; Van Velson 1967), some "critical legal scholars" (e.g., R. Gordon 1984; Kairys 1982; Livingston 1982; Trubek 1984), and recent work in law and anthropology (e.g., Comaroff 1989; Comaroff and Roberts 1981; Lazarus-Black and Hirsch 1994; Moore 1986, 1989; Nader 1989; Snyder 1981; Starr and Collier 1989; Stoler 1985, 1989; Vincent 1989; Westermark 1986) insist: law and legal processes are culturally construed. They are a constitutive means of structuring social life, and when they order "order," they do so as the negotiated outcomes of historically motivated social, political, economic, and ideological forces. Contemporary Antiguans continue the age-old tradition of using legal institutions to build, manage, and dissolve kinship ties. The long-term influence of these rules and the ways disputes are resolved are important to the individuals whose relationships have been realigned as a result of their experiences with the legal system. Consequently, the structure and organization of creole family ideology and structure reflects not only those local, regional, and international forces and events that influenced the making of creole society generally but also specific judicial rules and processes. These rules and processes, in turn, subsume litigants' and lawyers' individual idiosyncrasies as well as shared beliefs and norms about family that persist in the common order.

The fact that the magistrates' courts are used regularly for resolving kinship matters but mainly by one class—poor and unmarried women—is evidence that law continues to influence family patterns and the economy of households, even as it reproduces the legal disabilities associated with lower-class kinship patterns. The persistence of these two alternative legal channels for married and unmarried persons preserves the earlier hierarchical class structure—a fact that does not go unnoticed in the community. One effect of the present judicial structure is that family disputes of lower-class people are "managed" in a different setting with very different consequences than are the family disputes of the middle class or the local elite. As Donzelot suggests, we are still witnessing a "policing" of poor families. This policing consists of not only the actual administrative intervention but also the constraints its very existence imposes upon what people do in the common order.[32] Ironically, much of this policing is inept. Court cases regularly fall out of the system and court orders are irregularly enforced, leaving many children without weekly support from their fathers. Nevertheless, and despite the limitations of the present codes, unmarried Antiguan women often use the courts. As we see next, speaking out for the legal, social, and moral rights of their children is important to women (Lazarus-Black 1992:881–82).

In addition to portraying the ways in which the state (and other states) influence the structure of creole kinship within and between the social classes, my findings in this chapter bear on the theoretical issue initially raised by Gluckman (1967) about judges' interpretation of law in relation to indigenous morals, customs, and values.[33] As we have seen, however, Antiguan kinship laws of the 1980s sharply limited the discretionary power of magistrates. Sometimes beliefs about how honest men behave or ideas about the rights that children should enjoy can make or break a particular kinship case in the lower courts, but in general, the magistrates' powers were narrowly circumscribed. High Court judges, in contrast, enjoy greater discretionary power in interpreting the law. They have greater freedom, therefore, to stretch laws in accordance with changing mores and customs. Divorce and adoption are issues to the point. Even though the grounds for divorce have not changed significantly in more than fifty years, and hardly anyone believes that cruelty, adultery, and desertion have suddenly become rampant social problems, many more divorces are processed now than in the past. Similarly, the majority of legal adoptions occur even though the judges suspect the parents plan to migrate, a violation of the Guardianship of Infants Act.

These two examples notwithstanding, I conclude that the very nature of the game of law in Antigua—which requires the contestants to quote statutes and to cite precedents—in the main ensures judges' conformity to and compliance with legal texts. I hypothesize that a similar conservatism influenced judges in the past and that therefore the more important legal source for transformations in class, kinship, and gender organization over time lies with the lawmakers and not with the judicial interpreters. Unfortunately, the record to test such a hypothesis does not exist for Antigua.

Most litigants, of course, lack knowledge about either the legal process or the detailed definitions and regulations that comprise their own kinship codes. Instead, they come to court armed with culturally specific ideas about justice and about how persons in various familial roles should behave. Only by investigating the process of bringing a case to court within the wider context of the Antiguan community can we fully clarify the relation between law and social norms. I examine next why and when plaintiffs go to the courts and how they manage to convert family and other disputes into kinship cases for the courts to resolve. Most important, I focus on how ideas about justice alter the practices of everyday life and influence what is brought to court.

8

Cases, Courts, and Family Ideology in the Common Order

Justice is not a straight t'ing you know, is a crooked and curvy t'ing. It have to twis' and turn and ben' up . . . to get where it mus' get to.

—Thelwell 1980:53

Ideas about "justice" are part of what Geertz calls a people's "legal sensibility," that "method and manner of conceiving decision situations so that settled rules can be applied to decide them (as well, of course, of conceiving the rules)" (1983:215). These ideas are cultural constructions rooted in history and mediated by the social, economic, and political conditions that provide the contexts for life experiences. Certain ideas about justice—such as the notion that society should be governed by the rule of law—are shared by all Antiguans. Other ideas, especially about the extent to which justice prevails, vary among people of different classes. In this chapter, I am concerned with some ideas about justice that color relations between men, women, and kin and that allow us to understand why and when Antiguans take family cases to court. I discuss two types of kinship cases, child maintenance and divorce. These represent both tiers of the formal judicial system, involve people in different classes, and illuminate the content and structure of creole family and gender organization. They also clarify the continuing dialectic between kinship legalities and illegalities, and between kinship laws and family norms.

One common assumption will be firmly refuted. Academic, legal, and popular wisdom holds that West Indian women go to magistrate's court for money; that they are unemployed or underemployed with too many illegitimate children to raise and too few dollars with which to do so. They go to court because their babies' fathers don't support them or don't pay regularly enough (e.g., Durant Gonzalez 1982; Jackson 1982; Massiah 1982; Senior 1991). But when I asked one such woman if she went to court for money, her answer surprised me. She looked at me indignantly and said: "I carry my case up there for justice. I complain him for justice" (Lazarus-Black 1991:119).[1]

Ideas about justice are integral to the ideology and practice of family within and between the social classes of contemporary Antigua. They condition familial life in the common order, incorporating some of the legal and illegal kin behavior contained in kinship codes and negotiated in formal legal institutions. Two principles, in particular, establish the criteria for just familial relationships: the creed of gender hierarchy in the organization of familial roles and the principle of the equality of all human beings. These two principles are crucial to understanding relations between men and women, expectations between family members, and how intra- and interclass familial conflicts are managed.

The creed of gender hierarchy in the organization of familial roles permeates relationships between husbands and wives, women and their babies' fathers, brothers and sisters, and parents and children throughout the English-speaking Caribbean (e.g., Alexander 1973, 1984; P. Anderson 1986; Austin 1979, 1984; DeVeer 1979; Douglass 1992; Lazarus-Black 1990a, 1992; Powell 1986; R. Smith 1956, 1973, 1982a, 1984, 1987, 1988; Senior 1991; Sutton and Makiesky-Barrow 1977). Although West Indians emphasize and highly value individual autonomy and economic independence for both men and women, I found Antiguans repeatedly stressed the biological and social differences between men and women and used those differences to support the notion that there is a separate and "proper" domain for each sex. Both men and women distinguish between the "inside" world of women and the "outside" world of men, and neither views those two domains as "equal" in any respect. Among other things, gender hierarchy means women will love men, bear children, and then raise those children, whereas men will make choices about how much time and resources they will devote to the women they love and the children they father. The creed of gender hierarchy within the family contributes to the subordinate position of women in Antiguan society. As in Jamaica, "husbands, because they are men, are of superior social status to their wives, because they are women" (Douglass 1992:136). Moreover, some Caribbean laws still buttress women's subordinate status (Forde 1981; Senior 1991). Nevertheless, we shall find a highly developed sense of justice ensures there are limits beyond which a man may not assert the special privileges accorded to his sex.

My discussion of the second principle, the belief in human equality, stems from an argument made originally by Jayawardena (1968) (see Lazarus-Black 1990a) but recently reassessed by B. Williams (1991).[2] Jayawardena analyzes factors that contribute to the rise of egalitarian ideologies, demonstrates how different conceptions of egalitarianism evolve within disparate social and economic contexts, and shows how such beliefs condition forms of collective social protest. He distinguishes between two forms of egalitarianism: "the equality of political, economic, and other social rights and opportunities" and "the equality of men deriving from their intrinsic personal or human worth" (1968:413).

This second form of egalitarianism, the subject of Jayawardena's analysis, is exemplified in Shylock's insistence upon his humanity as a Jew in a Gentile world (ibid.:413). In practice, the two forms of equality are not mutually exclusive; one type or the other may be more or less developed in a particular society, or in a particular segment of a society (ibid.:414). Still, certain conditions are likely to contribute to the rise of the latter form:

> Intrinsic or human equality seems to prevail in inverse relation to the prevalence of social equality. Typically, notions of human equality are dominant in a sub-group to the extent that it is denied social equality by the wider society or its dominant class. The denial may be complete or only substantive in that actual conditions fall far short of the ideal of equal rights and opportunities proclaimed as the standard. . . . [Intrinsic equality] ideology prevails in a segment that stands in opposition to the social order that denies, or is believed to deny, to the group access to the sources of wealth, power and prestige in the society. (Ibid.:414–15)

Like the Indian plantation laborers of Guyana and the MaKah Indians of the U.S. Northwest described by Jayawardena (ibid.:415–27), Antiguan women remained politically, economically, and socially subordinate in their society in the mid-1980s, even if they held in theory the same constitutional rights as men. Women are also one group who strongly uphold the principle of human equality. This does not imply that lower-class Antiguan men do not embrace egalitarian norms; there is ample evidence that they do. I found, however, that women constantly espoused the principle of human equality in their relationships by insisting on being treated with "respect."[3] Women's egalitarianism is partially based on religious teachings, but it is also the consequence of their pragmatic experiences; women take care of one another and one another's children using female-based networks that cross social class.[4] Women value this labor and find it worthy of respect. Thus my research supports Jayawardena's hypothesis, but I find, additionally, that depending on the parties, the situation, and the context, norms regulating gender in Antigua act either in tandem with or in opposition to the principle of equality.

In the six case histories that comprise this chapter, and in the final section that specifically addresses kinship in relation to class, I demonstrate how the principles of gender hierarchy and equality mesh with law and legal processes. The cases provide further evidence for my argument that studies of kinship must encompass simultaneously the legal forms and forces of the state and the commonsense understanding of kin that evolves in local communities (Lazarus-Black 1991:119). These case studies exemplify the interaction between community norms and state forms and show that statutory rules and judicial processes governing kinship continue to frame and reshape the terms and content of contemporary family ideology and practice. I find, for example, role expectations for husbands and wives, lovers and friends, and fathers and children transcend social class. So, too, does at least anecdotal knowledge of law's strengths and limitations in respect to family strife. Not surprisingly, then, commonalities in creole family patterns outweigh class differences. A few class differences do exist: the degree of adherence to the legally sanctioned form of the family, the meaning of marriage in relation to other forms of union, and the individually determined pragmatic role of childbearing in alliance formation. Nevertheless, because class is a social relationship, class differences are tempered by such variables as gender, age and religion.

Carrying a Case for Justice: Family Ideology at the Magistrate's Court

Previously I discussed the structural, legal, economic, and ideological reasons only lower-class persons use the magistrate's court to resolve family issues. To reiterate briefly: local law stipulates that disputes over child support between unmarried persons, a very high percentage of whom are lower class, must be resolved at the magistrate's court. "Carrying a case" to one of these courts entails many inconveniences and a willingness to endure an invasion of family privacy and community gossip. The monetary costs of prosecuting a case are minimal, so that anyone can bring a suit, but the amount of support that is awarded is never enough to maintain a child. These reasons combine to keep middle-class persons from using the magistrate's court to resolve family disputes.

Indeed, the amount of child support is so low that it can make a difference only to the most indigent of women, and that fact is well known in the

TABLE 22   **Kinship Cases in St. John's and Cases of Arrears in Selected Years**

Year	Total Cases	New Cases in St. John's	Cases of Arrears
1963	1,031	N.A.	N.A.
1964	885	N.A.	N.A.
1978	2,170	N.A.	N.A.
1979	2,976	N.A.	N.A.
1980	2,733	167	2,566
1981	2,909	123	2,786
1982	2,024	165	1,859
1983	1,841	262	1,579
1984	1,492	196	1,296
1985	1,237	152	1,085
1986	1,377	117	1,260
1987	1,369	121	1,248

SOURCES: Great Britain, Colonial Office, *Antigua Report*, 1963–1964 and Magistrate's Court records.

community. Fifteen dollars a week,[5] I heard repeatedly, cannot feed a child. Moreover, if financial considerations were the primary reason women went to court, we would expect to see a sharp and steady rise in the number of cases filed after 1982, when the stipend was raised from seven to fifteen dollars. As Tables 22 and 23 show, that is not the case.

There was, however, an immediate but temporary rise in the number of requests for affiliation and maintenance in St. John's in 1983, right after the government increased the child-support stipend. As one might suspect, the publicity surrounding the change in the law encouraged some women with easy access to this court to apply for aid for the first time and others to request

TABLE 23   **Kinship Cases Adjudicated in Village Courts in Antigua, 1981–1987**

Year	Parham	All Saints	Bolans
1981	23	24	18
1982	29	28	14
1983	24	28	15
1984	12	35	17
1985	15	25	24
1986	15	20	9
1987	13	17	11

SOURCE: Magistrate's Court records.

increases in the aid they already received. Within two years, however, the number of new requests had fallen. The records reveal no radical changes in the number of new cases filed in any of the country courts.[6] Apparently neither urban nor village women were motivated to go to court for purely financial reasons. Doubtless other considerations guide their decisions to go to court.

The case histories, interviews with litigants and lawyers, and observations of trials, show women take men to court when those men violate local norms about respect, support, and appropriate relations between the sexes. Women invoke the state in the name of justice, using law and judicial processes to enact ritually the meaning, rights, and responsibilities of kin (Lazarus-Black 1991:126). Three case histories illustrate this phenomenon.[7]

Margaret Wilson, now a married woman, decided to take Johnny Thomas, a livestock farmer and butcher, to magistrate's court thirteen years after they had lived together. Margaret's child with Johnny was her fourth; her other son and two daughters were children of two earlier relationships. Margaret explained she and Johnny had lived together for more than a year, but she left him during her pregnancy because he beat her. She met her present husband when Johnny's son was just an infant. She and Mr. Wilson set up a household, although they did not marry for many years. Margaret and Johnny eventually resolved their differences, and he provided at least some financial assistance for the child.[8] At the time of the court case, Mr. and Mrs. Wilson pooled their resources to raise Johnny junior and one of Margaret's daughters. Margaret worked as a cleaning woman; her husband was retired and had a pension. This household certainly would have benefitted from regular child-support payments from Johnny, but money was not the issue that brought Margaret to court. Johnny upset Margaret because he cursed her in public:

MARGARET: I don really mind how it [money] come in. I'm not depending on that special to feed my chile. I just—I didn't really bring him just for the money. I brought him for the words that he give me. And seeing that is his chile'—why I have to get those words? I say, well, let I complain him to feed him. I didn't brought it for the money specially.

MLB: So, in other words, if he hadn't acted the way he had in the public market—

MARGARET: I didn't expect that from him!

MLB: It really was embarrassing?

MARGARET: It really was embarrassing! I was so ashamed that I had to cry. Because what really happened, right? My chile get damage at school, the Friday. He was playing ball and the ball hit him in his eye. And probably damaged the baby. And I take him to the doctor, the eye doctor from Guadeloupe. And they told me I have to make a reservation for him to go over to Guadeloupe.

Margaret explained she needed to fill a prescription for her son right away but did not have enough cash. She sent the child to his father to tell him to get the medication, but Johnny turned the boy away. At that point, she went herself:

> After he tell the chile that I said to him, "Johnny, the chile get damage at school and I take him to the doctor and the reason why I come here is because I was short of money to fulfill the prescription. So I am asking you if you could help him." As soon as I said that to him, he abuse me! [Margaret used a stream of curses here.] And I was so ashamed!

Johnny and Margaret had had a few disagreements before this incident at the public market. She annoyed him by asking for money on a previous occasion and by arranging tutoring for the boy on Saturday mornings when Johnny needed him at the market. She, in turn, was chagrined because he expected the boy to "work like a big man." But the incident that led her to court involved an infringement of a familial norm: inappropriate public abuse of a mother by the father of her child. Johnny's lack of respect, not money, persuaded Margaret to file complaints for insulting language and failure to maintain a child.

In some ways this trial was atypical; both parties hired attorneys, Margaret and Johnny were older than the usual parties in these disputes, and Johnny faced two charges. On the other hand, it was typical in that he acknowledged paternity immediately and agreed to pay fifteen dollars to support his son. Johnny pleaded guilty to using indecent language, for which he was reprimanded and discharged. In rendering his verdict, the magistrate expressed what is expected of Antiguan men concerning their treatment of their children's mothers:

> I think this incident is very unfortunate, especially since she is the mother of your child. Your lawyer has explained to me that it is not your habit to be a defendant in a criminal court. But she is the mother of your child and you should treat her with a bit more respect. In regard to this matter, I am not minded to make a fine. I'm more of a mind to reprimand and discharge, but you must treat her with respect in the future, especially as she is the mother of your child. You must not insult her in a public place. Try to be more careful in this matter in the future.

The magistrate's speech served several purposes. In the first place, "the reference to norms places the court and its decisions in a wide framework of legitimacy [and] it can camouflage any exercise of power as a simple exercise of authority" (Moore 1978:210). The invocation of norms justifies the existence of the court, the power to exercise authority, and the particular decision of the judge (ibid.:210). It removes the burden of the possible consequences of the order from the magistrate because it links an individual decision to the very essence of an orderly society. Finally, this particular lecture upholds two important tenets of creole family ideology: it asserts the principle of the equality of human beings and acknowledges community expectations of men toward women who have their children.

Ideally, men and women are treated as equals in the courts in contemporary Antigua; outside they are held to have distinctly different natures. They are different kinds of beings, associated with different spheres of activities.[9] Men and women love and need each other—children are one consequence of that fact—but because their natures are so different, men and women parent in different ways. Women nurture children, cook for them, wash them, teach them, and discipline them. Men may do some of these things, but their primary responsibility is to "feed a child," which means that the man maintains a particular kind of relationship with the child and the mother. An alliance exists in the first place because the man and the child share the same blood. Antiguan men are proud of their children and boast about their number. As another indication of their willingness to accept fatherhood, men rarely deny paternity at court, even if there are raging disagreements about how much they can afford in weekly payments. A child generally uses his or her father's surname in the community, even if not legally entitled to do so, and has the right to that man's attention and "support." Support may take the form of cash, gifts, food, clothing, school supplies, or services provided by either the man or members of his family. For example, a woman generally does not take a man to court if his mother babysits or makes clothing for her grandchild. In contrast to the law, community norms are flexible with respect to the amount and type of support due to an illegitimate child. Support may vary either in amount or kind from month to month, but it must be given with some regularity to maintain the alliance (Lazarus-Black 1991:127). For example, two of Margaret's children have the same father, a poor man who makes charcoal for a living. The charcoal man did not provide weekly cash or much time to help Margaret raise the children, but he "fed" his children as local norms prescribe:

MLB: How does he take care of them?

MARGARET: Well, he works. He do hard work. He burn coal, and I usually sell the coals. And when he get the coal money, he give them. He even start to give me money to be put into a house to build for both of dem.

In addition to support for children, family ideology holds that a man owes the mother of his child "respect." Like the notion of "feeding a child," "respect" embodies a host of expectations. It means that even after their separation, the man speaks politely about his child's mother and the people she is close to, that he acknowledges them publicly if the occasion arises, that he acts with discretion, and that he never flaunts a new relationship in her presence. Breaking these norms that govern relationships between men, women, and children[10] often results in a man being taken to the magistrate's court—as we saw quite clearly in Margaret's case. Margaret came to court for respect, not money. Her story speaks directly about principles of gender hierarchy and human equality in the lower class in St. John's. These ideas appear again in Emily and Josephine's histories.

In 1985 Emily was thirty-eight, unmarried, and had four children, each of whom had a different father. She supported herself and the children by cleaning offices two days a week and working in a private home one afternoon. Sometimes she sold candy, cigarettes, drinks, and other small items on a street corner from a tray perched on a styrofoam cooler. Her regular salary was only $95.00 per week (about U.S. $35) and she frequently asked assistance from her mother who worked at the poor house, or from her younger sister, a primary school teacher.

Her situation had improved somewhat a year later. She had a full-time cleaning job for which she earned $108.00 (about U.S. $40) per week. She also had obtained some funds from an American organization that assisted poor children. The composition of her household had changed as well. Her oldest daughter had returned to live with her and a little girl she was "minding" in 1985 had gone to live with her father's sister. One thing was unchanged: Emily had virtually no support for her children from their fathers. Yet Emily took only two of those men to court. The first man was a bartender, the second was a police officer. The other fathers were laborers.

Josephine's story reveals some interesting parallels to Emily's case. Her father, Tyronne, was a carpenter and electrician. Tyronne had no formal training, but he was a master at fixing and inventing things and could connect a house to the government electricity without detection. Tyronne ran a small shop and drove a big car. When he died in 1981, Josephine met siblings she had never known at his funeral.

Josephine's mother, Evelyn, worked as a domestic servant. Evelyn and Tyronne had not stayed together long and he stopped paying support after purchasing some baby clothes for Josephine. Evelyn became involved in several other relationships after they parted. When she married for the second time at the age of forty-four, she had had eight children by six different men. Only her first husband had consistently supported his two children. The other men, laborers and fishermen, went their separate ways. Only Tyronne, however, was taken to court. By coincidence, two other women also summoned Tyronne to court for maintenance on the same day, and the magistrate awarded each of them the maximum the law allowed.

The timing of Tyronne's cases may have been coincidental; the fact that he, two of the fathers of Emily's children, and one of Margaret's boyfriends were brought to court, was not. The case studies show that women use the courts selectively. The profiles of these men are keys to identifying ideas about family, gender, and status that explain why Antiguan women go to court and why these particular men received summons (Lazarus-Black 1991:126–27).

Consider the men Margaret, Emily, and Evelyn brought to court: the livestock farmer, the bartender, the policeman, and the electrician. These men share a stature that distinguishes them from the other fathers of Margaret's, Emily's, and Evelyn's illegitimate children. Locally, they are called "big men."[11] Margaret, in fact, specifically referred to Johnny as a "bigee bigee."[12] One becomes a big man partly through holding a respectable job with a steady income. Beyond this, a big man has won admiration from the community by virtue of his leadership qualities, command of language, intelligence, wit, education, and generosity. Big men can muster men and resources when they need to. They can maintain multiple unions, even when married, keep their women "in order," and father and "feed" many children. Big men, in short, uphold certain standards in their family relationships. They provide gifts to their wives and "outside" women and support all of their children in a manner which accords with their standing in the community.

Violating this code of behavior makes a big man an Antiguan woman's choice for a trip to the magistrate's court for a ritual shaming. The courtroom becomes for these men what Garfinkel (1965:89) calls a "degradation ceremony." When a man's name is called in court, his position as a big man is challenged. The trial indicates that he is not generous, not responsible, not a suitable father, and incapable of controlling his women.

By all accounts and my own observations, the shaming of men at the magistrates' court undeniably achieves this aim. Johnny Thomas specifically used the term "degradation" to describe his experience in court:

MLB: I think I could tell by the way you were on the stand that you were not pleased to be there?

J: No. It's in a way—in a way—a degradation of character. I mean personally, there are times that I jus give away more than fifteen dollars. In actual fact, they [Margaret and Johnny, Jr.] were getting thirty dollars, or, say, twenty-eight dollars, at the face value, every week, going into that house. There are some parents, their children have to help them without even getting an additional penny.

Johnny's feelings were not uncommon: men find it extremely embarrassing to be taken to court. That is why many of them amend their ways—at least temporarily—after a woman files a case, and that explains why some cases fall out of the system. The men who do come to court are chastised about their behavior, as Johnny was, and some are warned that they face prison if they fail to support their children. Others refuse to attend, but in that case the suit is adjudged in their absence and the effect upon their reputation in the community is the same. The shaming ceremony, then, renews and validates legally constituted kinship responsibilities while mitigating the prestige of a big man.

The court ritual that challenges a man's personal competence and his status among his peers also inverts the usual hierarchical status between men and women. When she brings a man to magistrate's court, a woman forces a conjuncture of the domestic and the public spheres; the dirty laundry is made public. During the case, she uses law, courts, forensic processes, and legal personnel to lay claim to the rights due her and her children. If only for the duration of the ritual, she is a status equal and the public spokesperson and representative for her children. Such behavior has its costs. A woman may be chided for going to court; she may be accused of "spite." Sometimes, too, a shamed big man provides even less child support after a court hearing than before. Nonetheless, the achievement of equality, the validation of rights, and the recognition of moral duty—central elements of Antiguan family ideology—are proclaimed during the trial. These constitute a vital part of the justice for which Antiguan women go to court (Lazarus-Black 1991:128).

Ironically, the expressed intent of the lawmakers—the regular provision of support for illegitimate children—is not nearly as effective as the threat or the actual performance of the shaming ceremony. As we have seen, the records show men pay child support intermittently. Most women wait weeks between receiving checks; some wait months. Those who take policemen to court face an added difficulty because officers are reluctant to hand warrants for failure to pay child support to fellow officers.

One last issue with respect to kinship cases at the magistrate's courts needs to be raised. There is a point at which a big man is too big a man to impugn in court, which accounts for the infrequency of interclass family disputes in the lower courts. At least three reasons shield upper middle-class men from the justice that lower-class women seek from the courts. First, charges of corruption against public officials occur frequently enough so that the lower class remains cynical about the justice poor people can expect at court when their opponents are wealthy and powerful people. In their view, pragmatism teaches that there is not much use in suing a middle-class man whose fancy lawyer will break your case or who is himself a friend of a friend of the judge. Second, rich and powerful men are likely to be married to rich and powerful women, who are formidable adversaries in their own right because they wield considerable influence over employment and educational opportunities in the community. Margaret Wilson, for one, told me she did not take the father of her first child to court "because he was a married man and you know, they say that if you take a married man to court, his wife gonna put you in trouble, some kinda ting, so, I never try to do it."[13] Finally, some lower-class women don't take the wealthy fathers of their illegitimate children to court because they cherish the hope that someday these men will "rediscover" their children, come to love them, and provide them with their rightful due. That hope is part of the ideology of creole family life and is crucial to understanding why an Antiguan woman has a child "for" a man.

To conclude, though a maintenance case is prima facie a request for cash, it is in fact a way to substantiate familial alliances and to shame men who purport to be big men but who break the big man's code of conduct. Nothing in the statutory code, of course, refers to big men; these cases exemplify the intersection of law and family ideology. A woman brings a case to magistrate's court to claim normative rights that regulate family, gender, and social hierarchy within the lower class. They rely on and use a literal translation of Antiguan kinship law to manage male behavior, to voice objections to their own inequality, and to reaffirm the rights of their children (Lazarus-Black 1991:129). They "carry" their cases for "justice," reversing the gender rules that instruct them to speak privately and to limit their politics to the domestic sphere.

Equality and Hierarchy at the High Court

Whereas maintenance cases reveal ideas about family and gender only within the lower class, divorce cases allow us to analyze familial beliefs and practices across class lines. In contrast to the magistrates' court, the High Court has served historically as a dispute forum for middle-class family crises. Its litigants often have property interests to protect in addition to issues of child custody and maintenance. Therefore, divorce cases not only provide insights about familial organization in all social strata but also identify norms pertaining to the division of labor and the exchange of commodities in families. Here, as in magistrates' court, family norms as well as law determine who brings complaints and when and why they do. Just as the meaning of a child-support case is tied to Antiguan notions about "feeding a child," "respect," and "big men," the meaning of divorce embodies such extralegal beliefs as "Christian union," "home," and "big women." We shall find also that the principles of human equality and gender hierarchy prevail at every rank in creole society; they establish benchmarks for just familial relationships. Thus the local divorce law, like the maintenance act, encompasses some of the central tenets of creole family ideology.

We saw earlier that women are more likely to initiate divorce than men, that they divorce most often on the grounds of desertion, and that they commonly ask for child support but not alimony, unless they are divorcing wealthy men. In the divorce cases I followed, women typically complained about several legal and extralegal matrimonial offenses, including adultery. One attorney estimated: "In 75 percent of the cases it's another woman." Another lawyer guessed adultery was the "real" reason behind every divorce he had taken to court. A young man, the father of two children, explained:

> From my own experience, men and women get along very good here in Antigua until one or the other decides to have another relationship with another woman or with another man. But to be honest, it is mostly Antiguan men—that I know, right—like to trouble a lot of women. So you always find them going out and troublin' a lot of women and that is where all the problems stem from.

The description is a very familiar one to Caribbeanists (e.g., DeVeer 1979:108; Douglass 1992:172; Senior 1991:171–73; R. Smith 1988:116–17). Still, it is an error to assume that a woman seeks counsel because her husband engaged in sexual intercourse with another woman. Discussions with members of the community uncovered very strong beliefs about proper male and proper female behavior, including social mores that tolerate a certain license for men's "playing around." Everyone agrees that men love women, and love to love women. Men take up with other women and their wives put up with it—until the man stops acknowledging their alliance. The important question for a wife is whether her husband has broken their accord by his lack of discretion, indicative of his lack of respect for her, or has violated the unwritten code between them that stipulates that he acknowledge their love with his gifts to her and to the children she has for him.[14] In other words, what brings women to magistrates' court sends them to a divorce lawyer: lack of respect, breach of familial norms, and flagrant "injustice." Mrs. Amanda Green's case history, in fact, includes two trips to magistrates' court for child support before testifying at the High Court for a divorce. Amanda's story sheds further light upon the issues with which we are concerned: expectations about marriage and a family home, inside and outside children, the flow of resources in families, the principle of human equality, the issue of respect, gender hierarchy, and Antiguan conceptions of justice.

Amanda became friendly with Evan Green, another Antiguan, while visiting her older sister in St. Croix. When they met she had already borne three children, each for a different man, but only the last child resided with her. Amanda rejected Evan's marriage proposals for several months; she was only twenty-three and felt she was still too young to marry. Eventually, however, she accepted his proposal. At first they lived in St. Croix, but Evan had trouble finding work and then they received word that his mother was ill. They returned to Antigua and settled in a rental house in the village in which Amanda had grown up. She cared for their new baby and her daughter and nursed his elderly mother. Evan found work as a carpenter in a distant village. Sometimes he slept there because of the difficulty of finding a ride home.

Several months later Amanda went to the village where Evan worked. A woman informed her that a girl in the village was pregnant with Evan's child. When she confronted him in the privacy of their home, Evan denied the baby was his. Nevertheless, he came home less frequently. Yet Amanda did not take her husband to court over that outside child:

MLB: Was it right after that child was born that you decided to take him to court?

AMANDA: No. First thing, I'll get pregnant, I tell him. I tell him you have—Dat time we have one kid, and that's Junior. I tell he if you have one outside to feed, then you have two mouths to feed inside. And I get pregnant with Polly.

MLB: On purpose?

AMANDA: On purpose. . . . Me say to he, "We prevent children to get a home—and you having children outside?" He na answer.

Thus Amanda's "revenge" for Evan's behavior consisted neither of threats to leave him nor a ritual shaming at the magistrate's court. Instead, she had the child she had been denying herself in the hope of trying to conserve cash to build a family home.

For the next two years, Evan played a role rarely discussed in the anthropological literature on Caribbean families: that of the "visiting husband."[15] He showed up occasionally to eat, sleep, change his clothes, visit with his children, and sleep with his wife—and then he disappeared for weeks. Late in 1975, however, Amanda and Evan had a serious "falling out" over his lack of attention to the family and he stopped sleeping at the house altogether. At first he continued to provide up to one hundred dollars a week for the children. The exact amount depended on how much work he had during the week. By 1981, however, Amanda had to go to Evan's place of employment to get child support. Tired of begging for assistance, behavior hardly befitting a married woman now employed and paying a mortgage, she filed and won cases at the magistrate's court on behalf of herself and the children.

Amanda always dealt with the matter of support with a characteristically Antiguan sense of justice. Once when she knew Evan had been out of work for a few months, she went to the courthouse and told the collecting officer to take his name off the list temporarily. She also personally paid bail for him on three occasions when the police threatened to take him to jail for failure to pay child support![16] On the other hand, in 1982, when she knew he was earning good money at one of the hotels but not sharing his good fortune with their children, she went back to the magistrate and asked for increases in maintenance. At that time, she relinquished her case for wife support because she was involved with another man.

Amanda filed for divorce in 1983, on the grounds of desertion, not adultery. She divorced Evan, she said, because

> he don live home. He don want to live [with me]. He don say I living back in [one of the villages] and he is not around. And I don see the use keeping somebody [keeping company with another man] and still married to him. You understand what I mean? Having a friend and still married to him.

Amanda told me the Monday of her divorce was the saddest day of her life; she had made a pledge to God to stay with her husband and she had had to break that vow. But her decision to divorce, and how and when she did, were completely in accord with the cultural logic of Antiguan marriage. Whatever his legal offenses against matrimony, Evan had blatantly disregarded several creole family norms. First, his behavior indicated that he was indifferent to her position as a "big woman"[17] in her village.

Like many lower-class Antiguan women, Amanda married only when she believed she was "grown" or "big" in the sense that she knew about life, could confidently perform the duties of a wife and mother, and felt ready to make a commitment to a man and to God. As a big woman, she was ready and entitled to run her own household. True, when she married Evan they did not yet have a "proper" home, still an important prerequisite for marriage in Antigua.[18] However, Evan was a steady worker and she was sure that they would soon acquire a house. Instead, Evan lost his job in St. Croix and they had to return to Antigua, where he divided his time between distant villages and his income between his wife, his children, his mother, and a new girlfriend. And, to add insult to injury, women in the villages were gossiping and Evan's girlfriend had the audacity to send her the message that she was "blind mice" [like a blind mouse]. Clearly Evan violated the principles of human equality and respect between husbands and wives.

Second, Evan's behavior eventually exceeded Amanda's definition of the limits of gender hierarchy. Like most women I interviewed, Amanda firmly believed wives should defer to husbands when a couple faces important decisions. She told me, for example, she would have moved to the village where Evan worked if he had asked her to, even though she much preferred to live near her own kin: "And I think, also, you supposed to live together. Not you in one place and ya husband in the next place. I don think that's fair, that's right. I always say, if I did wrong my husband and I have to bow, I would do it. But he wrong me, and he jus can't give in."

Amanda's words capture three examples of the operation of gender hierarchy in Antiguan marriage: (1) husbands usually provide the family home and have the final word about where wives and children live; (2) men regulate the amount of time, the type of labor, and the economic contributions they will make to the household; and (3) men rarely explain their comings and goings and they rarely apologize. These norms allow men to control the rhythm of the day and night, the pace of work and play, and the exchange of commodities in Antiguan families in ways that women cannot.[19] I never heard an Antiguan wife tell her husband what time to be home for dinner; she serves him when he appears. Nor is there a female counterpart to the "visiting husband." Yet as Amanda's case shows, women place limits on the principle of gender hierarchy; every person, regardless of sex, enjoys the right to command respect from others. Life in the common order teaches what is just and what is not; each woman decides for herself where the exact limits lie.

Finally, Amanda's decision to divorce was also partly motivated by Evan's having fathered an outside child during the marriage. Most Antiguan women and men readily accept outside children, unless that child is born in the midst of the marriage. (As we say, timing is everything.) A wife knows her husband will have to feed his outside child—she even grudgingly accepts that he should—but she does not want to share his wealth with additional outside children after their marriage. In Amanda's case, too, the outside child belittled her sacrifice in postponing having more children, made it impossible for them to build a "proper" home together, and caused others to treat her disrespectfully.

Amanda's lawyer, of course, kept all of this history out of the courtroom. He filed for divorce on the basis of desertion. Evan received the court papers and immediately filed a countersuit charging Amanda with adultery. His anger and charges were characteristic: men have fewer qualms about airing dirty laundry in public when they are sued or initiate divorce and are more likely to try to destroy their wives' reputations in court. In this case, however, the trial date was postponed for a year, during which time Evan withdrew his suit. He did not appear at the trial in 1985. Amanda testified Evan was "always sleeping out," that occasionally he beat her, and that they had not cohabited since 1975. She did not mention his outside child. After her testimony, Amanda's lawyer told the judge that he had filed a discretionary statement on her behalf. The judge read the document, raised his eyebrows, and then granted Amanda a divorce for Evan's desertion.[20] She retained custody of the children, but the judge reserved the question of weekly maintenance.

Amanda's case is representative of Antiguan divorces on several accounts. First, she tried a variety of alternatives to resolve her marital problems, including asking friends and relatives to speak to Evan and filing cases at magistrates' court to see if that wouldn't encourage him to amend his ways. Second, their many disagreements—most of which had little to do with the letter of the law—were handled outside the courtroom. In the end, however, their case was reconstructed so that the divorce could proceed rapidly, "civilly," and without discussion of other incidents.[21] Amanda's case was about thwarted dreams, a proper family home, the distribution of resources, adultery, outside children, lack of respect, and failure to feed lawful offspring—an accumulation of unjust behavior that transgressed the principle of human equality and the limits of gender hierarchy. Third, Amanda requested maintenance for her legitimate children and a "child of the family" who had lived with her and Evan over the years: such support was rightfully theirs. She did not request alimony, because she had a new boy friend who provided her with companionship and financial assistance for herself and a new baby.[22] Finally, this divorce was typical in that Evan's initial reaction to the case was to file a countersuit that defamed his wife's personal and moral character and threatened her status as a big woman.

Amanda is from the working class, but middle- and upper-class Antiguans share her expectations and values about marriage and family obligations. Consequently, there are similarities between Amanda's story and those of Mrs. Roberts and Mrs. Davis, two highly educated, professional, and financially secure women who were parties to divorce cases I followed.

The community was frankly shocked when Mrs. Lisbeth Roberts took her husband to court: they seemed the perfect couple. The Roberts married late in their twenties, after completing their university educations. He was an engineer working for the government, earning a substantial salary, and with friends in high places. She taught at one of the better schools. Neither had other children. They owned an elegant home and employed domestic help. Trevor Roberts worked long hours, but Lisbeth had her school duties, entertained friends, and practiced netball.

In their own home, however, Lisbeth and Trevor quarreled incessantly. The arguments began as soon as they married and escalated after the birth of their child. He insisted upon privacy in his social and business affairs and spent much time away from home. He also held very rigid expectations about women as mothers, wives, and daughters—and he found his wife inadequate in each of those roles. She was lax in her domestic duties, headstrong as a wife, dependent upon her parents, and incapable of providing a proper role model for their son. He hoped her parents might convince her to change her ways, but she seemed deaf to reason. For her part, Lisbeth found Trevor inattentive, suspected he saw other women, and resented his intrusions upon her domain—raising their child and running the family home. One day after a particularly upsetting quarrel, Trevor removed their son from school and announced he had no intention of returning to the matrimonial home. He filed for separation, and a bitter child-custody case, which was still unresolved when I left Antigua, ensued.

In the midst of the custody dispute, Lisbeth filed for divorce. At first she brought the case for mental cruelty, describing the anguish she suffered in losing the company of her child. After the papers were filed, her attorney learned Trevor was troubled about being charged with mental cruelty: it might hinder his career. The attorneys called each other and filed new papers. Lisbeth withdrew her original complaint and entered another for desertion. Trevor did not contest the second suit.

In the United States, the Roberts would have divorced for "irreconcilable differences."[23] Because they were in Antigua, they had to wait three years and prove a matrimonial offense. In actuality, their problems, like those of Amanda and Evan Green, had less to do with breaking kinship laws than they had to do with Antiguan familial and gender norms. Lisbeth and Trevor differed in their thinking about male and female domains, child rearing, and the limits of gender hierarchy. By Antiguan standards, Trevor was unusual in his avid interest in his child's daily routine and he overstepped the boundaries of a husband's familial role. From Lisbeth's perspective, his actions violated a relationship that should be based on mutual respect. Moreover, he "stole" their child! Given these circumstances, the norm that holds that a wife should conform to her husband's wishes no longer applied and it was necessary to divorce him. Lisbeth planned to ask for a substantial monthly maintenance check for their son, and, in contrast to Amanda, she asked for alimony from her wealthy husband.

The divorce case of Mr. and Mrs. Davis brought charges of both desertion and mental cruelty to the court. Henry Davis, a civil servant, sued his wife for divorce on the grounds that she treated him cruelly and that her act of changing the locks on the doors of their home justified his own act of constructive desertion. Theresa Davis, a registered nurse, fought the case: she denied committing any matrimonial offense. Theresa opposed divorce on religious grounds, but like some women who take men to magistrates' court, she was accused of "spite" for contesting the case. During the trial, Henry's lawyer charged:

> I'm suggesting this is all nonsense—that divorce is wrong in the eyes of the Lord. What you have in mind is that you don't want him to marry some one else! You don't want him, but you want to make sure nobody else is going to have him! First you say divorce is wrong except on the grounds of adultery only, then you say its wrong because the minister says its wrong. I'm suggesting you don't want him, but nobody else is going to have him. . . . This is something that is done all the time in Antigua; that if a woman doesn't want a divorce she goes and finds a church that doesn't believe in it.

All the churches in Antigua frown upon divorce,[24] but in any case, this attorney's assessment of Theresa's motives is at best superficial. Theresa Davis acted in accord with a creole sense of family justice. She came to court to protest her innocence and her actions exemplify middle-class women's use of the court as a forum to demand justice:

> Now, he was saying I should settle out of court. I tell him, "Settle what out of court?" I said, "What is there to settle out of court? You put me in court and what happened? You don't want to face the music? Look, you call the tune! Now the music is going to play!"

I interviewed both Mr. and Mrs. Davis at length. What was perhaps most striking about their marital history was Theresa's reluctance to set limits to the principle of gender hierarchy. Over the course of a very long marriage, she coped with financial debt and several outside children of whom she was unaware when she married. She moved several times to accommodate her husband's needs, grew accustomed to almost sole responsibility for the children, and, though they both had full time jobs, accepted that he alone enjoyed personal freedom in "spare" time. When she was served with divorce papers, Theresa had already resolved to live as contentedly as possible in the comfortable family home, to ignore rumors about her husband's girlfriend, and to confine her social life to activities at church. The attorney's generalization notwithstanding, religion deeply affected how she felt about marriage and about the relation between children and their fathers:

MLB: You opposed the divorce?

THERESA: Yes, because I don't really feel that it is in God's plan for people to divorce, OK? I feel that somewhere along the line there could be some reconciliation. . . . I had to put up with so much. . . . And no neighbor knows, you know? Those children did not know how much I was hurting because of their father's thing. . . . But I have told them they must respect their father no matter what. Because I have the blessing of my father. And I wouldn't like them to lose the blessing from God. Because the Bible says, "Honor thy Father and thy Mother," and they put "Father" first. So, even though—I use an expression—keep him at close distance. . . . But keep him as your father, because he is your father. Don't disrespect him.

As this passage makes clear, Theresa subscribes fully to the notion of "respect" between husbands and wives and between parents and children, to the principle of gender hierarchy, and to the belief that justice will prevail.

After several very long days of testimony, the judge disallowed Henry's charge of cruelty but granted his divorce for constructive desertion, citing the petitioner's inability to enter his home as a suitable reason for his finding a new one. Theresa's lawyer assessed the case as a "policy judgment": an example of a judge stretching the letter of the law to grant a divorce that would never have been proffered when divorce was less acceptable in Antiguan society.

To conclude, divorce cases, like paternity suits, reveal the continuing dialectic between kinship legalities and illegalities and between just and unjust treatment of familial members. They illustrate, too, how laws and kinship norms intersect. Today, as in the past, kinship law and judicial processes shape, as they are shaped by, family and gender ideology in the common order. Commonsense understanding of matrimony, home, and big women are integral to the making and breaking of Antiguan marriages; but so are the divorce law and the discretionary power of judges. Shared codes and norms foster commonalities in family ideology and practice within and across the social classes. Throughout these islands,[25] people share beliefs about the different natures of men and women, about the "fact" of gender hierarchy, about what constitutes just familial behavior, and about the equality of human beings, regardless of sex, before the court. Are there, then, class differences in family beliefs or practices?

Family and Class

Over the years, two opposing viewpoints on the relationship between class and kinship in the English-speaking Caribbean have emerged. One finds in the vast majority of earlier work the argument that middle-class people marry and that lower-class people fail to legalize their relationships. Many of these studies focused on lower-class families and researchers' attentions were drawn to the question of why West Indians said they favored marriage but failed to live in wedlock. Explanations for this phenomenon stressed the conflict between African and European values, the absence of the norm of legitimacy itself, the dire effects of slavery and poverty, migration, and the tendency of the lower class to generate its own institutions and values. A "middle-class" kinship pattern was then differentiated from a "lower-class" kinship pattern (e.g., Goode 1960; Henriques 1953; Herskovits 1958; Rodman 1971; M. Smith 1962; Patterson 1967). In the second view, which treats class, gender, and kinship as intersecting phenomena, the ensuing analyses become more complex (e.g., Alexander 1973, 1984; Austin 1979, 1984; DeVeer 1979; Douglass 1992; Fischer 1974b; Lazarus-Black 1990a; Moses 1981; Schneider and Smith 1973; Senior 1991; R. Smith 1978, 1982a, 1987, 1988; Sutton and Makiesky-Barrow 1981). My research in Antigua confirms that "class" is a necessary but insufficient cause to explain the alternative patterns that exist in this creole kinship system. As in Jamaica, "gender difference is highly elaborated" (Douglass 1992:9), but so too are the influences of religion (cf. Austin-Broos 1987, 1991; Clarke 1966:76; Fischer 1974a, 1974b; Roberts and Sinclair 1978) and aging (e.g., Glazier 1983; Wilson 1969, 1973). I consider three class differences and demonstrate how the principles of human equality and gender hierarchy, concern for individual salvation, and maturity affect those differences and thereby contribute to the systematic character of creole family life within and between the social classes.

In the first place, the so-called middle-class pattern, in which people marry legally and then have legitimate children, differs for men and women (Lazarus-Black 1990a:263).[26] The Davises are a good example: she had no children prior to her marriage while he had several. Moreover, after the marriage Theresa had children only for her husband while Henry fathered children with lower-class women. His life history presents an Antiguan example of the West Indian "dual marriage system" described by R. Smith (1978, 1982a, 1987, 1988). Moreover, the same behavior occurred in our working class couple, Amanda and Evan Green. Amanda bore a child for another man only after seven years of separation from Evan.

The two patterns, male and female, are partly consequences of very different cultural notions about what makes a "good woman" and what makes a "good man." Antiguans told me a good woman has only one sexual partner, takes care to see her children are respectful, very clean, and properly attired, and is kind and generous to her family and friends. She never "knuckles" [cuckolds] her man, she is not a "walkabout," and she refrains from gossiping.[27] A good man, on the other hand, is not subjected to so many behavioral strictures.

Quite simply, he is someone who "sees about his family." In part, too, the patterns differ because very different sanctions apply when people fail to conform to the ideal. Many women adhere to the rule that commands them to postpone having children until after they are married because of the severe repercussions that follow if they do not. Some of those sanctions apply to all women irrespective of social class, others are class specific. For example, any woman who becomes pregnant in Antigua is forced to leave school. If she is unmarried, she is initially ostracized by members of the community, and, depending on the church she attends, she may be "read" out of the congregation, denied the right to participate in certain church functions, or prohibited from holding office. Middle-class and elite women face additional sanctions. An older, middle-class woman whose sister had had an illegitimate child told me, "Well, if a girl got pregnant they would ship them out, send them to Dominica, to Britain, to cover up so society wouldn't know. It was as if it were a sin to have a girl 'fall,' as we call it, or to have an illegitimate child. It would ruin the family."[28]

Thus if they could afford it, middle-class parents sent pregnant daughters abroad. Alternatively, they arranged for an illegal abortion. If she kept the child, they might refuse to finance her education. Finally, in contrast to her lower-class sisters, an unmarried middle-class mother might find she jeopardized her future marital choices. Lower-class men think it is "natural" for a girlfriend to have a child, but middle-class men, people told me, are less willing to support other men's children. Unfortunately, I am unable to examine what consequences contemporary middle- and upper-class women now face in choosing motherhood without matrimony because none of my middle-class friends, acquaintances, or interviewees, or their female siblings, had a child out of wedlock during my fieldwork in 1985–87. I knew of one case in which the mother of a middle-class man was raising his outside child by a lower-class woman.[29]

In contrast to women's treatment, neither parents nor the formal institutions of society sanction men if they father children out of wedlock. They are not denied an education, they do not find their future careers jeopardized, they are not ostracized by the community, and the act of fathering a child has bearing on their church affiliation only if they are members of a fundamentalist sect. Indeed, as we have seen, fathering children contributes to a man's prestige as a big man in his community. In short, reproductive patterns in Antigua must be differentiated both by class and by gender.

A second difference between the classes concerns the meaning and function of marriage in relation to other forms of union. As we saw in Chapter 6, the churches have been only marginally and temporarily successful in raising the marriage rate, and unable to reverse the relationship between reproduction and marriage. Still, a singular perspective about the rights and duties of kinship permeates sermons that accompany baptisms, godparenthood, confirmations, marriages, funerals, weekly services, and Sunday school classes. Not surprisingly, then, people in all social strata in Antigua talk about religion when they discuss why they marry and are reluctant to divorce. But depending on class and gender, they offer different interpretations of the meaning of marriage and its relation to religion.[30]

I found that most lower-class Antiguans want to marry before they die in order to end life in a state of grace. One woman I knew well, a mother of three who had been involved in a visiting union with the same man for years, had difficulty at first in answering my question about the difference between a marriage and a long-term, nonlegal union. She paused for a long time and then decided she couldn't tell me, but "I *have* to be married before I die." I returned to the question later and she then reflected on the fact that her grandmother was constantly nagging her about why her boyfriend didn't marry her: "Maybe because she's a Christian and they believe you should get married. So I don't really know why you have to get married. Maybe it's a sin not to marry and to live with a man. . . . I believe so. I believe it is." This comment initially surprised me because my friend infrequently attended church and had previously seemed indifferent to religion. I came to understand that she believed that although a man and woman need not belong to, or be raised in the same church, what was important was that they both be Christian. Marriage sanctified by the church is an important component within the more general beliefs about what it means to "live a Christian life." Those beliefs mark a crucial difference for Antiguans between the long-term, nonlegal union and one that is legitimate both in the eyes of the state and the church. As one fellow told me, "Nobody wants to die and feel he's got some big sin on his head." In short, marriage becomes increasingly important in the lower class as people become older because each individual, regardless of sex, wants to make peace with his or her God.[31]

Middle- and upper-class Antiguans share this genuine concern for their soul, but they try to marry before or soon after they have children to secure their status in this world as well as in the next. Lisbeth Roberts, for example, believed in marriage for very pragmatic reasons:

> A long-term, nonlegal union puts the woman at a disadvantage because she is generally the one at a lower salary. She is the one bearing the children, and in terms of financial status in the home, she does not have a steady footing. She is dependent on the man, she has to be, or otherwise her next relationship *has* to involve a man who can give her financial support. So she may form a relationship not for any reason other than this financial support. Her ability to improve herself, educationally, is reduced, if not curtailed totally.

A prosperous male attorney provided this explanation of why people in his social class marry:

w: I think you have to break it down by subdivisions. For the upper middle and upper classes there are basically two reasons: First, it is expected of them. That's the first thing. It is the paramount thing. It is expected that one day they will. You could say it is a family tradition. And the second thing is prestige. It's the prestige of being Mrs. So-and-So. It goes with the accountants, lawyers, doctors, people like that. . . .

mlb: Why does it give status? In what way?

w: It's that you are looked upon differently in society if you are married. You can be accepted into certain clubs and associations, and into church life. And you know the church plays a very important role in this society. Married women are more readily accepted in certain categories of the church. Religion plays a very important role from top to bottom in our society. Prestige is an all-embracing term—it includes all of these things.

Lower-class Antiguan women do speak about the economic advantages of marriage when they are specifically asked, but in contrast to one sample of lower-class women in Jamaica (DeVeer 1979), I did not find financial security was foremost in their minds when they talked about getting married. More often than not, they delayed weddings until other things, like proper housing and schooling for the children, were taken care of. Lower-class men and women said getting married was one thing people did as they became "big people," but everyone denied that you had to be married to be a big man or a big woman. Middle-class Antiguans, in contrast, see marriage as a necessary attribute of a respectable family life, as they do in Jamaica (Alexander 1973, 1978, 1984; Austin 1979, 1984; Douglass 1992; R. Smith 1978, 1982a, 1987, 1988).

Thus the meaning of marriage shifts from its symbolic identity as a sign of grace and as an attribute of the person in the lower class to that of a sign of grace and of the hierarchical status of the family in the middle class. Members of different social strata differ in terms of the meaning and practice that religion and religious symbolism occupies in their everyday lives, and therefore marriage, a religious sacrament, will be differently evaluated (Fischer 1974a:9; Roberts and Sinclair 1978:17–19). Regardless of their class, however, Antiguan women, like those of Providencia (Wilson 1973:100–104), are much more likely than men to attend church regularly and to take charge of all the family celebrations at the church (baptisms, weddings, confirmations, and funerals). They are therefore much more likely to be intimately acquainted with their minister and to be subject to his gentle, or not so gentle, prodding to marry (see also Justus 1981). Finally, women are genuinely concerned with providing a good example, a Christian example, for their children. In my experience, they were also far more likely than men to cite religious and familial reasons as to why they want to marry. A woman attorney told me:

> I think people feel that if they don't marry there is a taint on the relationship, that it is immoral. And I suppose I will pass on that to my children—though of course I can't determine that they will accept my morals! (laughs) And then you have the case where the couple have been living together for years and everything is good. And the pastor comes to see them and says, "Why don't you get married?" And then they get reborn and they decide to marry. And then they say that's when the trouble started! And thirdly, there may be children involved. And they want to make sure that before they die the children have got a name.

Antiguan men also want to save their souls, and they agree that it is preferable for children to "grow" under the auspices of a married couple. Every male attorney told me that people in Antigua married because of religion and for respectability. Similarly, in Barbuda, fishermen, construction workers, and two ministers of religion told me that men marry "after a while" for religion and for the sake of "respect," for the children. However, men also have gender-specific reasons for marrying. Johnny Thomas, for one, provided this explanation as to why he planned to wed someday:

MLB: Do you think it is important to legally marry?

JOHNNY: Yes, I would say so.

MLB: Why?

JOHNNY: Well, I think that certain economic reasons. I think it's a good thing.

MLB: For certain economic reasons? Could you explain that?

JOHNNY: I think it, it helps exercise some control on the expenditure. I think other people, like other women, are apt to— Like fear of getting a child for a married man and so on. And it sort of protect you in a way. It does advise certain things.

Men of diverse socioeconomic backgrounds told me they married, or plan to marry, to get their economic affairs in order. They were well aware of the fact that because of the kinship codes, marriage confers a way for men to channel resources in specific directions. Like a will, marriage may "legitimize" behavior that departs from community norms. For some, it is a way to break a financial relationship with an "outside" woman.[32]

Finally, my observation is that whatever their class, Antiguan men feel ambivalently about marriage because it "tames" their nature and threatens their independence. One man involved in a divorce case I followed told me he had eventually married his girlfriend, the mother of two of his children, because he figured that it was finally time he "settled down."[33] Most men expect to marry eventually, but they are wary of the demands of wives on their cash and their time. Their ambivalence is expressed in story after story about how well couples get along until they marry, as mentioned in the comment by the woman attorney. A Barbudan man explained his theory about why relations between husbands and wives deteriorate:

MLB: You said a lot of times those who are not married do better than those who are. Why is that?

M: Those tend to hold better because you are bound by love. When you go to church you are bound by law. They know the fellow bound by law walks more easily, from my point of view. When they are bound by love, they don't walk. The ladies are a little more lenient if he wants to sow a few wild oats. He may sow a few wild oats and then go back home.

MLB: Is it at the point of marriage that she will no longer allow him to, as you say, sow his wild oats?

M: [nods.] Well, when they are not married and he goes out to sow a few wild oats, she either has to take him back or she has to let him go and she probably wouldn't want him to go, especially if she has children for him.

MLB: You said he is more likely to walk if he is married?

M: It is more likely that she will drive him away, fussing with him about this and that, so he goes.

In this account, marriage rules contradict a love that is unruled, natural. Marriage poses a most difficult and contradictory demand on Antiguan men: to become "too tame" is antithetical to man's nature and makes him vulnerable to caustic teasing. Thus, loving, having children, and getting married are quite separate activities that sometimes conflict because the culture simultaneously accepts a view of kinship manifest in the institutions of church and state and concedes that it is against man's nature to live by such codes. Perhaps this explains, too, why Antiguans, in contrast to middle- and upper-class Jamaicans (Alexander 1984:154–58; Douglass 1992:142), so infrequently told me that they marry specifically "for love."[34]

A third "class" difference in familial practices involves the alternative strategies people use to muster social, political, and economic resources as well as such intangible assets as "name" and "reputation." Today, as in the past, elite and middle-class Antiguans embrace marriage as a strategy for building alliances. Because marriage is sanctioned by the church, which gives both families its blessing, and the state, which protects the couple's property interests, it remains a highly desirable and useful way to elevate reputation and the family fortune. As Theresa Davis told me: "The people who own big businesses wouldn't want their children to marry somebody very down." She couldn't think of any marriages between men and women of radically different class backgrounds. On the other hand, lower-class women know that marriage restricts their ability to exercise certain options. Once married, they must rely on the resources of their own kin group and that of their husband's. Unmarried women, in contrast, have much greater leeway to choose their own "friends." Indeed, the severe strictures upon their activities and movements explain some women's desire to postpone marriage.[35]

Reproduction, of course, offers an alternative strategy for constructing alliances and one that spans each of the social classes. In the special sense that Mauss (1967) understood when he wrote about the nature of gifts and exchange in primitive societies, children are gifts in Antigua. Lévi-Strauss (1969) notwithstanding, a child, not a woman, is a gift that begins an alliance that is—at least theoretically—"forever." This is true for people in every socio-economic rank in creole society. Blood ties never "break," although blood can eventually "wash out" if a person is not careful.

Gender differences with respect to the role that children play in the formation of individual alliances are relatively clear-cut. As in Tortola (Dirks and Kerns 1976), Antiguan women always speak of having a child "for a man," and they characterize their children as their "insurance," emphasizing the open-ended character of the ties between their children, their men, their own, and their men's kin. As an astute friend explained:

MLB: Why does a woman have a child for a man?

S: Sometimes for love. Sometimes because of the man's position. Society.

MLB: Tell me about that.

S: OK. It might be for a family name. Not necessarily a rich family, but a big family, widespread throughout Antigua. . . . so it's nice having a child for him, a part of the B clan. . . . She can say my son is a B . . .

Children are a woman's wealth from the moment they are born.[36] They are links to a community of other women and men and caretakers in one's old age. (There was only one home for the destitute elderly in Antigua in 1987.) As we have seen, men also desire children and rarely deny paternity. Yet their children become more politically and economically important to them later in life, when they are themselves adults upon whom a big man can call. Through these children, a man earns respect from his peers (Wilson 1973:150).

In conclusion, some class differences in beliefs and practices of family life in Antigua can be discerned: on the whole, members of the middle class are more likely to marry before the birth of several children; the significance and meaning of marriage as a civil, religious, and economic institution changes for people at different ranks of society; and the pragmatic question of how to build alliances that will spread one's name and reputation is answered differently by persons in different classes. The state buttresses class differences by distinguishing between married and unmarried persons, and, until 1987, between legitimate and illegitimate children in law. Nevertheless, the cultural rules that contend men and women have different natures, the idea of being a Christian, belief in the equality of human beings, and knowledge about and access to kinship law, mitigate the effects of class differences.

A Final Note: Cases, Courts, and Creolization

Cases for affiliation and maintenance, like divorce suits, dramatize similarities and differences between the ideal of kinship contained in law and sanctioned by the church and the everyday beliefs and practices of men and women who participate in the creole kinship system of the common order. These cases reflect a variety of conflicts—only some of which have to do with kinship law or the reasons for strife found in the quantitative data from the court records. As we have seen, maintenance cases rarely have to do simply with money, and divorces infrequently concern genuine desertion, but both suits are constructed so that they seem to fall within the relevant courts' jurisdictions. Unwittingly, judges mediate disputes that entail such fundamental issues as human equality and the limits of gender hierarchy in the organization of familial roles. Nevertheless, their participation is a vital component of the creole family system.

Antigua's kinship courts, like its kinship cases, manifest the dichotomy between "colonial" and "creole" (E. Brathwaite 1971). True to their colonial origins, the magistrates' courts continue to pass orders to support illegitimate children, and they keep those children out of the poor house. Similarly, the High Court divides families and their property when evidence of matrimonial offenses is brought to public attention. And yet both courts now serve distinctly creole purposes. Paternity court functions in an especially important capacity for lower-class women because having children is the primary vehicle of alliance formation among the poor. Lower-class women use the magistrates' court to declare publicly alliances between men and their children and to shame men who purport to be big men but fail to conform to the big man's standard of behavior. Their belief in human equality and dignity gives them the courage to go to court; but they do not go there until men pass the limits of gender and intraclass hierarchical privilege. Theirs is a distinctly creole act, an act exemplifying the dialectical interaction between state forms and community norms. Similarly, because the High Court judge has discretion, people are now likely to obtain divorces when they wish to break their marriage contracts, despite lawmakers' refusal to rewrite the divorce law.

This analysis allows us to answer why Antiguan women participate heavily in kinship legalities. Lower-class women take men to court to right violations of norms that govern family, gender, and status hierarchy in the community.

These norms are shared by their middle-class sisters, but feelings of shame and fear about losing one's reputation preclude middle-class women from using the lower courts. Much more so than their lower-class sisters, these women learn to suffer silently. On the other hand, because marriage is the preferred form of alliance formation in the middle class, they are more likely to have legitimized their unions. If all else fails, the High Court allows them to dissolve their unions and fixes property settlements more equitably. Women may also prefer to crystallize their marital status at High Court because their culture places great emphasis on sexuality and "availability," whereas their religion frowns on both. Finally, the codes defining crimes of kinship—such as failure to support, desertion, cruelty, and adultery—may in fact be activities that men engage in more frequently than women. If so, then law enables women to prosecute and makes men defendants. Women's lawyers then help them to redefine their complaints "civilly" and without airing too much "dirty laundry" in public.

The changing functions of the courts and the role they play in ordering contemporary familial relationships are consequences of the historical transformation implied by the distinction between *colonial* and *creole*. After Antigua's independence in 1981, lawmakers began rewriting local kinship laws and readjusting legal processes to bridge the gap between the statutes and local conceptions about which ties create families and what meanings are attached to such relationships. Legislation to enable men to acknowledge legally illegitimate children, to protect such children's inheritances, and to end discrimination based on birth status offers further evidence of creolization.

9

The Present and Future
of Kinship Legalities

All these barriers were there because you didn't go to this
school, because you were born out of wedlock you can't
do most things and it use to create a lot of confusion in the
environment. Take for instance, in the villages, if you went
to Grammar School and your neighbor didn't go, it's a lot of
trouble you were having daily with those two parents
especially if they were friends when they were small. One start
to boo the other, "Look where my son is" and so on.
Sometimes they even say they are going to work obeah on
you. All these things used to happen. Confusion on
confusion because you were born in wedlock and could go to
a big school and these things must be stopped and every
child must be considered the same way.

—Antigua and Barbuda, House Debate, 4 December 1986

In a momentous synthesis at the end of 1986, the Parliament of Antigua and
Barbuda legally banished bastardy and made "illegitimacy" legitimate. Three
laws changed profoundly the interrelationship between kinship legalities and
illegalities in these islands.

The Status of Children Act,[1] and two companion measures, the Births Act[2]
and the Intestate Estates Act[3] herald the beginning of a new and third era in

the history of creole class, kinship, and gender relations. These bills redefine centuries-old kinship relationships and restructure the duties, obligations, and property rights of kin. For the first time, discrimination against a person on the basis of birth status is now illegal, men can acknowledge their illegitimate children by complying with a simple procedure, and all children so recognized inherit from their fathers' estates. Because some 80 percent of the children in these islands are born out of wedlock, these bills bear on the lives of a great many people.

In this chapter, I explain why these statutes and the events that contextualize their passage mark a critical turning point in the history of Antiguan family organization and in the use of family law as an instrument of class, kinship, and gender relations. Viewed historically and ethnographically, these changes in Antigua's kinship laws not only mark the evolution of the legal definition of family and the functions the state assigns kinship law but also signal changes in the character and forms of resistance to state power (cf. Foucault 1979; Abu-Lughod 1990; Stoler 1985, 1989).

The recent effort to banish bastardy belongs to the long struggle in Antigua for a more equitable division of labor and resources, representative government, and political autonomy (cf. Henry 1983, 1985, 1992). Examining the events surrounding passage of the latest kinship codes, I find that today, as in the past, family law reflects the socioeconomic backgrounds, religious interests, and political concerns of those who frame them. As in previous chapters, I examine the relationship between the political and economic dominance of particular groups and legislated rules and contend with how statutes interact with, but do not fully displace, norms and normative practices. In the case of the most recent legislative changes, however, actions by married women, people not normally influential to the law-making process in Antigua, were pivotal in the effort to banish bastardy and reconstitute the relationship between families and the state. The question centered on equal rights, an issue lawmakers thought noncontroversial, given the country's history of slavery, but which actually proved complex because kinship systems fundamentally affect the status of gender relations, as well as blood ties and property rights. In the reform of the bastardy laws, ideas about relationships between men and women, tempered by references to Christian ideals, influenced the content of the new kinship laws and the history of their passage (Lazarus-Black 1992:864–67). As we shall see, the principles of individual equality and gender hierarchy mediated the content and process of lawmaking, the dialectic between power and resistance.

The Context for Reforming the Kinship Statutes

The gradual transfer of political power from the planters began around 1918 with the first attempts to organize workers, raise wages, and repeal the Contract

Act. Carmody (1978) demonstrates how Antigua's long tradition of village organization and leadership served as the blueprint for the later development of trade unions and political parties. Leaders of the Ulotrichian Universal Union (1915) and the Antigua Progress Union (1918) provided welfare services for their members and served as unofficial bargaining representatives for workers in their continuing attempts to improve wages and working conditions on the estates before unions became legal (1978:155, 164). Meanwhile, posts in the civil service and commerce in Antigua were slowly filled by children of former indentured servants from Portugal, traders from the Middle East, and people from the working class who achieved social mobility primarily through teaching, the professions, and the church (Henry 1983b, 1985; Lowes 1993).

Throughout the 1930s, the world economy sank into depression and the price of sugar dropped dramatically. Antiguans faced severe hardships and violence seemed imminent. The British, alarmed at the possibility of open rebellion in its West Indian colonies, sent a Royal Commission to investigate.[4] The Moyne Commission arrived in Antigua in December 1938. One of the members, Sir Walter Citrine, held a public meeting in which he proposed the formation of a labor union. Two weeks later, the Antigua Trades and Labour Union was born (*Antigua and Barbuda Independence* 1981:15). The union was officially registered, and thus legitimated, on 3 March 1940. It negotiated a 50 percent increase in daily wages for its striking workers that same year (Henry 1985:82–87; Tunteng 1975:36–42). At first, union officials concentrated on organizing workers in the sugar industry. Later, they organized dock workers in St. John's and established units in the villages to bring self-employed small farmers and laborers into the organization (N. Richards n.d.:6–7). Some union leaders then moved directly into the political arena and formed the Antigua Labour Party. The party platform was partly inspired by the British Labour Party and partly by Marcus Garvey, because George Weston, an Antiguan, played a central role in the Garvey movement (Reisman 1964:21). During the 1940s, both the party and the union concentrated their efforts on improving conditions for the working people (Henry 1983b:297).

In 1951, the same year that saw a major strike by cane workers against the Antigua Sugar Syndicate,[5] Professor Simon Rottenberg published his lecture on "The Economy of Antigua." Sugar was still the principal crop, export, and source of employment (see Table 24). The 1945 census of agriculture in the Leeward Islands, for example, had found 3,196 farms of one acre or more in size in Antigua and sugar was the principal crop of 2,159 of them. Moreover, of 16,700 acres in crop, 12,600 harvested sugar (Rottenberg 1951:851). In addition to their reliance on a single crop, Rottenberg found a people living "at very low levels of income." Indeed, he continued, even "the 'rich' of Antigua are not very well-to-do" (ibid.:851, 854). Adult males working at the Antigua Sugar

TABLE 24   **Composition of Employed Labor Force of Antigua, 1951**

Industry	Percentage
Sugar[a]	49
Cotton[a]	27
Fishing	2
Manufacturing	12
Construction	4
Transportation	3
Trade	8
Services	17
Government (including work relief)	10
Domestic service	4
Other	3
Not classified	5

SOURCE: Adapted from Rottenberg 1951:854. These percentages do not add up to 100 percent, but Rottenberg offers no explanation for the discrepancy. Perhaps the figures reflect Antiguans' tendency to work several different jobs.
[a] With or without ground provisions.

Factory earned $10.67 per week; females earned $4.36 per week. About one in four Antiguans was unemployed. Young men drifted in the towns, resisting work in the cane fields "largely because of the low social prestige which attaches to this work, and, in some cases . . . to hold out for artisan work of a particular class for which they consider themselves qualified" (ibid.:853). Antigua's future deeply concerned Rottenberg, for productivity on the island was seriously low. He concluded: "It is probably true that no economy dominated by agriculture can support a population as thickly settled as Antigua's at anything but a low standard of living" (ibid.:853). Yet 1951 was also the year Antiguans finally won universal adult suffrage and increased political representation.[6]

Samuel Smith, the working man whom we met earlier, understood well how critical these changes were:

> In my mind, 1951 got to be the best year since the end of slavery. What happen that year set the stage for what was going to come. The union was also doing other serious business. It was advancing in politics. By then the Council had nominated members—planters—and elected members—from the union. The nominated members outnumbered the elected ones by three. The union got the Council to add three more seats to the elected side and got the number even. That was also when the rule was changed so that you could vote at age twenty-one, whether you could read and write or not. When the Council hold the elections in 1951 and the union got all the elected seats, the two sides really start to square up. (Smith and Smith 1986:149–50)

In 1956, the union won all eight of the elected council seats. The elected membership of the council increased from eight to ten in 1961.

Beginning in the 1960s, Antigua's economy moved away from rigid dependency on the agricultural sector and towards the service industries and tourism (Challenger 1981:13).[7] Table 25 suggests how much has changed economically since 1951.

Today, tourism is the country's biggest industry, providing employment for some five thousand people (*Antigua and Barbuda Independence* 1981:7). The government, however, remains the largest single employer, accounting for about 30 percent of the total employed work force.[8] Significantly, a large percentage of the government's payroll, almost 55 percent in 1982, represents payments to temporary laborers. Unemployment rates remained at about 20 percent in the period from 1978 to 1982 (World Bank 1985:3, 4).

Foreign businessmen and expatriates play important roles in the nation's economy, comprising an influential component of Antigua's economic elite. Between 1977 and 1982, for example, foreign savings financed approximately 60 percent of Antigua's total investments. Most of this reflected the flow of private capital into tourist and energy development and borrowings on commercial terms (ibid.:2). These entrepreneurs and investors are absent from the official political process (Henry 1983b:299).

A constitutional conference in London in 1966 was the occasion for the development of the first plans for limited autonomy from Britain. In 1969, Antigua and Barbuda became an Associated State with control over internal affairs but with defense and all foreign relations under British supervision. Almost immediately after this event, however, the islands were thrown into turmoil. Barbuda, unhappy in its relationship with Antigua, attempted to secede (Berleant-Schiller 1988:124–30). Next, the leaders of the Antigua Trades

TABLE 25   **Employed Labor Force by Economic Sector, 1981**

Economic Sector	Percentage
Agriculture, livestock, fishing	9.0
Mining and quarrying	.3
Manufacturing	7.4
Electricity, gas, and water	1.5
Construction	11.1
Distributive trades (hotels and restaurants)	22.4
Transport, storage, communications	11.1
Finance, banking, and business services	3.4
Other services	33.8
Total	100.0

SOURCE: Adapted from World Bank 1985:51.

and Labour Union disagreed, and George Walter and his followers created a separate union, the Antigua Workers Union (AWU), and a new political party, the Progressive Labour Movement (PLM). The PLM won the election of 1971 but subsequently lost favor (Sanders 1984; Henry 1983b, 1985), and the Antigua Labour Party returned to power. The Afro-Caribbean Liberation Movement party, whose leadership was strongly influenced by scholar, artist, and political activist C. L. R. James, offered an alternative political and economic agenda beginning in the 1970s and entered electoral politics in 1980. It has not as yet succeeded in gaining mass support (Henry 1992).

In contrast to earlier government by British appointees and planters, then, the contemporary political leadership is Antiguan born and locally educated. They are people who have "come up": the sons and daughters of overseers, peasant farmers, artisans, plumbers, shipwrights, stevedores, and clerks (Henry 1983, 1985; Lowes 1993). Moreover, a surprising number of them held jobs such as carpenter, artisan, time keeper, secretary, and clerk before assuming their posts in Parliament.[9] The exemplar is V. C. Bird, Sr., the Prime Minister, who has served continuously as chief executive since 1961, with the exception of 1971–76. Bird was born out of wedlock in an Antiguan slum, which meant that a secondary school education was out of the question "both because it was expensive and the schools did not permit entry to illegitimate children" (*Antigua and Barbuda Independence* 1981:28). He and his associates now in Parliament were active in the labor disputes and strikes of the depression, led the fight to legalize the unions, helped write Antigua's successive constitutions, and brought the nation to independence.[10] Those lawmakers are familiar not only with the commonsense understanding of family in Antiguan communities but also with the plight of illegitimate children (Lazarus-Black 1992).[11] Moreover, it was common knowledge in the legal community that Jamaica, Trinidad, and Barbados, nations with kinship histories similar to Antigua's, had revised their statutes to end discrimination against illegitimate children.[12] Soon after independence, the Antiguan political elite imagined a new role for kinship law in state reconstitution (Lazarus-Black 1992:886–87).

Restructuring the Kinship Codes: The First Debate about Illegitimacy

Antigua's newly independent government included a Status of Children Act on its list of "priority legislation" in 1982.[13] The solicitor general and his assistants wrote the first drafts of the Status of Children Act and Births Act the following year. The bills made all the rights, privileges, and obligations of children born out of wedlock identical to those of children born in legal unions and provided a procedure by which men might readily identify their illegitimate offspring. Neither bill addressed directly the subject of inheritance. By implication, however, any child legitimated by his father's signature on a certificate at the courthouse under the Births Act might inherit equally with the progeny of a marriage. Having secured the approval of the cabinet, and following usual procedure, the bills were then introduced to the House of Representatives for debate.

The transcript of the first parliamentary debate reveals the representatives immediately understood the overtly political significance of the newly proposed kinship codes. Champions of the bills made the issue of human equality their central argument. Proponents claimed the statutes protected individual rights and were just alternatives to discrimination based on birth status that had served the old social hierarchy. The attorney general declared that "when this bill is passed into law; it will be one of the most important pieces of legislation which this House would have passed" (Antigua and Barbuda, House Debate,

6 December 1984). Several legislators stated explicitly that kinship law could be wielded as a political tool and an instrument of class relations. One enthusiast, for example, called the bill "the outcome of the social revolution that started in 1939" with the efforts to legalize labor unions (ibid.). Members of the House recounted their own memories of illegitimate children being excluded from high schools on the island, cutting off an important route for social mobility. One recalled:

> Mr Speaker, the church and the school, especially secondary school, first started to get rid of this thing and I am going to refer to our church, the Moravian Church, because some years ago when I was small, well I happened to be one of the fortunate ones to be born in wedlock so I was baptized during the service . . . but the bastard children were baptized before the service. You could not mix them up at all. And the mothers who were married were blessed at a special service with a special hymn. And the mothers for the bastard children didn't get any blessing. (Ibid.)

The lawmakers also found practical value in the bills because they removed the obstacles and embarrassment people faced when they tried to secure documents to travel and work overseas. As one representative declared: "There have been too many cases of people who want to get their green card not being able to get it because of the fact that they were so-called bastards." Supporters also identified these measures with "progressive thinking." Even the leader of the opposition political party agreed "with certain principles" of the bills (ibid.).

In addition to evaluating the overtly political implications of recasting the kinship codes, the debate provided Antiguan lawmakers an opportunity to consider what familial norms and practices the bills ignored or actually undermined. Perhaps inadvertently, the discourse about kinship codes in the House drew to national attention how the newly proposed system of kinship legalities impinged upon the flourishing system of illegalities. A leader in the opposition political party, for example, concurred that it was unjust to refuse illegitimate children access to secondary schools, but he found some shortcomings in the proposed legislation. First, the lawmakers needed to amend procedures to accommodate the case of children born after their fathers' died. More importantly, they failed to address the problem of men who were "knuckled" or who were "given" children not their biological offspring:

> You know what can happen in some of these countries—that a child sometimes really—it might not be your father. It might be your mother, but that mother give that child to that particular father. But then, some of the parents— These are real facts, because some of the grandfathers and grandmothers would not accept those kinds of things. Because even if it is a fact that it is your child, you know how parents go sometimes. They say, Well look, I would not really use the word "knuckle" but I would have to say this. That sometimes the grandparents feel that that person [woman] was [not] a straightforward person to their husband. And if that child

belonging to that particular father, you know how it is, they have doubts in their mind. I am not going to let him inherit anything out of my will.

Mr. Speaker, Sir, you are dealing with a situation where I know you are going to have a lot of critics . . . because when you have a bastard child to have the same right as a lawful child to inherit what you have, I think you are giving a license to a lot of people to do some illegal things in this country. (Ibid.)

Antiguans use the term *knuckling* when one of the parties in a long-term, socially acknowledged relationship takes a lover. Someone who is knuckled might be married, living with someone, or in an established visiting union. People say that sometimes when a woman knuckles a man and becomes pregnant, she "gives" that child to her steady companion regardless of the child's biological paternity. If she is married, in fact, she is encouraged to do so by an Antiguan statute that declares that a married woman's child is her husband's child unless he proves a case of adultery against her.[14] If an Antiguan man's mother (or another female member of his family) suspects that his woman's child is not his biological offspring, however, she may visit the baby after the birth to determine whom the child resembles. Her opinion carries great weight, for it directly effects the man's reputation and honor in the community. If she finds he has been knuckled, he is unlikely to "take" the child.

On the other hand, as another representative pointed out, there are other circumstances in which men consciously take children who are not their biological relation:

It is a situation where sometime ago, I know a gentleman who took a child, it was not his and the reason he took it—he knew it was not his you know—but the reason he took it was because his friend was married to the friend's child. But to keep the wife away from the husband—these are some of the things we have in our society. (Ibid.)

This speaker used confusing terminology to avoid names. He is referring to a situation in which a man took a child for a male friend of his whose wife would have become irate if she had learned that he had fathered an outside child. Antiguans use the term *friend* to refer to platonic friends of both sexes or as a euphemism for a lover.

A legislator from one of the rural districts raised another familial practice that the proposed kinship codes undermined. He reminded the House of the humorous story about the working man who went to his paymaster before payday to try to collect his wages. The man claimed his father was in the hospital, so the paymaster helped him out. The very next week the fellow returned with the same excuse about a different patient: "But apparently he had two fathers in truth. By that I mean the right father's name was on [the birth certificate] and never supported him and the other father who was paying dear for his mother's company, had to be the father to support him (ibid.)."

The story refers to the norm that men support the children of their lovers; they become "fathers" to the children of their girlfriends. What was to be gained, asked this official, by concretizing the status of fatherhood? In the common order, after all, "father" is often a revolving status.

As it turned out, however, the most compelling critique of the Status of Children Act was that it threatened the privileged status of marriage and the inheritances of married women and their children—and it threatened these because of the familial and gender norms that encourage men to father outside children. The following comment proved prophetic:

> I understand that some wives are complaining that, imagine. That they have gone down the aisle, they have been blessed with the special blessing of holy matrimony, they have brought up their children in the fear of the Lord and the right way and so on, and some of the husbands go out and they have children out there. And now those children are going to come into the estate that we worked so hard for and so on. They better hold on to who they have inside from now on so that they do not go out. I hope and trust that the controls will put on from inside so that we do not have too many bastards outside to share in the estate. (Ibid.)

Notwithstanding a few members' reservations, the Status of Children Act and the Births Act passed the House without effort in 1984. It seemed to lawmakers that bastardy was about to be abolished and that the revolutionary transformation in the system of kinship legalities had begun (Lazarus-Black 1992:887, 888).

Legal Reform as Gendered Practice

Despite the enthusiasm in the House, however, the Status of Children Act and Births Act were never scheduled for Senate debate, making their enactment into law impossible. Why didn't the plan to legitimate illegitimacy succeed in 1984?

The attempt to banish bastardy made explicit the contradictory ideas contained in Antigua's legal culture. Relegislating the rights of individuals, but also of parents and children, the Status of Children Act raised the question about which of two opposing principles should prevail: should kinship law cherish first the rights of all individuals regardless of birth status or should it continue to encourage marriage and legally constituted families? The contradiction fueled an unexpected controversy that shifted the course of Antigua's kinship history, delaying for two years the Status of Children Act and the Births Act and causing legislators to draft a new Intestate Estates Act.

The Status of Children Act and Births Act of 1984 failed to reach the Senate because of lobbying by a group of married women who believed strongly in the equality of all children but who refused to ignore the practical consequences of family and gender norms in their community. Antiguan men's proclivity to father and provide for children outside of legal unions, together with the custom of holding a couple's marital assets in the man's name even if a wife works outside the home, suggested to them that the Status of Children Act and the Births Act posed possible social embarrassment together with considerable financial threat. A man's decision to legitimize a child born outside of the marriage could jeopardize his wife's own and her children's security. Alert to this possibility, the women initiated a political struggle over family law reform lasting two years, waged completely in accord with local kinship and gender norms, espousing human rights and the sanctity of marriage, and ultimately gaining for married women the legal protection they sought.

The struggle over these acts was particularly surprising and interesting because it involved married women. A review of the literature on women in the Caribbean finds "women do not actively participate in the political and policy-making arenas of their societies" and that women who are involved in decision-making positions are mainly middle- and upper-income women (R. Clarke 1986:147). As a group, Caribbean women have never been proportionately represented in government, political parties, or trade unions. They have had low membership rates in formal organizations generally, except for church groups, and some research suggests that when West Indian women do become involved in formal political efforts, their activities are often limited to such traditionally female tasks as fund raising and social welfare efforts (Anderson 1986; R. Clarke 1986; Durant Gonzalez 1982, 1986; Massiah 1986; Safa 1986; Senior 1991).[15] The Antiguan case is thus an exception to the view of Caribbean women that predominates in the literature.

Who were the married women involved in the struggle over Antigua's kinship codes? In an effort to protect the identities of the people I interviewed and those involved in the efforts to change the laws, I asked government officials not to name the protagonists. One member of Parliament referred to them as "certain married women," a description I adopted in later interviews.[16] I did not make this request during informal discussions of these events with lawyers who were acquaintances of mine, but no one volunteered their names. A few told me that the group included "some of the politicians' wives," which suggests their elite status. One member of Parliament said the group also included an office worker and a recently widowed owner of a shop. Another insisted that the group represented women of different classes and religious sects, some supported by their husbands:

> All of them. All of them would complain. Because, you see, why all women complain is that their children will not have—"Look [they would say] I am with my husband, I am working, he's working. Whatever the low, or the high, whatever we have, we

pool together. Usually, this is what happens and they feel that only their children should benefit. Now if he has children outside, well, why should that child come in and just benefit from what the married woman has worked for?" You see? And so all the women in that category, all married women, they were complaining. And I don't think that it's a popular bill among married people. (Interview, 21 April 1987)

Cognizant of the contradiction between the allegedly "protective" Status of Children Act, and the actual social and economic consequences for women and children of local conjugal and reproductive practices, the women achieved their goal in a manner that was strictly in accord with Antiguan gender ideology. Public display of political opposition to the rights of illegitimate children in a formal arena would have been viewed as inappropriate, as "rude" and "come up." Instead, the women wielded power quietly. They spoke to their husbands and ministers, made personal phone calls to officials and, importantly, a small group arranged a private appointment with the prime minister that was successful in convincing him of the validity of their claims.[17] Lobbying to restructure the kinship laws mostly took place outside the formal system; not once did the women become entangled in the legal process (Lazarus-Black 1992:888–90).[18]

Later, as they engaged in these efforts, the women garnered editorial support from the Antigua Trades and Labour Union. The union had on at least one occasion published an article chastising the government for delaying passage of the Status of Children Act.[19] Interestingly, the union's decision to speak in favor of the bills was motivated partially by pressure from Antiguan fathers living in America. Once again, other states impinged upon the state of Antiguan kinship:

> I think the main group in here [those who contacted the union] were men. Some women too. But there was a group in the United States who want us, who want us to do something about the Births and Deaths and Status of Children Act because they were all fathers of illegitimate children. They have applied to the United States [government] for [in] different states where they were [living] to be able to bring their children there. Well, [they are] having a big problem with immigration because they will have to give their children their name. . . . So they wrote to us. I think there were eleven of them, from the association—signed it as "worried Antiguan parents." So I took up the matter, that is when I went to the prime minister. . . . But the pressure came mainly from a group of men, there were some women too, who wanted to give some sort of legitimate status to the child, by giving it the father's name, but mainly this group from overseas, quite a few parents who wanted their children to come over there, be educated. (Interview, 29 April 1987)

This union leader explained to me that people had begun speaking about legitimizing illegitimate children at union headquarters as early as 1981 or 1982. He personally recalled talking about the need for such an amendment with a male taxi driver, two women who worked in a factory, a higgler, and another woman whose occupation was unknown to him. At that time, however, "there was no force put by any group to bring it to the public attention." This "force" was subsequently provided by vocal Antiguans living abroad who were irate at the problems they experienced in trying to bring their children to America.

Meanwhile, the concrete result of the women's efforts was a new Intestate Act offering financial protection to wives and legitimate children without seriously disadvantaging illegitimate children whose fathers had legally acknowledged them. According to this statute, if a man dies intestate, his wife gets one-third of his property and all of his personal effects, including automobiles, tools, jewelry, and household furnishings. The remaining two-thirds of the property are shared by his children, including those legitimized under the new Births Act. A man can defeat the provisions of the Intestate Act, however, if he makes other arrangements in a legal will. Hence there were now three kinship statutes to present to Parliament.

Most of the people I interviewed believed the women who opposed the Status of Children Act were motivated by personal financial interests. No doubt some were. To reduce these women's efforts to secure the Intestate Act to purely financial motives, however, is to misunderstand the familial and gender norms of the common order; it is analogous to misunderstanding why women take men to magistrates' court. A woman attorney presented a more comprehensive explanation:

> I've always agreed that the child born illegitimate should never suffer because of the parents. But there are other considerations to be taken. I don't think we have reached the stage where a wife, especially if she is a working wife, that she would be so broadminded that the [outside] child is not going to bother her. She says, "I'm working, I'm supporting this family. Why should your money go to support a child with another woman?" They don't call it the illegitimate child. It is a child with another woman. And they worry: "You will continue to see the other woman." Which poses a threat to them. That, that will take some time to erase. They see it as a threat to the marriage. So in this way, it is not a good law. . . . And again, on the question of inheritance, the same thing will happen. They say, "I work for it, and then you don't make a will and then my children don't get it." And these estates, most of them are very small and everything counts. There is a tendency to be insecure and they tend to see this as a threat to the marriage. From the illegitimate child's perspective, it is fair. But it is going to take some time to erase these kinds of feelings.

This interpretation is accurate, economical, and consistent with the practices and beliefs it purports to illuminate (cf. Scott 1985:139). It does not deny that women who opposed the bills experienced jealousy or that they were interested in protecting their resources, but it also alerts us to their other concerns. As we have seen, the birth of a child marks the beginning of a new alliance and a rupture in "oeconomia." That is why "they don't call it the illegitimate child.

It is a child with another woman." Such "contingencies" operationalize the principles of gender hierarchy and human equality, just as they restructure familial alliances and the compositions of households. Marriage gives Antiguan women incentives to work and scrimp and save for their families. When a husband becomes involved with an outside woman he undermines his wife's identity as a big woman and her power to negotiate status and resources within the networks she has so carefully forged and managed over time. Not surprisingly, then, when the Status of Children Act first appeared, it failed to resonate with married women's creole legal sensibilities.

Thus what had begun as a simple act to prevent discrimination against illegitimate children and to allow fathers to acknowledge legally their offspring generated a deluge of controversy in the common order. The Status of Children Act divided political conservatives and liberals, members of unions, Christians of various churches,[20] and married and unmarried women. Still, no one publicly opposed the principle of human equality that the bills purported to uphold and no groups organized publicly to oppose them. Married women's success in securing the Intestate Estates Act heralds their new political clout. This power, however, was wielded within the confines of everyday norms prescribing gender hierarchy. Gender hierarchy mediated lawmaking again in the next stage of reconstituting the kinship codes and changing the nature of state intervention in peoples' everyday lives.

The Second Debates

With the new Intestate Act drafted to the women's satisfaction, Antigua's legislators pressed ahead. The Births Act went back to the House on 5 June 1986. The "debate" was limited to three speakers, each of whom gave the bill his whole-hearted support. If any of the representatives noticed the bill had been modified in the intervening years, none brought it up.

Yet the 1986 Births Act shows that earlier concerns about how the new system of legalities might undermine certain familial practices in the common order had had an impact in the Ministry of Legal Affairs. In contrast to the version given to me in 1985, the 1986 Births Act prohibits a man's registration as the father of a child to constitute prima facie evidence of adultery.

The Senate, which officially had never seen the earlier draft, debated the act eleven days later. The clause regarding adultery drew attention:

> I was a bit confused by Senator Q, because he did indicate that he knows of cases where certain men have agreed to have their names registered as fathers of children, when they are in fact not fathers. I would take it by making that point he is in fact making this sub-section very necessary. Because the sub-section is saying that

by the mere expression of somebody as father, does not by reason of legislation, does not become prima facie evidence of adultery. I think that point is very well taken. (Antigua and Barbuda, Senate Debate, 16 June 1986)[21]

Senator Q responded:

> Mr. President, can I give him some information? What I am trying to tell him is this. That in my experience over the years, of fathers in the Caribbean, I have not come across—I don't know what year—a father never denies a child that he thinks is his.
>
> On the contrary, he may well put his name down for a child who he knows is not his, rather than deny a child. But if the man starts kicking up a lot, something funny. And all I will say, the magistrate may give him the child if he likes, but suppose some of his ancestors say that is not his breed, what do you do? And he is not sure. I am not talking about the title. As one man told the magistrate, "Whatever I did, was bought and paid for." What does that mean? The magistrate still gave him the child. (Ibid.)

The Hon. Mr. U then tried to clarify that the "real" purpose for the stipulation was to ensure that men could identify themselves as the fathers of their children. The issue of adultery between husband and wife was an entirely separate matter.

As this senator pointed out, however, a declaration of paternity is now lawful for certain purposes but not for others! The new clause protects a man who, for whatever reason, decides to "take" a child without his worrying about being accused of adultery. In decidedly creole fashion, the lawmakers had found a way to let men identify themselves as fathers of outside children while shielding them from lawsuits by irate wives! As married women had when the first versions of the Births Act and Status of Children Act appeared, some married men apparently had also spent some time negotiating a change in favor of norms in the common order. Men and women, however, had concerned themselves with different issues.

Six months later, the attorney general proffered the Status of Children Act and the Intestate Act to Parliament. Proponents emphasized again the need to protect the rights of every child regardless of birth status and expressed pride in being part of an effort to end discrimination. They associated these kinship laws with the political goal of promoting a more just society. Lawmakers lauded the bills as indispensable to a democratic nation.

Not surprisingly, the second House debate about kinship law, like the first, provoked a discourse about the natures of men and women. Several Parliamentarians, for example, blamed men for the country's high rate of illegitimacy:

> Mr. Speaker, Sir, I think this piece of legislation is very good. All children must be equal in status. This does not mean, however, that people should not be encour-

aged to get married. Neither should this bill be deemed as men have the right to sow their seed wild, over the place, breeding every woman they can get.

Mr. Speaker, again, you know there are some men who do not really care, so long as they look nice and have certain possessions they will have children all over the place. This bill is really trying to protect the rights of a lot of children but you should encourage some of these men to get married. (Ibid.)

Admonishments of this kind were typical and are to be expected, for West Indians regularly blame the "problem" of illegitimacy on the promiscuous natures of Caribbean men who have a proclivity "to love a whole lot of women" (e.g., Alexander 1977b, 1984; Barrow 1982; DeVeer 1979; Douglass 1992; Senior 1991; R. Smith 1987, 1988). On the other hand, as Edward Long had in 1774, one representative faulted married women for their husbands' philandering:

Mr. Speaker, I have had so many calls after the first reading of this bill from wives who said: "Are you supporting that bill?" I ask them: "Why shouldn't I?" What they are thinking about is they didn't send out their husbands to interfere with other girls and if something happens they should not be responsible for that child coming into the sharing of the family. I don't think that is a good way of thinking. If they look after their husbands properly they will not leave and go out, they will stay inside. (Ibid.)

Most of the Senators, however, praised the acts as indispensable to a truly democratic nation and protective of the "real" family:

Mr. Speaker, we have a state in this country where the attitude of our people must be changed. We are trying to change them from the top but they have to be changed from the bottom too. . . . I am saying even though we are talking about all children as one, we are also saying, Sir, that they must realize although they are one, their attitudes must be of the same nature. Don't let those from the married family feel they are higher up than those of the unmarried families. They all must go down the road together and behave and hug up one another. For instance, my son, a daughter, one in wedlock and one out of wedlock, they should be together, hug up and kiss up and so on. This is what we are trying to do, to bring together the family. (Ibid.)

Similarly, another man insisted that the bills would bring "half" siblings closer together: "They will now feel they are the same because they are going to benefit the same way unless the father decides to share up the estate a little differently by the will" (ibid.). Thus the state would strengthen family.

While acknowledging that many Antiguan children are born out of wedlock, the representatives insisted that protecting the rights of these Antiguan family members had nothing to do with condoning "immorality," condemning Christianity, or advocating African polygamy:

What I am saying, I hope that it is not in the spirit of creating all sorts of families here and there that this bill is brought here today. It is not a situation in Africa where one man can have two, three, four wives and all sort of concubines, although we have them here, and I hope we are not trying our best to encourage such. We do feel a Christian society is really a welcome one. (Ibid.)

The family the legislators hoped their new kinship system would protect was "Christian" in its ideal union and "Christian" in its tolerance of bastard children. In accord with the still pervasive influence of the churches, their rhetoric privileged marriage as a religious phenomenon, although not as fully determinative of a married man's resources. Lawmakers understood that the family they envisioned was one whose blood was thicker than water or any contract. The legislature reordered kinship law so that it would more closely resemble family in the Antiguan community, a family defined first through socially recognized blood ties (Lazarus-Black 1992:891–92).

The new model of kinship and the fresh meaning given to various kinship terms reflects the interests of today's working and middle classes. These laws capture the familial norms of the common order, which includes people in different ranks:

> The lobbying we should listen to is the lobbying of the working class, and this affects the working class. . . . I do not think that the introduction of this bill would make us any less unChristian-like in our mannerisms. But even the developed countries which look on themselves as being the civil society. They call them what, now, today? The cultural society. You find more and more children are being born out of wedlock. You find very well-to-do high class, middle class, people shacking up without marriage. (Ibid.)

These laws protect working-class families, yet, as this senator alludes, they also accord with the changing practices of local "cultural society." Formerly, elite and middle-class Antiguans avoided "shacking up" before marriage. Today, as middle-class women work for wages, maintain their own apartments, move away from their parents and their family ministers, and divorce, this practice is becoming more common and more acceptable.[22] The new laws also resonate with another very recent middle-class phenomenon referred to by a senator: "When professional people, secretaries, decide rather than get married, decide rather to have a child. This has been happening all the while in the modern cycle these days" (ibid.). For other middle-class lawmakers, these laws "hit home" in a literal sense. Some were themselves illegitimate children; others had fathered children outside of marriage. One announced he had already been to the courthouse to use the Births Act to register his name as the father of one of his children. He was concerned that the proper forms were not yet available (ibid.).

The Parliamentarians and the women's coalition left a critical contradiction unresolved, however, precisely because they shared the same cultural assumptions. The debates over illegitimacy divided women as they are often divided in the common order: at odds in their most-valued kinship roles as wives and mothers. As one representative noted in passing to Parliament:

> Mr. Speaker, whenever a father dies, especially if he is married, the mourners usually look on the illegitimate child or children and that sadness is extended to those children because of the fact that they know they are not sharing in the estate of the father. Now we are saying the child or children born out of wedlock will come into some part of the estate. This is a very good piece of legislation and I know that some wives are grumbling but many mothers are laughing. (Antigua and Barbuda, House Debate, 4 December 1986)

As is the case throughout the Commonwealth Caribbean (e.g., Senior 1991), socially acknowledged children are included within "family" in Antigua; baby mothers are usually not. For example, when I asked Antiguans what they meant by family and who they included in their families,[23] I found they always mentioned, without hesitation or reflection, individuals related to them by blood. An exception was sometimes made if there was "bad blood" between two persons—although the exception also proved the rule because the individual felt compelled to explain to me precisely why he had to omit that person from his family. Occasionally a person included a close friend as a part of his or her family (see below). On the other hand, people who were "only" baby mothers or baby fathers were usually excluded from a man or woman's discussion about family. Moreover, although some respondents included spouses as part of their families, others did not. The following examples were typical:

MLB: What do people mean when they use the term family in Antigua?

V: Same as what you use the word relative. It includes the wife, husband, aunts, etc. They would regard people who are family by the half-blood and whole-blood people. Family and relative connotes the same thing, although it should mean just the husband, wife, and children. Here we have "children of the family." So it is not just the unit of the husband, wife, and children. In Antigua, when we use the term family, you bring in all the relatives.

MLB: Is the mother of a child family to a man she has the child for?

V: Not really. She is not family to the man she had the child for.

In this case, the speaker was a male, in his sixties, and married. Another man, in his late forties, and also married, drew a diagram for me and explained: "If A and B conceive C, A is not a relative to B, whether or not they marry. A wife is not family [either]. She is in a category a little bit higher than that. And legally she has that status too. No, a wife is not family. Legally she is more than family as such." An elderly married white woman told me:

Q: I have this nephew. He married a woman in [another country] and then he left that woman and came back to Antigua where he has since had three children, with three different black Antiguan women.

MLB: Are they part of your family?

Q: Well, the children are, they have the blood, but the women are not part of the family at all.

A working-class woman in her late thirties who had had several children for a man she had loved a long time, did not consider that man her family. An unmarried man in his mid-twenties earning a middle-class salary first described his parents and sisters as comprising his family. When pressed to continue, he said, "Well, there is a guy, a very good friend, who I would say, if anybody asked me, I would say he's my brother. . . . Actually he lives with us." Queried again, he joked about his dog and then noted: "Well, if you want to, put down my fiancée, I'm engaged." Then he told me that he had two children, each with a different woman. Later in the interview I learned that he was on very good terms with these women and spoke to them regularly. He had not, however, thought to mention them when I asked about his family.

These several examples suggest the new legal model for kinship mostly accords with Antiguans' sense of family. Present lawmakers encoded kinship law to accommodate the cultural logic of the common order, attuned to norms that inform their understanding of justice, equality, gender, and family. That the lawmakers were also protecting the interests of the working and middle classes cannot be doubted. Political power had shifted away from the old colonial establishment, and the Parliamentarians understood that they were breaking the cement of the old social hierarchy. They were creolizing law according to a different image of family and society.

Concluding Notes: The Politics of Family Law Reform

Although legalities have always provided Antiguans with means to fashion, regularize, recognize, and break familial alliances, the sources for the most recent kinship laws represent a unique and complex coalescence of structural, ideological, and personal forms and forces.[24] The most important of these is the reformation of the class structure, a process that began in the 1930s with the first widespread efforts to organize workers, raise wages, and remove the Contract Act. Labor demands were met slowly; the Contract Act was not completely eliminated until 1937, and the first union, the Antigua Trades and Labour Union, was not legal until 1940. Since the 1940s, but especially after the collapse of sugar production in the mid-1970s, the government has concentrated efforts on diversifying the economy, promoting manufacturing, foreign investment, and tourism. The work force today has left the fields and is increasingly employed by government or tourist-related services (Henry 1985:88–91, 99–138; interview with attorney general, 27 August 1985).[25]

These economic changes and the concomitant redistribution of the work force coincided with "constitutional decolonization ... the delicate art of transferring formal power to a colonized people without radically altering the structure of the society or negating imperial economic interests" (Henry 1985:93). Antiguans won the right to administer their own affairs slowly and by a series of legal modifications before gaining full independence in 1981. Not surprisingly, the new state's lawmakers were initially preoccupied with amending the constitution and planning the economic future of the nation. My sources cited "writing the constitution," "getting the tourist industry on firmer ground," "replacing the income tax with other revenue bills," "amending the Medical Benefits Scheme, the Industrial Code, and the Industrial Courts," "getting more schools," and fixing "infra-structural problems" such as roads, electricity, and water as the major issues of the early 1980s. Still, the desire to create a new model for kinship ranked high on the legislators' list of priorities; it was encoded into law within five years of statehood.

The shift in political power to the advantage of the middle and working classes is critical to understanding the emergence of the new kinship codes. No reassessment of the legal implications and consequences of legitimacy, illegitimacy, marriage, and inheritance could occur until a local bourgeoisie emerged with strong identification and ties to the working class, an agenda for social and economic change, and the opportunity to put those plans into action (Lazarus-Black 1992:892). The rapidity with which these laws reached Parliament was also a consequence of the fact that the majority party, the Antigua Labour Party, and the union with the largest membership, the Antigua Trades and Labour Union, made the rights of illegitimate children a political cause. ALP officeholders talked about these kinship laws as the fulfillment of election promises and as a political coup for working people. Moreover, in 1986, the statutes were strongly supported by the Antigua Trades and Labour Union newspaper, vocal leaders, and the rank and file.

The "women's movement" had definite ideological and practical influence upon the Antiguan legislators. Women represent a significant portion of the contemporary electorate, and, as a member of Parliament told me, they are becoming a more vocal and viable political constituency. Another official reminded me that the United Nation's Decade of the Woman had just ended and that Antigua had sponsored a delegation to the U.N. Nairobi conference on women. Their participation had received favorable local publicity and had sensitized the nation to some of the special needs of women and children.

The activities of lawyers in other nations also swayed the men who drafted these bills and the members of Parliament who supported them. Recall that in 1985–87 most of Antigua's legal professionals trained abroad. They knew Jamaica, Barbados, Guyana, Trinidad, and Great Britain had ended discrimination against illegitimate children. Understandably, they felt some pressure to follow in the footsteps of nations whose legal systems are considered "progressive." After all, not to do so is to run the risk of having the country and the local bar association judged backward.

One must also acknowledge the efforts of particular individuals and the idiosyncrasies of biography to account fully for the sources for these kinship codes. Why does an individual devote his or her energies to working for the enactment of a kinship bill? A member of Parliament told me he had decided as a student that someday he was going to "do something" about the status of illegitimate children. While studying law in England, he had been moved by a case in which the children of a working man were denied his insurance monies because of their birth status. For this attorney, the Status of Children Act marked the fulfillment of a lifelong personal commitment.

Outlawing illegitimacy, Antiguan lawmakers outlawed condemnation of the kinship organization of the working people. Simultaneously, of course, they legitimated their own postcolonial rule—one which has not been without its critics (Henry 1985, 1992). Although Antigua's latest kinship statutes redefine kinship relationships and restructure the duties, obligations, and property rights of kin, they also emphasize individuals as "free agents," part of the legacy of the labor laws of the nineteenth century. The state, however, now enters into the lives of families in a radically new way in that law protects the illegitimate child from discrimination and allows that child to inherit. Today the state recognizes and supports a different definition of kinship—one that affects families in every social class. In addition, who can use the courts and for what purpose has changed.

The shift in political power has also changed the character and forms of opposition to the state (cf. Foucault 1979; Abu-Lughod 1990; Bolland 1981, 1992a; Comaroff and Comaroff 1991; Cooper and Stoler 1989; Stoler 1985, 1989). The events surrounding the passage of these laws reveal a complex web of power and resistance. The women's protest in Antigua makes clear that the same cultural logic informs "power" and "resistance." Just as the common order principles of human equality and gender hierarchy permeated discussions in Parliament about kinship law and families in the community, the cultural logic of gender relations shaped the form and content of the women's resistance. Given the slave history of these islands, no one would contest a demand for the legal equality of persons, and, thus, all welcomed the plan to banish bastardy as part of an effort to create a just and equitable society. And yet, given the long-held association between marriage and sacred Christian duties, married women could argue "legitimately" that wives must retain certain rights and privileges. Both the content of the new codes and the actions that brought them into law were structured by peoples' understanding of this history and by their creole understanding of kinship, class, and gender. As far as I can determine, this was the first time in Antiguan history that women exercised power successfully to resist bills that threatened their kinship status and social, political, and financial interests. They wielded power to change the character of state intervention in their everyday lives.

A conflict remains, however. In practice, the Intestate Act may divide women against each other in their roles as mothers and wives. This is because although socially acknowledged, albeit illegitimate, children are often included within a man's "family," their mothers are usually not once the couple's conjugal relationship ends. Thus, women who have children with men they do not remain with may find their children protected but their own situations tenuous. In 1987, however, the symbolic significance of these acts occupied the minds of their proponents; just what will be their actual practical, economic, and structural significance for men and women, and for Antiguan families, remains to be seen (Lazarus-Black 1992:892–93).

❧ Conclusions

Antiguan family ideology and structure evolved in the dialectic between legitimate acts and illegal encounters. It originated in the interplay of convention and conflict, old and new law, and the politics of domination and resistance. Family ideology and structure were inextricably tied both to the processes of class and state formation and to the countervailing actions and ideas that challenged the power and the inventions of lawmakers. The Antiguan case demonstrates that family patterns and values reflect changing arrangements of socioeconomic order, political authority, and legal sensibilities first developed in the seventeenth century during colonialism and slavery, altered momentously by emancipation in 1834, and most recently transformed again after independence in 1981. Antiguan family ideology and structure expresses the ways in which Caribbean people conceptualized and experienced order, hierarchy, and justice in the past and how they constitute these in the present.

My theoretical argument contends kinship ideologies and structures encompass simultaneously the legal forms and forces of the state and the commonsense understanding of kin that evolves in local communities (Lazarus-Black 1991:119). I found law and legal processes salient to the origin and development of Antiguan kinship organization—but without denying the significance of ideas and practices governing gender, labor, class, race, and hierarchy that also shaped commonsense understanding in the common order. By treating kinship laws as cultural texts, and by examining them historically through changing political and socioeconomic contexts, one can analyze the contents of those codes, demonstrate their formative role in the making of creole society, and document when, why, and by whom new rules are written. This approach addresses the relationship between agency and structure in kinship, class, and state formation, changes in the meaning, pervasiveness, and importance of kinship rules and processes to the people of the common order, and the interaction between the forms and forces of the state and normative kinship patterns.

Foucault's "systems of legalities and illegalities" (1979) provides a powerful framework for rethinking Caribbean kinship and the process of creolization more generally. Legalities were an essential part of the colonial experience: they allowed people—mostly men—to plan, organize, develop, and defend a new sociocultural order. Legalities provided means to fabricate a slave mode of production and the social arrangements that made it viable. Law selected, constructed, and legitimized certain social and property relationships but not others. Over time, too, lawmakers changed the definition of the *extralegal* and *illegal*, sometimes with dramatic consequences for the people of the common order. The formal legal rules and regulations defining and governing consanguineous and affinal relationships, and the judicial processes through which the state enacted and enforced its codes, were a critical part of this system of legalities. Kinship law designated specific relations of power over persons and things and facilitated the nature and extent of state intervention in peoples' everyday lives. Kinship laws also buttressed gender hierarchy.

Systems of legalities disclose relations of power between different groups in society, and between men and women, and alert us to the state's pivotal role in constructing the meanings, forms, and functions of kinship. Legalities, however, everywhere encourage opposition; they generate illegalities. Throughout the Commonwealth Caribbean, illegalities pervaded local economies, politics, and familial relationships within and between different social ranks. Illicit unions, miscegenation, concubinage, and bastardy were commonplace. Their regularity encouraged the rise of associated norms that were known and mostly respected across the ranks of creole society. These norms and practices, like the contents of the kinship codes and the use of formal legal institutions to regulate familial disputes, were incorporated into the people's legal sensibilities (Geertz 1983). Illegalities remind us that the designs and purposes of the state never completely dominate, that people live by custom as well as code, and that the relevance and experience of family law is altered by people's biographical situations and commonsense understanding. The domain of the illegal is a critical site for and of resistance to legalities, but, as we have noted, it is not itself free of domination.

This research explored historically and ethnographically the dialectic between legalities and illegalities, seeking a more comprehensive assessment of the origin, development, and present character of Antiguan family ideology and structure. That understanding, in turn, speaks to several themes in research on law and society: (1) the role of colonial states in shaping, maintaining, and changing kinship, class, and gender organization; (2) the value of investigating law and legal processes to better understand other cultures, historical change, and law's presence in everyday life; (3) how norms change the meaning and consequences of lawmakers' law and judges' judgments; and (4) the hegemony of law in relation to alternative forms of domination and resistance.

Kinship Legalities, Class, and State Formation in the English-speaking Caribbean

Studies of Caribbean family life have mostly neglected the historical development of indigenous kinship law and ignored the importance of legal rules and processes in everyday life. I found, however, that historically legal codes and judicial institutions shaped, and in turn were shaped by, local kinship norms and practices. Moreover, rules and judicial processes remain constituent of local family ideology and practice today.

Kinship organization, gender hierarchy, and social class were created simultaneously in Antigua, and, I suspect, elsewhere in the English-speaking Caribbean. In the first period of Antigua's kinship history, 1632–1834, settlers consciously maneuvered kinship laws to create and protect a new organization of labor and social hierarchy. Specific marriage and inheritance laws of this period were directed not only at controlling human reproduction but also at reproducing the social and economic structures of slavery and mercantile capitalism. Each new kinship rule in Antigua had specific implications for the ranking of persons; they were devised to differentiate individuals according to their role in the division of labor. Judicial codes and processes shaped, even as they were shaped by, family patterns within and between the social ranks. Locally crafted marriage laws, for example, influenced the evolution of familial patterns because they established particular meanings for the terms and relationships of marriage, legitimacy, illegitimacy, and inheritance. Kinship and labor codes created and reproduced the ranks of persons that solidified into social classes after emancipation.

As Weber understood, law was taught and practiced in Britain as empirical craft (1978:vol. 2, 785).[1] In the West Indies, the empirical craftsmen borrowed, changed, rejected, and played with the contents and forms of the past. Contrary to local assumptions, Caribbean kinship law never duplicated Great Britain's. Indeed, the record shows lawmakers departed from the customs and codes of England almost immediately. With few exceptions, Antiguan kinship laws were crafted locally. At first, lawmakers drafted laws to direct the marriage and reproductive practices of free colonists. Later, they produced a different set of rules for indentured servants and another for slaves. Antiguans wrote alternative models of rights, duties, and responsibilities for kinsmen in these different social ranks, established boundaries between them, and limited their interaction under penalty of fines, enslavement, or imprisonment. They also directed the formation of certain domestic groups and altered women's control over property and inheritance according to their class. Although Britain offered one main model of kinship, with variants for the inheritances of noble and royal titles and estates, Antigua encoded three different kinship models concurrently.

The case of Antigua demonstrates that colonial lawmakers tried to mold the form and content of familial relationships in directions that served the predominant mode of production. Because families of different classes performed different roles in the division of labor, the state had a greater interest in supervising the familial affairs of some strata than others. Therefore the nature and extent to which the state intervened in the lives of families differed for people in different social strata. Recall, for example, that the state protected newly imported indentured servant families in ways never offered to slave families. Moreover, because members of different classes had different access to and relationships with society's formal political, legal, and economic institutions, they manifested different degrees of adherence to lawful kinship. Even in 1987, unmarried women could not appeal to the High Court for financial assistance from their children's fathers. The codes specifically denied them access to this court. Still, all persons encounter and contend with kinship law, even if only at the birth of a child or at the death of a kinsman.

The Antiguan case shows, too, that over time the state varied its definition of kinship and the institutional support it afforded families in different classes. This appears vividly in laws enacted in the second stage of Antigua's kinship history, 1834–1986. Immediately before and after slavery was abolished, local kinship statutes and the administration of familial relations in the island were tied to the state's direct intervention through political management of poor laws, various welfare statutes, and labor codes. In the nineteenth century, the state "policed" as much as it "governed" families (Donzelot 1979). Faced with very high mortality rates and a shrinking local labor pool, the state sent its inspectors out into the villages to sanitize, immunize, and educate the masses. Restrictive marriage and fornication codes that had limited the reproductive freedom of this class no longer occupied the minds of lawmakers. Instead, social-welfare policies were tied to the needs of the local employers and the costs of maintaining a free labor force (cf. Fox-Piven and Cloward 1971; Lazarus-Black 1992:878).

The state now directly observed and intervened in the ways that parents socialized their children; it entered into the lives of families in a fundamentally new way. Lawmakers redrew the boundaries between the legal, the extralegal, and the illegal. Poor laws made any person related by blood or law to someone who applied for relief at the poor house legally responsible for keeping him or her out of there. When the slaves were freed, the responsibility for nonworking persons was shifted in law to an "extended" family that specifically included grandparents. This "family," defined by the state, was charged with supporting individuals in periods of adversity. On the other hand, when it came to labor, each person was on his own. Laborers were free to move on, free to stay, free to sign a contract, free to be punished for breaking one. This law, part of the Contract Act, forced nearly every laborer to sign a contract to work for the planter who owned the land where he or she resided. Nineteenth-century Antiguan law, in other words, required both the solidarity of families and the independence of laborers. Both precepts remain characteristic of commonsense understanding in the common order today.

Like Antiguan kinship law, Antiguan marriage developed a distinctly creole character. During the slave era, only free persons could marry legally, but that does not imply that marriage was a "white" institution. Free people of color in St. John's and its immediate environs readily embraced formal unions. Registers of the Anglican church show a high percentage of weddings per-formed between people of color between 1814 and 1826. Nevertheless, Antigua sustained a low marriage rate and a high illegitimacy rate after emancipation, when, at least theoretically, all persons could marry. I suggested several reasons to account for these figures, including the presence of alternative ways to define and participate in family, the much slower acceptance of Christianity in the hinterlands (in part because of the lack of ministers in rural areas), personal decisions not to marry in the Anglican church when that denomina-tion was the only available choice, resistance to this form of state intervention in one's life, and the fact that the meaning of marriage, like the idea of a suitable spouse, had acquired creole connotations. Both the historical sources and my ethnographic research lead me to conclude that the desire for individual Christian salvation, and sometimes for social status, are important factors in a person's decision to wed. Moreover, because both reasons become increasingly important as one grows older, marriage occurs later in life and after the earlier childbearing years. The idea that marriage should precede reproduction belongs mostly to law and Christianity, not to people's broader understanding of family in the common order. Concepts like "big man" and "big woman" express commonsense notions that allow and even encourage reproduction to precede marriage. As a result, some 80 percent of Antiguan children are born out of wedlock.

My research also suggests that the degree of consensus between the family presented in the state's kinship codes and the structure of families in the common order partly depends upon whether lawmakers identify with the practices of the masses or whether lawmakers' interests are better served symbolically or pragmatically by creating or maintaining a gap between kinship law and family practice.[2] The formation of a completely separate kinship system for slaves, with different marriage and inheritance rules, re-enforced differences between the masses and the elite. The slave kinship system depicted Africans and their descendants as uncivilized and pagan persons and also allowed planters to sell slaves without worrying about Christian or legal contracts.

The great gap between Antigua's kinship codes and local practices was retained after emancipation and until political power shifted to a new middle class late in the twentieth century. Antigua turned toward Crown colony government in two stages, in 1868 and 1898, and joined the Leeward Island Federation in 1871. As a consequence, authority over kinship codes was transferred to an interisland council that showed little interest in renovating family law to serve better the local populace. Two acts from this period, however, indicate that lawmakers continued to use kinship codes to serve their own class interests. The 1875 bastardy act and the 1913 divorce statute, unusual in that both were virtual carbon copies of earlier British laws, made poor men pay more support for their illegitimate children, thereby relieving the state of the burden, and allowed married people to dissolve their unions if they could afford to do so.

Antigua's present lawmakers, on the other hand, have not neglected kinship. Since independence in 1981, Parliament has passed major innovations in the nation's kinship codes to bring common practice in line with law. The Status of Children Act, the Births Act, and the Intestate Estates Act redefine kinship relationships and restructure the duties, obligations, and property rights of kin. Today it is illegal to discriminate against a person on the basis of birth status, fathers can acknowledge their illegitimate children by complying with a simple procedure, and all children so recognized may inherit from their fathers' estates. In addition to their symbolic importance and potential economic impact, these laws have changed who can go to court and for what purposes.

Antigua's new kinship codes reflect changes in the socioeconomic backgrounds of those who legislate and in the distribution of formal political power in this society. They also reflect women's changing roles in Antiguan society and the cultural logic of gender hierarchy and human equality. Once again, family law has become a powerful resource, but this time to protect married women and children, to prevent discrimination based on birth status, and to ensure a sense of justice more in tune with contemporary creole legal sensibilities than with those of the old colonial elite. Contemporary legislators wielded kinship law to break the boundaries between the classes, rather than to secure them. This concern to protect the rights of all individuals occurred only after the rise to power of a new political elite whose social origins were distinctly working class.

Because the relationship between legalities and illegalities is dialectical, changes in kinship legalities necessarily imply changes in the forms, contents, and meanings of kinship illegalities. It follows that we must reexamine the common presumption that "common-law marriage" is everywhere and always the same phenomenon. In the American colonies, for example, local laws brought common-law marriage into the system of legalities. Americans sanctioned a nonlegal union of seven years, protecting the property of the parties and legitimating the children. In contrast, Antiguan lawmakers never officially legalized common-law unions. In fact, they specifically refused to sanction any union not celebrated by a designated marriage officer. As in Jamaica, the unions designated as common law had "no more recognition before the law than the loosest of family associations" (Roberts 1979:265).[3] These West Indians, in other words, relegated common-law marriage to the system of illegalities. To refer to all relationships of long duration with cohabitation as common-law relationships therefore obscures the important point that the meaning and legitimacy of common-law marriage differs in different colonial and contemporary contexts.[4] As in Jamaica, nonlegal unions remain an intricate component of both class and kinship with illegitimacy expressing a relation of power between people of different social strata (cf. Alexander 1984; Austin 1984; Douglas 1992; R. Smith 1987).

Norms and Laws in the Contemporary Common Order

I draw three principal conclusions from my ethnographic research. First, my study demonstrates the value of investigating legal texts and processes to understand better other cultures. Like Cohn (1989), Rosen (1989a, 1989b), and Greenhouse (1986, 1989), I found "law" to be an important place for communicating meaning and cultural significance. Historical and contemporary conceptions of *man, woman, race, labor,* and *justice,* for example, pervaded law in Antigua. Second, I found that when Antiguans discuss and participate in family, they unconsciously assume specific components of the state's kinship system, borrow much official rhetoric, and incorporate a place for judicial processes and formal institutions. On the other hand, to understand how Antiguans conceptualize and act as members of families is to acknowledge that states only partially penetrate the forms and meanings of daily interactions between kinsmen. As we have seen, people commonly resort to the illegal and participate in the extralegal. Third, I uncovered a few class and gender differences in the ways that people experience family. These differences occur because men and women have different biographical situations, because religion is more important to some than others, because people have more or less contact with and concern for the rules and processes of the state's kinship system, and because, depending upon their sex and class, people are more or less and differently subject to the state's direct intervention in their families.

Certain ideas encoded in Antiguan law as early as the seventeenth century have left indelible marks on the historical consciousness of the people. Consider, for example, the legacies of the slave era found in local conceptions of laboring, law, and gender. In Antigua, the British conception of a "laborer" as an independent married man, the master of his own household but employed by another, exploded. Work acquired new patterns and discipline on slave plantations; it became estranged (Foucault 1979; Marx 1975). The slave laws devalued labor and the laborer simultaneously. Not surprisingly, a stinging association between agricultural labor and the condition of bondage remains today. During slavery, too, the majority of West Indians were alternatively "commodities" or "criminals" (Goveia 1970). In this sense, slaves lived outside the law while living under it. Nevertheless, as we have seen, they learned its rules, its possibilities, and its limits and used this knowledge to negotiate outcomes favorable to their own biographical situations. Today Antiguans sometimes poke fun at law and lawmakers, but they do not pay homage to "outlaws" as in Jamaica (Harrison 1988). A "big" man or woman in Antigua, an adult person, does not cultivate trouble with the law. Jamaicans and Antiguans have different legal sensibilities about outlaws. And, as a last example, early Antiguan laws projected contradictory images of women's place in society and of their relation to labor. The slave codes and indentured servant acts mostly pretended that laborers had no gender. With the exceptions of differences in their clothing and food allotments, and later rules applying to pregnancy, male and female slaves and indentured workers were not distinguished in law. Men and women experienced slavery differently, but the law mostly ignored those differences to suit planters' interests. On the other hand, the law specifically emphasized gender differences within the free population. English common law made free women subordinate to their fathers and husbands, and local Antiguan statutes made it possible for husbands to convey their wives' landed property and for the state to disregard the dower rights of widows of "ten-acre men." Such codes buttressed the operative system of gender stratification and also left a great many free women impoverished. The legacy of law for Antiguan women was the presumption of their equality with men in the fields coupled with the presumption of their subordination everywhere else (cf. Forde 1981; Brodber 1982). In short, commonsense understanding of labor, justice, and gender in contemporary Antigua incorporates many of the assumptions and contradictions of the old statutes, even if people do not consciously identify their origin or history.

Commonsense understanding of family in Antigua today uses several components of the state's kinship system: relationship is formed through blood or by marriage, marriage has higher status than nonformal liaisons, and legitimacy has long been associated with social and economic privilege. When people talked to me about family, they were deeply concerned, as is law, with rights and duties. The norm that a man should support his biological offspring finds support in legal kinship. As I have shown, Antiguans believe that men should feed their children and respect the women with whom they are allied. They also believe women's most important roles are kinship roles and there is continuity between law's depiction of these roles and women's experiences of them.

Still, family life in the common order is distinguished from judicial kinship in several important ways. In practice, family affiliates people to the social, economic, and political activities that comprise "life and living." It distributes people over different households, creates networks for sharing food and other material and nonmaterial resources, and determines who shall raise which children. Antiguan family structure allows for a diversity of relationships between men, women, and children and alternative household arrangements. Antiguan family ideology incorporates local ideas about alliance, loyalty, the different natures of men and women, generosity, big men and women, and Christian salvation. It includes the principles of human equality and gender hierarchy. Family ideology also embraces ideas about justice that are distinct from, and sometimes critical of, those found in law.

I have argued that the Antiguan kinship system is constituted by the rules and processes of the state and the extralegal and illegal norms and practices of the common order. These laws and most norms are shared across different social classes. Nevertheless, I uncovered some class and gender differences with respect to family beliefs and practices. As is true elsewhere in the Commonwealth Caribbean, the degree of adherence to the legally sanctioned form of the family differs in the middle and lower classes. Middle-class Antiguans are expected to legalize their relationships at an earlier age, and they generally do. Lower-class persons, on the other hand, are less likely to wed until later in their lives. The reason for this, as I have already noted, is that the meaning of marriage in family ideology is strongly linked to Christian beliefs and, perhaps more for the middle class, to a concern for social status. For the middle class, marriage is associated with adulthood, the establishment of a new household, and a respectable family life. Ideally, it should precede reproduction. Lower-class persons, in contrast, typically associate marriage with individual salvation. Although marriage is a sign of grace, of the decision to live as a Christian, it has little to do with having babies. When children begin to have "sense," however, their parents sometimes worry about the example they set if they fail to marry. Another class difference concerns alliance formation. Following a long historical pattern, those in the middle class use marriage to unite and protect legally persons and their properties. In the lower class, however, a new alliance typically begins when a woman has a child for a man. These alliances, unlike marriages, are constantly and consciously being renegotiated. They have to be based on love, generosity, and respect.

Different assumptions about and expectations of men and women modify somewhat these class differences. The ideal that marriage precede reproduction, for example, is much more frequently adhered to by Antiguan women. Middle-class men, in contrast to women, father children prior to marrying someone else, and some have "outside" children after their marriages. I attribute this gender difference to local norms about what constitutes a "good woman," in contrast to a "good man," and to the immediate severe sanctions imposed by families, schoolmasters, and ministers when middle-class women become pregnant out of wedlock. In addition, women's more frequent participation in church and concern to set a Christian example for their children makes them somewhat more desirous of marriage. Antiguan men, in contrast, struggle with the idea that marriage will "tame" them. Second, children play different roles in the lives of men and women regardless of class. Antiguan men love and want children and they are by no means marginal to men's lives. Still, I have called children women's special wealth. By this I mean not only the fact that Antiguans hold that the relationship between a woman and her child is somehow stronger and more enduring than that between a man and a child, but also that children are evidence of women's capacity to love, of having been loved, of adulthood, and of their ability to form and perpetuate alliances. Children are essential to women's identity and power in the common order.

Finally, Antiguan family ideology and structure, past and present, reveals some interesting differences from the model of marriage and family that scholars have described as typically "British" or "Western." For one thing, the "companionate" idea of marriage, in vogue in England at least since the fourteenth century (Laslett 1977; Macfarlane 1986), is not so strongly emphasized in Antigua. As is typical among working-class populations in the United States, (Aschenbrenner 1975; Komarovsky 1967; Rapp 1982, 1987; Schneider and Smith 1973; Stack 1974), the strong emphasis on gender differences in Antigua creates a situation in which men and women do not expect to be great friends with their spouses. In contrast to middle- and upper-class Jamaicans (Alexander 1978, 1984; Douglass 1992; R. Smith 1987), Antiguan informants rarely mentioned love first when I asked them about the prerequisites to marriage. A second difference between British and Antiguan family ideology is that the latter rejects the Malthusian notion that children are expensive and therefore should be limited in number (MacFarlane 1986:38–39, 51–78). Antiguan men and women value children for themselves and as evidence of a person's sexuality, love, and maturity. Children are also terribly important in one's old age. Without them, elderly Antiguans would be too lonely and too poor. Finally, neither the agents of the state nor the men from the missions have been successful in convincing Antiguans that one form of union, or one form of household, works for all human beings. Husband, wife, and children, set firmly apart in a separate establishment, the "Western" ideal, is only one of several possibilities for family in the Commonwealth Caribbean.

Of Judicial Codes and Processes

As a plethora of studies has shown, court cases are conditioned by the possibilities and constraints of legal codes and procedures, the idiosyncrasies of legal personnel and litigants, the history and sociology of the relationships between the parties, and local community norms and values (e.g., Comaroff and Roberts 1977, 1981; Conley and O'Barr 1990; Epstein 1967; Gluckman 1967; Merry 1979, 1986, 1990; Nader and Yngvesson 1973; Starr and Collier 1989; Van Velson 1967; Yngvesson 1985, 1988). I found in addition that the hierarchical organization of Antigua's courts perpetuates the class structure. Moreover, although judicial discretion eliminates some of the "gap" between old statutes and changing values and practices in the community, the most important source for transformation in the kinship system lies with state legislators, not with judicial interpreters. Nevertheless, as I explain below, judicial discretion plays an important part in the processing of cases. I discovered certain tenets of kinship codes and procedural rules make middle-class persons the main beneficiaries of judicial discretion. Magistrates, who hear most lower-class disputes, have had much less discretion in resolving kinship cases.

Antiguan women who take men to magistrates' court for child support do so most often to right a breach of the norms of the common order, not to remedy an offense in law. They are concerned with misconduct involving partnering, parenting, responsibility, respect, and social status. Typically, they are young, unmarried, caring for more than one child, and juggling a job and domestic responsibilities. Most have had a long-term relationship with the man they bring to court. Most are poor. In contrast to earlier studies that stressed that economics motivate women to take men to court for child support, I found Antiguan women carry a case to court to shame men who break the norms governing familial relationships in the community. They know the fifteen dollars a week they can get at court cannot "feed" a child. During litigation, however, they reverse the structure of gender stratification that prevails in everyday life and that they experience as unjust. The shaming ceremony renews and validates legally constituted kinship responsibilities while mitigating the prestige of big men. The achievement of equality, the validation of women's rights, and the recognition of moral duty are proclaimed during the trial. In other words, even if Antiguans alter the meaning, function, and significance of lawmakers' law, legalities continue to provide them with means to discuss, construct, maintain, and break alliances. Going to magistrates' court is a distinctly creole act.

The interpenetration of the legal and the normative became obvious, too, when Antiguans divorce, adopt children, and decide issues of inheritance. Divorce provides several examples of this process. For instance, divorce is granted in Antigua only for desertion, adultery, or cruelty. Attorneys confirm that adultery is the "real" reason behind most divorce suits, even though contemporary cases are most often prosecuted for desertion. Lawyers and litigants alike agree that desertion is the "best" complaint to file because it is easiest to prove, requires no witnesses, and complies with the local norm that proscribes discussing intimate relationships in public places. Second, a man's infidelity, technically a breach of kinship law, does not bring a woman to divorce court. Wives divorce their husbands for violations of family norms: for lack of respect, indiscretion, failure to feed children, and other injustices. Thus, it is impossible to understand Antiguan divorce without taking into consideration the creole meaning of *marriage, home,* and *big woman.* Third, most women who file for divorce have achieved at least minimal financial independence. When they go to court they ask for child support but not for alimony. This accords with family norms that hold that men and women should provide each other with gifts and services as a natural part of a loving relationship, that these exchanges end when love cools, and that, in any case, men are responsible for feeding the children they father.

The interpenetration of the legal and the normative appears again when Antiguans adopt children and write their wills. Informal adoption is common, as it is elsewhere in the Caribbean, but Antiguans readily effect legal adoption when the situation requires it. In the 1980s, this occurred most often when they wanted to take children abroad and had to conform to other nations' immigration policies. Nevertheless, as I explained, men have also used formal adoption to legalize their relationships with their own illegitimate children. Men used legal wills before 1987, too, to acknowledge illegitimate children and circumvent the inheritance law. Following family ideology, sons and daughters generally inherit property of equal value, with women sometimes receiving "domestic" property such as houses and jewelry and men acquiring property associated with outside labor, such as land, livestock, and farm equipment.

Until 1987, a man with both legitimate and illegitimate children generally left the former children family land and the matrimonial home, whereas the latter received property elsewhere on the island. Geographical distance indexed the social separation of distinct families. Allied by love, but not blood or law, the mothers of illegitimate children who live apart from their children's father are rarely mentioned in men's wills.

Like litigants, Antiguan judges and magistrates seek to reconcile kinship law and family norms. Judicial discretion allows them to blend a strong regard for legalities with a commonsense understanding of family and a creole sense of justice. For example, of West Indian if not Antiguan origin, High Court judges interpreted Antigua's divorce and adoption laws in 1985–87 to make it possible for people to end their marriages fairly easily and to facilitate adoption enabling children to go abroad. People explained to me that the secularization of the society, the higher standard of living that allowed more persons to travel, and women's intensifying participation in the paid work force all led to the rise in divorce and adoption rates. Certainly judges' willingness to hear these cases and to make unobstructed decisions about evidence brought before them also encouraged more suits. Without doubt, High Court judges give legalities flexibility and elasticity in tune with evolving norms and values. As times change, the phenomenon of judicial discretion allows some Antiguans to manage new family crises through old kinship processes.

Yet the issues and situations subject to judicial discretion differ in the two courts, which also determine how much discretion occurs. As Kairys points out, *stare decisis* is inherently political. Judges regularly use *stare decisis* to reverse themselves without appearing to do so (1982:11–13). I found in addition that High Court judges play with the ambiguous language of codes, interpreting laws in ways that better suit the needs of the new middle class. An example frequently cited to me, and which I observed in court, was the interpretation of acts as "cruelty" that had not been considered criminal offenses before.

Magistrates also exercise judicial discretion, but over different questions and to much less an extent than is true of High Court judges. In general, discretion in the lower courts stems from magistrates' relatively greater control over facts and the credibility of witnesses. On the other hand, they have the added institutional concern that their decisions can be readily reviewed (ibid.:15). In Antigua in 1985–87, discretion was also discouraged by the extremely detailed formal code of procedure and relative lack of ambiguity in the statutes applying to familial disputes. For example, although a magistrate could informally instruct a woman about the evidence she needed to prove a paternity suit before beginning the trial, he was bound by rigid rules once the trial began. Nor could he do anything about the small stipend awarded for child support.

In short, because the relationship between legal codes and legal processes differs inside the two courts, the forms and consequences of judicial discretion also differ. Further, because the High Court is the court that mostly serves the elite and middle class, and the magistrate the lower class, judicial discretion has class connotations. When judicial discretion makes kinship law do the work that Antiguan families require of it, it is mainly the middle class that benefits.

The Rule of Law and Other Organizations of Domination and Resistance

Systems of legalities are constituted by the rule of law, which is an organization of both domination and resistance. They regularly employ and allow certain species of power (see also Hirsch and Lazarus-Black 1994). Systems of illegalities, much less studied or understood, create alternative forms and ideologies of domination and resistance. In these, power is differently defined, utilized, and justified. Obeah exemplifies one such alternate organization of domination and resistance. In this final section, I present some concluding thoughts about the power of law, other structures of domination and resistance, and the nature of legal consciousness.

Turk identifies five forms of the power of law: (1) direct physical violence, as in war or police power; (2) political power, or control over decision making; (3) ideological power, in influencing definitions of and access to knowledge, beliefs, and values; (4) economic power, command of the means of production and of allocation and use of material resources; and (5) diversionary power, the power to influence human attention and living time (1976:280–84). Based on the research presented here, I would add two others. Missing from Turk's analysis is the fact that the power of law permeates beliefs and practices usually labelled "personal": it enters into peoples' thinking about what to expect of a spouse, how to "mind" the children, and how much schooling to give them. It is an integral part of the "discourse of familiarity" (Bourdieu 1977:18). Second, the power of law is highly discretionary, from the naming of what shall constitute an offense, to the question of who stands before the bench and who sits behind it, and to the literal and not-so-literal interpretation of statutes in courts. This power of law is manifest in social relations and practices intrinsic and extrinsic to formal dispute processes (cf. Comaroff and Roberts 1977, 1981).

The history of kinship law in Antigua leads one inescapably to the conclusion that lawmakers used kinship statutes to structure an organization of domination that directly served and legitimized class relations. Lawmakers made the model of family contained in law hegemonic, defining and maintaining certain relations of domination and subordination. Indeed, the kinship of Antiguan law easily meets two criteria essential to create an effective instrument of consent:

> First, it must claim that the system of privilege, status, and property it defends operates in the interest not only of elites but also of subordinate groups whose compliance or support is being elicited. To do this it must, in effect, make implicit promises of benefits for subordinate groups that will serve as the stake which they too have in the prevailing social order. Second, as Gramsci realized, the dominant class must make good on at least a portion of these promises if it is to have the slightest hope of gaining compliance. That is, hegemony is not just a symbolic bone tossed to subordinate groups; it requires some actual sacrifices or restraint by the dominant groups. (Scott 1985:337)

E. P. Thompson made a similar point. The rule of law, he eloquently explained, is characterized not only by its "instrumentality as mediating and reinforcing existent class relations and ideologically, as offering to these a legitimation" but also by the indisputable fact that the given "class relations [are] expressed, not in any way one likes, but through the forms of law" (1975:262). The rule of law constrains and enables the people of the common order:

> We reach, then, not a simple conclusion (law = class power) but a complex and contradictory one. On the one hand, it is true that the law did mediate existent class relations to the advantage of the rulers.... On the other hand, the law mediated these class relations through legal forms, which imposed, again and again, inhibitions upon the actions of the rulers. (Ibid.:264)

Like Thompson, I have been struck, but not made starry-eyed, by the remarkable capacity of people to struggle about the rule of law from within the rule of law (ibid.:266). The people of the Antiguan common order very quickly became adept at using the rule of law for their own material, practical, ideological, and symbolic purposes. Antiguan slaves brought masters before magistrates, indentured servants held employers to the terms of their contracts, and black women made white men accountable for executing wills according to the directions of their deceased lovers. The poor and disadvantaged regularly used legalities to resist the power wielders' attempts to stray beyond the legal limits they set for themselves, to check the elites' assumptions and privileges, and to demand a justice born of their own experiences. The investigation of law and forensic processes therefore proved as invaluable to the social history and anthropology of the economically powerless as it was to the study of the elite.

The most subordinated of people regularly find a place for protest within the rule of law. Guyanese workers used the courts when the conditions of their labor proved unbearable (Rodney 1981), Jamaican leaders turned to law to secure the right to unionize laborers (Post 1978), and English commoners of the eighteenth century took great delight in sending noblemen to the gallows (Hay 1975). Writing about the antebellum American South, Genovese understood well the extraordinary ideological and practical ramifications stemming from the fact that slaves were governed by the rule of law:

> The slaves grasped the significance of their victory with deeper insight than they have usually been given credit for. They saw that they had few rights at law and that those could easily be violated by the whites. But even one right, imperfectly defended, was enough to tell them that the pretensions of the master class could be resisted. Before long, law or no law, they were adding a great many "customary rights" of their own and learning how to get them respected. . . . The slaves forced themselves upon the law, for the courts repeatedly sustained such ostensibly extralegal arrangements as having the force of law because sanctioned by time-honored practice. (1972:30, 31)

Thus legalities often provide fuel and form for resistance to the rules of law, and resistance is then incorporated into the system of hegemony sustained by the law.[5]

Although historians point to the intellectual and practical achievements of elites in creating legal systems, and observe that the masses use legalities to demand or defend their rights, they mostly ignore conceptions of power, order, justice, and structures of domination and resistance forged within systems of illegalities. If we investigate systems of legalities *and* illegalities, however, a much more complicated picture emerges. Structures and ideologies of power may be legal, illegal, or extralegal. Therefore, the rule of law both controls and empowers the masses, creating an internal dialectic within the system of legalities. Structures and ideologies of power are negotiated as well in systems of illegalities and in the domain of the extralegal. As we have seen, these systems continually interact. Finally, efforts to resist domination may incorporate legalities, illegalities, or both.

Because people live simultaneously within systems of legalities and illegalities, they learn to identify and manipulate more than one organization of domination and resistance. The nature and extent of an individual's participation in one or more of these systems depends on class, gender, and other aspects of biographical situation, such as the number and strength of one's alliances, political connections, and financial independence. Lower-class Antiguan women, for example, regularly use courts to establish affiliation and maintenance, increase support orders, and deny their husbands cohabitation. Women commonly use legalities to manage relationships between kin: they initiate formal procedures to name, maintain, and break alliances. Some legalities, then, give women power over certain relationships. There are times, however, when class intervenes, when big men are too big to take to court. If legal codes and processes fail them, if the law does not hold an offense to be a "crime," or if they prefer privacy, women may search for justice in their social relationships by resorting to illegalities, including obeah.

I investigated obeah as an indigenous ideology of power and justice, part of the system of illegalities whose conceptual opposition is not Christianity, as previous studies have suggested, but rather an entire system of legalities. Obeah should not be reduced to an African survival, a form of magic or religion, or a political act of the underclass. Obeah is empowering knowledge and enabling practice. Distinctly creole, it may be directed against an exploiting class, but the justice it expresses also permeates relationships between neighbors, lovers, and kin. Obeah often deals with the problem of injustice and hierarchy between men and women and within and between different social ranks.

As Weber noted, "Every domination both expresses itself and functions through administration" (1978:vol. 2, 948). Outside the realm of the rule of law, power is differently constructed, administered, experienced, and justified. Obeah belonged first to the slaves. It belonged to the slaves collectively, but it also differentiated power and social prestige among them. Slave masters understood that obeah posed a serious threat to their social order. They made it illegal and tried to eradicate it. All attempts to destroy obeah, however, failed. After slavery, obeah men and women worked ordeals to determine the guilt or innocence of suspected thieves and adulterers, and to predict the consequences of different courses of action. Obeah is still practiced by persons of all social and economic backgrounds and by both men and women. In one of its rites, "tying a man," obeah contends directly with inequality between men and women. In the rite, women strengthen their alliances with men and claim rights for their children. Tying a man, like going to court, reverses the order of gender stratification in the common order. In both cases, women work their power through their relationships.

Finally, this analysis of alternative forms of domination and resistance is also relevant to recent theoretical discussions about the nature of legal consciousness. Critical legal scholars[6] have identified three characteristics of legal consciousness that account for the hegemony of law in the United States: (1) people regard their legal institutions as legitimate and therefore acquiesce to their rule, (2) law promulgates its own legitimacy by creating an illusory image of itself as objective and neutral through various processes of "mystification," and (3) there is a pervasive belief that existing legal arrangements are both fixed and inevitable (Sarat and Felstiner 1989:1664). Some further qualifications and additions to these characterizations can be made based upon the research presented here. Critical legal scholars have investigated legal consciousness "from the top down," assuming an organization of domination without resistance. The hegemony of law in Antigua, however, is strengthened by the fact that commonsense understanding includes the knowledge that the system of legalities contains within itself means for resistance. Thus it is not only that Antiguan law is mystified as "objective" or "neutral" but also that it is sometimes experienced as a "weapon of the weak" (Scott 1985).[7] Moreover, legal consciousness is conditioned, and the hegemony of law perpetuated, by the fact that whatever are lawmakers' overt intentions as they frame a law or establish a court, such legalities will be reworked continually to serve other purposes and other sensibilities of justice. In practice, the state's rules and courts have ideological and pragmatic value to people in the common order. Finally, discussions of legal consciousness have been limited to legalities. Critical legal scholarship has thus far failed to investigate historically how ideas about justice and injustice develop in accord with, but also in opposition to, the rule of law.

As Thompson suggests, the rule of law is a remarkable legacy (1975). It is remarkable for both its generative force and its capacity to contain. In Antigua, the predominance and pervasiveness of legalities since the earliest days of colonialism have been greatly responsible for the persistence and consistency of its political, legal, social, and economic structures and for much of the content and flow of ideas in the common order. Certainly, legalities have been central to the origin and development of class, kinship, and gender in Antigua. But if legalities mostly provide a stabilizing and conservative influence in history, the tension between legalities and illegalities serves as an important locus for the internal contradictions that compel historical innovation and change.

❧ Notes

Preface

1. The last official census, conducted in 1960, recorded 54,304 persons; a partial census in 1970 estimated a population of 64,794. The 1991 census surprised Antiguans, because throughout the 1980s officials estimated the population to be more than 80,000. The 1991 figures include 29,638 men and 31,202 women, of whom 60,148 were living in private households, 609 resided in institutions, 78 were long-term guests in hotels, and 5 were considered vagrants. The sex ratio is presently 105 females for every 100 males. The census enumerated 19,501 households, as compared to 13,615 in 1960. The average household size has dropped from 4.12 persons in 1960 to 3.08 in 1991 (Antigua and Barbuda, *1991 Population and Housing Census: Preliminary Report* 1991:3, 4).

2. Later *Statistical Yearbooks* do not give unemployment rates.

Notes on Sources, Methods, and Terminology

1. Formal education beyond secondary school is not readily available in Antigua. The experience of going overseas to take a "course" is fairly widespread, consequently, in the middle class. Antiguans used *course* in the same way that I do. Taking a course is a way to further one's education.

2. Lowes analyzes the Antiguan "nonwhite middle class," a description she also finds "fraught with difficulties," but that avoids "such imprecise, and inaccurate, terms as brown or mulatto, or such value-laden ones as black or Afro-Caribbean. . . . I have chosen nonwhite, knowing that it too is biased because it defines everything in terms of not being white" (Lowes 1992:3).

261

3. Contributors to the volume *Decolonizing Anthropology* (1991), edited by Faye V. Harrison, confront this issue in analytically interesting ways. Articles by D'Amico-Samuels and Harrison will be of particular interest to Caribbeanists.

4. I employ E. P. Thompson's definition of class as a historical category "defined by men as they live their own history" (1978:146). Thompson's argument that "class struggle" precedes a people's discovery that they constitute a "class" accurately describes class formation in the Caribbean. As he explained: "People find themselves in a society structured in determined ways (crucially, but not exclusively, in productive relations), they experience exploitation (or the need to maintain power over those whom they exploit), they identify points of antagonistic interest, they commence to struggle around these issues and in the process of struggling they discover themselves as classes, they come to know this discovery as class-consciousness. Class and class-consciousness are always the last, not the first, stage in the real historical process" (ibid.:149). During slavery, Antigua was marked by "class struggle," but "classes" as such emerged only after all productive relations were "freed." This usage conforms with the view that "class" in its modern sense arose within industrial capitalist societies (ibid.:148).

Introduction

1. Following local custom, I refer to the nation of Antigua and Barbuda as Antigua.

2. I use the term *state* to refer to the actors who control the political, economic, technological, and ideological apparatus of government, as well as their enabling institutions. States are historically constituted, varying greatly in their power and techniques of rule from place to place and in the same place over time. My research analyzes the ways states become "integral states" (Forgacs 1988:423), producing both coercion and consent. As Moore noted: "It is a truism that the state is not only the site of politics and legislation, but purchaser, seller, employer, money lender, and manufacturer of ideology, as well as a host of other things. . . . The institutional subsystems of different purposes overlap, intersect, become one another in different situations" (1986:8). I take a similar position when I analyze obeah as a phenomenon of traditional anthropological analyses.

3. This study focuses on Antigua, but throughout the text I draw on materials from elsewhere in the English-speaking Caribbean. Although I agree with Trouillot that "domination of English on Caribbean studies reflects and reinforces boundaries and rankings inherited from the colonial past, as well as current U.S. domination" (1992:35), my decision to trace three hundred years of family law from mostly primary sources forced some limitations of comparative cases. I use *British West Indies, English-speaking Caribbean,* and *Commonwealth Caribbean* to refer to former British colonies.

4. In the past two decades, these issues have been central to the anthropology of law (e.g., Abel 1979; Benda-Beckmann 1981; Cohn 1965, 1983, 1989; Cohn and Dirks 1988; J. Comaroff 1985; J. L. Comaroff 1980, 1982, 1989; Comaroff and Comaroff 1986; Comaroff and Roberts 1986; Cooper and Stoler 1989; Fitzpatrick 1980; Goveia 1970; Lewin 1987; Martinez-Alier 1974; Moore 1978, 1986, 1989; Nader 1989; Nader and Todd 1978; Rosen 1989; Salamone 1983; R. Smith 1982, 1984, 1987; Snyder 1981; Starr and Pool 1974; Starr and Collier 1987, 1989; Stolcke 1984; Stoler 1985, 1989; Vincent 1989; Westermark 1986). For reviews of recent theoretical trends in the field, see Starr and Collier (1987, 1989) and Hirsch and Lazarus-Black (1994). In addition, Merry provides a comprehensive overview of research contending with "legal pluralism" (1988) and "colonialism and law" (1991). Earlier studies investigated the impact of European law upon indigenous peoples, pointing especially to the interaction between divergent normative orders (e.g., Bohannan 1989, 1965; Burman and Harrell-Bond 1979; Cohn 1959, 1965; Galanter 1968; Gluckman 1955, 1965; Jayawardena 1963; Kidder 1979; Pospisil 1979, 1981). To my knowledge, anthropologists of law have not previously had the opportunity to examine lawmaking "in progress" as gendered practice, as I did (Lazarus-Black 1992:865 n. 2).

5. The argument developed here was influenced most by Foucault (1979, 1980, 1991) and Donzelot (1979, 1991), and independently of both Moore (1986:128), who once noted the analytical importance of approaching the legal and illegal domains as parts of a single system, and Fitzpatrick (1983a, 1983b), who also contends that we must investigate law as constituent of social life and family relationships. Fitzpatrick makes the point in the context of building a "radical theory of legal pluralism" (1983a). My analysis, in contrast, shows by concrete example how the state and families intersect dialectically over time and makes commonsense understanding of kin and gender central to the study of those processes. In my view, the concept of legal pluralism does not go far enough in delineating contested domains of power (Lazarus-Black 1992:865 n. 7).

6. Following Comaroff and Roberts, a *norm* is "a statement of rule that is indigenously regarded as relevant to the regulation of social conduct" (1981:28). By "normative kinship order," I mean individuals' commonsense understanding and use of language, attitudes, and behaviors considered appropriate for individuals who define themselves as family.

7. Caribbean planters' use of laws to regulate reproduction and marriage shares similarities with the deployment of kinship rules regulating indentured sugar laborers in Deli, Indonesia, in the early twentieth century (Stoler 1989). There are other interesting parallels between Antiguan and Brazilian marriage, divorce, and inheritance laws (see Lewin 1981, 1987). This research emphasizes law's generative as well as its oppressive character.

8. Ideologies express historically specific forms of consciousness that derive from, but also condition, material life. They are rooted in *practice*, the intentional activities through which men labor to produce their subsistence and reproduce themselves as material and social beings (Larrain 1979:41–44). I do not use *ideology* in the sense of false consciousness. By *structure* I imply a construct designed to illuminate persisting social relationships between groups or individuals that endure over time. The structural relationships with which I am concerned are intended to clarify historical patterns.

9. Merry shows that in practice, law may be comprised of several discrete "discourses": legal, moral, and therapeutic (1990:110–33).

10. It is possible, however, to think of other structures of domination, neither legal nor illegal. Several examples are provided in Bourdieu's discussion of the "elementary form" of domination practiced directly between one person and another (1977:191). Many of the everyday practices that express Antiguan women's subordination to men fall under the category of the extralegal. For example, I noticed men in visiting unions often made their girlfriends wait at home for them, sometimes for hours, despite the availability of telephones.

11. In the English-speaking Caribbean, the term *creole* was first used to refer to "a person of pure white blood born in the colonies, as distinguished from one born in Europe." Later the connotation was generalized to distinguish "any person born, or thing produced, in the colonies from a person or thing of the same kind, born or produced elsewhere" (Pares 1950:348). Sociologists, anthropologists, linguists, historians, and nonacademics living in the region, however, have altered the meaning of the term (e.g., Hannerz 1987, 1991; Mintz and Price 1985:6–7). In my view, C. L. R. James and Raymond T. Smith best capture the meaning of creole society. James explains: "Wherever the sugar plantation and slavery existed, they imposed a pattern. It is an original pattern, not European, not African, not a part of the American main, not native in any conceivable sense of that word, but West Indian, sui generis, with no parallels anywhere else" (cited in Henry and Buhle 1992:55). For Smith, creole society "was rooted in the political and economic dominance of the metropolitan power, it was colour stratified, and was integrated around the conception of the moral and cultural superiority of things English" (1967:234). Creole culture involves a shared ideology that emphasizes "the importance of Christianity, of education, respect of the law, 'good' as opposed to 'rough' or 'bad' behaviour, the need for moral upliftment, and the importance of using proper language; all factors which emphasized not only the de facto power of the Europeans, but also the superiority of English culture" (ibid.:235). For further discussion of the meaning of creole society and the process of creolization, see Brathwaite (1971), Brereton (1979), Craton (1978), Decamp (1971), Dominguez (1986), Drummond (1980), Hannerz (1987), Jayawardena (1963), Lowenthal (1972), Mintz (1967), Robotham (1980), Rodney (1981), and R. Smith (1966, 1992).

Bolland compares and contrasts some of these and other studies of creolization, deftly delineating their strengths and limitations. He also demonstrates how the image of the creole society is "linked to the process of decolonization and nation-building" (1992b:52).

12. Boggs summarizes Gramsci's concept of hegemony as "the permeation throughout civil society—including a whole range of structures and activities like trade unions, schools, the churches, and the family—of an entire system of values, attitudes, beliefs, morality, etc. that is in one way or another supportive of the established order and the class interests that dominate it. . . . To the extent that this prevailing consciousness is internalized by the broad masses, it becomes part of 'common sense'" (in Greer 1982:305). Greer argues, correctly, that the consequences of the Gramscian approach are that it no longer makes sense to view law as merely a reflection of the power of the ruling class, as the inevitable logic of capitalism, as an autonomous system of rules, or as a product of compromises between capitalists and members of other social classes, although this latter perspective accords with some Gramscian principles. Instead, one conceptualizes law as a constitutive force of state power, or as it happens in this case, as "constitutive of the capitalist state power" (ibid.:308). For discussion of the relation between ideology and hegemony, see Comaroff and Comaroff 1991. For further debate about law, hegemony, and resistance cross-culturally see Lazarus-Black and Hirsch 1994.

13. Weber first defines *domination* as "the probability that a command with a given specific content will be obeyed by a given group of persons" (1978:vol. 1, 53). The presence of probability rather than surety, however, allows an opposing organization of resistance. In another context, Weber made domination "identical with authoritarian power of command," a situation in which "the manifested will (command) of the ruler or rulers is meant to influence the conduct of one or more others (the ruled) and actually does influence it in such a way that their conduct to a socially relevant degree occurs as if the ruled had made the content of the command the maxim of their conduct for its very own sake. Looked upon from the other end, this situation will be called obedience" (1978:vol. 2, 946).

14. I investigate obeah in Chapters 2, 4, and 6.

15. In "Common-Sense and Scientific Interpretation of Human Action," Schutz's best-known work, historicity is "sedimented" in objects and institutions: "All cultural objects—tools, symbols, language systems, works of art, social institutions, etc.—point back by their very origin and meaning to the activities of human subjects. For this reason we are always conscious of the historicity of culture which we encounter in traditions and customs. This historicity is capable of being examined in its reference to human activities of which it is the sediment" (1962:10). Thus although he insisted upon the social origin of knowledge, Schutz was not specifically concerned with the sources or historical transformations of specific ideas. He left the examination of the "transcendent infinity" of the social and natural worlds to a "philosophical anthropology" (ibid.:330, 356). Geertz (1983) is far more sensitive to the historical and generative character of commonsense knowledge, but my sense of common sense is that it is less totalizing than Geertz imagines.

16. Only one sentence mentioning gender differences appears in Schutz's *Collected Papers*: "The determination of what is worthwhile and what is necessary to communicate depends on the typical, practical, and theoretical problems which have to be solved, and these will be different for men and women, for the young and for the old, for the hunter and for the fisherman, and in general, for the various social roles assumed by the members of the group" (1962:349). The same point, also undeveloped, appears in *On Phenomenology and Social Relations* (1970:79, 246–47). Geertz (1983) can be criticized as well for failing to elaborate how gender conditions commonsense knowledge.

17. I first argued this in Lazarus-Black 1990a. Later I learned that Foucault made a similar point: "It is the tactics of government which make possible the continued definition and redefinition of what is within the competence of the state and what is not, the public versus the private and so on; thus the state can only be understood in its survival and its limits on the basis of the general tactics of governmentality" (1991:103).

18. See Reddock (1988:126–31) for a recent re-evaluation of Higman's quantitative analysis. As she points out, the character of the relationships between men and women changed over time, as did the notion of what constituted "women's work" and "men's work" (ibid.:131, 110).

19. This study contributes to a growing number of works that emphasize the importance of situating one's fieldwork in a historical anthropology. A few examples include J. Comaroff 1985; Comaroff and Comaroff 1991; Merry 1990; Moore 1978, 1986; Nader 1989, 1990; R. Smith 1982a, 1984, 1987, 1992; J. Stolcke 1984; and Stoler 1985, 1989.

20. For example, Moses describes women's legal rights in Montserrat based on contemporary legislation, interviews with public officials and other informants, and 1974 crime statistics. She concludes that Montserrat's laws buttress a male dominance ideology that also pervades the home, schools, and jobs (1976, 1981). Durant Gonzalez found Jamaica's Status of Children Act, which protects the rights of illegitimate children, produced some unintended personal and financial hardships for married women. While giving all of a man's children the right to inherit his property, it also took away mothers' exclusive custody rights and redistributed goods to children without reference to wives' priorities (1982:5–7). Jackson uses Jamaica's Family Court records from 1976 to 1980 to discuss tensions women experience raising children, maintaining relationships with boyfriends and husbands, and coping with their personal needs under conditions of limited finances (1982:28–62). Cumper and Daly's handbook on domestic law in the Commonwealth Caribbean (1979) gives an overview of law for the general public.

21. Austin also finds Jamaican schools are important instruments for perpetuating a hegemonic world view (1984:214). More recently, she explores how denominational and evangelical religions legitimize class relations in Jamaica (1987, 1991, 1992). She does not address the role of law in perpetuating the dominant ideology about kinship. B. Williams investigates with great sophistication the deployment of cultural hegemony in modern Guyana (1991), but, again, without elaboration of the forms or forces of law.

22. In de Certeau's words: "I call a *strategy* the calculation (or manipulation) of power relationships that becomes possible as soon as a subject with will and power (a business, an army, a city, a scientific institution) can be isolated. It postulates a *place* that can be delimited as its own and serve as the base from which relations with an *exteriority* composed of targets or threats (customers or competitors, enemies, the country surrounding the city, objectives and objects of research, etc.) can be managed. As in management, every 'strategic' rationalization seeks first of all to distinguish its 'own' place, that is, the place of its own power and will, from an 'environment'" (1984:35–36).

23. In 1981, Comaroff and Roberts identified two basic paradigms in the anthropology of law. Briefly summarized, the "rule-centered" paradigm directs attention to order, judgments, and judges, whereas the "processual" paradigm leads scholars to focus on conflict, forensic processes, and litigants (1981:5–17). Starr and Collier's (1989) volume marks a turning point in the development of the latter paradigm. The newly evolving processual paradigm shares with the former certain epistemological assumptions: the notion that conflict is endemic to society, that dispute is as natural as consensus, that humans cooperate when it is in their interests to do so ("interests" being varyingly defined), and that the dynamics of social control lie in social processes. However, *process* has been reconceptualized to include broad historical and sociopolitical processes. With Starr and Collier, I welcome anthropology's progression from a concern with legal rules and local disputing processes to investigations of power and history in the study of law.

24. Discussion of the advantages and limitations of using legal cases and statutes as historical sources can be found in Higginbotham (1978:7–9); Jordan (1968:587–88); Lazarus-Black (1994); and Schwarz (1988:35–58). A more extensive treatment of subordinated people's use of law in relation to power, hegemony, and resistance appears in Hirsch and Lazarus-Black (1994).

25. For further discussion, see Lazarus-Black 1994, in which I argue that examining trial materials and alternative legal arenas sheds light on the origins and development of West Indian legal hegemony.

26. The "socially powerful role of linguistic ideology as it intersects with and regiments linguistic practice" (Mertz 1992:325) was made startlingly clear to me during the months I worked

for Beth Mertz analyzing language ideology and practice in law schools in the United States. For further discussion, see Mertz 1994.

27. Chapter 1 discusses Antigua's slave codes and provides sources for studies of slave statutes elsewhere in the region. Some excellent accounts of the power of law to protect special interests in the postemancipation period include: Rodney's compelling narrative of a capitalist/planter class' use of law to regulate labor in Guyana (1981), Post's biting discussion of the conversion of the problems of surplus labor and underdevelopment in Jamaica into issues of civil liberties (1978:419–20), Bolland's (1981, 1992a) histories of systems of land and labor control in Belize, and Trotman's (1986) examination of crime in Trinidad between 1838 and 1900. Mahabir traces with rich detail legal response to Trinidad's 1970 "state of emergency," finding "the function of the emergency regulations was political survival on the one hand, and the preservation of the existing political, social and economic structure of Trinidadian society on the other" (1985:117). She also provides an important contribution to our understanding of Trinidad's early legal history (ibid.:15–56) (see also E. Williams 1962). These studies are unusual in addressing analytically the complex play between legal processes and social and economic structures in the Caribbean. None focuses specifically on kinship and gender.

28. Seventeenth-century English society was, of course, decidedly hierarchical. At the apex were men whose status increasingly depended upon their ability to generate and use capital, rather than upon their landed interests and titles. "Blue blood" was "purchasable," and wealthy merchants discovered long "lost" family crests (Hill 1969:51, 54). The "peasantry" was more heterogeneous than it had been in the previous century. Besides subsistence husbandmen, there were farmers (many renters with long-term leases) producing wool for local and European markets and employing wage laborers (ibid.:70). A new strata of peddlers and traders appeared in the countryside, even as the common folk still bore the brunt of the gentry's and the gentlemen's attempts to better an already dominant position. A clause in the Statute of Artificers (1563–1694), for example, reserved the skilled crafts for the sons of landowners, and the Act of Settlement (1662) prohibited the poor from moving freely about the countryside in search of either work or trouble. Still, by the seventeenth century, the property rights of "the meanest" in England could be defended by law (Hill 1969:49). Moreover, there were no rules forbidding intermarriage between different ranks: one could marry "up" or "down," and people frequently did (Macfarlane 1986:254–57).

29. The number of capital offenses in England grew from about fifty to more than two hundred in the years between 1688 and 1820 (Hay 1975:18). People who stole, pilfered, or committed adultery a second time faced death (Corrigan and Sayer 1985:81, 155).

30. One economic crisis after another marked the century (Hill 1969:14). The Thirty Years War (1618–48) curtailed the export market. There was an especially severe depression 1620–24, and enclosure acts worsened conditions throughout the countryside. Poor markets within Europe led merchants "to shift their theatre of action to the colonies" (Sheridan 1973:75–76, 80). Britain won the monopoly for carrying slaves to the Spanish Americas after the War of Spanish Succession (1701–13).

31. Genovese finds: "At their eighteenth-century peak, the West Indian sugar islands accounted for one-fifth of British imports, one-sixteenth of British exports, and one-eighth of total British trade, in comparison with figures of one-ninth, one-eleventh, and one-tenth respectively for the North American mainland" (1971:27).

32. Curtin distinguishes the ethnocentric perspectives that characterized early British views of Africans from the "full-blown pseudo-scientific racism which dominated so much of European thought between the 1840s and the 1940s. The difference lay in the fact that 'science,' the body of knowledge rationally derived from empirical observation, then supported the proposition that race was one of the principal determinants of attitudes, endowments, capabilities, and inherent tendencies among human beings" (1964:29). When the seventeenth-century Antiguan colonists described their slaves, they did so with obvious color prejudice, fear, and disdain. Jamaican Edward Long's scientific racism, however, was not yet in vogue. Long's 1774 *History of Jamaica* claimed scientific proof for the argument that Europeans and Africans belonged to different species. The book was widely read throughout the Americas and in Europe (ibid.:36, 43–45). R. Smith (1982b)

compares Long's ideas about race with those of another famous scholar of Jamaican history, Bryan Edwards, and traces the relation between race and class in the postemancipation Caribbean. For a more recent discussion of European images of Africa and Africans, see Comaroff and Comaroff 1991.

33. The panopticon was adapted from a scheme pioneered by Jeremy Bentham's brother, Samuel, who drew up the plan while supervising Prince Potemkin's dockyard workers in Russia (Corrigan and Sayer 1985:156).

34. E. P. Thompson describes task-oriented labor as more "humanly comprehensible" than timed labor. Communities in which it is practiced "show the least demarcation" between work and life (1967:60). Yet "to men accustomed to labour timed by the clock, this attitude to labour appears to be wasteful and lacking in urgency" (ibid.:60). On the plantation, the demarcation between work and life was structured to obliterate most of the time that could be devoted to life. Even so, masters regularly complained about their slaves' "waste" of time.

35. Years after I had written this line I discovered a chapter in Richard Wade's *Slavery in the Cities* entitled "The Lash and the Law" (1964:180). Wade writes sensitively about the implications of corporal punishment: "It came to be a social gesture embodying discipline, deterrence, and degradation" (ibid.:186). He points out that it was unlikely that any slave in the United States could have reached maturity without at some time having experienced corporal punishment: "Getting into trouble was just too easy; a brush with the law was almost certain" (ibid.:195). What is clear from his chapter is that the combination of physical violence and law made life terrifying in a way most of us will never understand. See also Mintz (1992:274) on this point.

36. Beckles makes a similar point with respect to the transformation of indentured servitude in Barbados: "The traditional socio-legal framework of English indentured servitude reflected the ideology of ruling-class paternalism, with its guiding concepts of 'mutual obligation' and 'duty.' . . . Barbudan servitude was shaped not by the moral and social ideas of mutual obligation and responsibility, but by clearly defined contractual arrangements determined by market forces" (1989:79).

37. In its modern sense, the idea of "the individual" dates from the late sixteenth or early seventeenth century; it was popularized with the spread of Protestantism (cf. Weber 1958; Hill 1969:40). In comparison to earlier times, individuals in the early seventeenth century were more responsible to their God and somewhat less accountable to their kin and neighbors, but they had not yet been fully "freed" in their relations to capital or the state. As Durkheim recognized, individualization and state formation are part of a dual transformation—only "through the state is individualism possible" (cited in Corrigan and Sayer 1985:187). With the emergence of nation-states and, later, industrial capitalism, ideas about the individual would incorporate specific notions about time, work, and self-discipline (cf. Thompson 1967; Comaroff and Comaroff 1986a, 1986b, 1988, 1990; Foucault 1979), issues important to the development of Antigua and its kinship system.

38. Grossberg's *Governing the Hearth* is an exemplary study of the history of American family law from colonialism through the nineteenth century. Even so, Grossberg does not fully address the ways in which class and race permeated the decision-making process. His account only touches on slave codes and miscegenation laws.

Chapter 1: Fashioning a Creole Society

1. The classic work demonstrating that slavery and the slave trade generated enormous capital and financed England's Industrial Revolution is Eric Williams's *Capitalism and Slavery*. Williams calls the West Indies interest the *"enfant terrible* of English politics until American Independence struck the first great blow at mercantilism and monopoly" (1944:96).

2. Goveia (1965) first described the contradictory features of political organization in the Leeward Islands. More recently, Henry characterized Antigua's early capitalist state as "a compromise between the local elites and the imperial directorate which favored the latter; and a situation

of class/race subjugation that made the labor of the imported African population available to the local elites" (1985:26). He explains: "The need to embody these two situations . . . gave the colonial state its peculiar mix of military, democratic and authoritarian features" (ibid.:26).

3. St. Kitts became an exclusively English colony by the Treaty of Utrecht in 1713. The Treaty of Paris (1763) gave Grenada, St. Vincent, Dominica, and Tobago to the British. Peace lasted until 1793, when the French declared war again. They lost Trinidad in this fray. The last major battles before slave emancipation were waged against Napoleon's forces, but left Antigua untouched.

4. Many of the island's earliest statutes include urgent pleas for Britain to send more soldiers and to assist the colonists in expanding and providing for their local militia (Microfilm No. 1; *Laws of Antigua* 1690–1790:87–88).

5. For example, Roman-Dutch law prevailed in the colonies of Demerara, Essequebo, and Berbice for almost thirty years after they were ceded to the English (Shahabuddeen 1973). The Jamaican case, however, shows a seemingly simple guideline for establishing law in a colony could in practice be subject to a variety of interpretations. Jamaica was seized from Spanish colonists but was subsequently redefined as an "uninhabited place" when the British drove the Spanish from the island (Edwards 1819:199; Patchett 1973:17; Morrison 1979:46–47).

6. See Great Britain, *The English Reports,* King's Bench Division, LXXVII:398. These guidelines were reconfirmed by the decision in Blankard v. Galdy in 1694 (Greaves and Clarke 1897:1).

7. E. Williams (1944:178–96) and Goveia (1965:335–36) concur that the humanitarian movement to end the slave trade and slavery occurred only as the economic power of the West Indian sugar interests waned: "If the British West Indian sugar industry had not been in severe difficulties from the beginning of the nineteenth century, it appears most unlikely that the humanitarians could have succeeded in abolishing either the British slave trade or British colonial slavery. For they failed in their demands for effective reform whenever these demands were supported only by appeals to humanitarian principles, and they succeeded only when their humane objectives coincided with practical political and economic circumstances favourable to their achievement" (ibid.).

8. For a detailed description of the cumbersome process of disallowing a colonial law, see C. Clarke (1834:41–45) and Higham (1921:226–28).

9. One disallowed bill attempted to abolish the General Legislature of the Leeward Islands; another was a statute permitting slave evidence to be used against free men. The latter bill has been discussed in detail by Gaspar (1985a:43–62). Great Britain also disallowed an Antiguan measure that would have extended civil rights to Roman Catholics.

10. In 1625 Charles I granted Barbados and "the whole of the Caribbee Islands" to the Earl of Carlisle and his heirs forever. However, Charles II repurchased those rights for the Crown in 1663 and placed Francis Lord Willoughby of Parham in charge of administering the islands. Barbados was separated from the Leewards in 1671.

11. The governor-in-chief also served as chancellor and vice-admiral and appointed members of the judiciary in each island. Those positions paid poorly, but men welcomed them because of the status and political clout they bestowed upon incumbents. The governor-in-chief also appointed clergymen to vacant benefices. In these matters, it was politic, but not mandatory, for him to consult with the bishop of London.

12. For a brief period, between 1816 and 1832, Antigua, Barbuda, and Montserrat had their own governor general, separate from the executive head of St. Kitts, Nevis, Anguilla, the Virgin Islands, and Dominica. Each island retained its own lieutenant governor and House of Assembly (C. Clarke 1834:123, 127).

13. During Queen Anne's reign (1702–14), the colonists sent a petition requesting that the assembly be eliminated altogether, but their plea was rejected (*Laws of the Leeward Islands* 1791–1804:6).

14. To vote for the vestry board one had to be a free born male, a native or naturalized subject of Great Britain, twenty-one years of age, and in possession of ten acres or a house and land valued at ten pounds currency (Goveia 1965:90). Voting qualifications were changed periodically, in line with changes in the economy. In 1718, for example, the property qualification was raised

to possession of ten acres of land or a house renting for twenty pounds per year (Microfilm No. 1; Goveia 1965:90).

15. In comparison to the other Leeward Islands, Antigua had more than its fair share of trained lawyers. "Between 1675 and 1775, 21 of the 37 West Indians admitted to Gray's Inn came from Antigua. All but 10 of the 37, however, were admitted after 1740" (Sheridan 1973:371). Barrister Rowland Burton, the first professional to attain that office, was appointed chief justice of Antigua in 1786 (Goveia 1965:63). Serious attempts to alter the procedures and practices of Antiguan courts to bring them into greater conformity with those of England did not occur until Antigua adopted the Crown colony form of government. For example, An Act to amend the Court Acts (1868) permitted Antiguan courts to adopt the rules and practices of the Court of Common Pleas in England, although it also allowed "such alterations or variations as may be applicable to the state condition and circumstances of this Colony." An Act for assimilating the Law of this Colony respecting certain Treasonable offenses to the Law of the United Kingdom passed in the same year (Microfilm No. 9).

16. There is an alternative view held by some lawyers that the common law "is a system of immemorial existence, not made by judicial action, merely 'declared'" (Patchett 1973:31). Patchett, an authority on West Indian law, disagrees, as does American legal historian Lawrence Friedman.

17. Morrison notes this provision was a basis for Imperial control of the local Jamaican assembly in the early years (1979:50).

18. The clause was a thinly disguised attempt to use slave evidence to convict free men. Great Britain never disallowed this bill, although the Colonial Office later discredited an act that would have permitted slave testimony to be used against freed black men (Gaspar 1985a:58–61). According to the preamble of the 1694 statute, Jews were instigating Antiguan slaves to commit thefts against their masters (*Laws of Antigua* 1791–1804:4; Microfilm No. 1). The Antiguans repealed the bill in 1701 after the Jews petitioned the governor, his council, and the assembly. They claimed the bill had caused "great suffering" and promised "due obedience" in the future, especially "in case of Warr" (Microfilm No. 1; Gaspar 1985a:271).

19. Catholics were welcomed back later in the eighteenth century, when free Antiguans began emphasizing skin color rather than religion as the basis for social solidarity. In 1798, at the same time that the General Legislature of the Leeward Islands voted to ameliorate the working and living conditions of the slaves, it passed a bill extending the franchise and other civil liberties to white Roman Catholics. Great Britain disallowed the Antiguan act and Antiguan Catholics did not gain their full civil rights until the nineteenth century (*Laws of Antigua* 1791–1804:499; Goveia 1965:91–93; Oliver 1894:vol. 1, cxlii).

20. Beckles found that the selling price of indentured servants, like the selling price of slaves, varied by sex, skills, and nationality. Planters in Barbados, for example, paid lower prices for Scottish servants and disliked Irish Catholics (1984:14).

21. Sugar production in Antigua expanded dramatically throughout the eighteenth century, "increasing from the average of 4,900 tons for the decade 1711–1720 to 9,200 tons for the decade 1761–1770" (Henry 1985:20). In the year 1770, Antigua exported 430,216 pounds of sugar to Great Britain, 35,551 to North America, and 230 to other islands (Watkins 1924:35).

22. Throughout the eighteenth century, legislators tried continually to increase the number of white settlers. An Act for the Encouragement of, and Maintaining White Women Servants, and preserving, and increasing the Number of White Inhabitants in this Island (1767), for example, states frankly that bills of 1716, 1740, and 1755 to encourage immigration had not had the "good effects hoped for . . . our Numbers of White People having rather decreased than otherwise, which has been Chiefly occasioned by Women not being allowed to pass and reckon as Servants, in the Public Accounts for the Tax on Slaves." But this was not the only cause for the lack of increase among Antiguan whites. The lawmakers also complained that too many overseers and agricultural servants remained celibate, "their Wives beeing deemed as Burthens upon such Plantations." Officials were annoyed, but not completely surprised, that servants continued to emigrate (*Laws of Antigua* 1690–1790:385–86, 388).

23. In England, families mostly lived together and divided labor. A large percentage of households in the seventeenth century, however, also contained young unmarried servants. Perhaps some 60 percent of the English population aged fifteen to twenty-four were servants in the period 1574 to 1821 (Macfarlane 1986:86). Service was so common, in fact, that one historian has suggested it was "a stage in the life cycle for large numbers of people" (Laslett 1977:34). On the average, coresident domestic groups included 4.75 persons (Laslett 1972:126).

24. Demographer Wells reports that the men who took colonial censuses used *household* and *family* but "never bothered to make a distinction between them, and may have considered them the same. Although it is not certain, the evidence suggests that when the colonists referred to a family or a household they meant an independent, economic unit, the members of which lived in one dwelling or in close proximity. The members of such a unit included all those who lived under the control of the 'master of the family'" (1975:42). As Wells points out, this definition differs from modern American usage in which *family* implies kinship and *household* implies common residence but without the same concept of control (ibid.:42). Wells retains the eighteenth-century definition of family in reporting mean household size and composition for the Leeward Islands (ibid.:220–35). He reports average household sizes of 33.7 persons for 1753–56, of whom 3.4 were white (2.5 adults and .9 children) and 30.4 were slaves (ibid.:220). The data do not allow us to determine lines of consanguinity and affinity. Wells found the composition of all households was affected by the age of the household head, with the largest households led by whites ages 35–44. Wealth was a second factor influencing household size; poor persons lived in small households and were more likely to be without children (ibid.:226–28).

25. I have conducted fieldwork in Antigua, Barbuda, and, to a much more limited extent, Barbados. In all three islands, people of different social classes, and men and women, attributed the high rate of female-headed households in the Caribbean to the legacy of slavery. My research contributes to a growing number of studies that find slavery only partially explains eighteenth-century household structure and headship in these islands.

26. Mintz, however, finds little evidence to suggest that women predominated in marketing before emancipation (1974:216–17). He believes female marketing in Jamaica developed with the spread of peasant agriculture.

27. Slave owners were compelled by law to maintain certain proportions of white men to slaves on their estates. In 1692, every master of ten slaves had to keep one white servant man in his employ (Microfilm No. 1). After 1716, each man possessing fifteen slaves furnished one white man for militia duty and one additional recruit for every twenty slaves thereafter (Microfilm No. 1). A bill of 1740 declared each estate owner responsible for one white man or two white women for every thirty slaves owned. The penalty for failing to comply with the regulation was forty pounds. It grew increasingly difficult to maintain these proportions, however, and lawmakers were forced to change them. By the 1790s, planters needed to employ only one white man for every forty slaves (*Laws of Antigua* 1791–1804:131, 409, 439). These "deficiency laws" remained on the books until just before emancipation (Horsford 1856:88).

28. An English act of 1547 made loiterers and idlers "not applying themselves to some honest labour" liable to be "marked with a hot iron in the breast with the letter V" and then enslaved to the person bringing him in for two years" (Chambliss 1973:139).

29. The Spanish carried the earliest slave code to the West Indies as part of their thirteenth-century common law, the *Siete Partidas* (Goveia 1970:10–17). In the *Siete Partidas*, a slave was defined as an unfortunate person bound in servitude. He or she was nevertheless part of "la familia." Spanish custom and law made it possible for a slave to arrange an agreement with a master (coartación) that fixed terms for the slave's eventual release (Ibid.:11–15). In contrast, laws in the English colonies held that slaves were commodities, the absolute property of the owner. Another difference that partially explains the contrasting forms of social organization that developed in the Spanish and English colonies derives from the contrasting sources for colonial legislation. Spanish lawmakers lacked daily experience with slavery because the institution never played a major role in the Spanish economy. Because the Spanish government retained a firm grasp on colonial law and held relatively liberal notions about slavery, the kinds of police measures

that the English colonists found "indispensable" did not appear in the Spanish colonies. On the other hand, because Englishmen upheld their right to legislate according to local conditions, slave owners made slave laws (ibid.:16, 19).

30. There is a vast literature on slavery in the American mainland colonies. Jordan (1968) and Higginbotham (1978) provide excellent and classic overviews and comparisons of the different colonies.

31. This legal status was probably as significant to free women as it was to slave social organization. Slaves were included as part of a widow's dower rights and could be sold from an estate only when there were no other assets to pay debts (Microfilm No. 1). Inadvertently, then, the law protected widows by allowing them to run estates without fear that the executors of their husbands' wills might deprive them of their labor force. The law that made slaves inseparable from land must also have promoted social cohesion among them. It must have encouraged long-term relationships among slaves on stable estates even though it was common practice for seventeenth-century planters to try to dissuade slaves from forming emotional ties by employing tactics such as purchasing individuals who spoke different languages.

32. Slaves in South Carolina outnumbered free settlers by 1708 and remained in the majority throughout the colonial period. South Carolina's white population included a large percentage of migrants from Barbados. Not surprisingly, then, South Carolina's codes borrowed many of the severe strictures of the slave codes of that Caribbean colony (Higginbotham 1978:152).

33. The slave codes of the Leeward Islands are discussed at length by Goveia (1965, 1970) and Gaspar (1979, 1985a).

34. Beckford (1983) argues cogently how the plantation system transformed colonial societies to conform to a peculiar stasis. This description builds on R. Smith's (1967) application of Goffman's concept of the "total institution."

35. Betty's Hope Estate is under excavation and is open to visitors. According to information provided at the site, the work force included 255 slaves in 1751. Six hundred of the estate's 870 acres were planted in cane. Sixty women and 40 men comprised the first gang; 46 children were "weeders or grasspickers." There were 9 coopers, 15 carpenters, 6 masons, and 3 smiths.

36. See Mintz (1985:48–61 for an astute review of the plantation's pre-industrial and industrial features. Descriptions of the organization and functioning of sugar plantations in Antigua appear in Goveia (1965), Sheridan (1957, 1973, 1977), D. Hall (1971), and Henry (1985).

37. Slave markets were critical throughout the Caribbean (e.g., Mintz 1974; Patterson 1967; Rodney 1981; M. Smith 1965b). For sources pertaining to the slave economy in Antigua see Sewell 1861, Phillips 1926, D. Hall 1971, Carmody 1978, and O'Laughlin 1959.

Chapter 2: Legal Sensibilities in the Common Order

1. St. John's courthouse was designed in neoclassical style by architect Peter Harrison. The building was constructed at the site of the first market, at Long and Market streets. Completed in 1750, it was funded by a tax levied on all slave owners for six years and with funds lent by the executors of Jonas Langford and Samuel and Thomas Watkins. Courts were held on the lower floor, and the second story provided meeting rooms for the council and assembly. The building was also used for charity balls, official dinners, lectures, and other civil gatherings. The Historical and Archaeological Society of Antigua created a museum in the courthouse in 1985 (Historical and Archaeological Society Pamphlet).

2. In research on postemancipation Trinidad, Trotman (1986:230) claims former slaves and their descendants respected the rule of law and voluntarily sought the jurisdiction of the courts. He also suggests, however, that the former slaves had no choice "since their own legal institutions had either been destroyed or undermined and drained of validity. The law was used as a weapon to destroy, and the process of criminalization was used to deny validity and integrity to their cultural institutions" (ibid.:230–31). Trotman recognizes that the Trinidadian masses used the

courts to resolve disputes, but his emphasis on the courts as instruments of oppression does not allow him to appreciate fully their constituent role in the evolution of Trinidadian legal consciousness.

3. Interestingly, Schwarz also found that in eighteenth-century Virginia an increase in certain major crimes committed by slaves was "a leading indicator of the coming of a regional scare, plot, or outbreak as opposed to isolated insurgencies or mutinies" (1988:259). Slave murder of whites, for example, "prefigured insurrectionary scares and events" (ibid.:259).

4. *Coromantee* was a generic term referring to slaves who came through a Dutch fort at Kormantin on the African Gold Coast. The largest ethnic groups in that area belonged to the Akan language family (Gaspar 1985a:89–90). By the time of the 1736 conspiracy, slaves born in Antigua probably outnumbered those born in Africa. However, the expansion of the Ashante state during this period led to an increase in the number of Akan-speaking captives sold to European traders for resale in the West Indies. Of slaves born in Africa but living in Antigua, there existed a sizable number of these captives. Additionally, many slaves born in the island must have had Akan-speaking parents (ibid.:234, 236).

5. Gaspar found: "Though outnumbered by the Creoles, the Coromantees were a sizable minority of the Antigua slave population in 1736; and while many of these Africans were acculturated and skilled, the majority seem to have been unacculturated and field hands. Like most Creoles, acculturated and skilled Coromantees could often manipulate their privileged status in the interest of resistance, but ultimately, and more than any other factor, perhaps, it was [the slave leader] Court's charismatic influence and the memory and image of Africa that drew them into the plot, along with common Coromantee field hands" (1985a:234).

6. Gaspar interprets the bill to allow freedmen to be convicted on the evidence of slaves as indicative of a change in the Antiguans' associations between class and color. Whereas the English "conveyed a conception of freedom that was based on class . . . that of the island legislature . . . was based on race and class. Whites saw freedmen and slaves as branches of the same troublesome tree. . . . The overwhelming tendency was to emphasize the slave origins of freedmen rather than incline toward according them the full free status of whites" (1985a:60, 61). Recall, however, that in 1694 the colonists had also indicted Jews on "any such evidence" as a justice might deem sufficient.

7. Poisoning raised such fears among slave masters in Virginia, for example, that in 1748 they passed a special law condemning to death without benefit of clergy "any negroe, or other slave," administering "any medicine whatsoever" unless granted approval to do so by a white authority. As in the West Indies, Virginian slaves died accused of poisoning both their masters and other slaves (Schwarz 1988:97). Poisoning was not just a crime of slaves, however. The English made it treason punishable by boiling to death under Henry VII's reign (ibid.:97).

8. For Henry, for example, obeah in Antigua is the result of a "magicization of the belief sector" of African peoples. It is a world view that has lost its "basic ontology" and "mythologies that explained the creation of the world, the place of man in it, etc." (1985:33, 34). Gaspar's treatment is more extensive, and he pays greater attention to obeah's political functions during the 1736 slave coup (1985a:246–48), but he, too, treats obeah as an African survival.

9. Although our separate research focuses on different Caribbean countries and different historical periods, Trotman and I both found obeah suppressed and criminalized in order to ensure the cultural hegemony of the planters. My discussion of obeah differs from Trotman's in two respects. First, Trotman continues to treat obeah as a phenomenon of religion and magic; indeed, he locates the source of obeah's power to resist planter hegemony in its capacity to function as a religion (1986:223, 227). Second, Trotman fails to point out that although obeah and law were once in veritable opposition, they are today both components of a broader West Indian legal sensibility.

10. Mullin (1977) points out that in comparison to slaves on the mainland, Caribbean slaves had greater autonomy, manifested less evidence of paternalism, and sometimes participated in separate legal arenas. See Lazarus-Black 1994 for further discussion.

11. Newton's (1979) bibliography of legal sources available at the law library in Barbados, for example, includes mainly twentieth-century sources and a few nineteenth-century law reports from Guyana. Greaves and Clarke's *Report of Cases Relating to Barbados* mentions just three cases

from the slave era; two address the question of the reception of English law in the colonies while the third involves a debt for slaves and court costs (1897:1–3). Catterral's series on legal cases and American slavery includes only one eighteenth-century law report from the West Indies, which she excerpts but hardly analyzes (1968:349). Chutkan's (1975) paper takes the conventional view in arguing that Jamaican courts were capricious and corrupt, but her work is important in drawing our attention to law as a contributing factor in the Morant Bay Rebellion and for bringing to scholarly attention the fact that Jamaicans used alternative courts, even if they were ignored by the planters. Dodd (1979) presents interesting data about the development of the legal system in Guyana that includes descriptions of alternative legal forums and practitioners. Unfortunately, his argument is by today's standards unacceptably pejorative. Brana-Shute and Brana-Shute (1980) edited ten papers pertaining to crime and punishment in the Caribbean in the 1970s. They, too, note the "paucity of material on the sociological and historical aspects of crime in the Caribbean (ibid.:v) I found the poor, women, people of color, and slaves brought cases to courts as early as the last quarter of the eighteenth century (Lazarus-Black 1994).

12. N. Hall (1972) finds planters in Barbados used the courts to serve their own class interests and purposefully limited poor peoples' access to those courts. For example, there was a hefty "economic qualification" to bring suit in the court of appeals (ibid.:27). Moreover, free colored persons were unable to give evidence in court in Barbados until 1817, and then only if they had received a Christian baptism (ibid.:40). Trials for criminal and civil offenses committed by slaves were conducted by magistrates who served as "both judge and jury" (ibid.:42). Although I have no doubt that fraudulent practices obtained in courts throughout the Caribbean, my point is that the courts became increasingly important over time as an arena for common folk to voice resistance and to pursue rights.

13. In the 1702 act, a single justice of the peace tried slaves accused of minor offenses, and two justices heard slaves charged with "heinous crimes." The justices relied upon their own discretion in meting out punishment. Slaves' evidence against free persons was not admitted, although the justices could decide if other slaves should testify (Gaspar 1985:150).

14. Interestingly, the sample of cases contained no instances of black men suing white men. There is simply not enough evidence to determine if this represents a pattern, or is simply a feature of this selection of cases.

15. These committees had been formed in lieu of 1817 instructions from Britain to each of the colonies to keep annual registers describing the condition of the slaves (*Laws of Antigua* 1804–17:257–61). The Antiguans found it "too difficult" to keep the accounts up to date and instituted the Councils of Protection instead. It is not clear how they managed to get away with this, but it does help explain the dearth of slave records in Antigua. One of the commissioners commented that orders from the councils and orders from Great Britain were probably equally disregarded, but another, Fortunatus Dwarris, was impressed with the condition of Antiguan slaves: "I do not find the slave starved, wretched, and habitually ill treated" (Great Britain, Commission of Inquiry, 1826:vol. 3, 28, 117).

16. My thanks to John Comaroff for clarifying this point.

17. Discussing the 1868 Register of Complaints for the state of Louisiana, "one of the single most complete and extensive sources on the Freedmen's Bureau complaint system and how it affected, and was affected by, black women," J. Jones (1985:331) found that of all complaints initiated by blacks, 39 percent were brought by women. In addition, "the percentage of cases initiated by freedwomen (as opposed to freedmen) increased along a rural-urban continuum, reflecting the fact that a larger proportion of city women bore complete responsibility for their own welfare and that of their children" (ibid.:331).

18. Yngvesson explains that in western Massachusetts women use courts to punish husbands or lovers and to contend with rebellious children: "There is no evidence that complainants in these domestic abuse cases use the legal system in order to terminate a relationship. They use it rather to restructure and continue the relationship" (1985:641, 642). Merry argues that working-class women in the United States are "more likely to take their neighbors, husbands, lovers, and children to court than are men because they are relatively powerless in these relationships" (1990:4).

19. Trotman's history of nineteenth-century Trinidad convinces us that the island's courts, magistrates, judges, and police were corrupt, abusive, and class and race biased. Nevertheless, he reports "Trinidadians respected the rule of law" and "voluntarily sought the jurisdiction of the courts in some of their disputes" (ibid.:230). Trotman responds to this contradiction only partially convincingly. He proposes that (1) the very corruption of the courts "demystified the law and, ironically, served to encourage participation"; (2) some people went to court because they had no choice, "since their own legal institutions had either been destroyed or undermined and drained of validity"; and (3) respect for law "developed partly from fear of its coercive powers" (ibid.:230, 235). My critique of this explanation is that it focuses on the ways in which law oppresses and suppresses without attending to its generative and inclusive character, and capacity to express resistance.

20. Bourdieu said of law that it is "the quintessential form of the symbolic power of naming that creates the things named, and creates social groups in particular. It confers upon the reality which arises from its classificatory operations the maximum permanence that any social entity has the power to confer upon another, the permanence which we attribute to objects" (1987:838).

Chapter 3: Antiguan Family Law, 1632–1834

1. Catharine of Aragon had married Henry VIII's older brother, Arthur, who died shortly after. Henry VII, unwilling to let Catharine return to Spain with her enormous dowry, betrothed her to his son, Henry VIII. Henry VIII, in search of a son, charged their marriage was incestuous (Durant 1957:535–36).

2. There was one exceptional period, 1653–57, during the English Civil War, when the formalities of marriage were temporarily transferred to civil magistrates. The century was marked by increasing resistance to the clergy and the ecclesiastical courts (Gillis 1983:263).

3. The Marriage Act of 1823 amended the conditions under which a marriage became voidable. A marriage was not voided if the persons unknowingly and unwittingly married in an inappropriate place or without due publication of the banns. The 1823 statute remained the principal act governing marriage formalities in Great Britain for more than 125 years (Bromley 1981:37).

4. English and North American lawmakers did not begin awarding custody of young children to their mothers until the nineteenth century. In England, Talfourd's Act (1839) empowered the courts to give a mother custody of children until the age of seven and access thereafter until maturity unless there was evidence of her adultery (Bromley 1981:284). In the United States, the "tender years doctrine" held young children were more appropriately placed in a mother's care if there was no evidence challenging her fitness as a parent (Grossberg 1985:248–49).

5. In seventeenth-century England, particularly in rural areas, men and women postponed marriage and reproduction until they could support their own households. Illegitimacy was relatively rare, affecting less than 3 percent of the population, although it varied by region and in different periods. It was, for example, unusually high early in the century but unusually low at its midpoint (Laslett 1977:104–5, 114, 126). Until about 1700, about one in ten brides was pregnant at marriage, having become so after their betrothal ceremony (Macfarlane 1986:305). As a rule, women had their first children relatively late, "both in the life experience of the mother and also in the period of fecundity" (Laslett 1977:13). Spouses were similar in age, but oftentimes wives were slightly older than their husbands.

6. The law of primogeniture also excluded second sons from inheriting their fathers' estates. However, society provided the means for them to acquire property by their own efforts and accorded them permanent rights to that property. Women's property holdings were generally temporary unless their fathers arranged marriage settlements for them or they were widowed. Alternatively, a woman's status with respect to property could be altered by gifts given to her alone or through special trusts administered on her behalf. Marriage settlements, trusts, and gifts of real property, of course, were legalities confined mainly to England's and Antigua's "well-to-do."

7. Dower rights in England were amended in 1833 in an act that provided that "dower should not attach to any land which the husband disposed of during his lifetime or by will and that the wife's right to dower out of his estates of inheritance in respect of which he died intestate should be barred if he made a declaration to this effect by deed or will. As a quid pro quo the Act gave the wife dower in her husband's equitable freeholds in respect of which he died intestate, if he had not barred her right by declaration" (Bromley 1981:411). Dower was abolished altogether in 1925 (ibid.:417).

8. I analyze Antiguan poor laws and their relationship to the governing of families after emancipation in Chapter 5. Poor relief legislation in England began with the breakup of feudalism. The first laws regulated individual alms giving, repressed begging and vagrancy, and restricted laborers from leaving their parishes. An act of 1531 licensed the poor and aged to ask for alms, but five years later another statute prohibited begging altogether. The new proposal arranged for local collection and distribution of charity to the "needy poor" (including bastard infants), provided jobs for willing workers and apprenticeships for children, and enforced punishments for those who refused to work. The success of these various projects was thwarted, however, by the lack of finances to support them. In 1572, lawmakers addressed that issue by passing an act empowering local officials to collect payments for poor relief within the parishes. The Poor Law Act of 1576 held both parents responsible for the illegitimate child. An act of 1601 specifically appointed "overseers of the poor," selected by justices of the peace, and required each parish to levy a poor relief tax. Financial responsibility for illegitimate children in England was reassessed in acts of 1809, 1834, 1844, and 1872 (Pipkin 1934; Jacobs 1932).

9. As described in Chapter 1, each colony had a "reception date," at which time they received, at least theoretically, the whole of English statutory and common law. After that date, and following the creation of a local assembly, laws made in England were not binding in a colony unless expressly framed for it by Parliament.

10. There is a vast literature on slavery in the English-speaking Caribbean, almost all of which attends at least briefly to slave laws. Statutes governing the family lives of free settlers and servants, on the other hand, have not received nearly as much attention. Higman's (1984b) comparative study provides an excellent overview of the peoples, economies, politics, and social organization of the Caribbean in the slave era with some attention to local laws. For further discussion of Jamaica's marriage and family laws in this period, see Curtin 1955; Edwards [1819] 1966; Higman 1973, 1976, 1984; Long [1774] 1970; Patterson 1967; and R. Smith 1987, 1988. Goveia (1965) compares and contrasts the slave codes and the social, economic, and political structures of the Leeward Islands. Elsewhere (Goveia 1970) she compares British slave codes to French, Spanish, and Dutch statutes. Gaspar (1985a) analyzes Antiguan slavery to 1736. Beckles (1989) describes kinship statutes and practices in Barbados. Henriques (1974) traces miscegenation law in the Caribbean, Latin America, the United States, and Africa. Morrissey (1989), Beckles (1989), and Bush (1990) focus on the experiences of slave women. Most of these studies are confined to a more limited time period than is provided here for Antigua; none focus in depth upon the dialectical interplay of legalities and illegalities in the making of class, kinship, and gender.

11. Martinez-Alier's *Marriage, Class, and Colour in Nineteenth-Century Cuba* (1974) provides one of the most persuasive illustrations of how law, and especially kinship law, is used to create, facilitate, and sustain a system of domination. Cuba embarked on widespread importation of slaves and expanded its sugar economy after the British takeover of Havana in 1762 (ibid.:2). Beginning in 1806, Cuban political authorities issued a proclamation requiring interracial couples who wanted to marry to obtain a special dispensation from the state. Initially, permission to marry was granted to interracial couples if both were members of the lower class. They did not, however, grant permission for such a marriage to the relative of a priest or an official (ibid.:4, 20–26). By the 1860s, when the growing abolitionist and independence movements threatened the livelihood of the politically dominant planting interests, all such marriages were denied. Most Cuban planters and colonial powers associated class endogamy with color segregation and the ban on interracial marriages was not lifted until slavery was abolished (ibid.:5, 31, 38).

12. One specialist on English family law guessed that the statute requiring a minister to witness a marriage ceremony "probably never applied outside England and Ireland; it certainly does not apply where compliance with it would be impossible, difficult or even inconvenient" (Bromley 1981:29). Yet instead of waiving that legal stricture, Antiguans preserved the special legal privileges and rights of marriage for an exclusive few by transferring the formalities of marriage to civil authorities.

13. Edward Long wrote in 1774: "Formerly, the custom in these islands was, to be married by the justices of the peace; for in those days a clergyman was not always at hand. ... And it is certain, that a marriage, celebrated in this manner in Jamaica, even now, if according to the form of words in our liturgy, would be valid in law, and support the right to dower or thirds. The Jamaica law restrains none from performing the ceremony, except ministers not qualified ... and the penalty, imposed upon others who solemnize without banns or license, does not tend to declare such marriages void" (1970 2:238).

14. In the act of 1908, incest was defined as sexual intercourse between parents and children, siblings, and a man and his granddaughter. An offender faced between three and seven years of penal servitude or up to two years imprisonment with or without hard labor (N. Anderson 1982).

15. Gaspar incorrectly concludes that "the marriage law could not have achieved much, to judge only from the gradual increase in the number of freedmen of mixed ancestry in the years after 1702, and the large number of mulatto slaves on the island's plantations and in the towns" (1985b:144). He conflates the practices of miscegenation, concubinage (which may or may not involve interracial unions), and marriage. As I show in the next chapter, these were very different creole phenomena and were subject to different norms and laws. Gaspar also underestimates the impact of the kinship codes for the developing creole society.

16. For a discussion of the legal regulation of sexual and marital behavior between slaves, servants, and free persons in the North American mainland colonies, see Higginbotham 1978.

17. On the other hand, a man could eliminate his wife's right to dower in his will, though his widow retained the right to take the matter to court. Dower is precluded by the Intestate Estates Act (1945) (*Laws of Antigua* 1962:vol. 1, 289–96.)

18. Much as they lamented the number of illegitimate children in the colony, the legislators were vehemently opposed to abortion. An 1815 act increased the penalties against any woman who attempted to abort or who tried to kill an unborn child who would have been illegitimate. A woman accused of this crime was tried by the rules of evidence applicable to murder. Any person who attempted to hide a still-born illegitimate child could be sentenced to two years in prison (*Laws of Antigua* 1804–17:348, 349). Flannagan specifically attributed the passage of these acts to several incidents in which young unmarried women practiced infanticide to preserve a newly ingrained sense of "honor" (1967:vol. 2, 95). Abortion was practiced elsewhere in the Caribbean (Morrissey 1989:112), and most likely it was also practiced in Antigua.

19. Except in Nevis, Leeward Island slaves were chattels only in cases of debt and when other assets were unavailable (Goveia 1965:152–53).

20. These "pronatalist" policies were similar to provisions of a law passed in Jamaica in 1792. The Jamaican statute, however, also provided monetary rewards to owners and overseers of estates on which there was a natural increase in the slave population (Roberts 1979:235–37).

21. The French handled these matters differently in their colonies. Edward Long, a scholar of Jamaican history, reports that the Code Noir of 1685 commanded all slaves be baptized and denied lawful marriage only to persons not baptized. Free men who had children with their slaves, and masters who allowed such behavior, were fined two thousand pounds of sugar. A master having children with his slave was deprived of both the children and their mother; they were forfeited "to the use and benefit of the hospital, with disability of their becoming enfranchised." Alternatively, the master might marry his concubine, an act that freed her and the children and gave them legitimate status (Long 1970:vol. 3, 923–24). At least in law, the French encouraged slave marriages consented to by masters and disallowed the separation of husbands, wives, and young children (ibid.:924, 932). Like the British, however, the French traced slave status through women. The Code of Martinique, for example, declares: "Children who are born of the marriages

of slaves are slaves and belong to the masters of the women slaves and not to those of their husbands. Should a male marry a free female, the children, whether boys or girls, will have the condition of their mother and be free like her . . . and if their father is free and the mother is a slave, the children will equally be slaves" (cited in Cousins 1935:37, my translation). According to Cousins, "Female descent of slave-status was not due to illegitimacy, or to a practical difficulty in discovering the identity of the father. Transcending the paternal rights implied by marriage stood the ancient law that the child of the freewoman is free and the child of the bondwoman is a slave" (ibid.:37). One of the consequences of the differing slave and free kinship laws, as Cousins correctly notes, would be the "struggle between the 'male' and 'female' types of family structure" (ibid.:55). In contrast to Cousins, I argue that neither of these two types were replicas of African or European patterns, and that they constitute one indigenous creole system.

22. Common practice in the islands allowed slaves to keep whatever goods they might acquire from the sale of provisions grown on the estates in their "own" gardens and during their "own" time. Some masters let slaves earn cash by hiring themselves out. Slaves did, of course, leave inheritances for their children in whatever forms were available to them.

23. Jones (1990) has recently argued that sale or threat of sale away from one's family were among the harshest and most effective forms of social control used by masters in the North American colonies. His argument is based on research on South Carolina, the mainland colony whose economic, political, and social conditions were in several ways similar to Antigua's. Slaveholders in South Carolina borrowed West Indian slave codes, established very large plantations manned by hundreds of slaves, and created a "black majority" in the state (Higginbotham 1978:151–215).

24. As Morrissey correctly points out, of course, legal equality "did not translate into equity among slaves precisely because slave masters treated male and female slaves differently" (1989:13). Caribbean slave men almost always had greater access to skilled positions, hiring out, and subsistence plots, and they held some authority over slave women and children. On the other hand, slave women's greater access to manumissions, domestic work, sexual unions with masters, and potential for bearing free children gave them other forms of power and advantages (ibid.:13–14). Nevertheless, law had greater influence in shaping kinship ideology and practice over time than Morrissey supposes.

25. I found nothing in the Antiguan record analogous to the 1826 Jamaican statute that allowed for the solemnization of marriages among slaves, protected their property rights, and gave them the right to receive bequests and legacies (Roberts 1979:242–43). After they were freed, Antiguan slaves incorporated the ritual of Christian marriage, but, as we shall see, the meaning of marriage had been forever altered.

Chapter 4: Legalities, Illegalities, and Creole Families

1. Referring to the "slave insurrection" in Antigua in 1831, Flannagan reports: "The cause of this disaffection among the black population was, the suppression of the Sunday markets, and the omission on the part of the authorities of the island, to provide a day instead of the Sabbath, in which the negroes might bring the produce of their gardens and poultry yards into the capital to sell" (1967:vol. 1, 146). The rebellion was repressed and its leader executed, but the planters agreed to allow the slaves to market their wares on Saturdays.

2. Neither I nor Gaspar, who made an exhaustive study of Antiguan records for the period up to 1763, located any documents describing trials of Antiguan slaves (1985a:190). However, Gaspar found compensation claims by owners whose slaves were executed between 1722 and 1763 and several estate records showing thefts, burglaries, felonies, and running away were the most common crimes committed by slaves against masters. Almost 51 percent of the compensation claims were for runaways executed or killed in flight, but there were also twenty-seven slaves condemned to death for having murdered other slaves (Gaspar 1985a:191–92, 194, 197). Almost sixty

years later, officials in Antigua reported to the Commissioners of Inquiry on the Administration of Justice in the West Indies that slaves "frequently" called upon magistrates to resolve their disputes (1826:131). As I argued in my discussion of obeah, there were culturally constituted legalities and illegalities within the slave community in Antigua, as well as between slaves and masters. Jones (1990:99) and Schwarz (1990:90–91) mention the lack of research on violence and crime among slaves in studies of North American slavery.

3. Goveia first pointed out that British settlers in the West Indies assigned their slaves two personas: they were either commodities or potential criminals (1970:25). More recently, Harrison (1988) discusses the meaning and use of social outlawry as a form of political protest and resistance in contemporary Jamaican society.

4. In a survey of Commonwealth Caribbean historiography, Higman points out that little is known about the social organization of free white and colored settlers in the early colonial period (1985: 5). However, R. Smith has argued for quite some time that a "dual marriage system" characterized West Indian societies from their inception (1982a:12). Dunn's (1972) discussion of the differences in family and household organization between Bridgetown and Provincetown and Beckles's (1981) and Romero's (1977) studies of indentured servants in the West Indies are other important contributions to this historiography.

5. Some important differences were: (1) Massachusetts Bay was settled initially as a Puritan refuge, but people journeyed to Antigua to make their fortunes as quickly as possible; (2) the varying modes of production in the two colonies; (3) the dissimilarities in Puritan and Anglican ideas about marriage; (4) the degree of formal institutional support for marriage provided by the church and state in each colony; and (5) the laws designed to regulate reproductive practices and gender relations in each locale. Together, these factors shaped the context for two quite different kinship systems. Their similarities and differences deserve much more elaboration than I can provide here.

6. Sheridan reports 698 of 3,652 white inhabitants were servants in 1720: 471 men, 140 women, 45 boys, and 42 girls (1973:196).

7. My thanks to Arthur Stinchcombe for drawing this to my attention. Interestingly, the Dutch employed the same tactic as the Antiguans years late in Sumatra: "In the late nineteenth century, the major tobacco companies neither accepted married applicants nor allowed them to take wives while in service" (Stoler 1989b:143). Later they relaxed this prohibition and permitted marriage after five years of service and evidence of solvency. As Stoler points out, "By refusing to employ married men, the estate industry virtually legislated a broad system of interracial concubinage into existence" (ibid.:143).

8. A 1672 account of the Leeward Islands mentions there were some sixty Quakers in Nevis and Antigua (Oliver 1894, vol. 1:liii). Irish immigration to Antigua declined and Scottish immigration increased in the next century.

9. Although certainly not commonplace in the seventeenth and eighteenth centuries, we shall see in the next chapter that divorce occurred more frequently in England before the 1857 Divorce Act than is usually imagined. Divorce was impossible in Antigua until the twentieth century, but John Luffman witnessed one trial for "criminal conversation," the eighteenth-century charge for adultery, at the Court of Common Pleas in St. John's in 1788. The case was brought by a schoolmaster against his wife and a young planter. The teacher won his suit, but when the jury learned that he himself "had been an industrious laborer in vineyards of seduction and prostitution," they awarded him only five hundred pounds in damages instead of the several thousand pounds he had requested. Luffman noted "to the honor of the island, it is worthy of remark, that this trial is the only instance for the aforementioned offence, for the last forty years" (1789:168–70). One presumes, of course, that adultery was more common than the legal record suggests.

10. For example, nineteenth-century Cuban marriage law prohibited marriages between persons related to the fourth degree, and custom dictated that persons allied by ritual kin ties should not wed. A papal dispensation was required before such persons could marry, yet these marriages were fairly common. There were two usual patterns, each serving a different purpose: marriage

between a man and his deceased wife's sister ensured the continued alliance between the two families, and marriage between a man and his brother's or sister's daughter solidified the consanguineous family's fortune (Martinez-Alier 1974:87–91).

11. Martin published *An Essay Upon Plantership* in 1750. The composition, which contains instructions to novice sugar planters, is the work of an erudite and pragmatic man of the times.

12. At the first census of the Leeward Islands in 1678 there were 176 males for every 100 females, with a comparable ratio among blacks of 107 males to 100 females. By 1720 there were only 108 white men for every 100 white women. The ratio fell again in 1756 to 104 white males to every 100 white females (Wells 1975:218). Antigua's African and colored population had 87 males per 100 females in 1817 and 90 males per 100 females in 1831 (Higman 1984b:116).

13. Contemporary Market Street in St. John's was formerly called "Scotch Row" because, according to Samuel Smith, "it was the business centre and all the business on both sides of it stretching from South Street at the southern end to Newgate Street in the north use to belong to Scotchmen" (Smith and Smith 1986:94). Lowes (1993:81–87) gives further details of the history of the street and its retailers.

14. In the English-speaking Caribbean, a *mulatto* was the child of a white man and a black woman, a *quadroon* was the child of a mulatto woman and a white man, and a *mestee* (*mustee*) was the child of a quadroon and a white man (Braithwaite 1971:167). *Mustee* was also used to describe a person who was part Indian, usually Indian and black (Jordan 1968:168–69).

15. Gaspar refers to the "very slow growth of the free non-white or freedmen, population of mixed (mulattoes), or unmixed (Negro) ancestry" before 1750 (1985b:135), but later figures do not suggest a slow growth rate! Indeed, the rapid growth of this population is interesting because the white settlers' fertility rates were low, mortality was high, and the group maintained their numbers mainly through the regular importation of adults, many of whom were servants (Wells 1975:214–17). Free black adults, on the other hand, were not imported into Antigua until after the end of the slave trade. Therefore, the free nonwhite group could have increased from a total of 17 persons in 1707 to 531 persons twenty years later, and to 1,230 persons in 1787 only through manumissions—for which there is little evidence—or through high fertility rates. My guess is that children were highly valued and that in Antigua, as in Barbados (Handler 1974:21) and Jamaica (Wells 1975:200), a high percentage of the total population of freed slaves were minors. There is also the possibility, of course, that the census figures are estimates. Higman calculates that in 1830 Antigua's population consisted of 80 percent "slave," 14.9 percent "freedman," and 5.1 percent "white" (1984b:77).

16. White women may have also chosen not to marry, or they may have been widowed. The 1753 survey of households showed 34 percent headed by women.

17. Free women of color outnumbered men of their own grade throughout the Leewards in the eighteenth century. For example, there were eighty-one women and thirty-seven men with this status in Montserrat in 1788, and the proportion of free colored women to men in Nevis was said to be nine to four (Goveia 1965:216). In Barbados, too, free black and colored women outnumbered men, but the ratios changed over the years. In 1801–2 women constituted 58 percent of the freed population, but that number dropped to 49.6 percent in 1809 (Handler 1974:22).

18. Moravian marriage records from the slave period in Antigua are not available, but Moravian ministers did sometimes marry slaves—in the eyes of the church if not the law. For example, Mary Prince, the slave of Mr. and Mrs. Wood of Antigua, married Daniel James in December 1826 at the Spring Gardens Moravian Church in St. John's. James was a carpenter and cooper who purchased his freedom. Mary's owners flogged her for marrying James without their permission, but they later relented and allowed him to live with her in their yard (Ferguson 1987:16, 74–75).

19. The petitioners also asked for a repeal of the White Servants' Act (an act found only in Antigua and Jamaica that prevented men of color from engaging in agricultural pursuits), to serve as plantation managers and overseers, to hold militia commissions, to sit as Grand and Petit Jurors, and to be allowed to participate in coroners' inquests (Oliver 1894:vol. 1, clii).

20. In Trinidad charitable associations such as the Trinidad Purity Alliance, which had the "formidable object of fighting illegitimacy and illicit unions, and campaigning for individual and

social 'purity,'" were run by upper-class men and women. The Anglican bishop chaired the alliance (Brereton 1979:57).

21. Sir George Thomas was the son of Colonel George Thomas and Sarah Winthrop, the only daughter of the Quaker deputy governor of Antigua. From the perspective of West Indian whites, his was an ideal and admirable career. Sir George inherited the estates of North Sound, Winthropes, Popeshead, and Five Islands from his uncle, William Thomas. He served in the assembly and the Council of Antigua and then was appointed lieutenant governor of Pennsylvania. He held that office from 1738 to 1747. In 1753, Sir George became governor of the Leeward Islands. He remained in the Caribbean until 1766, when he retired to England (Sheridan 1957:3).

22. Coleridge found that in Montserrat, Protestants and Catholics got along very cordially: "Indeed the faithful Catholic here has anticipated the fruits of emancipation; he considers it highly absurd to suffer himself to be deprived of great political advantages for the sake of a few oaths. . . . They intermarry, and in most cases the Abbe' loses; a thing which the Abbe' should look into, for the reverse takes place in England" (Coleridge 1826:169–70).

23. Higman reports: "Most urban slaves worked as domestics. In 1834 they accounted for 71 percent of the total slave population of Roseau [Dominica], 66 percent in Kingston [Jamaica], 60 percent in St. Johns [Antigua], and 49 percent in St. George [Grenada]" (1984b:227).

24. The Church of England was disestablished by Act No. 7 of 1873. From that date, public revenues could no longer be used to support the church. The church retained the right to organize assemblies, to govern itself, and to oversee its financial affairs and property. It lost the right to tax (*Laws of Antigua* 1920:77).

25. According to Olwig, slave households were small (1.9 to 3 persons) and marriage remained uncommon in the Danish possession of St. John until after emancipation. At that time, the Danes made changing one's residence illegal unless one were joining a spouse on another plantation. They also made fathers legally responsible for their children. In the 1860s, the Moravian church, which claimed as adherents about 90 percent of the population, joined the government in an effort to promote marriage and agreed that only legitimate children would be baptized (1981:68). As they anticipated, the result was a steep increase in the number of marriages (from 15 percent of the population in 1846 to 65 percent in 1880). Certainly not foreseen was the membership increase in the Lutheran church, whose ministers would baptize illegitimate children.

26. In Jamaica, Moravians and Anglicans tended mainly to the upper class, whereas Methodists and Baptists recruited wide followings among slaves (Fischer 1974a:30). The latter two denominations faced a great deal of discrimination when they first arrived. See Turner (1982) for a historical analysis of missionary activity in Jamaica.

27. Two critically important studies of the dialectical interplay of Christianity and African forms and forces include J. Comaroff (1985) and Comaroff and Comaroff (1991).

28. Although Roberts and Sinclair note that the association between religion and the family did not constitute the focus of their study, they drew attention to the significance of Christian baptism, confirmation, marriage, and burial, "to the understanding of the family within a society [Jamaica] which clings closely to Christianity" (1978:1). They emphasize that theirs is not "an attempt to put forward a kind of religious determinism of the family. It merely emphasizes the relevance of the religious setting in any analysis of the West Indian family, especially where such analysis involves the question of its 'origins'" (ibid.:2). Roberts and Sinclair find baptism of greater religious importance than marriage to Jamaicans—which accords with the emphasis given to baptism as opposed to marriage in the eighteenth and nineteenth centuries (ibid.:10–11). Nevertheless, the link between religion and the desire to marry emerges repeatedly throughout their text (ibid.:16, 18, 65) and fully accords with my findings for Antigua.

29. The relation between Christianity and marriage is discussed in greater detail in Chapter 6. During my fieldwork in Barbuda, I discovered that several people I interviewed had married following a major Christian revival that happened to coincide with some of the worst hurricanes and earthquakes in this century. These men and women felt they had been saved from disaster and from their own damnation.

Marriages in Barbuda

1970	2	1976	0	1982	4
1971	2	1977	0	1983	2
1972	1	1978	3	1984	0
1973	9	1979	6	1985	0
1974	5	1980	1	1986	5
1975	4	1981	0	1987	1

SOURCE: High Court records, St. John's, Antigua.

Interestingly, in 1772 a very destructive hurricane brought many new devotees to the Moravian church in Antigua (Simpson 1978:34). Roberts also found a link between marriage rates and natural disasters in Jamaica: "An outstanding feature of marriage in the island was the very high level attained after the destruction of Kingston by earthquake and fire in 1907. The rate reported at that time . . . was the highest ever recorded in the island. This dramatic rise following a natural disaster, strongly suggests a heavy involvement of religious feeling, unmarried mothers were evidently motivated to seek religious, and only incidently, legal sanctions to their union. . . . In any event, this high level of marriage proved to be of very short duration. By 1908, the rate had returned to its traditional low level" (1985:23; 1979:287–88). Finally, Brereton reports Trinidad's marriage rate was unusually high in 1854, when cholera struck the island and "terrified people married in droves to avoid dying in a state of sin" (1979:120).

30. Some of the most radical differences in law's treatment of the children of interracial unions occur between the French, Spanish, Dutch, and English-speaking islands. Among others, see especially discussions of miscegenation and racial ideologies in Curtin 1964, Genovese 1972, Higginbotham 1978, Jordan 1968, and Mintz 1974. For Jamaica, see Alexander 1977a, 1984; Austin 1979, 1984; Curtin 1955; Douglass 1992; Henriques 1953, 1974; and R. Smith 1982b, 1987, 1988.

31. As Art Stinchcombe noted to me, the comparison between the Jamaican and Antiguan estates is imperfect on two accounts. First, Jamaica's terrain is rougher than Antigua's, leading to more wasted acreage on each estate and influencing the number of slaves actually needed to tend the cane. Second, Antigua was one of the older sugar colonies and these used more slaves per acre. Nevertheless, the combined demographic evidence anticipates ethnographic reality; Antiguans are mostly phenotypically dark skinned (Senior 1991:3). More importantly, in sharp contrast to the findings of anthropologists who have worked in Jamaica, miscegenation did not loom large in the kinship ideology articulated by Antiguans I interviewed.

32. Lowes (1993) constructs a convincing body of evidence to prove that the small nonwhite middle class in Antigua at abolition had almost disappeared a century later. Earlier (1982) she remarked that "color" is differently emphasized in different classes in Antigua.

33. As D. Hall (1964) explains, people were absentee proprietors of West Indian estates for a variety of reasons. An unprecedented era of prosperity beginning around 1750 made it possible for many Caribbean planters to retire in England. After 1775, and until about 1815, many estates lacked resident owners because they were inherited by men who had never been to the islands and who never cared to go there. These heirs were interested only in the estates' revenues. Following the Napoleonic Wars and the abolition of the slave trade, a large number of estates fell into the hands of overseas creditors (Ragatz 1931:7). Antiguan society suffered from absenteeism in its very early history, but in later periods, according to Ragatz, it was the exception that attested to the "true significance of absenteeism as a factor in affecting the ruin of the British Caribbean" (ibid.:24). Sheridan (1973:206) finds merit in Ragatz's thesis, but stresses that Antigua differed from its sister colonies in degree, rather than kind.

34. Handler sees a "general pattern in the British West Indies wherein manumissions were very infrequent" (1974:50). Just over 1 percent of Antigua's 29,537 slaves had been manumitted in

1831–32. In 1826–27, .8 percent of the total slave population was manumitted. The figures for 1817, 1820, and 1823–24 were .7 percent, .4 percent, and .6 percent, respectively.

35. Jamaican slave women, in contrast, counted on "love and affection" when consideration of their manumission arose. Returns of manumissions in Jamaica between 1808 and 1823 show two-thirds of the slaves freed in that period were women and children. In the majority of cases, the children were listed as being a lighter shade than their mothers (Cousins 1935:47, 49). A reviewer suggested to me that perhaps women were socially but not legally freed. Although I certainly allow for this possibility, nothing in the historical record from Antigua supports the argument that that was a regular practice.

36. The spokesman from Dominica professed that he scarcely understood the question. He told the committee: "A male slave marrying a white female, or a white male marrying a female slave, I have never yet met with. A male white owner marrying his own slave, would, I conceive, virtually enfranchise her, and the progeny would be free of course. But a conmixture of white and slave does not render either the slave or issue free from servitude" (1826:vol. 2, 247–48). The representative from St. Vincent admitted that a 1756 law decreed that "all persons more than three degrees removed in a lineal descent, from a negro ancestor, should be deemed white, and should have all the privileges and immunities of His Majesty's white subjects of those colonies, if free and brought up in the Christian religion." However, that act, similar to one in Jamaica, had been suspended in 1802, five years before the end of the slave trade.

37. Antigua actually had a slightly higher percentage of urban slaves than Jamaica did in 1810 and 1820. By 1830, however, the percentage was the same (8 percent) (Higman 1984b:68–70).

38. The Antiguan case is more like that of Barbados. Handler found: "In striking contrast to the legal code of Jamaica, where miscegenation was apparently much greater, the Barbadian code did not contain provisions which permitted freedmen, after a certain generation or with primarily Caucasian features, to be defined as white" (1974:68–69). The Barbadian lawmakers made things easier on themselves: in an act of 1721 they debarred from basic civil rights any one "whose original extraction shall be proved to have been from a Negro" (ibid.:68).

39. In a discussion trying to reconcile our different experiences, Lowes and I agreed that genealogies are politicized and may shift to accommodate the impact of events such as the black power movement of the 1960s and 1970s. As a result, different generations may espouse different myths of origin. The Antiguan middle class of the nineteenth and early twentieth centuries may indeed have originated in the unions of black women and white men. The contemporary middle class in Antigua has a different origin and history and seems to place genealogical emphasis differently (Lazarus-Black 1990a:chap. 6; Lowes 1982, 1987, 1993).

Chapter 5: The Postemancipation Period, 1834–1986

1. See, for example, Rodney (1981:69–70) for Guyana and Post (1978:121) for Jamaica. Thome and Kimball reported that in Antigua in 1837 "the commonest petty crime of the time was 'breaking canes to eat,' but crimes of a heinous nature were very rare" (in Nicholson 1984:15).

2. Trotman (1986:271–72) argues that the "plantocrats labelled as criminal those activities that reflected the contradictions of the [plantation] system" they struggled to retain. The same argument holds for Antigua in the immediate postemancipation period.

3. The new assembly's twenty-four members included the solicitor general, treasurer, attorney general, colonial secretary, eight men nominated by the governor, and twelve elected representatives. A year later, an executive council was appointed to assist the governor (Microfilm No. 9).

4. D. Hall argues that emancipation was indirectly responsible for the loss of local legal autonomy because one reason Antiguan legislators voted to become a Crown colony was the planters' fear that the emancipated population would gain too much control in the House of Assembly (1971:175–77). Brereton's work on Trinidad suggests over the course of the nineteenth century the Crown and local Caribbean elites shared common interests: "The central fact about

politics in Trinidad in the later nineteenth century is that the planter-merchant community was able to exercise a very considerable influence on policy making, despite the formally autocratic Crown Colony constitution" (1979:24).

5. The 1872 statute made Antigua, Montserrat, St. Christopher, Nevis, Dominica and the (British) Virgin Islands a single colony. The island secretary and the attorney general of the Leeward Islands became members of the Legislative Council of Antigua. An executive council continued to assist the governor. In 1898, the Legislative Council was reorganized to consist of eight "official" and eight "unofficial" members appointed by the queen and serving at her pleasure. After 1899, the eight official members included the colonial secretary, the attorney general, and the auditor general of the Leeward Islands, the treasurer of Antigua, and four other public officials. Unofficial members were private citizens (Microfilm No. 10).

6. After the surrender of local autonomy, Antigua only occasionally passed a measure affecting kin relations. Two examples are the Absconding Guardians ordinance of 1919 (Maintenance of Children Act, Cap. 49), which protected children whose parents or guardians were leaving the island without making adequate provision for their maintenance and care (*Laws of Antigua* 1920:618–20; Cumper and Daly 1979:20), and the Children Emigration Protection Ordinance (1919), which prevented guardians from removing a child from the state unless they could show just cause (*Laws of Antigua* 1962:vol. 2, 1215–16). I found several cases in the magistrates' books for 1981–87 in which the former statute had been invoked to prevent fathers from leaving the island. The Children Emigration (Protection) Ordinance was repealed in 1974 (*Laws of Antigua* 1974:No. 25).

7. As Lowes points out, only Sheridan (1961) and Dunn (1972) have conducted research on the composition of the Antiguan plantocracy. Reanalyzing their data, she finds that discontinuities are as striking as continuities. For example, by 1829 only thirteen of sixty-five leading families in 1730–75 remained estate owners, and of these, three were absentee (1992:9 n. 6). Lowes (1993:99–113) describes the colonial service occupational ladder, of which the Leeward Islands "were only one rung—and a very lowly rung at that" (ibid.:99). The colonial posts were filled by "gentlemen," hardly ever including white West Indians, not to mention people of color. In the first election after emancipation, the Antiguan assembly was elected by a total of only 323 men, because the property qualifications for voting were so high (ibid.:108–9). By 1897, however, the planting interest in government was beginning to erode, and seven of the twelve elected members were nonwhites. Not surprisingly, this Legislative Council voted itself out of existence the following year, following a warning from the secretary of state for colonies that the planters would get no further assistance until the elected element to the council was eliminated (ibid.:117–19).

8. The full title of the Contract Act was: An Act For The Better Adjusting And More Easy Recovery Of The Wages of Servants In Husbandry And Of Artificers, Handicraftsmen And Other Labourers Employed Upon Estates; And For The Better Regulation Of Such Servants, Artificers, Handicraftsmen And Other Labourers (1835) (*Laws of Antigua* 1864:183–86). Great Britain disallowed some of the more abominable clauses of Antigua's Contract Act immediately. Other clauses were repealed in 1855 and 1865 (Microfilm No. 6; Microfilm No. 9; D. Hall 1971:27–28). Still, the Contract Act remained law until 1937.

9. In other British colonies, only slaves under six years of age were freed in 1834; others had to serve their former masters as apprentices for six years. All Antiguan slaves, in contrast, were set free on 1 August 1834. D. Hall explains that the legislators voted for immediate emancipation because they were sure that the transition would be peaceful, there was hardly any available land for purchase and therefore they expected the freedmen would remain on the estates, and they believed wage labor would prove cheaper than slave labor (1971:19–24). As it turned out, the apprenticeship system proved unworkable and it was abandoned by 1838. Bolland (1981) suggests the Antiguan Contract Act served as a model to control labor elsewhere in the British colonies.

10. An amending act of 1865 explains: "All Servants in Husbandry, or Artificers, Handicraftsmen or other Laborers who shall be employed to work upon Estates shall, in the absence of sufficient proof to the contrary, be considered as employed under a 'General Hiring'" (Microfilm No. 9).

11. Chinese immigrants were originally indentured for three years, but this was altered to one year in 1880 at the same time that funds were set aside to defray the costs of an anticipated group (Microfilm No. 10). As far as I can tell, very few Chinese immigrants arrived in Antigua. The census of 1946 lists eighty "Asiatic" persons on the island, but the category included both "Syrians" (seventy-seven) and "Chinese" (three) (Jamaica, Central Bureau of Statistics, 1948:xvi).

12. The few blatant attempts to attract white laborers, and especially white women, met very limited success. Great Britain disallowed An Act To Encourage The Immigration And Settlement Of European Farm And Other Servants And Mechanics (1844) the following year. That law had encouraged employers to import married servants and mechanics by paying special bounties for these men, their wives, and children (Microfilm No. 7). It was replaced two years later by a statute to bring workers from "the Azores, Madiera, the Canaries or the Cape de Verd Islands." That act received royal assent but contained no economic incentives to encourage employers to find families who would emigrate together. Importers may have been discouraged from recruiting women under this scheme because they earned only two-thirds the bounty earned for bringing in men (Microfilm No. 8).

13. See, for example, Rodney's discussion of the indentured-servant codes in Guyana (1981:34–40). Brereton (1979:178–81), Trotman (1986:191–95), and E. Williams (1962:102–5) are among those describing the uses and abuses of indentured-servant codes in Trinidad.

14. The 1834 bill to punish rogues and other disorderly persons was finally repealed by Federal Act No. 15 of 1876 (*Laws of Antigua* 1920:xvi). However, it was only one of several repressive measures of the nineteenth century. For example, an act of 1854 instructs constables to arrest people for offenses such as "furious riding or driving," "posting bills," "prostitutes," "indecent song or figure," "kite or game," "placing coals or cart in thoroughfare," "removing night soil," "name on vehicle," and "mischievous or disorderly conduct." Each of these crimes carried a forty-shilling penalty. Five-pound fines were charged against persons keeping "a house of ill fame," against those who "knowingly permit drunkenness" or who "suffer prostitutes or persons of notoriously bad character to meet together and remain therein" (*Laws of Antigua* 1864:314–18). A law of 1858 made it unnecessary to prove the intention of the offender in cases of disorderly conduct; proof of the act was deemed a punishable offense (*Laws of Antigua* 1864:370).

15. The lawmakers took these steps in the same month that they abolished slavery! They explained: "It is highly expedient and necessary that the police Establishment of this Island and the laws regulating the same should be altered and modified so far as to make these more suitable to the changes in the social conditions and circumstances of the colony" (Microfilm No. 6).

16. In 1854, the force included sixty-eight men, and the police magistrate held court three days a week. Mounted police joined the force in 1858. A second police magistrate was hired in 1860 and a third in 1867. The first resident magistrate to Barbuda was appointed in 1871 (Microfilm No. 7; Microfilm No. 9; Microfilm No. 10).

17. Other Antiguan bills to prevent "riotous and disorderly conduct" appear in 1841 and 1842 (Microfilm No. 7). In 1859, the maximum penalty for involvement in riots was changed to five years in prison (Microfilm No. 9). The Legislative Council of the Leeward Islands further reduced these penalties in 1897 (*Federal Acts of the Leeward Islands* 1897:No. 23).

18. The first postemancipation registration law I encountered is An Act For Registering Births And Deaths (1856) (Microfilm No. 9). The preamble, repeated in later statutes, rationalizes the count this way: "Evidence of title to property may be more easily obtained and statistical information afforded for purposes of public interest and utility, and whereby also crime may be more readily discovered and more efficiently suppressed" (Microfilm No. 9). Other registration or census laws passed in 1861, 1868, 1870, 1880, and 1885 (Microfilm No. 9; Microfilm No. 10; *Laws of Antigua* 1864:335–40; *Laws of Antigua* 1920:46–62). Data was collected from Barbuda after 1868 (Microfilm No. 9).

19. It is still illegal to fail to obtain the services of a midwife: "It shall be the duty of the husband, and where a man and a woman who are unmarried are living together in the same house or room as husband and wife it shall be the duty of such man, to secure the attendance of a duly qualified medical practitioner or a registered midwife at the confinement of his wife

or such woman, as the case may be, and the failure on the part of such husband or man to secure such attendance shall be an offence under this ordinance" (*Laws of Antigua* 1962:vol. 3, 1927).

20. The first Board of Health was established in 1854. Acts to prevent the spread of infectious diseases appeared in 1888 and 1895 (Microfilm No. 10). A board to maintain the cleanliness of public roads, slaughterhouses, markets, houses and yards, and towns and villages, was appointed in 1902 (*Laws of Antigua* 1920:369–79).

21. The British Infant Felons Act (1840) allowed the court to assign custody of a juvenile convicted of a felony to any person willing to care for him if such referral were deemed in the youth's best interests (Bromley 1981:390). Antigua's juvenile apprentice act was amended in 1867 so that males between the ages of ten and sixteen could be apprenticed as agricultural laborers for up to five years as long as an immigration agent countersigned the Indenture of Apprenticeship. Acts of 1869 and 1870 empowered magistrates to apprentice persons under age sixteen and "convicted of certain Larcenies and Misdemeanours" (Microfilm No. 9). These various Antiguan acts were consolidated in the Apprentices Act of the Leeward Island Federation (1882) (*Federal Acts of the Leeward Islands* 1914:vol. 2, 7–8).

22. The act declared: "It shall be lawful for any parent or any other person having the legal custody of any child under the age of five years to require the Management to receive such child into their care in the Nursery for any period of time between sunrise and sunset upon payment of the fee applicable to the case. . . . Provided always that the Management shall not be required to receive any child into the nursery if in the discretion of the Management it appears that the parent or other person having the legal custody of such child is in a position to take proper care of such child outside the nursery" (Microfilm No. 10).

23. Under the Juveniles Act in force during my fieldwork in 1985–87, "neglect" meant failure to provide "adequate food, clothing, rest, medical aid or lodging" for a child, but only if the parent is able to do so. The act protects the right of "any parent, teacher or other person having the lawful control or charge of a juvenile," to punish him. Any parent who finds a child beyond his control may ask the Juvenile Court for assistance. Ironically, however, the Juveniles Act does not define "parent" (Cumper and Daly 1979:18, 19, 22).

24. Lowes (1993:239–80) provides an excellent discussion of the history of education in Antigua, describing the education arena as a "terrain of struggle, first between free and unfree, then between whites and nonwhites" (ibid.:240). Brereton (1979:64–85) discusses the importance of education for social mobility in postemancipation Trinidad.

25. English common law and equity recognized parents' moral duty to give their children an education suitable to their station in life. However, there was no legal means to enforce that obligation. In 1870, Parliament took steps to build public elementary schools. The Elementary Education Act of 1876 required all parents to ensure that their children received instruction in "reading, writing, and arithmetic" (Bromley 1981:312).

26. Antigua began revising its system for educating the poor before the Act of Emancipation. In that act, the British government made provision to pay religious bodies to run schools for the freedmen. After 1845, West Indian governments and laborers had to pay for their own educational programs. Nevertheless, the British continued to send advice to the colonies about how best to educate the former slaves. They suggested "grammatical English," enough arithmetic to allow peasants to keep accounts, instruction in agricultural techniques and improvements, loyalty to the Crown, and social responsibility (Augier and Gordon 1962:164, 166, 182–83; Henry 1985:63–64; Lowes 1993:241–42).

27. The Employment Of Children Prohibition and the Employment Of Women, Young Persons And Children were put into effect during the Great Depression (*Laws of Antigua* 1962: vol. 5, 2807–8, 2809–13). These prohibited employment of children under the age of twelve except if they were engaged in domestic or agricultural work for parents or guardians and the employment of children under fourteen from any "industrial undertaking" whatsoever. These rules were replaced in 1975 by the comprehensive Antigua Labour Code (*Laws of Antigua* 1975:No. 14). Today children may not be employed during school hours, for more than eight hours in any day, or without a medical examination. They are also restricted from certain industrial and night jobs.

28. The law was entitled An Act To Authorize The Payment Of A Subsidy In Aid Of The Education Of The Middle And Upper Classes Of The Population Of Antigua. A similar scheme to assist the middle classes in educating their children was proposed in British Guiana in 1853. There, too, secondary schools were too expensive for most people (Augier and Gordon 1962:184–85). Trinidad also educated differently the children of the rich and the poor, and excluded illegitimate children from its colleges (Brereton 1979:64–85, 81–82).

29. The first government-owned secondary school in Antigua was the Princess Margaret School, which opened in 1955. The government acquired the Antigua Grammar School and the Antigua Girls High School in 1964 (N. Richards n.d.:11). Further details about the history of the latter two schools in relation to the struggle of the nonwhite middle class to educate its children can be found in Lowes (1993:254–80).

30. To take one early example, England had introduced the Speenhamland system of poor relief in 1795, which gave allowances to individuals whose wages fell below a certain level. The scale of the subsidy was tied to the price of bread and assured the poor a minimum income whatever their earnings. However, the act also impeded the development of the working class and eventually impoverished the people of the countryside (Polanyi 1944:78–83). In 1834, the Poor Law Reform Act "did away with this obstruction to the labor market: the 'right to live' was abolished" (ibid.:82). In contrast to the British, Antiguans ignored Speenhamland altogether and experimented instead with several different poor-relief schemes.

31. Sidney and Beatrice Webb's *English Poor Law Policy* (1963b) never clearly defines *relatives* or what legal responsibilities relatives held with respect to the poor. As far as I can determine, when nineteenth-century English poor-law commissioners and guardians discussed making "relatives" accountable for poor persons, they usually had in mind legal responsibilities between husbands, wives, and children (e.g., Webb and Webb 1963b:3, 4, 126). That fact, of course, is illustrative of the very different kinship systems with which British and Antiguan lawmakers were concerned. Those who drafted the English Poor Law of 1834 were primarily concerned with the "able-bodied poor," men capable of being employed in the workhouses. They assumed those men's dependent wives and children would follow them to the workhouses (ibid.:3, 15, 36, 100–101). "Wives" were further differentiated into several different classes, including widows, deserted wives, those whose husbands were in His Majesty's service, beyond the seas, imprisoned, or insane and with or without children (ibid.:40–41, 100–104, 174–78). Never-married women with illegitimate children comprised a relatively small percentage of England's paupers. Before 1834, they were given relief in their own homes. Each parish was responsible for trying to find putative fathers to recover what relief had been given their children. The 1834 poor law exempted putative fathers from the responsibility of reimbursing the parish. Instead, the commissioners recommended that a bastard child be "what Providence appears to have ordained that it should be, a burden on its mother, and where she cannot maintain it, on her parents" (cited in Webb and Webb 1963b:7). It is not clear, however, if this recommendation was enforced because Parliament "contented itself with giving the Central Authority wide powers and almost unfettered discretion in the use of them" (ibid.:12). After 1844, it became illegal to provide outdoor relief to women with illegitimate children, but again the discretionary power of local authorities produced geographical diversity in practice (ibid.:23, 83–84). A circular of 1871, a 1875 policy recommendation of the Manchester Board of Guardians, and an 1873–74 annual report suggested the inspectorate try harder to get contributions from relatives of people receiving relief (ibid.:150, 152, 229). I found only one nineteenth-century English law that specifically imposed legal obligation upon a group for persons not their spouse or offspring. The Married Women's Property Act (1882) made a married woman with separate property responsible for maintaining her husband, children, and grandchildren (ibid.:175) (Lazarus-Black 1992:879 n. 18).

32. The 1876 Vagrants Act of the Leeward Island Federation retained much of the language of this act. It reclassified any person "being able, wholly or in part, to maintain himself or herself, or his or her family, by work or other means, and willfully refusing or neglecting to do so" into an "idle and disorderly person" subject to a one month in prison. Moreover, "every person running

away and leaving his wife or his or her child or children" was deemed a "rogue and a vagabond," subject to three months of hard labor (*Federal Acts of the Leeward Islands* 1914:vol. 1, 125–28).

33. There is an earlier version of this clause in the 1852 act that created the Poor House but it did not specify which relationships carried legally binding responsibilities as precisely as the later law. Moreover, whereas the 1852 law required only the mother of a bastard child to maintain that child until age fourteen, the 1855 version made both parents responsible for illegitimate children. The penalty for failing to support one's relative was up to three months in jail with or without hard labor (Microfilm No. 8).

34. I am referring to informal adoptions; children now considered "children of the family" in British and Antiguan law. There were no legal adoptions in the Leeward Islands until 1944, even though these became possible in England in 1926 (*Federal Acts of the Leeward Islands* 1944:No. 18; *Laws of Antigua* 1962:vol. 7, 1505–17; Bromley 1981:336).

35. Some of the tenets of Jamaica's 1869 Maintenance Law sound similar to the Antiguan statutes I have described here. The Jamaican law passed during the depression of the 1860s and was obviously designed to prevent an increase in persons eligible for poor relief. Nevertheless, as Boxill notes, "this law was unique in its recognition of the reality of family relationships in Jamaica" (1985:12). Roberts, however, called the Jamaican act "a dead letter because it had no provision for fixing paternity" (1979:252).

36. The 1899 revision of this law also assigned legal responsibilities on the basis of near or remote consanguineous or affinal ties (Microfilm No. 10). Moreover, like the poor laws, these medical acts gave magistrates authority to penalize people who neglected or refused to maintain kin for whom they were legally responsible. Today, section 25 of the Offences Against the Persons Act (Cap. 58) makes willful refusal to maintain kin a misdemeanor. A social security system providing stipends for old age, sickness, unemployment, maternity leave, and funeral and survivors' benefits has been in operation since 1972 (*Laws of Antigua* 1972:No. 3).

37. Women with illegitimate children in England gained the right to apply for maintenance orders to be paid to themselves in 1844 (Bromley 1981:5, 595). That law was amended in the Bastardy Laws Amendment Act of 1872, which probably served as the model for the Leeward Islands statute.

38. Most of the changes since 1875 have been amendments in the amount and duration of support that a magistrate may order a man to pay or in the procedures to facilitate processing cases. For example, after 1881 a magistrate could assign putative fatherhood even if the man could not be brought to trial. At that time, illegitimate children received 1s.6d. per week in support until age 13 *(Federal Acts of the Leeward Islands* 1881:No. 16). After 1920, maintenance orders could be sent to England, Ireland, and elsewhere in the Commonwealth (*Laws of Antigua* 1962:vol. 8, 2457–64). Two years later child support was raised to 5s. per week (*Federal Acts of the Leeward Islands* 1921:No. 11; 1923:No 10; 1924:No. 13). Following the Magistrate's Code of Procedure (Amendment) Act (1953), a wife could apply for an order for noncohabitation if her spouse abused her or the children, for a weekly sum not exceeding $10.00 (Eastern Caribbean), and for $2.40 per week for each of the "children of the marriage." These included "every child (whether legitimate or illegitimate) whom the applicant or defendant is liable under any law to maintain and who has been living with them as part of the husband's family." Maintenance continued until the children were fourteen years old. A nonmarried woman applying for maintenance for her offspring, however, could obtain only $1.50 per week in support (*Federal Acts of the Leeward Islands* 1953:No. 13). Discrimination in the amount of the stipend based on the legitimacy status of the child was finally eliminated in 1973, at the same time that the ceiling was raised to $7.00 per week until the child reached sixteen. Wives could obtain up to $15.00 per week for their own support (*Laws of Antigua* 1973:No. 19). A further amendment to the Magistrate's Code of Procedure Act (1982) substituted $25.00 for support for a wife separated from her husband and $15.00 for support for each dependent child (*Laws of Antigua* 1982:No. 11). The 1982 statute remained in effect in 1992.

39. Stipends were payable directly to the mother, and she had to apply for arrears within thirteen weeks or they were forfeited. The magistrate also had discretionary power to order the father to pay the costs of the case, a payment to the midwife, and funeral expenses if the child

died. He could appoint a guardian for a child if the mother died, was of unsound mind, or went to prison.

40. In 1885, Bishop Nuttall led a conference to discuss the problem of illegitimacy in Jamaica. The members drew up several petitions, including one asking the governor to require registration of fathers of illegitimate children and to appoint an officer to ensure that every child was registered—with or without the mother's consent. When the governor failed to act, the bishop issued a pamphlet that included the perceptive comment that this "social evil" could not be attributed to vice among the natives, or solely to the lower classes (R. Smith 1987:186–87; 1988:104–5). Given the date of the amendment to enforce the bastardy law (1886), Nuttall and his associates may have wielded greater influence than previously imagined. Registration of fathers of bastard children has never been a popular idea in Jamaica. In March 1898, the Legislative Council rejected a similar proposal by Henry Clarke (Salmon n.d.:22).

41. Other bills affecting kinship legalities after the creation of the Leeward Federation also show direct British influence. Some examples, discussed in later chapters, include the Guardianship of Infants Act, 1949 (*Federal Acts of the Leeward Islands* 1949:No. 9), the Legitimacy Act, 1929 (*Federal Acts of the Leeward Islands* 1929:No. 9; *Laws of Antigua* 1962:vol. 5, 3029–35), and the Intestates Estates Act, 1945 (*Federal Acts of the Leeward Island* 1945:No. 4; *Laws of Antigua* 1962:vol. 1, 289–96).

42. In a study of early English divorces, Wolfram (1955) found 325 cases of divorce by private acts of Parliament between 1700 and 1857, when the Matrimonial Causes Act created the Divorce Court. These acts reveal demographic profiles of the parties and enable Wolfram to disprove these long-held assumptions: (1) divorce was until recently the privilege of the wealthy in England, (2) it was always extremely costly, and (3) its steady increase can be attributed to women's liberation. Wolfram found that divorces between titled and aristocratic persons constituted 77 percent of divorce cases between 1700–1750, but they accounted for only about 65 percent of all cases between 1750–1857. After 1830, the aristocracy almost disappears from the divorce roll and 20 percent of divorces were granted to lower-class persons. Women prosecuted four cases.

43. These included: (1) incestuous adultery, (2) bigamy with adultery, (3) adultery coupled with cruelty, (4)sodomy or bestiality, (5) adultery with desertion for two years or more, or (6) conviction for rape (Bromley 1981:187). Only after 1923 could wives petition for divorce on the single issue of adultery.

44. Recall that the common law granted fathers custody of their children, but that Talfourd's Act (1839) empowered the Court of Chancery to give mothers custody of children until age seven and access to them thereafter—unless a mother had been found guilty of adultery (Bromley 1981:284). An act of 1873 later gave mothers custody of children until age sixteen and ignored the issue of adultery. Antigua's Guardianship Of Infants Act (1887), modeled on the English act of 1886, declares: "The mother of an infant shall have the like powers to apply to the Court in respect of any matter affecting the infant as are possessed by the father" (*Laws of Antigua* 1962:vol. 5, 3025–28).

45. Jurisdiction over divorce in England was transferred to the High Court and assigned to the Probate, Divorce and Admiralty Division in 1875. The Administration Of Justice Act (1970) renamed this court the Family Division of the High Court and directed probate business to the Chancery Division and admiralty cases to the Queen's Bench Division. Since the 1950s and 1960s, however, the volume of family cases in England has made it necessary to hear noncontested divorce cases in county courts. The Family Division has powers to grant custody and maintenance orders, but its authority does not extend to decisions regarding paternity and maintenance of illegitimate children (Bromley 1981:2–4).

46. The Matrimonial Causes Act (1878), for example, allowed a wife to refuse to cohabit with her spouse if he had been convicted of assaulting her and gave the court authority to award her maintenance and custody of the children. Over the next half-century, a series of acts collectively known as the Summary Jurisdiction (Separation and Maintenance) Acts (1895 to 1949), extended the grounds for which wives could apply for maintenance orders, enabled the courts to order married men to pay higher sums for child support, and eventually gave husbands the right to

apply for matrimonial relief. These laws, in turn, were overhauled by the Matrimonial Proceedings (Magistrates' Courts) Act of 1960, which increased again magistrates' powers with respect to the custody and maintenance of children (Bromley 1981:5).

47. Cumper and Daly point out, for example, that "the *Marriage (Prohibited Degree of Relationship) Act* (Cap. 349) removes the restriction of affinity from the family of the deceased spouse, but declares that it shall remain in the cases of persons whose marriage has been terminated by divorce. The proviso to section 11 of the *Matrimonial Causes Act* (Cap. 52) confirms this. It states that 'It shall not be lawful for a man to marry the sister and/or half-sister' of his wife from whom he has been divorced during the lifetime of this wife, and there is a similar prohibition governing marriage by a divorced wife to the brother or half-brother of the man who had been her spouse during his lifetime. The law of England has lifted this ban on the remarriage of divorced persons, but in the face of the explicit legislative prohibitions quoted above, this cannot be taken to be applicable in Antigua" (1979:4). Antigua's laws derive from Leeward Island Acts No. 7 of 1912 and No. 8 of 1934.

48. The vast increase in divorce in England after World War II reflected changing attitudes and new economic factors: "Legal aid had opened the doors of the divorce court to many who could not previously have afforded it; the attitude of society towards divorced spouses (particularly 'guilty' spouses) had changed; and many religious bodies were taking a far less rigid attitude. More than 90 percent of all petitions were undefended and some of these undoubtedly amounted to divorce by consent" (Bromley 1981:188–89). Antigua has no legal-aid system, but many attorneys accept reduced fees for divorce suits from clients whom they know are economically impoverished.

49. Interestingly, because there is no record of earlier divorces, the council declared the law "applicable since the sixteenth day of June, nineteen hundred and thirteen" (*Federal Acts of the Leeward Islands* 1948:No. 1). A year later, it passed the Matrimonial Causes (War Marriages) Act, which applied only to unions celebrated after 3 September 1939. Clearly intended to address the special circumstances of the war years, the law allowed the Supreme Court to divorce couples who were married less than three years or who might not be domiciled in the colony (*Federal Acts of the Leeward Islands* 1949:No. 1). It was repealed in 1974 (*Laws of Antigua* 1974:No. 25).

50. A lawyer may satisfy the judge that his client is suffering exceptional hardship or depravity on the part of the spouse and so convince the judge to hear the case sooner.

51. Divorces obtained in Barbados, the British Virgin Islands, Dominica, Grenada, Guyana, Montserrat, St. Christopher-Nevis, Anguilla, St. Lucia, St. Vincent, Trinidad and Tobago, and the United Kingdom of Great Britain and Northern Ireland are recognized automatically. Decrees from other countries are accepted only if the petitioner can demonstrate the divorce was obtained legally and the respondent was both aware of the proceedings and given the opportunity to testify in his or her own behalf (*Laws of Antigua* 1975:No. 25). In practice, this means that only those who can afford to travel abroad can sever their marital ties on the basis of "irretrievable breakdown."

52. Lewin (1987) encountered a similar phenomenon in Brazil.

53. There were a few exceptional circumstances in the nineteenth century in which married women in England could control property. The Matrimonial Causes Act of 1857 allowed a woman legally separated from her husband to be deemed a *femme sole*. A deserted wife could also apply for a protection order to prevent her husband or his creditors from seizing goods she acquired after she was deserted. An act of 1886 allowed women assaulted by their husbands, and therefore granted noncohabitation orders, to deploy all property acquired after the separation (Bromley 1981:415, 486). Antiguan women had recourse to another legal remedy after 1862: if a woman's husband was declared a lunatic, if he were in prison, or if he were living overseas, she could apply to the court to dispense with his permission in managing property and to execute all acts and deeds as if she were a *femme sole*. As in England, a deserted Antiguan wife could apply to a magistrate to protect the belongings she acquired after her husband abandoned her (*Laws of Antigua* 1864:571).

54. I have argued elsewhere that members on both sides of the debates preceding passage of the 1870 Married Women's Property Act perceived that the relationship between kinship and property among the poor was different from that relationship among the wealthy. Indeed, this

perceived difference was crucial to the success of the bill's proponents. Mr. Russell Gurney of the House of Commons, for example, explained the 1870 act primarily as a remedy for the poor. Wealthy women, he believed, were adequately protected by marriage settlements. Lord Shaftesbury of the House of Lords agreed: he thought the law should apply only to the wages of working wives. Similarly, Lord Cairns emphasized that the bill would "do for the poor what the Court of Equity did for the rich" (Lazarus-Black 1982:40, 44). The Parliamentarians drew upon a stereotypical image of working-class marriage to make their case. They viewed working-class men as "given to drunkenness and dissipation" but working-class wives as forming the "core of the family" because they were capable of earning wages and spending them wisely. Therefore, some remedy for those abused working-class women was necessary. In other words, the 1870 bill addressed "exceptional cases" in which husbands did not live up to their "natural" obligations.

55. In 1985–87, the High Court housed uncataloged, disintegrating records from scattered years of this century in its basement. It was impossible for me to investigate those materials during my fieldwork, but the next generation of researchers may uncover trial data relevant to this question. Today the Married Women's Property Act has been adapted for use in Antigua primarily to deal with problems women face because of local kinship practices. Women and their lawyers invoke this statute as a consequence of the common practice by which married couples hold their joint property in the husband's name. Several attorneys explained to me that the law is used when (1) couples want to separate but not divorce, (2) a marriage has failed before the three years required to be eligible for divorce but the spouses have parted, (3) there are no legal grounds to file for divorce but the spouses have parted, or (4) a wife suspects her husband plans to leave her and wants to establish her contribution to their joint property. Hence the custom that presupposes a man's control over matrimonial property causes women's lawyers to use an 1887 code when there is trouble in the marriage (Lazarus-Black 1992:882).

Chapter 6: Family Life in the Common Order after Slavery

1. For recent reassessments of the political, economic, and cultural conditions influencing *The Meaning of Freedom* in the United States and the Caribbean, see McGlynn and Drescher (1992). Contributors to the volume find emancipation nowhere—except perhaps in Haiti—ushered in an era of radically changed political or socioeconomic circumstances for former slaves, but situations differed from place to place. See, for example, articles by Mandle (1992:69–84) for the American south and Bolland (1992:113–46) for the British Caribbean. In the same collection, Wright notes: "The legal and financial dimensions of postemancipation labor systems have been understudied in comparative terms" (1992:105). An excellent account of black American women's experiences in slavery and freedom is found in J. Jones (1985).

2. These are a few of the Jamaican cults discussed in West Indian histories. Schulyer, for example, believes myalism is "the first documented Jamaican religion cast in the 'classical' African mold" (1979:66). Her research shows that the movement began as early as the 1760s to protect slaves against European sorcery. The more recent Jamaican Cumina Cult holds dances at deaths, christenings, and marriages, and to pay respect to ancestors. During the rites, members are possessed by ancestral spirits called *zombies*. Followers believe in a pantheon of sky and earthbound gods (Simpson 1976:294–95). Adherents of the Convince Cult are called *bongo men*. They communicate with the spirits of people who once belonged to their cult (Dobbin 1986:145–46). Simpson dates both the Convince Cult and pocomania among the revivalist cults that began in the late eighteenth century (1976:295). Members of both groups are "polytheistic in orientation" (ibid.:295–96). Today, pocomania attracts a wider following than the Convince Cult (R. Smith pers. comm. 1990). Curtin (1955) provides an excellent description of the rise of the Native Baptists and the ensuing 1831 "Baptist War"; Turner (1982) concentrates on the role of the missionaries in that war. See Simpson 1978 for a general summary of Caribbean cults, and Austin-Broos for

a rich analysis of Christianity "as a structuring element" that has been reinterpreted over time by Jamaicans (1992:222).

3. Britain's trade policy was "freer" in some respects than it had been earlier, but as Polanyi (1944) points out, such policies are carefully regulated, not "free."

4. That was not the case, however, in later periods (Lowes 1987:10). Lowes's (1993) study of twenty-four nonwhite, middle-class Antiguan families from the 1830s to 1930s shows the second generation after emancipation was less prosperous and less prominent than its predecessor. The causes were economic and sheer race prejudice. Scottish, Portuguese, and other immigrants arrived in the 1850s and 1860s and moved into the niches once dominated by nonwhite Antiguans.

5. Lowes documents that drought, a recession, and the turn to U.S. markets in the 1890s hurt Antiguan planters badly. The value of exports in 1895, for example, was half that of 1892, and government deficits continued over the next decade (1993:87–88).

6. See Laurence (1971) for an overview of immigration schemes in different islands. Shortages of agricultural laborers were most chronic in Jamaica, Trinidad, and Guyana because in these places the former slaves could leave the estates and take advantage of unsettled lands by purchasing plots, renting, or simply squatting. The land shortage in Antigua prevented the majority of freed slaves from leaving the estates. Yet as Laurence explains, laborers were imported not only because there were too few people to work on the estates but also to ensure that competition between the workers would force down wages. Although the laws governing indentured servants shared many similarities across the English-speaking Caribbean, wages, housing conditions, access to medical care, etc. differed from place to place.

7. African and American black indentured servants are difficult to trace in the records. Laurence reports that they intermarried with local villagers and even the officials eventually ceased to regard them as special immigrants (1971:15). There is no count of how many East Indians or Chinese arrived in Antigua as part of these schemes (ibid.:26), although boxes of indentured-servant contracts exist in the Antigua National Archives. Only a handful of persons of East Indian or Chinese descent lived in Antigua in 1985–87. Since 1990, a new community of Chinese-born immigrants, some of them part of a former government bridge-building project, have settled in Antigua.

8. The record is difficult to read: "Super inpedimentum consanguinitats second gradus in linea [nieta?]."

9. In 1864 the priest married C. E., the illegitimate son of M, to P, the legitimate daughter of M. B. In 1871, he married "the unlawful son of M" to a woman who was a lawful child. The third case involved a widower from St. Kitts who married an illegitimate Antiguan girl in 1873 (Catholic Church Records, St. John's, Antigua).

10. Marriage by license was a mark of status in England in the eighteenth and nineteenth centuries. It was much more expensive, but it gave the couple privacy (Gillis 1985:192–93). As we saw in the case of Gilbert and Hart in Chapter 4, marriage licenses were also status markers in Antigua. Of the three men in this sample who married by license, one was a barrister, the second was a wealthy merchant, and the third was a "clerk," a job title suggesting at least middle-class rank in Antigua.

11. Earlier accounts of West Indian kinship structure characterize it as "matriarchical" or "matrifocal" rather than as "patriarchical." See R. Smith (1956, 1973, 1988) for the original meaning of the term *matrifocal* and for a critique of later uses and abuses of the phrase by anthropologists, sociologists, and historians.

12. This accords with Higman's finding that "in the old sugar colonies, at least, probably a majority of slave mates belonged to different masters" (1984b:369). Baptismal records from the Wesleyan church (1816–34) and the Moravian church (1817–33) in Antigua show that 19.5 and 67.2 percent, respectively, of mates registering children belonged to different owners (ibid.:370). Higman explains: "In general, the proportion separated increased along with population density and creolization" (ibid.:369).

13. Higman suggested that barracks were mostly a postemancipation development (1984b:220). Those described by Samuel Smith recall the shacks put up by the major sugar companies in

"Sugartown" Jamaica to house cane workers. The Jamaican companies originally intended them for single men, but they were sometimes occupied by whole families (E. Clarke 1966:23). Similar housing conditions existed on estates in Antigua in the 1960s.

14. See Carnegie (1987) for several views of the origin and development of Afro-Caribbean villages after emancipation.

15. Dirks and Kerns argue, for example, that "the level of marriage and extra-legal alliances expressed in Afro-Caribbean communities is a dynamic adjustment to economic environment" (1976:35). They also found that migration had a major impact on marital frequency in Rum Bay, Tortola (ibid.:44). The Antiguan case supports instead Schneider and Smith's (1978), Roberts and Sinclair's (1978), and R. Smith's (1982, 1984, 1988) arguments that lower-class kinship patterns are not consequences of their economic situation. See also Douglass (1992:15–16).

16. The short-term effect of the transition from sugar to tourism caused high unemployment and underemployment. Approximately 4,000 persons were employed in the sugar industry in the peak years of the 1950s, but only 1,235 jobs were available in the tourist industry in 1968. The official unemployment rate in 1973 was 20.46 percent; in 1979 it remained at 20 percent. Inflation reached a record high in 1973, when it escalated to 22 percent, but between 1976 and 1980 it averaged about 12 percent per year (Henry 1985:136). Unemployment stood at 20.7 percent in 1980 and at 20.8 percent in 1981 (*Statistical Yearbook* 1983:50). According to the 1985 *Statistical Yearbook*, unemployment remained at 20.9 percent between 1982 and 1984 and rose slightly in 1985 to 21.1 percent (1985:53). The 1987 *Yearbook*, which includes statistics for 1986, does not give unemployment rates. Everyone I interviewed agreed social and economic conditions have improved greatly since the 1950s. The most recent *Statistical Yearbook*, for 1988, was unavailable when I conducted my fieldwork. It gives a marriage rate of 4.85 for that year. The recent increase in the marriage rate could be due to a number of factors, including: (1) the continuing strong influence of the churches and fundamentalism; (2) a rise in the number of people who now divorce and then remarry (see Chapter 7); (3) the effect of a statute encouraging tourists to marry in Antigua (see Chapter 9, note 12), but who are probably not differentiated from Antiguans in the data collected by the Statistics Department; or (4) further changes in the internal composition of Antigua's middle class. There is no reason to believe that the economy shifted the marriage rate from 1985 to 1988.

17. The recent increase in the marriage rate could be due to a number of factors, including: (1) the continuing strong influence of the churches and fundamentalism; (2) a rise in the number of people who now divorce and then remarry (see Chapter 7); (3) the effect of a statute encouraging tourists to marry in Antigua (see Chapter 9, note 12), but who are probably not differentiated from Antiguans in the data collected by the Statistics Department; or (4) further changes in the internal composition of Antigua's middle class. There is no reason to believe that the economy shifted the marriage rate from 1985 to 1988.

18. Their behavior is more similar to the pattern described by Gutman (1976) for former slaves in North America.

19. There were 221 marriages in 1957, including 102 in St. John's parish, 118 in the five other parishes, and 1 in Barbuda. In St. John's parish, fundamentalist ministers performed 17 ceremonies, the registrar united one couple, and the major denominations married 84 couples. In the other parishes, only 10 ceremonies were performed by fundamentalists. The wedding in Barbuda was registered by the Pilgrim Holiness church (Antigua, *Registrar General's Report for the Year 1957* 1958:Table J).

20. In 1965, the Seventh Day Adventists registered 1 marriage, Pilgrim Holiness recorded 2, Zion Church performed 2, and Church of God celebrated one in St. Paul's parish. The fundamentalists registered another 21 marriages in St. John's parish and 5 others in the remaining parishes. The Anglican church celebrated 3 of the 6 Barbudan weddings; Pilgrim Holiness joined the other couples. In all, 1965 witnessed 213 marriages on Antigua and Barbuda.

21. My comment about the clergy's views is based on interviews with ministers from Anglican, Methodist, Baptist, Catholic, Seventh Day Adventist, and three fundamentalist churches in Antigua and Barbuda conducted in 1985–86 and 1987. Without exception, these ministers advocated marriage, were against divorce except in the most extraordinary circumstances, found "common-

law" unions disgraceful, and bemoaned the high rate of illegitimacy. Some of the fundamentalist ministers do not believe in going to court and counsel their parishioners to "forgive and forget" or to "turn the other cheek." Overall, however, in the mid-1980s their perspectives on marriage and kinship accorded with those of the state.

22. Fundamentalism is far more influential in Antigua than Rastafarianism. Antiguans often use the term "rasta man" disparagingly, to imply uncouth or rude behavior. This is in sharp contrast to Jamaica where Rastafarianism became "a vehicle of nationalist politics" and gained respectability among the middle class in the 1970s and 1980s (Austin-Broos 1987:6; see also Austin Broos 1991, 1992).

23. In his research on Trinidad, Trotman found: "During the period July 1868 to December 1871, there were fourteen prison commitals for Obeah, including two women. The prison terms ranged from one month to as many as six months, and some received as many as thirty-six lashes. In the period 1875–99, another thirty-nine persons were imprisoned for practicing Obeah" (1986:224).

24. I have not yet had the opportunity to investigate old police records to determine when Antiguans were last convicted for obeah. No cases to prosecute obeah appear in the magistrates' records for 1980–1987, nor could people working at the St. John's court, some for more than a decade, recall a defendant charged specifically with obeah. A few lawyers recalled a case in which a man charged with homicide claimed his victim was practicing obeah against him. (He was convicted anyway.) In 1992, I began collecting data about legal cases in which obeah plays some role, even though evidence of its practice is carefully suppressed in court by astute attorneys. In Montserrat, which shares Acts of the Leeward Islands with Antigua, cases of obeah were prosecuted as late as 1959 and 1961. The defendants were found guilty in both instances and sentenced to two months in prison. They were fortunate in comparison to a man who was convicted of obeah in 1913: he received six strokes with the cat-o-nine and a year in prison with hard labor. Both men and women were accused of practicing obeah in Montserrat, but male arrests outnumbered female arrests by three to one (Dobbin 1986:14, 15, 20).

25. An early reference to obeah's role in mediating intersex conflicts in the Caribbean is contained in R. Smith's classic study of Guyana (1956:219). Smith found that Guyanese women used obeah to retain the attention of lovers and husbands and to keep their sons at home (ibid.:114, 120). I did not find this latter practice in Antigua, but it fully accords with the argument presented here.

26. Rubenstein made a similar point in his discussion of "hangings" or mock trials in St. Vincent (1976:774). None of the Antiguans I asked had ever heard of mock trials.

27. Foner described similar characteristics of obeah participants in rural Jamaica (1973:95–99).

28. Bourguignon suggests women join cults to serve as a balance to the predominantly masculine institutions in the societies in which they live (in Simpson 1978:139). Women are more active in Antiguan churches than men, but that does not stop them from participating in other formal institutions. Simpson, who argues that Caribbean cults arose and persist due to a combination of "cultural, structural or socioeconomic, and psychological variables," noted in passing that cult members hope "to reduce their suffering, combat the 'meaninglessness' of their lives, or overcome injustice" (ibid.:16, 286).

Chapter 7: Making and Breaking Alliances

1. See Merry (1979, 1986, 1990, 1994) and Yngvesson (1985, 1988, 1994) for the use of court as a measure of last resort by lower-class Americans.

2. Government records are not clear whether the total number of offenses against the penal code includes kinship cases; nevertheless, the yearly sum of approximately 100 to 150 new paternity suits filed at the St. John's magistrates' court argues that these cases represent a significant proportion of court time. The total number of criminal prosecutions reported by the commissioner

of police for 1983 to 1987 are 777 in 1983, 815 in 1984, 564 in 1985, 379 in 1986, and 583 in 1987 (*Statistical Yearbook* 1987:49).

3. The "ethnographic present" is 1985–86, and the summer of 1987. In the fall of 1992, I returned to Antigua for the first time in five years. Of course, some things had changed; much remained the same. The lower courts are air-conditioned now, and the shoe saloon under the magistrates' courthouse has been replaced by a furniture store. Antigua has four new magistrates. They sometimes hear family cases at different times during the week and have eliminated the practice of posting "Orders in Bastardy" on Thursdays. Overall, the bar has expanded, and many of the new lawyers are women. Indeed, the feminization of the profession in Antigua was one of the most frequently cited explanations of how the bar had changed during my absence. Five lawyers interviewed by me in 1985–86 have passed away, and three others now practice law in other places. The organization of the courts and the character and processing of the cases remain much the same. The divorce law and the statute that gives a woman just $15.00 E.C. to support her illegitimate child were in effect in 1992.

4. For discussion of the dissonance between law, legal practitioners, and colloquial understanding in American small-claims courts, see Conley and O'Barr (1990). Their case studies "dismantle the stereotype of 'the judge' as impassive arbiter" (1990:111). Examples of the complexities of lawyer-client interaction in American divorce cases can be found in Sarat and Felstiner (1986, 1988, 1989) and Felstiner and Sarat (1992).

5. Bastardy and maintenance laws in England were first associated with poor laws and classified as "criminal" cases that had to be proved according to the rules of evidence applicable in criminal as opposed to civil cases. The standard of evidence requires that they be proved "beyond reasonable doubt" instead of by "a preponderance of the evidence."

6. The data for this discussion is partially based on my survey of twenty-five of the thirty-four legal professionals practicing in Antigua in 1985–86 (Lazarus-Black 1987).

7. The solicitor general and other members of the office of the attorney general draft the statutes that go to Parliament. I do not wish to imply that these officers are unaware of legislation in other Caribbean islands; on the contrary, many are well informed about current legislation in nearby states. However, English codes most influenced those who practiced law and adjudicated cases in the mid-1980s. Nine of ten lawyers participating in my survey who gave examples for changes they wanted to see in kinship codes cited English statutes as models (Lazarus-Black 1987).

8. This is changing. There are two law schools in the English-speaking Caribbean, in Jamaica and Trinidad. Antigua is a contributing member to the school. Increasingly, the generation of lawyers building practices in Antigua in the 1990s is being trained at these institutions.

9. How the gender of the attorney or judge influenced the processing of maintenance and divorce cases was not a question I investigated specifically in 1985–86. My survey of legal professionals focused on the types of cases lawyers handled, characteristics of litigants, family norms, and opinions about needed law reform. My field notes and interview transcripts, however, reveal both male and female litigants expected women to be more compassionate to female complainants and some women specifically chose other women to represent them; one man in search of a divorce lawyer deliberately chose a smart woman. Moreover, my subsequent reading (see Henderson 1991 for a recent discussion of the patriarchy of law) and research on American divorce cases convinces me gender very much matters in the processing of kinship cases. In the United States, gender influences how litigants choose their attorneys, their expectations of the process, and what they seek from their lawyers (Lazarus-Black 1990b). My thanks to William L. F. Felstiner and Austin Sarat for permission to use their data for my pilot study.

10. The magistrates' jurisdiction is given in Cap. 48, part 5, of the *Laws of Antigua and Barbuda* and as amended most recently by No. 11 of 1982 (*Laws of Antigua* 1962:417–25).

11. The characterization of the magistrates' court as "a poor person's court" was first drawn by Cumper and Daly (1979:10). A few attorneys and some of the court personnel felt it was problematic to portray the court in this fashion. In their minds, it is a court with jurisdiction over illegitimate children—the majority of whom, coincidentally, are born to poor parents. Never-

theless, they conceded that the vast majority of persons with family disputes at the magistrates' court belong to the lower class.

12. Monetary values in this and the next chapter are given in local currency, the Eastern Caribbean dollar. One U.S. dollar is worth $2.67 E.C.

13. The legal personnel with whom I spoke in 1985–86 did not believe that increases in the maximum amount of child support that a magistrate can award would change greatly the numbers of people using these courts or persuade persons from other ranks of society to utilize them for all of these reasons. Research begun late in 1993 will test this hypothesis, for the law was amended in February 1993 to allow greater discretion.

14. I discuss why Antiguan women take men to the magistrate court in the next chapter.

15. Beautifully written and sophisticated accounts of the relations between law, culture, and fundamentalism in the U.S. appear in Greenhouse (1986, 1989).

16. Only a few hundred Rastafarians lived in Antigua in 1985. They appeared before the court occasionally on charges of possession or sale of marijuana, but I observed only two cases involving Rastafarians during my fieldwork and only one attorney I spoke with had heard of Rastafarians involved in child support cases.

17. The total number of cases from year to year, therefore, depends partially on how often these men are prosecuted. In 1985–87 magistrates summoned men to pay support every five or six weeks, notifying them that an arrest warrant would soon be issued. This convinced most to pay up. A review of the Bastardy Arrears Books in 1992 shows delinquent fathers were prosecuted less often that year than in 1985: warrants for arrears were issued once every two to three months instead of every five to six weeks. The drop in the number of cases between 1981 and 1982 was also due to a change in the frequency of issuing warrants. Interestingly, 1981 is the year Antigua gained independence; 1982 is when the government raised the child support stipend (See chapter 9).

18. There were three magistrates in Antigua during my first fieldwork; two men and one woman. I observed all three in court, but use the pronoun "he" to preserve anonymity.

19. Readers will be interested to learn that when I returned to Antigua in 1992, I discovered in the court records that this complainant successfully prosecuted her case against the father of her two children in 1988!

20. As an aid in assessing evidence, and as a source for English precedents, the magistrates turn to *Stone's Justices' Manual.* The volume explains various legal terms, procedures, and past rulings that have guided English judges. Magistrates are advised, for example, that "where there is evidence that over a long period, including the term of conception, the mother and the alleged father had associated together as sweethearts, and no evidence that she had associated with any other man, the justices are entitled to treat this as corroboration of the mother's statement. . . . Corroboration involves something more than possibility; it involves evidence which tends to show probability"(Fanner and Latham 1971:1365, 1366).

21. Of twenty-two complete trials in St. John's entailing requests for maintenance for children, I observed only one instance in which child support was denied. That case involved a married woman with two teenage sons, neither of whom were the natural children of the defendant, although both were legally "children of the family." A shrewd attorney established that both boys received some assistance from their biological fathers. Of the remaining twenty-one cases, fourteen ended in orders for support at the maximum the law allowed.

22. To substantiate a matrimonial offense in court, "there must be proof beyond reasonable doubt . . . though not proof of the standard required in a criminal case." The court recognizes that "in civil cases the proof required is by a preponderance of probability, but that there are degrees of probability within that standard, and that the degree depends on the subject-matter" (Fanner and Latham 1971:1404). For the legal definitions of "desertion," "adultery," and "cruelty," see the summary in Lazarus-Black (1990a:222–23) or Fanner and Latham (1971:1392–94, 1403–6).

In Antigua, a divorce is litigated in public, but custody and division of matrimonial property are privately resolved in the judge's chambers on another date. In reaching those decisions, a High Court judge follows the English guideline that the wife and children should not be relegated to a standard of living significantly lower than that of the husband and that his living allowance should not fall below subsistence level. Divorce settlements are not intended to be punitive measures (ibid.:1423, 1424).

23. There were 106 divorces between 1951 and 1959, but I have not included these in the chart because the cause for the divorce is unknown for 62 percent of those cases. Of cases for which data was available, 13 percent of the divorces were for adultery, 14 percent were for desertion, and 5 percent were for cruelty. Less than 6 percent of the cases were granted on the basis of two offenses.

24. In addition to discussing divorce at length with twenty-five attorneys, magistrates, and judges, I observed divorce cases at the High Court and collected data on twenty-two such suits. Of these, fourteen were adjudicated, six were adjourned "sine die," and two were continued for hearing. In six instances, I interviewed one or both of the litigants, discussed the situation with their attorneys at length, and read the case files.

25. There are no available statistics; my comment stems from my fieldwork at the High Court. I would hazard a guess that wealthier Antiguans, whatever their background, divorce abroad, where the codes are much more lenient and there is more privacy.

26. Men, in contrast, are the mediators of family quarrels outside the courtroom. I asked men and women, "To which relative would a person most likely turn to resolve a dispute?" They named "father," "parents," "brother," "uncle," "aunt," "grandparents," "grandfather," and "a respected relative"—just about every relative except mother and sister! No one relative, however, is culturally designated as the appropriate person for resolving grievances (Lazarus-Black 1987).

27. Most Caribbean ethnographers mention the pervasiveness of informal adoption. See, for example, Brodber (1974 and 1981) and E. Clarke (1966) for Jamaica, Rodman (1971) for Trinidad, Barrow (1986) for Barbados, R. Smith (1956) for Guyana, S. Gordon (1987) for Antigua, and Powell (1986) and Senior (1991) for a comparison of adoption practices in Barbados, Antigua, and St. Vincent. Brodber refers to temporary informal adoption as "passing on." She views the abandonment of children in Jamaica as the final step in an already familiar West Indian pattern (1974:49).

28. In Chapter 9 I describe the passage of the Births and Deaths Registration (Amendment) Act that allows men to readily acknowledge their illegitimate children—and also greatly simplified things with American immigration authorities. Given this new law, and the rationale behind many formal adoptions up to 1987, I expected to find a decrease in the number of legal adoptions in Antigua after that date. The record showed there were fifteen adoptions in 1988, twelve in 1989, nine in 1990, seven in 1991, and twenty in 1992.

29. The matter of who gains letters of administration is not published—which sometimes leads to wrongdoing. For example, John claims he is the only legitimate heir to old Fred, his recently deceased mother's brother. In fact, John has an older half-brother, Roy, who moved to the United States. The registrar, newly arrived from another Caribbean island, has no way of determining that John is a cad and he gives him letters of administration. Roy will never know that he is legally a beneficiary unless he visits Antigua and inquires about Uncle Fred.

30. See Carnegie 1987 for a more recent review of the concept of "family land" in relation to other forms of land tenure. Carnegie astutely critiques M. Smith's rigid separation of customary and legal patterns of land tenure, arguing land tenure displays an intersystemic character.

31. In 1987 Parliament changed the inheritance law so that an illegitimate child who has been legally acknowledged by his father is entitled to a portion of his deceased parent's estate. I elaborate the circumstances surrounding the passage of this bill in Chapter 9. During the summer of 1987, I discussed the possible ramifications of the new law with several people, but it was too early to determine the act's effect upon inheritance practices. Work in progress in 1993 investigates the meaning, function, and consequences of this new legislation.

32. My thanks to R. Smith (pers. comm. 1990) for clarifying this point.

33. Gluckman coined the phrase "the reasonable man" to describe how Barotse judges arrive at decisions. He argues that judges ask: "What would an ordinary, prudent or reasonable man have done in the circumstances of the case?" He suggested American judges go through similar processes and that "the law of economically more developed societies is concerned with specialized rights and duties: hence the reasonable man is a judicial fiction to assess whether, where and

how duties lie in relation to others' rights" (1967:391). Gluckman's concept has been critiqued (e.g., Gluckman 1967; Moore 1969; Epstein 1973) and we need not reopen those debates here. My point is to bring attention to how written codes constrain action, including magistrates' desires to conform to local norms. I found Antiguan law mostly prevented magistrates from even considering how "the reasonable man," not to mention the "reasonable woman," they most often confronted, would act. One might also say that much to their disgust, law sometimes prevented them from acting reasonably.

Chapter 8: Cases, Courts, and Family Ideology in the Common Order

1. That people go to court in search of justice seems self evident—and yet it continues to surprise social scientists. I am persuaded by Merry and Silbey's argument as to why that is the case: "The concept of dispute reflects the desire for clearly delineated and identifiable common units of analysis but inadvertently incorporates a bias toward secular and rationalist orientations and interpretations of action. Emphasizing free choice, individualism, autonomy, and advantage, and assuming instrumental rather than normative and religious orientations of social action, the concept seems to describe the culture of professional elites rather than the residents of [American] urban/ethnic neighborhoods" (1984:177). For other discussions of contemporary Americans' search for justice in court see Conley and O'Barr (1990), Merry (1979, 1986, 1990, 1994), O'Barr and Conley (1988), and Yngvesson (1985, 1988, 1994).

2. B. Williams refines Jayawardena's argument, placing both forms of equality within an ideological field that includes competing hierarchical precepts (1991:97, 194–97). Her sophisticated analysis of the competing and contradictory ideological notions of egalitarianism and hierarchy in Guyana emphasizes how these play out between persons in the village of Cockalorum and among different ethnic groups in the nation-state. The focus of my analysis, in contrast, is on how these same competing principles structure gender and familial organization in the common order.

3. In 1969 and 1973, Wilson developed the distinction between Caribbean men's concern for "reputation" and women's greater emphasis upon "respectability." Wilson argued "reputation" was an indigenous structural principle that promoted egalitarian norms, whereas "respectability" was metropolitan and encouraged class differences and inequality. Wilson has been criticized for failing to integrate these conflicting principles, for claiming women were more closely tied to an old colonial mentality, and for neglecting the power relations that obtain between men and women (e.g., Austin 1983:223; Barrow 1976:116; Douglass 1992:251–52; Glazier 1983:352; Trouillot 1992:26). My argument concerning women's ideas about "respect" differs from Wilson's thesis. As I explain in the text, "respect" is a component of egalitarianism that operates either in tandem with or in opposition to the principle of gender hierarchy, depending upon the parties and their circumstances. The Antiguan concern with being a "big woman" contradicts Wilson's notion that "reputation" is unimportant to women (see also Barrow 1976 on this point). As in Barbados, Antiguan women value highly autonomy and independence, but as Barrow found, these terms are not necessarily coterminous: "autonomy implies interdependency found among a number of individuals" (in Bolles and D'Amico-Samuels 1989:176). Antiguan gender hierarchy much resembles that of Montserrat (Moses 1977, 1981).

My findings differ from those of DeVeer (1979), who discovered occupation can alter women's perceptions about the extent of equality that obtains in Jamaica. In general, my interviewees were much less preoccupied with class and race and much more preoccupied with the church. These differences are consequences of the fact that Jamaica is much more highly stratified and internally differentiated by race and ethnicity than Antigua and Barbuda.

4. The pattern is widespread in the English-speaking Caribbean (e.g., Barrow 1986; Bolles 1983; Bolles and D'Amico-Samuels 1989; Colen 1986, 1990; Douglass 1992; Massiah 1986; Powell

1986; Safa 1986; Senior 1991; Sutton and Makiesky-Barrow 1977, 1981). As Justus puts it, "Women are socialized to be resourceful" (1981:447).

5. As in Chapter 7, monetary values are given in local currency, the Eastern Caribbean dollar.

6. Records were not available for Magistrate's District C, Barbuda, for 1981 or 1982. No kinship cases were filed in Barbuda in 1983, 1985, 1986, or 1987. Seven cases, however, were filed in 1984! Unfortunately, I am unable to fully account for this anomaly. I conducted my first fieldwork in Barbuda in January and February, 1986, unaware that the 1984 case load was so unusual. During brief visits to Barbuda in 1992 and 1993, I learned some of the women who brought cases in 1984 had discussed their decisions with one another. Hence, they may have given one another mutual support. These same women, however, had trouble actually collecting maintenance for their children. That problem may have then dissuaded other women from bringing new cases to the Barbuda court for maintenance.

7. I have changed the names and occupations of the parties and some details of the cases described in this chapter to preserve the respondents' identities.

8. In her interview, Margaret complained that the support had been limited and intermittent. In contrast, Johnny claimed he sent thirty or forty dollars to her every month, paid his son twenty dollars a week when he assisted him at the market on Saturday mornings, brought gifts whenever he went overseas, and took all his sons to the cricket matches every year.

9. Alexander claims the contrast between men and women in Jamaica expresses a dichotomy between nature and culture; that is, women are women by nature but men are as they are because they are "Jamaican" (1973:237, 238). Antiguan informants, in contrast, stressed biological and psychological differences between the sexes. Interestingly, both men and women used the phrases "that's Antigua!" and "that's Antiguan!" to comment on the breakdown of essential public services and the general inability (and irresponsibility?) of government officials to do the job they are supposed to do.

10. In another context, Colen (1986, 1990) found the lack of respect American women show their West Indian domestics, who are used to concern and respect for their family situations, causes great unhappiness for these women.

11. Carmody discusses Antiguan "big men" in overtly political roles. She finds they are "first among equals": leaders come from the villages and identify with local needs and values. Carmody argues that "big men" assume leadership positions by virtue of wit, intelligence, and "mouth" (rhetorical skill), but do not differ from other men in terms of "control and manipulation of personal wealth." In this respect, and because they do not organize competing factions, Carmody distinguishes Antiguan "big men" from the political type described by Sahlins for Polynesia (1978:326–27).

As Carmody predicted, the decade separating our respective fieldwork has witnessed Antiguans' increased attention to formal education, occupation, and income and these are eminent when people discuss what makes a man a "big man." Still, "personal wealth" continues to include such things as "title" (surname) and the effectiveness and extent of one's links to local families who wield social, economic, and political power. The "big man" to whom I refer in this paper, then, need not be an overt political leader and should not be confused with either Carmody's or Sahlins's models. As in Guyana, "big man" is a status category that changes in different social contexts: "It is, in part, the ability to retain one's status as a big man as one moves from one social context to the next, even when the change means a move from regional to national to international circles, that distinguishes 'truly big men' from 'small big men'" (B. Williams 1991:78). See B. Williams (ibid.:78–83) for further discussion.

12. Johnny Thomas is in many ways the typical lower-class Antiguan "big man." He inherited his butchering business, livestock, and several parcels of land from his father and is a hard-working entrepreneur expanding his operations. Yet Johnny still resides in one of the roughest sections of St. John's. He described his own class position this way: "Well, we just livin', just a little above the others in a reasonable property. We never get back down in the low thing, but I would say, the upper bracket? We weren't able to manage the height of living, in that bracket

there." In 1987, Johnny supported his mother, the woman he lived with, their four children, and, to varying degrees, six other children.

13. Unfortunately, I did not ask the occupation of the father of Margaret's first child and at the time of the interview I had not recognized the significance of her fear of antagonizing his wife. It is possible that either he or his wife were too powerful to risk taking to court. Margaret may have been afraid that his wife would ostracize her in public, with community approval, or that she might practice obeah.

14. This is common throughout the English-speaking Caribbean. For example, Barrow found that in Barbados "women recognized and indeed often accepted as a fact of life their partners' involvement in other affairs whether married or not. But they drew the line at the point where they and their children are neglected, particularly financially, in favor of outside women. The problem and their embarrassment are compounded by court procedures for support" (1982:7). Similarly, in Jamaica: "Male unfaithfulness is a focus of the culture, but male unfaithfulness is no more or less a betrayal of the marital commitment than fiscal irresponsibility, cruelty, or a variety of other stresses and strains" (Alexander 1973:217). Douglass also found that "adultery rarely led to divorce as long as the man showed respect for his wife by carrying out his affairs discreetly" (1992:173).

15. Gonzalez mentions this phenomenon among the Black Caribs of Livingston, Guatemala (1981:426).

16. For an example of this phenomenon from Jamaica, see Senior (1991:136–37).

17. The phrase is widely used in the English-speaking Caribbean. Writing about Jamaica, Durant Gonzalez explains: " 'Big woman' refers to a stage in the life cycle which is related to chronological age, but is not solely determined or limited by it. 'Big woman' status is based on configuration of age, territorial possession, personal achievements, formal life cycle events, and economic factors" (1986:53).

18. Many anthropologists have written about the symbolic importance of the home in the English-speaking Caribbean. Some examples include Austin 1979, 1984; Brodber 1975; DeVeer 1979; Dirks and Kerns 1976; Douglass 1992; Henriques 1953; Mintz 1974; R. Smith 1988; and B. Williams 1991. Antiguans speak about "home" in much the same way that Jamaicans do: the home is a sanctuary and a place of privacy. Its location, size, and contents mark the success or failure of its inhabitants against the yardstick of the social hierarchy. Depending on the context in which it is discussed, "home" symbolizes family, class, or both. Most Antiguans do not marry until they can set up an independent home; a great many couples move into new homes first and marry later.

19. Increased attention to gender relations in the Caribbean by anthropologists in recent years is yielding interesting data about male and female use of time and money within and beyond households (e.g., Bolles and D'Amico-Samuels 1989).

20. A discretionary statement explains when and why a plaintiff has been guilty of a matrimonial offense. The statement is confidential and is only opened by the judge at the trial. Amanda's discretionary statement informed the judge that she had given birth to a child for another man the previous year.

21. At one point Evan's new girlfriend called the police about Amanda. Amanda went to the woman's home to collect clothes she had bought Evan when they lived together. Much to the girlfriend's embarrassment, the police allowed Amanda to carry off her property! Amanda's behavior provides another example of why women fear the wrath of their boyfriends' wives.

22. Amanda invited me to attend the in-camera hearing for maintenance for the children, but the session was continually deferred. The magistrate's support orders remained in effect in 1987. Evan's girlfriend sometimes brought the money to the courthouse for his children.

23. For a study of contemporary American divorce law, see Jacob 1989. Weitzman (1985) investigates the social and economic consequences of modern divorce law, particularly for women and children.

24. The ministers I interviewed all try to dissuade couples from divorcing, and most specifically preach against divorce in church. Mrs. Davis's Methodist minister, whom she referred to as her

"spiritual leader," informed her (and me) that divorce is only acceptable under the extreme situation of adultery. He also prohibited divorced persons from holding offices in the church.

25. The circumstances leading to Amanda's divorce, as well as her decision to file her case for desertion rather than adultery, for example, replicate a pattern found in Jamaica (R. Smith 1982a:122). Jamaica's divorce statistics are strikingly similar to those of Antigua. In 1985, for example, 84 percent of Jamaican divorces were granted for separation or desertion—10 percent for cruelty and 2.9 percent for adultery (cited in Douglass 1992:196).

26. The middle-class pattern I describe here, with its associated gender differences, also describes the Grenadian elite of the 1950s (M. Smith 1965d:183–87) and the Jamaican elite of the 1980s (Douglass 1992:175–91).

27. This concurs with Jagdeo's description: "A good girl establishes a stable liaison with one boy, avoids sex if she can but, in the event that she cannot, she avoids 'pregnancy.'. . . If a girl has a stable relationship of the prescribed type and becomes pregnant, her family will not be in the embarrassing position of not knowing who the father is. The possibility that a boy may say that the 'baby aint his' weighs more heavily on the apprehensions of parents than the fact of pregnancy itself" (1984:59). Some notions about "respectability," then, differ by class and gender.

28. M. Smith (1965d) describes a similar phenomenon among the elite in Grenada in the early 1950s. Elite women in Grenada did not bear illegitimate children—it was "unthinkable." If they did, and remained on the island, they suffered a great loss of status (ibid.:183–84, 203).

29. The sanctions women face in Antigua, and how parents of middle-class and elite girls respond if their daughter becomes pregnant, resonates with the reactions M. Smith found in Grenada in the early 1950s (1965d). In 1992, I learned of three middle-class women who decided to have children without marrying, certainly not a large enough sample from which to generalize! In passing conversations, however, I ascertained that community reaction to these births was decidedly mixed. One woman explained that she believed such behavior was still much frowned upon in the middle class, although people were more "liberal" if the woman was older.

30. A survey of 491 Antiguan women conducted in 1980 as part of the Women in the Caribbean Project showed the likelihood of marriage increased dramatically with the age of the respondent, although researchers also found that more women were marrying at a younger age (Powell 1986:86, 87). Investigating kinship in Jamaica in the 1950s, E. Clarke also found that "religious considerations provide the strongest motive for marriage" (1970:76). Interestingly, a rationale for not marrying that Jamaicans told Henriques in the early 1950s was never voiced to me in Antigua: "The Old Testament stories of concubines and handmaidens have become part of the lives of the people so that they have Biblical sanction for their behavior which is in contradiction to the teaching of the churches. This may explain the . . . lack of a sense of contradiction between their social behavior and Christian morality" (1953:91). For further discussion of the influence of religion on marriage to Jamaica see Roberts and Sinclair (1978:1–18).

31. Wilson (1969:78) points to the correlation between old age and marriage. Critiquing Wilson's thesis, Glazier suggests that "it may be necessary to modify Wilson's notion of respectability so as to emphasize age and sex and deemphasize wealth as a factor" (1983:352).

32. Many discussions of marriage in the English-speaking Caribbean have emphasized that women want to marry for financial security. Johnny's comments give us another viewpoint. Interestingly, the two individuals whom Fischer quotes in his discussion of the legal/economic advantages of marriage in rural Jamaica were both men (1974b:10–11).

33. DeVeer gives an apt description of how Jamaican small tradesmen and factory workers contrast marriage with the freedom of "the sportin' life." She finds: "For a man, home, marriage, and 'inside' mean the destruction of a man's world, a world 'outside' which is based on male friendship and the sharing of resources" (1979:5). Middle-class men also stress the difference between "inside" and "outside," but their perspective is altered by their socioeconomic status: "Espousing middle class norms and emphasizing those norms which mark such middle class membership are more important to these men than espousing norms of male domination and control over women as the primary organizing principles of social life" (ibid.:13, 14, 106–9). Alexander (1973, 1977b, 1978, 1984) discusses in depth middle-class Jamaicans' concerns about men's

lack of responsibility to their families. Austin (1979) explains the broader symbolic connotations of "inside" and "outside" for Jamaicans.

34. DeVeer (1979:108–9) and R. Smith (1988:115–17) also find that "love" is only one of several reasons why West Indians marry. In contrast, Douglass discovered elite Jamaicans place great emphasis on marrying for love, often unaware of a pattern in which: "Women marry 'up' and men marry 'down'" (1992:136).

35. Henriques (1953:87) and Moses (1981:509) make this point about women and marriage in Jamaica and Montserrat, respectively. Douglass (1992:74–76, 243–47) describes beautifully and with clear analytic insight how contemporary Jamaican women move physically through space to accommodate a culture that differentiates "ladies" from "women."

36. Powell surmised that "women's childbearing will vary in terms of the nature of their interaction in social networks" (1982:154), but almost a decade later we still know relatively little about women's networks (Senior 1991:140). It does seem that the size and durability of these alliances change over time. For example, Gussler demonstrated that women in St. Kitts face their most difficult years when they are very young mothers and there are relatively few individuals with whom they can exchange goods, services, and jobs. They know, however, that their young children are an "investment"; part of the expanding network that one builds with age (Gussler 1980:201). Senior also describes children as women's "resources" (1991:67). As one woman put it, "Hand wash hand" (ibid.:140).

Chapter 9: The Present and Future of Kinship Legalities

1. The Status of Children Act eliminates the legal disabilities of illegitimate children. The statute declares "the status and rights, privileges and obligations of a child born out of wedlock are identical in all respects to those of a child born in wedlock" (*Laws of Antigua and Barbuda* 1986).

2. Until the Births and Deaths (Registration) (Amendment) Act became law, an unmarried woman who gave birth to a child in Antigua was compelled to register that child as a bastard. The mother's surname was recorded on the child's birth certificate, but the father's name was omitted. By law, the child was fatherless. The new act facilitates the process by which a man becomes the legal father of a child and diminishes the importance of marriage in assigning paternity. A man and woman may jointly register their child at birth, and no person need be stigmatized as a bastard because his or her parents have not wed. The statute also allows the registrar to reregister a child whose father's name does not appear on his original birth certificate. Once a man places his name on a birth certificate, he is legally responsible for the food, clothing, shelter, education, and general well-being of that child. Antiguans expect this act will greatly increase the number of children in the country with legal fathers.

3. The Intestate Estates (Amendment) Act recognizes every child's right to inherit from his or her father whether or not the parents are married; it specifically includes children born out of wedlock but legally acknowledged for distributing property on intestacy. Under the new law, "child" or "issue" in relation to the deceased means a child of the marriage, a person judged by a court to be the issue of the deceased, or a child acknowledged under the Births Act. The "brothers" and "sisters" of an intestate now include "any child of the father or mother of the intestate." The law also spells out the amount and type of property to be distributed to persons in various kinship statuses. The act covers only those cases in which the deceased has failed to make a legal will. According to the lawyers I interviewed in Antigua, however, the vast majority of Antiguans die intestate. Thus the economic consequences of this new law may prove significant.

4. For a complete account of the events of this period in Jamaica, see Post 1978.

5. The Antigua Syndicate Estates had acquired most of the estates in Antigua by this time and it operated the single sugar factory. In 1951, the syndicate placed its tenant land in reserve and tried to rid itself of resident workers. As N. Richards reports: "A monumental struggle ensued between the Antigua Syndicate Estates and the Trades and Labour Union in 1951 embroiling the

sugar workers, the waterfront, and other commercial interests. It was a struggle that saw the importation into the island of the 'Welsh Fusiliers,' a detachment of British soldiers, and the setting up of a Board of Enquiry under Sir Clement Malone. The Board recommended that the tenancy lands should be sold by the syndicate estates to the Government for extension of small farmers land settlement. This was eventually agreed to" (n.d.:9–10).

6. Recall that the Crown colony system of 1898 provided for all nominated members in the legislature. The constitution of 1938 allowed only five elected representatives.

7. The government made no attempt to develop an alternative to sugar until a recovery program was put into effect in 1938. Cotton made some headway as a result, but small producers faced myriad problems, including lack of control of the cotton ginnery (Lowes 1993:361). For the effects, social, political, and economic, of the coming of the Americans to Antigua in March 1941, see Lowes 1993:400–434. In a nutshell, American military presence on the island provided a host of new and higher-paying jobs—along with a new kind of blatant racism.

8. According to Henry, the state has had to play a leading role in economic development because of the underdevelopment of the local bourgeoisie (1982:13). Henry also finds recent state control over the work force has included several repressive techniques. During the 1970s, the government issued juridical measures "to control and reduce the power of the working class. Chief among these has been the Labour Code. This trend continued with the re-introduction of the Industrial Court under the ALP. Both of these have greatly affected the process of collective bargaining. This juridization of the class conflict has done two things: it has improved the 'investment climate' and it has weakened the trade unions" (1981:10). These actions contradict the working-class ideology that most current lawmakers espouse. But then no government rules only by the ideology it espouses (Stinchcombe 1975).

9. Lowes (pers. comm. 1989) researched the backgrounds of twenty-one members of Parliament in 1985, including information about "father's occupation" in sixteen cases. Of these, four were peasant farmers or overseers on estates, five were artisans (including two carpenters, a plumber, a shipwright, and a taxi driver), and five held occupations such as "time keeper," "teacher," and "civil servant," suggesting possible middle-class status. Only two, an "estate owner" and an "estate manager" may have belonged to the upper stratum. The backgrounds of these Parliamentarians reflected an "old guard," who were active in the union, held working class jobs, and were educated locally, and a younger group of men (and one woman) who gained social mobility through education. Of the twenty-one members, eleven were schooled only in Antigua, and ten others, mostly the younger generation, obtained university or vocational training abroad. Their previous employment histories include artisan, three; white-collar job (e.g., accountant, secretary, civil servant), ten; teacher, three; business interests, three; engineer, one; and doctor, one.

10. The Antigua Trades and Labour Union elected V. C. Bird as one of its first executives and made him president in 1943. Two years later, he won a seat on the Antigua Legislative Council. Except for 1971–76, Bird has served continuously as chief executive. In 1987, two of his sons were very active in politics. Vere Bird, Jr., was Minister for Communications, Information, and Public Works. Lester Bird was Deputy Prime Minister and Minister of Economic Development, External Affairs, Tourism, and Energy. He assumed leadership of the ALP in 1993.

11. Nevertheless, as Henry noted, the structure of the movement for independence and decolonization was not itself very democratic: "It was essentially bureaucratic in nature, with a charismatic leader at the top . . . a pattern of organization that resulted in a rather low level of internal democratization. Consequently, as the years went by and success attended the movement, these tightly controlled positions of leadership were subjected to processes of elite formation" (1983b:303). Henry attributes the present "post-colonial crisis of Antiguan society" (1992:242) to government failure to disband fully the plantation economy, continued high levels of foreign ownership and control, and the transformation of the unions and political parties into instruments of middle-class rule (ibid.:243).

12. Recall that most of the lawyers practicing in Antigua in 1985–87 trained in Great Britain. All the attorneys I interviewed knew other Caribbean nations had already altered their statutes to ban discrimination against illegitimate children. During the parliamentary debates, members

of the House and Senate also voiced concerns about appearing "backward" if they failed to eliminate such discrimination.

13. The very first laws explicitly related to marriage passed by the independent government were technical responses to specific economic and social developments that made parts of the old code untenable. The Magistrate's Code of Procedure (Amendment) Act (1982) and the Marriage Ordinance (Amendment) Act (1984) modified technicalities in earlier statutes without altering the meaning of kinship terms or the duties and obligations of kin. The 1982 amendment raised the maximum amount of child support from seven to fifteen dollars E.C. per week, reflecting increasing employment opportunities, a new minimum-wage act, and, in general, a higher standard of living. The 1984 law gave women the right to preside as marriage officers and validated those unions already celebrated by "a female Minister of the Christian Religion who was appointed or purported to be appointed by the Governor-General as a Marriage Officer." This amendment followed the Anglican church's decision to allow women to enter the ministry and the subsequent arrival of one such minister in Antigua. Another clause in the same act reduced to three days the time required for couples to reside within the state before applying for a marriage license. As a magistrate informed me, the new rule encouraged tourists, now the mainstay of the economy, to spend their honeymoon dollars in Antigua. Lawmakers also changed the age at which a person could marry without parental consent from twenty-one to eighteen years, conforming to an earlier decision to make eighteen the age of majority. A member of Parliament explained: "People at eighteen are earning big salaries and why prevent them from entering into contract and so?"

14. As the solicitor general explained to me: "A child born in wedlock, the law presumes that the husband is the father. It is the presumption. It can be rebutted, but you have to show evidence that the husband was away in India for the last year and could not have been around at the time of conception. But there is the presumption, so you have no problem with paternity. The husband is the father. The big problem with a child born out of wedlock is to establish with some certainty the father, who is the father of the child" (interview, 9 November 1985).

15. Antigua established a "Women's Desk" in 1980 as part of the responsibilities of the Ministry of Education, Culture, and Youth Affairs. The desk designs and sponsors projects to augment women's income-generating activities, health, nutrition, and family life. Lack of resources, however, severely limits what the small staff can accomplish. In 1985–86, Antigua had one woman senator but no women in the House. One former member of the House was no longer active in politics (R. Clarke 1986:118, 119, 122).

16. Antigua is a very small country, and its citizens value highly their privacy. During my fieldwork, I always assured the people I interviewed that I would protect their anonymity. I chose not to depart from my usual practice when I asked questions about the married women who struggled to obtain the new Intestate Act.

17. I have little information about one small group trying to organize a delegation to meet with the prime minister on behalf of the bills in 1985, during the period in which they failed to reach the Senate. This group consisted of three, and possibly four, highly educated and professional women. At least two were married with grown children. I declined their invitation to participate in their mission.

18. Penetrating the silence of other cultures is a difficult but extremely important task. As Santos noted years ago: "Silence is not equally distributed across cultures, nations, or even groups and classes in the same society. Silence is a scarce resource and the ruling classes in every society tend to allocate it according to their convenience and their cultural postulates" (1977:32). My case study shows that although women have been silenced in some ways by the cultural logic of gender relations in Antiguan society, they can work within silence to effect successful political strategies. A study from France by Susan Rogers gives another illustration of how women exercise power in covert and informal ways (cited in Scott 1990:52). Evaluating this work, Scott reminds us: "That such women's power can be exercised only behind a veil of proprieties that reaffirm men's official rule as powerholders is a tribute—albeit a left-handed one—to the men's continued control of the public transcript. To exercise power in the name of another party is always to run the risk that the formal titleholder will attempt to reclaim its substance as well as its form" (ibid.:52).

Although I agree with this point, it is also useful to consider that men need not listen. The fact that they did in the Antiguan case suggests a shift in the balance of power. As one elected official told me, Antiguan women vote in ever-increasing numbers and are not adverse to discussing their opinions with their representatives.

19. *Workers Voice* explained the reason for the delay in terms of continuing class struggle: "The Status of children Act 1984 [*sic*] was passed by the Lower House in 1984, but was never sent to the Senate, as certain influential persons in the society presurized [*sic*] their respective ministerial representatives to withdraw the Bill" (*Workers Voice,* 21 June 1986, p. 1). It called for immediate action to protect the rights of illegitimate children. A more widely read paper, the *Antigua and Barbuda Herald,* recorded that the Status of Children Act and the Intestates Act had passed the House on 10 December 1986. This brief article described the bills as "social legislations." The attorney general and the finance minister were quoted briefly, both emphasizing that it was right to abolish the legal distinctions between legitimate and illegitimate children (*Antigua and Barbuda Herald,* 19 December 1986, p. 2). There was no discussion in this article about why the bills had been delayed. The Senate debate of the Status of Children's Act, however, makes it clear that some "religious Christians" had also talked to Parliamentarians about whether these acts might discourage matrimony. I would hazard a guess that some were married women (Antigua and Barbuda, Senate Debate, 22 December 1986).

20. During the debates, one member of Parliament announced: "The dean's wife abused the Bishop last night in front of everybody when the service finish. She said that they should put them [those in favor of the Status of Children Act] in a barrel and roll them back to Jamaica." None of the churches, however, publicly opposed the bills.

21. The Senate debate had not been transcribed when I completed fieldwork in 1987. My discussion is based on long-hand notes by a court stenographer and the opportunity I had to listen to taped recordings of the session. My thanks to the court stenographers and the Clerk to Parliament, Mr. Dowe, for access to these materials. It is possible that I did not hear every speaker because one stenographer, who may have recorded some of the debate, was on a special assignment and I was unable to contact her. Her tapes remained in her personal possession. My sense is that even if I missed one or two speakers, my overall summary is accurate because there was no opposition to the bills.

22. A 1980 survey of 504 Antiguan women aged 20 to 64 in 1980, conducted as part of the Women in the Caribbean Project, found 51.4 percent of the women questioned had never married, 39.9 percent were married, 4.3 percent were widowed, and 4.4 percent were divorced or legally separated. Only 11 percent described themselves as participating in a "common-law" relationship, but another 23 percent were involved in "visiting" relationships. The breakdown on marital status in Antigua was almost identical to that of the sample from Barbados (White 1986:67). Antiguan women, however, were more likely than Barbadians to be employed outside the home: 47 percent of the Antiguan women surveyed were "employed by others," whereas 26 percent were "employed in home services." In Barbados, the figures were 43.5 percent and 34.2 percent, respectively (ibid.:69). Of 492 households in Antigua, "woman, partner, and children" was the most common type (33 percent). In 10.9 percent of the households women and children lived by themselves. Women lived on their own in 3.4 percent of the sample. These figures were also very close to those found in Barbados (ibid.:72).

23. As I analyzed my field notes, I discovered that in the early months of my research I had often asked people what they meant by "relatives" and who they included as their relatives, rather than what they meant by "family." I would now posit that for many Antiguans these are different questions. The examples I give in the text specifically reflect responses to the questions: "What is family in Antigua?" and "Who are the people in your family?" The strong emphasis on consanguineous relations in Antigua follows the pattern found in Jamaica and Guyana (e.g., Alexander 1973, 1976, 1978; Austin 1979, 1984; Douglass 1992; R. Smith 1956, 1973, 1988).

24. Lewin (1981, 1987) presents a fascinating and impressive account of how sociological, ideological, economic, and political forms and forces impinged upon the writing of kinship law in Brazil. Reform of the inheritance laws, to take one example, corresponded to a decline in

patriarchy and reliance upon a landed economy: "As the 1920s indicated, once commerce, industry, and the professions provided the majority of a *parentela's* [extended family's] membership with their livelihoods, then the dependence on a pattern of joint and contiguous land ownership by members of the same family declined. . . . The parallel reform of inheritance law, one that granted new impetus to individualism at the expense of a family collectivity, accelerated the demise of the elite family's quasi-corporate identity by rendering patrimony more varied and disposable" (1987:424).

25. I do not mean to overemphasize the extent of structural change in the economy. As Henry points out, Antigua remains heavily dependent on foreign assistance and ownership, exports, and seasonal tourism. Tourism provides even fewer jobs than sugar, and unemployment remains high (1985:133–36). Nevertheless, "what has changed and continues to change in the structural framework of state-class relations is not the basic hierarchical patterns but the relative distribution of power within the hierarchy." Thus while foreign capitalists continue to exert a critical role in capital accumulation and the direction of economic policy, local people have all experienced improved material conditions (ibid.:162–63).

Conclusions

1. Weber continues: "Not only was systematic and comprehensive treatment of the whole body of the law prevented by the craftlike specialization of the lawyers, but legal practice did not aim at all at a rational system but rather at a practically useful scheme of contracts and actions, oriented towards the interests of clients in typically recurrent situations" (1978, vol. 2:787).

2. Lewin (1981, 1987) describes how the ideological revolt against patriarchy and parentally imposed marriages gave Brazilian leaders impetus for reworking kinship codes in the era of the Old Republic (1889–1930). As in Antigua, reforms in Brazil's kinship codes can be explained by examining changes in the composition of its law-making class.

3. Moreover, as Roberts points out in another discussion, a "nice question" may be raised about whether the threefold typology of dividing West Indian relationships into "married," "common-law," and "visiting" unions, as has been usual at least since the census of 1943, "can also be applied satisfactorily to males" (1985:25).

4. Barbados changed dramatically the meaning of "common-law marriages" in 1981, when it brought unions of five years' duration into its system of legalities. "The 1981 reform legislation includes in the definition of 'spouse' not only legally married couples but those parties in a common-law union who have been living together for five years at least" (Senior 1991:85). Persons in unions of five years or more are liable to maintain one another and their children.

5. Although extensive comparison is beyond the scope of this argument, some very preliminary research suggests the value of investigating and comparing systems of legalities and illegalities cross-culturally. For example, as was true in the West Indies, North American slave codes differed in what rights and protections they offered to slaves and so partially determined the extent and nature of slaves' participation in legalities. Colonists in Massachusetts, for instance, granted black servants and slaves "the same legal rights as white servants in terms of their ability to petition the court for protection against their masters, and their ability to obtain the same panoply of legal protections available to whites when they were criminal defendants" (Higginbotham 1978:72). Not surprisingly, slaves in Massachusetts began suing for their freedom by the close of the French and Indian War. After 1783, Massachusetts courts refused to protect slavery (ibid.:84–85, 96–97). In Pennsylvania, slaves and white servants were tried in the same courts and received similar punishments until 1700, at which point lawmakers initiated a separate court for all blacks, whether slave or free (ibid.:272, 281). New York offered some legal protections to slaves, but also developed a segregated judicial system that persisted after the importation of slaves was prohibited in 1785 (ibid.:124, 139–40). In Virginia, in sharp contrast to the Yankee colonies, "nonwhites alone were legally deprived of all basic human rights" (ibid.:38). Virginian slaves were denied the right to

sue their masters for ill treatment in 1680–82. However, because a slave was allowed to testify in court in disputes involving people of color, it is not entirely accurate to conclude, as Higginbotham does, that "no part of the legal process was his ally, the courts not his sanctuary" (ibid.:58).

Although we know a great deal about American slave codes, we have barely begun to investigate slaves' engagements with legalities in the United States (Friedman 1990). Like Caribbean judges, however, North Americans also processed cases involving brutal masters and overseers, sending slaves signals about the usefulness of courts under certain conditions (cf. Genovese 1972; Schwarz 1988:24; Wade 1964:183). Further comparative research along these lines is needed to reveal similarities and differences in slaves' uses of law in different times and places, to illuminate better the relationship between legal codes and judicial processes, and to contribute to our understanding of the making of hegemony. Finally, we need to explore other systems of legalities in relation to their systems of illegalities.

6. For an introduction to the critical legal studies movement, see Kairys (1982), Livingston (1982), and Trubek (1984). Critical legal scholars treat law as a political phenomenon, emphasizing its distinctly ideological role in maintaining and legitimizing capitalist relations. They have been taken to task, however, for writing about legal consciousness as if it existed apart from particular times and places, for focusing upon doctrine while neglecting empirical investigations, and for failing to address the roles that racism and sexism play in shaping the hegemony of law (e.g., Crenshaw 1988; R. Gordon 1984; Silbey and Sarat 1987; P. Williams 1991). Legal consciousness bears the stamp of particular times and places, but also of class, color, and patriarchy. In all Caribbean cases I have examined thus far, the rule of law has been devised and controlled primarily by and for men (cf. MacKinnon 1987).

7. Scott does not, however, mention courts as a "weapon of the weak."

⁊◍ Works Cited

General Sources

Baker, E. C.
> 1965 *A Guide to Records in the Leeward Islands*. Oxford: Basil Blackwell.

Goveia, Elsa V.
> 1980 *A Study on the Historiography of the British West Indies to the end of the Nineteenth Century*. Washington, D.C.: Howard University Press.

Newton, Velma
> 1979 *Legal Literature and Conditions Affecting Legal Publishing in the Commonwealth Caribbean: A Bibliography*. Cave Hill, Barbados: Institute for Social and Economic Studies.

Patchett, Keith and Valerie Jenkins
> 1973 *A Bibliographical Guide to Law in the Commonwealth Caribbean*. Cave Hill, Barbados: University of the West Indies and Faculty of Law.

Sources at the Faculty of Law, University of the West Indies, Cave Hill, Barbados

Acts of Assembly passed in the Charibbee Leeward Islands from 1690 TO 1730
> 1734 Printed by Order of the Lords Commissioners of Trade and Plantations, by John Baskett, printer to the King's most Excellent Majesty.

Antigua and Barbuda, Consolidated Index of Statutes and Subsidiary Legislation to 1st January 1984
> 1984 Index compiled at the Faculty of Law Library, University of the West Indies, Cave Hill, Barbados. West Indian Legislation Indexing Project. (WILIP). Florida: Wm. W. Gaunt & Sons.

Federal Acts of the Leeward Islands
> 1914 2 vols. Prepared under and by virtue of the Statute Laws (Revised Edition) Act, 1909. By Sir Frederic Mackenzie Maxwell, KT., K.C., Chief Justice of the Leeward Islands. St. John's, Antigua: Government Printing Office.

The Federal Acts of the Leeward Islands containing the Acts of the General Legislative Council in force on the 31st Day of December, 1927
> 1930 Revised Edition. Prepared under the authority of The New Edition of the *Statutes Act, 1928*. By H. H. Trusted, Attorney General of the Leeward Islands. Leeward Islands: Government Printing Office. Additional Bound volumes: 1881, 1889, 1897, 1899, 1912, 1921, 1923, 1924, 1925, 1929, 1930, 1934, 1944, 1948, 1949, 1953, 1954, 1955.

Great Britain
> 1907 *The English Reports*, King's Bench Division. London: Stevens and Sons.

> 1826 *The Report of the Commissioners of Inquiry into the Administration of Civil and Criminal Justice in the West Indies*. 3 vols. Ordered, by The House of Commons, to be Printed, 11 December 1826.

The Laws in Force in Antigua: Acts of the Leeward Islands from the Year 1690 to the Year 1798, and the Acts of Antigua from the Year 1668 to the Year 1864
> 1864 Volume in the collection of the Faculty of Law, University of the West Indies, Cave Hill, Barbados.

Laws of Antigua and Montserrat
> 1668–1900 Records of the Colonial Office. Collection of the University of the West Indies, Law School, Cave Hill, Barbados. Microfilm Collection: No. 1. (1668–1721); No. 2. (1721–1753); No. 3. (1753–1772); No. 4. (1772–1795); No. 5. (1795–1829); No. 6. (1829–1837):No. 7. (1837–1846); No. 8. (1846–1852); No. 9. (1852–1869); No. 10 (1869–1900).

Semper, Dudley Henry, and Alan Cuthbert Burns
> 1911 *Index of The Laws of the Federated Colony of the Leeward Islands and of The Several Presidencies Comprising the Same*. London: Sweet and Maxwell.

Unpublished Sources and Locally Printed Texts at the University of the West Indies, Cave Hill, Barbados

An Abstract of Statistics of the Leeward Islands, Windward Islands and Barbados
> 1971 University of the West Indies. Institute of Social and Economic Research.

Works Cited

Fraser, H. Aubrey
1971 "The Law and the Illegitimate Child." Lecture delivered 30 June 1971 at the Centre of Multi-Racial Studies, Cave Hill, Barbados.

O'Loughlin, Carleen
1964 "Financial and Economic Survey of the Hotel Industry in Antigua." University of the West Indies. Institute of Social and Economic Research (Eastern Caribbean).

Salmon, Verleta
N.d. "Nullius Filius: A Historical Study of His Quest for Legal Recognition and Protection in Jamaica." LL.B. thesis, Faculty of Law, University of the West Indies, Cave Hill, Barbados.

Sources at the National Archives of Antigua and Barbuda, St. John's, Antigua

Acts of Assembly, Passed in the Charibbee Leeward Islands, From 1690 to 1730
London: Printed, by order of the Lord's Commissioners of Trade and Plantations by John Baskett.

Great Britain, Colonial Office, *Antigua Report*
For years 1957–1958; for years 1959–1960; for years 1961–1962; for years 1963–1964.

Laws of Antigua
Vol. 1, 1690–1790; Vol. 2, 1791–1804; Vol. 3, 1804–17. Bound manuscripts in the Antigua and Barbados Archives.

The Laws of the Island of Antigua: Consisting of the Acts passed by the Captain-General, Council, and Assembly, from 26th May, 1804, to 13th June, 1817 with an Analytical Table of the Acts; and a Copious Digested Index. Vol. III
1804–18 Prepared by the Legislature of Antigua and printed by their order under the Revision of Anthony Brown, Esq. Colonial Agent in London, by Samuel Bagster, Paternoster-Row, London.

Leeward Islands. *Blue Books.*
For year 1891; for year 1899; for year 1900; for year 1905; for year 1906; for year 1909. St. John's, Antigua: Government Printing Office.

Oliver, Vere Langford
1894–99 *The History of the Island of Antigua . . . from the First Settlement in 1635 to the Present Time.* 3 vols. London: Mitchell and Hughes.

Record of Common Pleas, 1823–1829
St. John's Anglican Church Records
  Baptism June 9, 1814 to December 31st, 1826, Marriages June 24th, 1814 to November 13th, 1826, Burials June 9th to December 21st, 1826.
  7th September 1840–31st December, 1853

Sources at the High Court, St. John's, Antigua

Antigua and Barbuda
 1962 *The Revised Laws of Antigua*. Prepared under the authority of the Revised
   Edition of the Laws Ordinance, 1951. 8 vols. London: Waterlow and Sons.

Antigua. Registrar General's Office.
 Report on the Vital Statistics of the Colony of Antigua. For the Year 1939 (January
   1940); For the Year 1951 (September 1952); For the Year 1953 (February 1954);
   For the Year 1954 (February 1955); For the Year 1955 (March 1956); For the
   Year 1957 (March 1958); For the Year 1958 (March 1959); For the Year 1959
   (n.d.). St. John's, Antigua: Government Printing Office.

Antigua. Registrar's Office.
 1968 *Report on the Vital Statistics of the State of Antigua for the Year 1965*. St. John's,
   Antigua: Government Printing Office.

Antigua. Registrar General's Office.
 1925–85 *Marriage Registers*. By Parish (St. John, St. Mary, St. George, St. Philip,
   St. Peter, St. Paul, Barbuda).

Jamaica, Central Bureau of Statistics
 1948 *The Census of the Leeward Islands, 1946*. Printed in Kingston, Jamaica.

Sources at the Magistrates' Court, St. John's, Antigua

All Saints Criminal Register, 1981–87
Barbuda Criminal Register, 1982–87
Bolans Criminal Register, 1981–87
Parham Criminal Register, 1981–87
St. John's Criminal Register, 1980–87

Records at Parliament, St. John's, Antigua

House Debate, *Births and Deaths Registration (Amendment) Act and Status of Children
 Act*, 6 December 1984
House Debate, *Births and Deaths Registration (Amendment) Act*, 5 June 1986
House Debate, *Intestate Estates (Amendment) Act and Status of Children Act*, 4 Decem-
 ber 1986
Senate Debate, *Births and Deaths Registration (Amendment) Act*, 16 June 1986
Senate Debate, *Intestate Estates (Amendment) Act and Status of Children Act*, 22 Decem-
 ber 1986

Church Records

Anglican Church Marriage Registers, Barbuda, 1925–85
Anglican Church Marriage Registers, St. John's, Antigua, 1956–87

Catholic Church Marriage Registers, St. John's, Antigua, 1862–1985 (scattered holdings)
Central Baptist Church Marriage Registers, St. John's, Antigua, 1972–84
Methodist Church Marriage Registers, St. John's, Antigua, 1955–87 (scattered holdings)
Moravian Church Marriage Registers, St. John's, Antigua, 1925–85
Pentecostal Church Marriage Registers, St. John's, Antigua, 1948–85
Seventh Day Adventist Marriage Registers, St. John's, Antigua, 1963–85

Newspapers and Magazines in Antigua and Barbuda

Antigua and Barbuda Herald
Nation's Voice
Outlet
Workers Voice

Secondary Sources

Abel, Richard L.
  1979 "Western Courts in Non-Western Settings: Patterns of Court Use in Colonial and Neo-Colonial Africa." In *The Imposition of Law.* Edited by Sandra B. Burman and Barbara E. Harrell-Bond. New York: Academic Press.

Abu-Lughod, Lila
  1990 "The Romance of Resistance: Tracing Transformations of Power through Bedouin Women." *American Ethnologist* 17:41–55.

Alexander, Jack
  1973 "The Culture of Middle-Class Family Life in Kingston, Jamaica." Ph.D. diss., University of Chicago.

  1976 "A Study of the Cultural Domain of 'Relatives'." *American Ethnologist* 3:17–38.

  1977a "The Culture of Race in Middle-Class Kingston, Jamaica." *American Ethnologist* 4:413–35.

  1977b "The Role of the Male in the Middle-Class Jamaican Family: A Comparative Perspective." *Journal of Comparative Family Studies* 8:369–89.

  1978 "The Cultural Domain of Marriage." *American Ethnologist* 5:5–14.

  1984 "Love, Race, Slavery, and Sexuality in Jamaican Images of the Family." In *Kinship Ideology and Practice in Latin America.* Edited by Raymond T. Smith. Chapel Hill: University of North Carolina Press.

Anderson, Benedict
  1983 *Imagined Communities: Reflections on the Origin and Spread of Nationalism.* London: Verso.

Works Cited

Anderson, Nancy F.
  1982 "The 'Marriage with a Deceased Wife's Sister Bill' Controversy: Incest Anxiety and the Defense of Family Purity in Victorian England." *Journal of British Studies* 21 (2):67–86.

Anderson, Patricia
  1986 "Conclusion: Women in the Caribbean." *Social and Economic Studies* 35 (2):291–324.

Andrews, Evangeline Walker and Charles M. Andrews, eds.
  1934 *Journal of a Lady of Quality; Being the Narrative of a Journey from Scotland to the West Indies, North Carolina, and Portugal, in the years 1774 to 1776.* By Janet Schaw. New Haven: Yale University Press.

Anonymous
  1903 *Antigua 1903.* Unsigned typed MS in the possession of Mr. John Fuller, Attorney-at-Law, St. John's, Antigua.

Antigua and Barbuda
  1974 *The Barbuda Local Government Act, 1974* St. John's, Antigua: Government Printing Office.

  1981 *The Antigua and Barbuda Constitution Order, 1981.* London: McCorquodale Printers.

  1984 *Status of Children Act.* Draft presented to the House of Representatives. St. John's, Antigua: Government Printing Office.

  1991 *1991 Population and Housing Census: Preliminary Report.* St. John's, Antigua: Department of Statistics.

Antigua and Barbuda Independence
  1981 Official Independence Magazine. St. John's, Antigua: Ministry of Foreign Affairs, Economic Development, Tourism, and Energy.

Antigua and Barbuda *Statistical Yearbook*
  1982, 1983, 1985, 1987, 1988 St. John's, Antigua: Statistics Division. Ministry of Finance.

Aschenbrenner, Joyce
  1975 *Lifelines: Black Families in Chicago.* Prospect Heights, Ill.: Waveland Press.

Augier, F. R., and Shirley C. Gordon
  1962 *Sources of West Indian History.* London: Longman Group.

Austin, Diane J.
  1979 "History and Symbols in Ideology: A Jamaican Example." *Man* 14 (3):497–514.

  1983 "Culture and Ideology in the English-speaking Caribbean: A View from Jamaica." *American Ethnologist* 10 (2):223–40.

  1984 *Urban Life in Kingston, Jamaica: The Culture and Class Ideology of Two Neighborhoods.* New York: Gordon and Breach Science Publishers.

Austin-Broos, Diane J.

1987 "Pentecostals and Rastafarians: Cultural, Political, and Gender Relations of Two Religious Movements." *Social and Economic Studies* 36 (4):1–39.

1991 "Religion and the Politics of Moral Order in Jamaica." *Anthropological Forum* 6 (3):293–319.

1992 "Redefining the Moral Order: Interpretations of Christianity in Postemancipation Jamaica." In *The Meaning of Freedom.* Edited by Frank McGlynn and Seymour Drescher. Pittsburgh: University of Pittsburgh Press.

Baker, Charles E.

1882 *Husband and Wife: and the Married Women's Property Act, 1882.* London: Frederick Warne and Co.

Barrow, Christine

1976 "Reputation and Ranking in a Barbadian Locality." *Social and Economic Studies* 25 (2):106–21.

1982 "Male Perceptions of Women in Barbados." Paper prepared for the Women in the Caribbean Project Conference, Barbados, September 1982.

1986 "Autonomy, Equality, and Women in Barbados." Paper presented at the Annual Caribbean Studies Conference, Caracas, Venezuela, May 1986.

1986 "Male Images of Women in Barbados." *Social and Economic Studies* 35 (3):51–64.

Beckford, George L.

1983 *Persistent Poverty: Underdevelopment in Plantation Economies of the Third World.* London: Zed Books.

Beckles, Hilary

1981 "Rebels and Reactionaries: The Political Responses of White Labourers to Planter-Class Hegemony in Seventeenth-Century Barbados." *Journal of Caribbean History* 15:1–19.

1984 *Black Rebellion in Barbados: The Struggle Against Slavery 1627–1838.* Bridgetown, Barbados: Antillo Press.

1989 *Natural Rebels: A Social History of Enslaved Black Women in Barbados.* New Brunswick, N.J.: Rutgers University Press.

Beckwith, Martha Warren

1929 *Black Roadways: A Study of Jamaican Folk Life.* Chapel Hill: University of North Carolina Press.

Bell, Hesketh J.

1889 *Obeah Witchcraft in the West Indies.* London: Sampson Low, Marston, Searle and Rivington.

Benda-Beckmann, Franz von

1981 "Some Comments on the Problems of Comparing the Relationship between Traditional and State Systems of Administration of Justice in Africa and Indonesia." *Journal of Legal Pluralism* 19:165–75.

Berleant-Schiller, Riva

1977a "The Social and Economic Role of Cattle in Barbuda." *Geographical Review* 67 (3):299–309.

1977b "Production and Division of Labor in a West Indian Peasant Community." *American Ethnologist* 4:253–72.

1988 "Ecology and Politics in Barbudan Land Tenure." In *Land and Development in the Caribbean.* Edited by Jean Besson and Janet Momsen. Warwick University Caribbean Series. London: Macmillan.

Besson, Jean

1987 "Family Land as a Model for Martha Brae's New History: Culture Building in an Afro-Caribbean Village." In *Afro-Caribbean Villages in Historical Perspective.* Edited by Charles V. Carnegie. Jamaica: African-Caribbean Institute of Jamaica.

1992 "Freedom and Community." In *The Meaning of Freedom.* Edited by Frank McGlynn and Seymour Drescher. Pittsburgh: University of Pittsburgh Press.

Blackstone, William

[1765–69] 1979 *Commentaries on the Laws of England.* 3 vols. Chicago: University of Chicago Press.

Bohannan, Paul

1965 "Ethnography and Comparison in Legal Anthropology." *American Anthropologist* 67:401–18.

[1957] 1989 *Justice and Judgment Among the Tiv.* Prospect Heights, Ill.: Waveland Press.

Bolland, O. Nigel

1981 "Systems of Domination after Slavery: The Control of Land and Labor in the British West Indies after 1838." *Comparative Studies in Society and History* 24 (4):591–619.

1992a "The Politics of Freedom in the British Caribbean." In *The Meaning of Freedom.* Edited by Frank McGlynn and Seymour Drescher. Pittsburgh: University of Pittsburgh Press.

1992b "Creolization and creole societies: a cultural nationalist view of Caribbean social history." In *Intellectuals in the Twentieth-century Caribbean.* Edited by Alistair Hennessy. Warwick University Caribbean Series. London: Macmillan.

Bolles, A. Lynn

1983 "Kitchens Hit by Priorities: Employed Working-Class Jamaican Women Confront the IMF." In *Women, Men, and the International Division of Labor.* Edited by J. Nash and M. P. Fernandez-Kelly. Albany: State University of New York Press.

Bolles, A. Lynn, and Deborah D'Amico-Samuels
1989 "Anthropological Scholarship on Gender in the English-speaking Carib-bean." In *Gender and Anthropology: Critical Reviews for Research and Training.* Edited by Sandra Morgen. Washington, D.C.: American Anthropological Association.

Bott, Elizabeth
1957 *Family and Social Network.* London: Tavistock Publications.

Boucher, Marcia
1987 "The men, women in calypso." *Sunday Sun* (Jamaica), 21 June.

Bourdieu, Pierre
1977 *Outline of a General Theory of Practice.* Translated by Richard Nice. Cam-bridge: University Press.

1987 "The Force of Law: Toward a Sociology of the Juridical Field." *Hastings Law Journal* 38:805–53.

Boxill, Eileen
1985 "Developments in Family Law Since Emancipation." *West Indian Law Journal* (October): 9–20.

Braithwaite, Lloyd
1953 "Social Stratification in Trinidad." *Social and Economic Studies* 2:5–175.

Brana-Shute, Rosemary, and Gary Brana-Shute, eds.
1980 *Crime and Punishment in the Caribbean.* Gainesville, Fla.: Center for Latin American Studies.

Brathwaite, Edward
1971 *The Development of Creole Society in Jamaica 1770–1820.* Oxford: Clarendon Press.

Brathwaite, Joan, ed.
1973 *Handbook of Churches in the Caribbean.* Prepared for the Inauguration of the Caribbean Conference of Churches. Published by Christian Action for Development in the Caribbean (CADEC), an agency of the Caribbean Conference of Churches.

Braudel, Fernand
1980 "History and Social Sciences: The Long Duree." In *On History.* Translated by Sarah Matthews. Chicago: University of Chicago Press.

Brereton, Bridget
1979 *Race Relations in Colonial Trinidad 1870–1900.* Cambridge: Cambridge Uni-versity Press.

Brodber, Erna
1974 *Abandonment of Children in Jamaica.* Mona, Jamaica: University of the West Indies, Institute of Social and Economic Research.

1975 *A Study of Yards in the City of Kingston.* Mona, Jamaica: University of the West Indies, Institute of Social and Economic Research.

1982 *Perceptions of Caribbean Women.* Women in the Caribbean Project. Joycelin Massiah, gen. ed. Cave Hill, Barbados: University of the West Indies.

Bromley, P. M.
　1981 *Family Law.* London: Butterworths.

Burman, Sandra B., and Barbara E. Harrell-Bond, eds.
　1979 *The Imposition of Law.* New York: Academic Press.

Bush, Barbara
　1990 *Slave Women in Caribbean Society 1650–1838.* Bloomington: Indiana University Press.

Candler, John
　1965 "John Candler's Visit to Antigua." *Caribbean Studies* 15 (3):51–57.

Carnegie, Charles V., ed.
　1987a Afro-Caribbean Villages in Historical Perspective. Mona, Jamaica: African-Caribbean Institute of Jamaica.

　1987b "Is Family Land an Institution?" In *Afro-Caribbean Villages in Historical Perspective.* Edited by Charles V. Carnegie. Mona, Jamaica: African-Caribbean Institute of Jamaica.

Carmody, Caroline
　1978 "First Among Equals: Antiguan Patterns of Local Level Leadership." Ph.D. diss., New York University.

The Caribbean Yearbook
　1977–78 Toronto, Canada: Caribook.

Caribbean Resource Kit for Women
　1982 Women and Development Unit. Extra-Mural Department. University of the West Indies. The Pine, St. Michael, Barbados.

Cassidy, F. G., and R. B. LePage
　1980 *Dictionary of Jamaican English.* Cambridge: Cambridge University Press.

Catterall, Helen Tunnicliff, ed.
　[1926] 1968 *Judicial Cases concerning American Slavery and the Negro. Cases from the Courts of States north of the Ohio and west of the Mississippi Rivers, Canada, and Jamaica.* (Vol. 5). New York: Negro Universities Press.

Challenger, Brian
　1981 "The Antiguan Economy: 1967–1981." *Bulletin of Eastern Caribbean Affairs* 17 (5):12–19.

Chambliss, William
　1973 "Vagrancy Law in England and America." In *The Social Organization of Law.* Edited by Donald Black and Maureen Mileski. New York: Seminar Press.

Chroust, Anton-Hermann
　1965 *The Rise of the Legal Profession in America.* 2 vols. Norman: University of Oklahoma Press.

Chutkan, Noelle
　1975 "The Administration of Justice in Jamaica As A Contributing Factor in the Morant Bay Rebellion of 1865." *Savacou* 11/12:78–85, 112–13.

Clarke, Charles
  1834 *Summary of Colonial Law, the Practice of the Court of Appeals from The Plantations, and of the Laws and Their Administration in All the Colonies with Charters of Justice, Orders in Council, etc.* London: S. Sweet.

Clarke, Edith
  1970 *My Mother Who Fathered Me: A Study of the Family in Three Selected Communities in Jamaica.* London: Allen and Unwin.

Clarke, Roberta
  1986 "Women's Organisations, Women's Interests." *Social and Economic Studies* 35 (3):107–55.

Codrington Family Archives
  N.d. Gloucestershire Records Office. Codrington Family Archives. Microfilm Collection. Gloucester, England. (Family Papers relating to the West Indies.)

Cohn, Bernard S.
  1959 "Some Notes on Law and Change in North India." *Economic Development and Cultural Change* 8:79–93.

  1965 "Anthropological Notes on Disputes and Law in India." *American Anthropologist* 67 (6):82–122.

  1981 "Anthropology and History in the 1980s." *Journal of Interdisciplinary History* 12:227–52.

  1983 "Representing Authority in Victorian India." In *The Invention of Tradition.* Edited by Eric Hobsbawm and Terence Ranger. Cambridge: Cambridge University Press.

  1985 "The Command of Language and the Language of Command." In *Subaltern Studies IV: Writings on South Asian History and Society.* Edited by Ranajit Guha. Oxford: Oxford University Press.

  1989 "Law and the Colonial State in India." In *History and Power in the Study of Law.* Edited by June Starr and Jane F. Collier. Ithaca, N.Y.: Cornell University Press.

Cohn, Bernard S. and Nicholas B. Dirks
  1988 "Beyond the Fringe: The Nation State, Colonialism, and The Technologies of Power." *Journal of Historical Sociology* 1 (2):224–29.

Colen, Shellee
  1986 "'With Respect and Feelings': Voices of West Indian Child Care and Domestic Workers in New York City." In *All American Women.* Edited by Johnnetta B. Cole. New York: Free Press.

  1990 "'Housekeeping' for the Green Card: West Indian Household Workers, the State, and Stratified Reproduction in New York." In *At Work in Homes.* Edited by Roger Sanjek and Shellee Colen. American Ethnological Society Monograph Series. No. 3. Washington, D.C.: American Anthropological Association.

Coleridge, Henry N.
1826 *Six Months in The West Indies, in 1825*. London: John Murray.

Comaroff, Jean
1985 *Body of Power, Spirit of Resistance: the Culture and History of a South African People*. Chicago: University of Chicago Press.

Comaroff, Jean and John Comaroff
1986a "Christianity and Colonialism in South Africa." *American Ethnologist* 13:1–22.

1986b "The Madman and the Migrant: Work and Labor in the Historical Consciousness of a South African People." *American Ethnologist* 14:191–209.

1988 "Through the Looking-glass: Colonial Encounters of the First Kind." *Journal of Historical Sociology* 1 (1):6–31.

1991 *Of Revelation and Revolution: Christianity, Colonialism, and Consciousness in South Africa*. Chicago: University of Chicago Press.

Comaroff, John L.
1980 "Class and Culture in a Peasant Economy: The Transformation of Land Tenure in Barolong." *Journal of African Law* 24 (1):85–113.

1982 "Dialectical Systems, History and Anthropology: Units of Study and Questions of Theory." *Journal of Southern African Studies* 8 (2):143–72.

1989 "Images of Empire, Contests of Conscience: Models of Colonial Domination in South Africa." *American Ethnologist* 16:661–85.

Comaroff, John L. and Simon Roberts
1977 "The Invocation of Norms in Dispute Settlement: The Tswana Case." In *Social Anthropology and Law*. Edited by Ian Hamnett. New York: Academic Press.

1981 *Rules and Processes: The Cultural Logic of Dispute in an African Context*. Chicago: University of Chicago Press.

Comitas, Lambros
1964 "Occupational Multiplicity in Rural Jamaica." In *Proceedings of the American Ethnological Society*. Edited by E. Garfield and E. Friedl. Seattle: University of Washington Press.

Conley, John M., and William M. O'Barr
1990 *Rules versus Relationships: The Ethnography of Legal Discourse*. Chicago: University of Chicago Press.

Conley, John M., William M. O'Barr, and E. Allan Lind
1978 "The Power of Language: Presentational Style in the Courtroom." *Duke Law Journal* 78:1375–99.

Cooper, Frederick and Ann L. Stoler
1989 "Tensions of Empire: Colonial Control and Visions of Rule." *American Ethnologist* 16 (4):609–21.

Corrigan, Philip, and Derek Sayer
1985 *The Great Arch: English State Formation as Cultural Revolution.* New York: Basil Blackwell.

Cousins, Winifred M.
1935 "Slave Family Life in the British Colonies: 1800–1834." *Sociological Review* 27:35–55.

Craton, Michael
1978 *Searching for the Invisible Man: Slaves and Plantation Life in Jamaica.* Cambridge: Harvard University Press.

1980 "The Passion to Exist: Slave Rebellions in the British West Indies 1650–1832." *Journal of Caribbean History* 13:1–20.

1982 *Testing the Chains: Resistance to Slavery in the British West Indies.* Ithaca, N.Y.: Cornell University Press.

Crenshaw, Kimberle Williams
1988 "Race, Reform, and Retrenchment: Transformation and Legitimation in Antidiscrimination Law." *Harvard Law Review* 101 (7):1331–87.

Cumper, Gloria and Stephanie Daly
1979 *Family Law in the Commonwealth Caribbean.* Jamaica: University of the West Indies.

Curtin, Philip D.
1955 *Two Jamaicas: The Role of Ideas in a Tropical Colony 1830–1865.* Cambridge, Mass.: Harvard University Press.

1964 *The Image of Africa: British Ideas and Actions, 1780–1850.* Madison: University of Wisconsin Press.

D'Amico-Samuels, Deborah
1991 "Undoing Fieldwork: Personal, Political, Theoretical and Methodological Implications." In *Decolonizing Anthropology.* Edited by Faye V. Harrison. Washington, D.C.: Association of Black Anthropologists, American Anthropological Association.

Darnton, Robert
1985 *The Great Cat Massacre: And Other Episodes in French Cultural History.* New York: Vintage Books.

Decamp, David
1971 "Introduction: The Study of Pidgin and Creole Languages." In *Pidginization and Creolization of Languages.* Edited by Dell Hymes. Cambridge: Cambridge University Press.

de Certeau, Michel
1984 *The Practice of Everyday Life.* Translated by Steven Randall. Berkeley: University of California Press.

DeVeer, Henrietta
1979 "Sex Roles and Social Stratification in a Rapidly Growing Urban Area—May Pen, Jamaica." Ph.D. diss., University of Chicago.

Dirks, Robert, and Virginia Kerns
1976 "Mating Patterns and Adaptive Change in Rum Bay, 1823–1970." *Social and Economic Studies* 25 (1):34–54.

Dobbin, Jay D.
1986 *The Jombee Dance of Montserrat: A Study of Trance Ritual in the West Indies.* Columbus: Ohio State University Press.

Dodd, David J.
1979 "The Role of Law in Plantation Society: Reflections on the Caribbean Legal System." *International Journal of the Sociology of Law* 7:275–96.

Dominguez, Virginia
1986 *White By Definition: Social Classification in Creole Louisiana.* New Brunswick, N.J.: Rutgers University Press.

Donzelot, Jacques
1979 *The Policing of Families.* Translated by Robert Hurley. New York: Pantheon Books.

1991 "The Mobilization of Society." In *The Foucault Effect.* Edited by Graham Burchell, Colin Gordon, and Peter Miller. Chicago: University of Chicago Press.

Douglass, Lisa
1992 *The Power of Sentiment: Love, Hierarchy, and the Jamaican Family Elite.* Boulder: Westview Press.

Drummond, Lee
1980 "The Cultural Continuum: A Theory of Intersystems." *Man* 15 (2):352–74.

Dunn, Richard S.
1973 *Sugar and Slaves: The Rise of the Planter Class in the English West Indies 1624–1713.* New York: W. W. Norton.

Durant, Will
1957 *The Story of Civilization: Part VI. The Reformation.* New York: Simon and Schuster.

Durant Gonzalez, Victoria
1982 "The Realm of Female Familial Responsibility." In *Women and the Family.* Edited by Joycelin Massiah. Women in the Caribbean Project. Cave Hill, Barbados: University of the West Indies, Institute of Social and Economic Research.

1986 "Evolution of a Research Methodology." *Social and Economic Studies* 35 (2):31–58.

Durkheim, Emile
[1893] 1964 *The Division of Labor in Society*. Translated by Georg Simpson. New York: Free Press.

Edwards, Bryan
[1819] 1966 *The History, Civil and Commercial, of the British West Indies*. 5th ed. New York: AMS Press.

Epstein, A. L.
1967 "The Case Method in the Field of Law." In *The Craft of Social Anthropology*. Edited by A. L. Epstein. London: Tavistock Publications.

1973 "The Reasonable Man Revisited: Some Problems in the Anthropology of Law." *Law & Society Review* 7 (4):643–66.

Evans-Pritchard, E. E.
1967 "The Morphology and Function of Magic: A Comparative Study of Trobriand and Zande Ritual and Spells." In *Magic, Witchcraft, and Curing*. Edited by John Middleton. Garden City: Natural History Press.

[1937] 1976 *Witchcraft, Oracles, and Magic among the Azande*. Abridged. Edited by Eva Gillies. Oxford: Clarendon Press.

Fanner, P. D., and C. T. Latham, eds.
1971 *Stone's Justices' Manual*. London: Butterworth and Company.

Felstiner, William L. F.
1974 "Influences of Social Organization on Dispute Processing." *Law & Society Review* 9 (1):63–94.

1975 "Avoidance as Dispute Processing: An Elaboration." *Law & Society Review* 9 (4):695–706.

Felstiner, William L. F., and Austin Sarat
1992 "Enactments of Power: Negotiating Reality and Responsibility in Lawyer-Client Interactions." *Cornell Law Review* 77 (6):1447–98.

Felstiner, William L. F., Richard L. Abel, and Austin Sarat
1981 "The Emergence and Transformation of Disputes: Naming, Blaming, Claiming . . ." *Law & Society Review* 15 (3/4):631–54, 883–910.

Femia, Joseph V.
1975 "Hegemony and Consciousness in the Thought of Antonio Gramsci." *Political Studies* 23:29–48.

1981 *Gramsci's Political Thought: Hegemony, Consciousness, and the Revolutionary Process*. Oxford: Clarendon Press.

Fergus, Howard A.
1978 "The Early Laws of Montserrat (1668–1680): The Legal Schema of a Slave Society." *Caribbean Quarterly* 24 (1/2):34–43.

Ferguson, Moira, ed.
1987 *The History of Mary Prince A West Indian Slave Related by Herself*. London: Pandora.

Fischer, Michael M. J.

   1974a "Value Assertion and Stratification: Religion and Marriage in Rural Jamaica." Part 1. *Caribbean Studies* 14 (1):7–37.

   1974b "Value Assertion and Stratification: Religion and Marriage in Rural Jamaica." Part II. *Caribbean Studies* 14 (3):7–35.

Fitzpatrick, Peter

   1980 *Law and State in Papua New Guinea.* New York: Academic Press.

   1983a "Law, Plurality and Underdevelopment." In *Legality, Ideology and the State.* Edited by D. Sugarman. New York: Academic Press.

   1983b "Marxism and Legal Pluralism." *Australian Journal of Law and Society* 1 (2):45–59.

   1984 "Law and Societies." *Osgoode Hall Law Journal* 22 (1):115–38.

Flannagan, Mrs.

   [1844] 1967 *Antigua and the Antiguans: A Full Account of the Caribs to the Present Day, Interspersed with Anecdotes and Legends. Also, An Impartial View of Slavery and the Free Labour Systems; The Statistics of the Island, and Biographical Notices of Principal Families.* 2 vols. Reprint. London: Spottiswoode, Ballantyne & Co.

Foner, Nancy

   1973 *Status and Power in Rural Jamaica.* New York: Teachers College Press.

Forde, Norma Monica

   1981 *Women and the Law.* Edited by Joycelin Massiah. Women in the Caribbean Project. Cave Hill, Barbados: University of the West Indies.

Forgacs, David, ed.

   1988 *An Antonio Gramsci Reader: Selected Writings, 1916–1935.* New York: Schocken Books.

Forsythe, Dennis

   1975 "Race, Colour and Class in the British West Indies." In *The Commonwealth Caribbean into the Seventies.* Edited by A. W. Singham. Montreal: McGill University Centre for Developing Area Studies.

Fortes, Meyer

   [1949] 1970 "Time and Social Structure: An Ashanti Case Study." In *Time and Social Structure.* Edited by Meyer Fortes. New York: Humanities Press.

Foucault, Michel

   1979 *Discipline and Punish: The Birth of the Prison.* Translated by Alan Sheridan. New York: Vintage Books.

   1980 *The History of Sexuality. Vol. I. An Introduction.* Translated by Allan Sheridan. New York: Vintage Books.

   1980 *Power/Knowledge: Selected Interviews and Other Writings 1972–1977.* Edited by Gordon Colin. Translated by Colin Gordon, Leo Marshall, John Mepham, and Kater Soper. New York: Pantheon Books.

   1991 "Governmentality." In *The Foucault Effect.* Edited by Graham Burchell, Colin Gordon, and Peter Miller. Chicago: University of Chicago Press.

Fox-Genovese, Elizabeth
　　1988 *Within the Plantation Household: Black and White Women of the Old South.*
　　Chapel Hill: University of North Carolina Press.

Fox-Piven, Frances, and Richard A. Cloward
　　1971 *Regulating the Poor: The Functions of Public Welfare.* New York: Vintage Books.

Friedman, Lawrence M.
　　1973 *A History of American Law.* New York: Simon and Schuster.

　　1990 "Turning the Tables: Slaves and the Criminal Law." *Law and Social Inquiry*
　　15 (3):611–23.

Galanter, Marc
　　1971 "The Displacement of Traditional Law in Modern India." *Journal of Social
　　Issues* 24 (4):65–91.

Garfinkel, Harold
　　1956 "Conditions of Successful Degradation Ceremonies." *American Journal of
　　Sociology* 61:420–24.

Gaspar, David Barry
　　1979 "Runaways in Seventeenth-Century Antigua, West Indies." *Boletin De
　　Estudios Latinamericanos y Del Caribe* (26):3–13.

　　1985a *Bondmen and Rebels: A Study of Master-Slave Relations in Antigua.* Baltimore:
　　Johns Hopkins University Press.

　　1985b "'A Mockery of Freedom': The Status of Freedmen in Antigua Slave Society
　　Before 1760." *Nieuwe West-Indische Gids* 59 (3/4):135–48.

Geertz, Clifford
　　1973 "Religion as a Cultural System." In *The Interpretation of Cultures.* New York:
　　Basic Books.

　　1983 *Local Knowledge: Further Essays in Interpretive Anthropology.* New York:
　　Basic Books.

A Genuine Narrative of the Conspiracy of the Negroes at Antigua
　　[1737] 1972 Extracted from an Authentic Copy of a Report, made to the Chief
　　Governor of the Carabee Islands, by the Commissioners, or Judges appointed
　　to try the Conspirators. New York: Arno Press.

Genovese, Eugene D.
　　1971 *The World the Slaveholders Made.* New York: Vintage Books.

　　1972 *Roll, Jordan, Roll: The World the Slaves Made.* New York: Pantheon Books.

Gibson, Marston
　　1984 "Pluralism, Social Engineering and Some Aspects of Law in the Caribbean."
　　Bulletin of Eastern Caribbean Affairs 10 (3):56–87.

Gillis, John R.

1983 "Conjugal Settlements: Resort to Clandestine and Common Law Marriage in England and Wales, 1650–1850." In *Disputes and Settlements*. Edited by John Bossey. Cambridge: Cambridge University Press.

1985 *For Better, For Worse: British Marriages, 1600 to the Present.* Oxford: Oxford University Press.

Glassman, Jonathon

1991 "The Bondsman's New Clothes: The Contradictory Consciousness of Slave Resistance on the Swahili Coast." *Journal of African History* 32:277–312.

Glazier, Stephen D.

1983 "Cultural Pluralism and Respectability in Trinidad." *Ethnic and Racial Studies* 6 (3):351–55.

Gluckman, Max

1965 "Concepts in the Comparative Study of Tribal Law." *American Anthropologist* 67:349–73.

[1955] 1967 *The Judicial Process Among the Barotse of Northern Rhodesia (Zambia).* New York: Humanities Press.

Goode, William J.

1960 "Illegitimacy in the Caribbean Social Structure." *American Sociological Review* 25:21–30.

1961 "Illegitimacy, Anomie, and Cultural Penetration." *American Sociological Review* 26:910–25.

Gonzalez, Nancie L. Solien

1970 "Toward a Definition of Matrifocality." In *African-American Anthropology: Contemporary Perspectives*. Edited by Norman E. Whitten, Jr., and John F. Szwed. New York: Free Press.

1981 "Household and Family in the Caribbean: Some Definitions and Concepts." In *The Black Woman Cross-Culturally*. Edited by Filomina Chioma Steady. Rochester, Vt.: Schenkman Books.

Gordon, Robert W.

1984 "Critical Legal Histories." *Stanford Law Review* 36:57–125.

Gordon, Sally W.

1987 "I Go to 'Tanties': The Economic Significance of Child-Shifting in Antigua, West Indies." *Journal of Comparative Family Studies* 18 (3):427–44.

Goveia, Elsa V.

1965 *Slave Society in the British Leeward Islands at the End of the Eighteenth Century.* New Haven: Yale University Press.

1970 "The West Indian Slave Laws of the 18th Century." *Chapters in Caribbean History* 2. Edited by Douglas Hall, Elsa Goveia, and Roy Augier. Aylesbury, England: Ginn and Company.

Greaves, W. Herbert, and C. P. Clarke
1897 *Report of Cases Relating to Barbados to be found in the English Law Reports and of Certain Cases Argued and Determined in the Local Courts.* Barbados: T. E. King.

Greenhouse, Carol J.
1986 *Praying for Justice: Faith, Order, and Community in an American Town.* Ithaca, N.Y.: Cornell University Press.

1989 "Interpreting American Litigiousness." In *History and Power in the Study of Law.* Edited by June Starr and Jane F. Collier. Ithaca, N.Y.: Cornell University Press.

Greer, Edward
1982 "Antonio Gramsci and 'Legal Hegemony.' " In *The Politics of Law: A Progressive Critique.* Edited by David Kairys. New York: Pantheon Books.

Greven, Philip J., Jr.
1973 "Family Structure in Seventeenth-Century Andover, Massachusetts." In *Interpreting Colonial America.* Edited by James Kirby Martin. New York: Dodd, Mead.

Grossberg, Michael
1985 *Governing the Hearth: Law and the Family in Nineteenth-Century America.* Chapel Hill: University of North Carolina Press.

Gulliver, P. H.
1969 "Dispute Settlement Without Courts: The Ndendeuli of Southern Tanzania." In *Law in Culture and Society.* Edited by Laura Nader. Chicago: Aldine.

Gussler, Judith D.
1980 "Adaptive Strategies and Social Networks of Women in St. Kitts." In *A World of Women: Anthropological Studies of Women in the Societies of the World.* Edited by Erika Bourguignon. New York: Praeger.

Gutman, Herbert G.
1976 *The Black Family in Slavery and Freedom, 1750–1925.* New York: Vintage Books.

Hall, Douglas
1964 "Absentee-Proprietorship in the British West Indies, to About 1850." *Jamaican Historical Review* 4:15–35.

1971 *Five of the Leewards 1834–1870.* Barbados: Caribbean Universities Press.

Hall, N. A. T.
1983 "Louis Rothe's 1846 Report on Education in Post-Emancipation Antigua." *Caribbean Journal of Education* 10 (1)55–62.

Hammick, James T.
1887 *The Marriage Law of England: A Practical Treatis on the Legal Incidents with the Constitution of the Matrimonial Contract.* London: Shaw and Sons.

Handler, Jerome S.

1974 *The Unappropriated People: Freedmen in the Slave Society of Barbados.* Baltimore: Johns Hopkins University Press.

Hannerz, Ulf

1987 "The World in Creolization." *Africa* 57 (4):546–59.

1991 "The State in Creolization." Paper presented at the American Anthropological Association, Chicago, 20–24 November.

Harrison, Faye V.

1988 "The Politics of Social Outlawry in Urban Jamaica." *Urban Anthropology* 17 (2/3):259–77.

1991 "Ethnography as Politics." In *Decolonizing Anthropology.* Edited by Faye V. Harrison. Washington, D.C.: Association of Black Anthropologists, American Anthropological Association.

Harrison, Faye V., ed.

1991 *Decolonizing Anthropology.* Washington, D.C.: Association of Black Anthropologists, American Anthropological Association.

Haw, Reginald

1952 *The State of Matrimony: An Investigation of the Relationship between Ecclesiastical and Civil Marriage in England after the Reformation with a Consideration of the Laws relating thereto.* London: S. P. C. K.

Hay, Douglas

1975 "Property, Authority and the Criminal Law." In *Albion's Fatal Tree: Crime and Society in Eighteenth-Century England.* Edited by Douglas Hay, Peter Linebaugh, John G. Rule, E. P. Thompson, and Cal Winslow. New York: Pantheon Books.

Hedrick, Basil C., and Jeanette E. Stephens

1977 "It's a Natural Fact: Obeah in the Bahamas." University of Northern Colorado, Museum of Anthropology. *Miscellaneous Series* No. 39.

Henderson, Lynne

1991 "Law's Patriarchy." *Law & Society Review* 25 (2):411–44.

Henriques, Fernando

1953 *Family and Colour in Jamaica.* London: Eyre & Spottiswoode.

1974 *Children of Caliban: Miscegenation.* London: Secker and Warburg.

Henry, Paget

1981 "State-Class Relations in Antigua." *Bulletin of Eastern Caribbean Affairs* 7 (5):7–19.

1982 "The Antigua and Barbudan Political System: Trends and Prospects." *Antigua and Barbuda Forum* 1 (1):13–18.

1983a "Decolonization and Cultural Underdevelopment in the Commonwealth Caribbean." In *The Newer Caribbean: Decolonization, Democracy, and Development.* Edited by Paget Henry and Carl Stone. Philadelphia: Publication of the Institute for the Study of Human Issues.

1983b "Decolonization and the Authoritarian Context of Democracy in Antigua."
In *The Newer Caribbean: Decolonization, Democracy, and Development.* Edited
by Paget Henry and Carl Stone. Philadelphia: Publication of the Institute
for the Study of Human Issues.

1985 *Peripheral Capitalism and Underdevelopment in Antigua.* New Brunswick,
N.J.: Transaction Books.

1992 "C. L. R. James and the Antiguan Left." In *C. L. R. James's Caribbean.* Edited
by Paget Henry and Paul Buhle. Durham, N.C.: Duke University Press.

Henry, Paget and Paul Buhle
1992 "Caliban as Deconstructionist: C. L. R. James and Post-Colonial Discourse."
In *C. L. R. James's Caribbean.* Edited by Paget Henry and Paul Buhle.
Durham, N.C.: Duke University Press.

Herskovits, Melville J.
1937 *Life in a Haitian Valley.* New York: Alfred A. Knopf.

[1941] 1958 *The Myth of the Negro Past.* Boston: Beacon Press.

1966 "The Contribution of Afroamerican Studies to Africanist Research." In *The
New World Negro.* Edited by Frances S. Herskovits. Bloomington: Indiana
University Press.

Heuman, Gad J.
1981 "White Over Brown Over Black: The Free Coloureds in Jamaican Society
During Slavery and After Emancipation." *Journal of Caribbean History*
14:46–69.

Higginbotham, A. Leon, Jr.
1978 *In the Matter of Color: Race and the American Legal Process.* New York: Oxford
University Press.

Higham, C. S. S.
1921 *The Development of the Leeward Islands Under the Restoration* 1660–1688.
Cambridge: University Press.

Higman, B. W.
1973 "Household Structure and Fertility on Jamaican Slave Plantations: A Nineteenth-century Example." *Population Studies* 27:527–50.

1976 *Slave Population and Economy in Jamaica, 1807–1834.* Cambridge: Cambridge
University Press.

1977 "Methodological Problems in the Study of the Slave Family." In *Comparative
Perspectives on Slavery in New World Plantation Societies.* Edited by Vera Rubin
and Arthur Tuden. *Annals of the New York Academy of Science* 292:591–96.

1979 "African and Creole Slave Family Patterns in Trinidad." In *Africa and the
Caribbean: The Legacies of a Link.* Edited by Margaret S. Crahan and Franklin
W. Knight. Baltimore: Johns Hopkins University Press.

1984a "Terms for Kin in the British West Indian Slave Community: Differing Perceptions of Masters and Slaves." In *Kinship Ideology and Practice in Latin America*. Edited by Raymond T. Smith. Chapel Hill: University of North Carolina Press.

1984b *Slave Populations of the British Caribbean 1807–1834*. Baltimore: Johns Hopkins University Press.

1985 "Theory, Method and Techniques in Caribbean Social History." *Journal of Caribbean History* 20:1–29.

Hill, Christopher
1969 *Reformation to Industrial Revolution*. Baltimore: Penguin Books.

Hirsch, Susan F.
1990 "Gender and Disputing: Insurgent Voices in Coastal Kenyan Muslim Courts." Ph.D. diss., Duke University.

1994 "Kadhi's Courts as Complex Sites of Resistance: The State, Islam, and Gender in Post-Colonial Kenya." In *Contested States: Law, Hegemony, and Resistance*. Edited by Mindie Lazarus-Black and Susan Hirsch. New York: Routledge, Chapman and Hall.

Hirsch, Susan F., and Mindie Lazarus-Black
1994 "Performance and Paradox: Exploring Law's Role in Hegemony and Resistance." In *Contested States: Law, Hegemony, and Resistance*. Edited by Mindie Lazarus-Black and Susan F. Hirsch. New York: Routledge, Chapman and Hall.

Hogg, Donald W.
1961 "Magic and 'Science' in Jamaica." *Caribbean Studies* 1 (2):1–5.

Horsford, Rev. John
1856 *A Voice from the West Indies: Being a Review of the Character and Results of Missionary Efforts in the British and Other Colonies in the Caribbean Sea. With Some Remarks on the Usages, Prejudices, etc. of the Inhabitants*. London: Alexander Hejlin.

Howard, John Henry
1827 *The Laws of The British Colonies, in The West Indies and other parts of America concerning Real and Personal Property and Manumission of Slaves; with A View of the Constitution of Each Colony*. 2 vols. London: William Henry Bond, Law Bookseller.

Jacobs, A. C.
1932 "Illegitimacy." *Encyclopaedia of the Social Sciences*. Edited by Edwin R. A. Seligman. 7:579–86. New York: Macmillan.

Jackson, Jean
    1982 "Stresses Affecting Women and their Families." In *Women and the Family.* Edited by Joycelin Massiah. Women in the Caribbean Project. Cave Hill, Barbados: University of the West Indies.

Jacob, Herbert
    1989 *Silent Revolution: The Transformation of Divorce Law in the United States.* Chicago: University of Chicago Press.

Jagdeo, Tirbani
    1984 *Teenage Pregnancy in the Caribbean.* New York: International Planned Parenthood Federation.

Jayawardena, Chandra
    1960 "Marital Stability in Two Guianese Sugar Estate Communities." *Social and Economic Studies* 9:76–100.

    1963 *Conflict and Solidarity in a Guianese Plantation.* London: Athlone Press.

    1968 "Ideology and Conflict in Lower Class Communities." *Comparative Studies in Society and History* 10:413–46.

Jones, Jacqueline
    1985 *Labor of Love, Labor of Sorrow: Black Women, Work, and the Family from Slavery to the Present.* New York: Vintage Books.

Jones, Norrece T., Jr.
    1990 *Born a Child of Freedom, Yet a Slave: Mechanisms of Control and Strategies of Resistance in Antebellum South Carolina.* Hanover, N.H.: University Press of New England.

Jordan, Winthrop D.
    1968 *White over Black: American Attitudes Toward the Negro, 1550–1812.* Baltimore: Penguin Books.

Justus, Joyce Bennett
    1981 "Women's Role in West Indian Society." In *The Black Woman Cross-Culturally.* Edited by Filomina Chioma Steady. Rochester, Vt.: Schenkman Books.

Kairys, David
    1982 "Legal Reasoning." In *The Politics of Law: A Progressive Critique.* Edited by David Kairys. New York: Pantheon Books.

Kidder, Robert J.
    1979 "Toward an Integrated Theory of Imposed Law." In *The Imposition of Law.* Edited by Sandra B. Burman and Barbara E. Harrell-Bond. New York: Academic Press.

Kincaid, Jamaica
    1985 *Annie John.* New York: New American Library.

Kunstadter, Peter
    1968 "Division of Labor and the Matrifocal Family." In *A Modern Introduction to the Family.* Edited by Norman W. Bell and Ezra F. Vogel. New York: Free Press.

Larrain, Jorge

1979 *The Concept of Ideology.* Athens: University of Georgia Press.

Laslett, Peter

1965 *The World We have Lost.* New York: Charles Scribner's Sons.

1972 "Mean Household Size in England Since the Sixteenth Century." In *Household and Family in Past Time.* Edited by Peter Laslett. Cambridge: Cambridge University Press.

1977 *Family Life and Illicit Love in Earlier Generations.* Cambridge: Cambridge University Press.

Laurence, K. O.

1971 *Immigration into the West Indies in the 19th Century.* Aylesbury, England: Ginn and Company.

Lazarus-Black, Mindie

1982 "Whole Bloods, Half Bloods, and Persons with Power: The Victorian Jural Legacy to Kinship Studies." Master's thesis, University of Chicago.

1987 "Working in the Courts: Legal Professionals on the Past and Present Role of Family Law, Antigua and Barbuda, West Indies." Paper presented to members of the Antigua and Barbuda Bar Association, April 1987.

1989 Review of *History and Power in the Study of Law.* Edited by June Starr and Jane F. Collier. Ithaca, N.Y.: Cornell University Press. *APLA Newsletter* 12 (2):8–12.

1990a "Legitimate Acts and Illegal Encounters: The Development of Family Ideology and Structure in Antigua and Barbuda, West Indies." Ph.D. diss., University of Chicago.

1990b "Between You and Me: The Salience of Gender In and Around the Divorce Lawyer's Office." Paper presented to the Law and Society Association, 1 June 1990, San Francisco, California.

1991 "Why Women Take Men to Magistrate's Court: Caribbean Kinship Ideology and Law." *Ethnology* 30 (2):119–33.

1992 "Bastardy, Gender Hierarchy, and the State: The Politics of Family Law Reform in Antigua and Barbuda." *Law & Society Review* 26 (4):863–99.

1994 "Slaves, Masters, and Magistrates: Law and the Politics of Resistance in the British Caribbean, 1736–1834." In *Contested States: Law, Hegemony, and Resistance.* Edited by Mindie Lazarus-Black and Susan F. Hirsch. New York: Routledge, Chapman and Hall.

Lazarus-Black, Mindie, and Susan F. Hirsch, eds.

1994 *Contested States: Law, Hegemony, and Resistance.* Edited by Mindie Lazarus-Black and Susan F. Hirsch. New York: Routledge, Chapman and Hall.

Lévi-Strauss, Claude
   1969 *The Elementary Structures of Kinship.* Edited by Rodney Needham. Translated by James Harle Bell, John Richard von Sturmer, and Rodney Needham. Boston: Beacon Press.

Lewin, Linda
   1981 "Property as Patrimony: Changing Notions of Family, Kinship and Wealth in Brazilian Inheritance Law from Empire to Republic." Paper presented to a conference on Theoretical Problems in Latin American Kinship Studies, Mexico.

   1987 *Politics and Parentela in Paraiba: A Case Study of Family-Based Oligarchy in Brazil.* Princeton: Princeton University Press.

Lewis, Gordon K.
   1983 *Main Currents in Caribbean Thought: The Historical Evolution of Caribbean Society in Its Ideological Aspects, 1492–1900.* Baltimore: Johns Hopkins University Press.

Lewis, M. G.
   [1815–17] 1929 *Journal of a West Indian Proprietor.* Edited by Mona Wilson. London: George Routledge & Sons.

Livingston, Debra
   1982 "Round and 'Round the Bramble Bush: From Legal Realism to Critical Legal Scholarship." *Harvard Law Review* 95 (7):1669–90.

Long, Edward
   [1774] 1970 *The History of Jamaica, or General Survey of the Ancient and Modern State of That Island: With Reflections on its Situations, Settlements, Inhabitants, Climate, Products, Commerce, Laws and Government.* 3 vols. London: Frank Cass.

Lowenthal, David
   1972 *West Indian Societies.* London: Oxford University Press.

Lowenthal, David, and Colin G. Clarke
   1977 "Slave-Breeding in Barbuda: The Past of a Negro Myth." In *Comparative Perspectives on Slavery in New World Plantation Societies.* Edited by Vera Rubin and Arthur Tuden. *Annals of the New York Academy of Science* 292:510–35.

Lowes, Susan
   1982 "From Free Colored to Middle Class: The Development of a Segment of the Population in Antigua, British West Indies, from 1830 to 1930." Paper prepared for the American Historical Association, Washington, D. C.

   1987 "Time and Motion in the Formation of the Middle Class in Antigua, 1834–1940." Paper presented to the American Anthropological Association, Chicago, November 1987.

   1992 "They Couldn't Mash Ants: The Decline of the White and Nonwhite Elites in Antigua, West Indies, 1834–1900." Paper presented in Denmark. Forthcoming in *Small Islands, Large Issue.* Edited by Karen Olwig. London: Frank Cass.

1993 "The Peculiar Class: The Formation, Collapse, and Reformation of the Middle Class in Antigua, West Indies, 1834–1940." Ph.D. diss., Teachers College, Columbia University.

Luffman, John
1789 *A Brief Account of the Island of Antigua, Together with the Customs and Manners of its Inhabitants, As well White as Black: As Also an Accurate Statement of the Food, Cloathing, Labor, and Punishment, of Slaves. In Letters to a Friend. Written in the Years 1786, 1787, 1788.* London: T. Cadell.

Lukes, Steven
1974 *Power: A Radical View.* London: Macmillan.

Lurry-Wright, Jerome Wendell
1987 *Custom and Conflict on a Bahamian Out-Island.* New York: University Press of America.

Macfarlane, Alan
1986 *Marriage and Love in England: Modes of Reproduction 1300–1840.* New York: Basil Blackwell.

MacKinnon, Catharine A.
1987 *Feminism Unmodified: Discourses on Life and Law.* Cambridge: Harvard University Press.

Mahabir, Cynthia
1985 *Crime and Nation-Building in the Caribbean: The Legacy of Legal Barriers.* Cambridge: Schenkman Publishing.

Mandle, Jay R.
1992 "Black Economic Entrapment after Emancipation in the United States." In *The Meaning of Freedom.* Edited by Frank McGlynn and Seymour Drescher. Pittsburgh: University of Pittsburgh Press.

Marshall, Woodville K., ed.
1977 *The Colthurst Journal.* Millwood, N.Y.: KTO Press.

Martin, Col. Samuel
1750 *An Essay upon Plantership Humbly inscribed To all the Planters of the British Sugar-Colonies in America.* Antigua: T. Smith. (Rare Book Room, New York Public Library).

Martinez-Alier, Verena
1974 *Marriage, Class and Colour in Nineteenth-Century Cuba: A Study of Racial Attitudes and Sexual Values in a Slave Society.* Cambridge: Cambridge University Press.

Marx, Karl
1975 *Early Writings.* Translated by Rodney Livingstone and Gregor Benton. New York: Vintage Books.

Marx, Karl and Frederick Engels
1977 *The German Ideology.* Edited by C. J. Arthur. New York: International Publishers.

Massell, Gregory J.
1968 "Law as an Instrument of Revolutionary Change in a Traditional Milieu: The Case of Soviet Central Asia." *Law & Society Review* 2:179–228.

Massiah, Joycelin
1982 "Family Structure and the Status of Women in the Caribbean with Particular Reference to Women Who Head Households." In *Women and the Family.* Edited by Joycelin Massiah. Women in the Caribbean Project. Cave Hill, Barbados: University of the West Indies.

1984 "Indicators of Women in Development: A Preliminary Framework for the Caribbean." In *Women and Work.* Edited by Joycelin Massiah. Women in the Caribbean Project. Cave Hill, Barbados: University of the West Indies.

1986 "Women in the Caribbean Project: An Overview." *Social and Economic Studies* 35 (2):1–29.

Mather, Lynn, and Barbara Yngvesson
1980 "Language, Audience, And The Transformation of Disputes." *Law & Society Review* 15 (3/4):775–910.

Matthews, Lear, and S. C. Lee
1975 "Matrifocality Reconsidered: The Case of the Rural Afro-Guyanese Family." In *Family and Kinship in Middle America and the Caribbean.* Edited by Arnaud F. Marks and Rene A. Romer. Willemstadt: Institute of Higher Studies in Curaçao.

Mauss, Marcel
1967 *The Gift.* Translated by Ian Cunnison. New York: W. W. Norton.

McGlynn, Frank, and Seymour Drescher, eds.
1992 *The Meaning of Freedom: Economics, Politics, and Culture After Slavery.* Pittsburgh: University of Pittsburgh Press.

Merry, Sally Engle
1979 "Going To Court: Strategies Of Dispute Management In An American Urban Neighborhood." *Law & Society Review* 13 (4):891–925.

1986 "Everyday Understandings of the Law in Working-Class America." *American Ethnologist* 13:253–70.

1988 "Legal Pluralism." *Law & Society Review* 22 (5):869–96.

1990 *Getting Justice and Getting Even: Legal Consciousness Among Working-Class Americans.* Chicago: University of Chicago Press.

1991 "Review Essay: Law and Colonialism." *Law & Society Review* 25 (4):889–922.

1992 "Anthropology, Law, and Transnational Processes." *Annual Review of Anthropology* 21:357–79.

1994 "Courts as Performances: Domestic Violence Hearings in a Hawaii Family Court." In *Contested States: Law, Hegemony, and Resistance.* Edited by Mindie Lazarus-Black and Susan F. Hirsch. New York: Routledge, Chapman and Hall.

Merry, Sally Engle, and Susan S. Silbey
  1984 "What Do Plaintiffs Want? Reexamining the Concept of Dispute." *Justice System Journal* 9 (2):151–78.

Mertz, Elizabeth
  1992 "Linguistic Ideology and Praxis in U.S. Law School Classrooms." *Pragmatics* 2:325–34.

  1994 "Recontextualization as Socialization: Text and Pragmatics in the Law School Classroom." In *Natural Histories of Discourse*. Edited by Michael Silverstein and Greg Urban.

Middleton, John, and E. H. Winter
  1963 "Introduction." *Witchcraft and Sorcery in East Africa*. New York: Frederick A. Praeger.

Mintz, Sidney W.
  1967 "Caribbean Nationhood in Anthropological Perspective." In *Caribbean Integration: Third Caribbean Scholars' Conference, Georgetown, Guyana*. Edited by Sybil Lewis and Thomas G. Mathews. Puerto Rico: University of Puerto Rico, Institute of Caribbean Studies.

  1971 "The Caribbean as a Socio-Cultural Area." In *Peoples and Cultures of the Caribbean: An Anthropological Reader*. Edited by Michael M. Horowitz. New York: Natural History Press.

  1974 "The Origins of the Jamaican Market System." In *Caribbean Transformations*. Baltimore: Johns Hopkins University Press.

  1974 *Caribbean Transformations*. Baltimore: Johns Hopkins University Press.

  1985 *Sweetness and Power: The Place of Sugar in Modern History*. New York: Viking.

  1992 "Panglosses and Pollyannas; or, Whose Reality Are We Talking About?" In *The Meaning of Freedom*. Edited by Frank McGlynn and Seymour Drescher. Pittsburgh: University of Pittsburgh Press.

Mintz, Sidney W., and Sally Price, eds.
  1985 *Caribbean Contours*. Baltimore: Johns Hopkins University Press.

Mintz, Sidney W., and Richard Price
  1976 *An Anthropological Approach to the Afro-American Past: A Caribbean Perspective*. Philadelphia: Institute for the Study of Human Issues.

Mohammed, Patricia, and Catherine Shepherd, eds.
  1988 *Gender in Caribbean Development*. Mona: University of the West Indies Women and Development Studies Project.

Moore, Sally Falk
  1969 "Law and Anthropology." In *Biennial Review of Anthropology*. Edited by B. J. Siegel. Stanford: Stanford University Press.

  1978 *Law as Process: An Anthropological Approach*. London: Routledge & Kegan Paul.

  1986 *Social Facts and Fabrications: "Customary Law" on Kilimanjaro*. Cambridge: Cambridge University Press.

  1989 "History and the Redefinition of Custom on Kilimanjaro." In *History and Power in the Study of Law*. Edited by June Starr and Jane F. Collier. Ithaca, N.Y.: Cornell University Press.

Morgan, Edmund S.
   [1942] 1973 "The Puritans and Sex." In *Interpreting Colonial America*. Edited by
   James Kirby Martin. New York: Dodd, Mead.

Morrish, Ivor
   1982 *Obeah, Christ and Rastaman: Jamaica and its Religion*. Cambridge: James
   Clarke & Company.

Morrison, Dennis
   1979 "The Reception of English Law in Jamaica." *West Indian Law Journal* (October): 43–61.

Morrissey, Marietta
   1989 *Slave Women in the New World: Gender Stratification in the Caribbean*. Lawrence: University Press of Kansas.

Moses, Yolanda
   1976 "Female Status and Male Dominance in Montserrat." Ph.D. diss., University
   of California, Riverside.

   1981 "Female Status, the Family, and Male Dominance in the West Indian Community." In *The Black Woman Cross-Culturally*. Edited by Filomina Chioma
   Steady. Rochester, Vt.: Schenkmen Books.

Mullin, Michael
   1977 "Slave Obeahmen and Slaveowning Patriarchs in an Era of War and Revolution (1776–1807)." In *New World Plantation Societies*. Edited by Vera Rubin
   and Arthur Tudin. New York: Academy of Sciences.

Nadel, S. F.
   1952 "Witchcraft in Four African Societies: An Essay in Comparison." *American
   Anthropologist* 54 (1):18–29.

Nader, Laura
   1989 "The Crown, the Colonists, and the Course of Zapotec Village Law." In
   History and Power in the Study of Law. Edited by June Starr and Jane F.
   Collier. Ithaca, N.Y.: Cornell University Press.

   1990 *Harmony Ideology: Justice and Control in a Zapotec Mountain Village*. Stanford:
   Stanford University Press.

Nader, Laura, and Barbara Yngvesson
   1973 "On Studying the Ethnography of Law and its Consequences." In *Handbook
   of Social and Cultural Anthropology*. Edited by J. J. Honigmann. Chicago:
   Rand McNally.

Nader, Laura, and Harry F. Todd, Jr., eds.
   1978 *The Disputing Process: Law in Ten Societies*. New York: Columbia University Press.

Nicholson, D. V.
   1983 *The Story of the Arawaks in Antigua and Barbuda*. London: Linden Press.

Nicholson, D. V., ed.
  1984 *The Progress and Effects of Emancipation in Antigua and Barbuda*. Antigua: Antigua Archives Office.

O'Barr, William M., and John M. Conley
  1988 "Lay Expectations of the Civil Justice System." *Law & Society Review* 22:147–52.

O'Loughlin, Carleen
  1959 "The Economy of Antigua." *Social and Economic Studies* 8:229–64.

Olwig, Karen Fog
  1981 "Women, 'Matrifocality' and Systems of Exchange: An Ethnohistorical Study of the Afro-American Family on St. John, Danish West Indies." *Ethnohistory* 28 (1):59–78.

Pares, Richard
  1950 *A West India Fortune*. London: Longmans, Green.

Patchett, K. W.
  1973 "Reception of Law in the West Indies." *Jamaican Law Journal* (April): 17–35; (October): 55–67.

Patterson, Orlando
  1967 *The Sociology of Slavery*. Rutherford, N.J.: Fairleigh Dickinson University Press.

  1973 "Slavery and Slave Revolts: A Sociohistorical Analysis of the First Maroon War, 1665–1740." In *Maroon Societies: Rebel Slave Communities in the Americas*. Edited by Richard Price. New York: Anchor Books.

  1982 "Persistence, Continuity, and Change in the Jamaican Working-Class Family." *Journal of Family History* 7:135–61.

Phillippo, James M.
  [1843] 1969 *Jamaica: its Past and Present State*. London: Dawsons of Pall Mall.

Phillips, Ulrich B.
  1926 "An Antigua Plantation, 1769–1818." *North Carolina Historical Review* 3 (1):439–45.

Pipkin, Charles W.
  1934 "Poor Laws." *Encyclopaedia of the Social Sciences*. Edited by Edwin R. A. Seligman. 12:230–34. New York: Macmillan.

Polanyi, Karl
  1944 *The Great Transformation: The Political and Economic Origins of Our Times*. Boston: Beacon Press.

Pospisil, Leopold
  1979 "Legally Induced Culture Change in New Guinea." In *The Imposition of Law*. Edited by Sandra B. Burman and Barbara E. Harrell-Bond. New York: Academic Press.

  1981 "Modern and Traditional Administration of Justice in New Guinea." *Journal of Legal Pluralism and Unofficial Law* 19:93–116.

Post, Ken
    1978 *Arise Ye Starvelings: The Jamaican Labour Rebellion of 1938 and its Aftermath.* The Hague: Martinus Nijhoff.

Powell, Dorian
    1982 "Network Analysis: A Suggested Model for the Study of Women and the Family in the Caribbean." In *Women and the Family.* Edited by Joycelin Massiah. Women in the Caribbean Project. Cave Hill, Barbados: University of the West Indies.

    1986 "Caribbean Women and their Response to Familial Experiences." *Social and Economic Studies* 35 (2)83–130.

Procacci, Giovanni
    1991 "Social Economy and the Government of Poverty." In *The Foucault Effect.* Edited by Graham Burchell, Colin Gordon, and Peter Miller. Chicago: University of Chicago Press.

Ragatz, Lowell Joseph
    1931 "Absentee Landlordism in the British Caribbean, 1750–1833." *Agricultural History* 5:7–24.

Ranger, Terence
    1983 "The Invention of Tradition in Colonial Africa." In *The Invention of Tradition.* Edited by Eric Hobsbawm and Terence Ranger. Cambridge: Cambridge University Press.

Rapp, Rayna
    1982 "Family and Class in Contemporary America: Notes Toward an Understanding of Ideology." In *Rethinking the Family: Some Feminist Questions.* Edited by Barrie Thorne. New York: Longman.

    1987 "Urban Kinship in Contemporary America: Families, Classes, and Ideology." In *Cities of the United States: Studies in Urban Anthropology.* Edited by Leith Mullings. New York: Columbia University Press.

Reddock, Rhoda
    1988 "Women and the Slave Plantation Economy in the Caribbean." In *Retrieving Women's History.* Edited by S. Jay Kleinberg. Berg: Unesco.

Reisman, Karl
    1964 "'The Isle is Full of Noises': A Study of Creole in the Speech Patterns of Antigua, West Indies." Ph.D. diss., Harvard University.

    1970 "Cultural and Linguistic Ambiguity in a West Indian Village." In *African-American Anthropology.* Edited by Norman E. Whitten, Jr., and John F. Szwed. New York: Free Press.

Richards, Audrey
    1971 "Introduction: The Nature of the Problem." In *Councils in Action.* Edited by Audrey Richards and Adam Kuper. Cambridge: University Press.

Richards, Novelle
    N.d. *Trade Unionism: Its Effects upon the Antigua and Barbuda Society.* St. John's, Antigua: Antigua Archives Committee.

Richards, Vincent A.
  1982 "The Antigua and Barbudan Economy: Trends and Prospects." *Antigua and Barbuda Forum* 1 (1):30–36.

Richardson, Ronald Kent
  1987 *Moral Imperium: Afro-Caribbeans and the Transformation of British Rule, 1776–1838.* New York: Greenwood Press.

Riessman, Catherine Kohler
  1990 *Divorce Talk: Women and Men Make Sense of Personal Relationships.* New Brunswick, N.J.: Rutgers University Press.

Roberts, George W.
  [1957] 1979 *The Population of Jamaica.* Millwood, N.Y.: Kraus Reprint.

  1985 "Some Observations on the Social Background: The Family Law in the Caribbean." *West Indian Law Journal* (October): 21–28.

Roberts, George W., and Sonja A. Sinclair
  1978 *Women in Jamaica: Patterns of Reproduction and Family.* Millwood, N.Y.: KTO Press.

Robinson, May
  1893 "Obeah Worship in East and West Indies." *Folklore* 4:207–13.

Robotham, Don
  1980 "Pluralism as Ideology." *Social and Economic Studies* 29:69–89.

Rodman, Hyman
  1971 *Lower-Class Families: The Culture of Poverty in Negro Trinidad.* New York: Oxford University Press.

Rodney, Walter
  1981 *A History of the Guyanese Working People, 1881–1905.* Baltimore: Johns Hopkins University Press.

Romero, Patricia
  1977 "The Slave Traders' Images of Slaves." In *Comparative Perspectives on Slavery in New World Plantation Societies.* Edited by Vera Rubin and Arthur Tuden. *Annals of the New York Academy of Science* 292:286–92.

Rosen, Lawrence
  1989a *The Anthropology of Justice: Law as Culture in Islamic Society.* Cambridge: University Press.

  1989b "Islamic 'Case Law' and the Logic of Consequence." In *History and Power in the Study of Law.* Edited by June Starr and Jane F. Collier. Ithaca, N.Y.: Cornell University Press.

Rottenberg, Simon
  1951 "The Economy of Antigua." *Caribbean Commonwealth Monthly Information Bulletin* 4 (12):851–55.

Rubenstein, Hymie
    1976 "Incest, Effigy Hanging, and Biculturation in a West Indian Village." *American Ethnologist* 3:765–81.

Safa, Helen I.
    1986 "Economic Autonomy and Sexual Equality in Caribbean Society." *Social and Economic Studies* 35 (3):1–21.

Salamone, Frank
    1983 "The Clash between Indigenous, Islamic, Colonial and Post-Colonial Law in Nigeria." *Journal of Legal Pluralism and Unofficial Law* 21:15–60.

Sanders, Ronald
    1984 *Antigua and Barbuda, 1966–1981: Transition, Trial, Triumph.* St. John's, Antigua: Archives Committee.

Santos, Boaventura de Sousa
    1977 "The Law of the Oppressed: The Construction and Reproduction of Legality in Pasargada." *Law & Society Review* 12:5–126.

Sarat, Austin, and William L. F. Felstiner
    1986 "Law and Strategy in the Divorce Lawyer's Office." *Law & Society Review* 20 (1):93–134.

    1988 "Law and Social Relations: Vocabularies of Motive in Lawyer/Client Interaction." *Law & Society Review* 22 (4):737–69.

    1989 "Lawyers and Legal Consciousness: Law Talk in the Divorce Lawyer's Office." *Yale Law Journal* 98 (8):1663–88.

Schneider, David M.
    1972 "What is Kinship all about?" In *Kinship in the Morgan Centennial Year.* Edited by Priscilla Reining. Washington, D.C.: Washington Anthropological Society.

    [1968] 1980 *American Kinship: A Cultural Account.* Chicago: University of Chicago Press.

    1984 *A Critique of the Study of Kinship.* Ann Arbor: University of Michigan Press.

Schneider, David M., and Raymond T. Smith
    1973 *Class Differences and Sex Roles in American Kinship.* Englewood Cliffs, N.J.: Prentice-Hall.

Schuler, Monica
    1979 "Myalism and the African Religious Tradition in Jamaica." In *Africa and the Caribbean: The Legacies of a Link.* Edited by Margaret E. Crahan and Franklin W. Knight. Baltimore: Johns Hopkins University Press.

    1980 *"Alas, Alas, Kongo": A Social History of Indentured African Immigration into Jamaica, 1841–1865.* Baltimore: Johns Hopkins University Press.

Schutz, Alfred

    1962 *Collected Papers: I. The Problem of Social Reality*. Edited by Maurice Natanson. The Hague: Martinus Nijhoff.

    1970 *On Phenomenology and Social Relations: Selected Writings*. Edited by Helmut R. Wagner. Chicago: University of Chicago Press.

Schwarz, Philip J.

    1988 *Twice Condemned: Slaves and the Criminal Laws of Virginia*. Baton Rouge: Louisiana State University Press.

Scott, James C.

    1985 *Weapons of the Weak: Everyday Forms of Peasant Resistance*. New Haven: Yale University Press.

    1990 *Domination and the Arts of Resistance: Hidden Transcripts*. New Haven: Yale University Press.

Scott, Joan W.

    1986 "Gender: A Useful Category of Historical Analysis." *American Historical Review* 91 (5):1053–75.

Senior, Olive

    1991 *Working Miracles: Women's Lives in the English-speaking Caribbean*. Bloomington: Indiana University Press.

Sereno, Renzo

    1948 "Obeah: Magic and Social Structure in the Lesser Antilles." *Psychiatry* 11 (1):15–31.

Sewell, William G.

    1861 *The Ordeal of Free Labour in the British West Indies*. New York: Harper and Brothers.

Shahabuddeen, M.

    1973 *The Legal System of Guyana*. Georgetown: Guyana Printers.

Sheridan, Richard B.

    1957 "Letters from a Sugar Plantation in Antigua, 1739–1758." *Agricultural History* 31:3–23.

    1961 "The Rise of a Colonial Gentry: A Case Study of Antigua, 1730–1775." *Economic History Review*, 2d ser. 13 (3):342–57.

    1971 "Planters and Merchants: The Oliver Family of Antigua and London 1716–1784." *Business History* 13 (2):104–13.

    1973 *Sugar and Slavery: An Economic History of the British West Indies 1623–1775*. Baltimore: Johns Hopkins University Press.

    1977 "The Role of the Scots in the Economy and Society of the West Indies." In *Comparative Perspectives on Slavery in New World Plantation Societies*. Edited by Vera Rubin and Arthur Tuden. *Annals of the New York Academy of Sciences* 292:94–106.

Silbey, Susan S., and Austin Sarat
  1987 "Critical Traditions in Law and Society Research." *Law & Society Review* 21 (1):165–74.

Simpson, George Eaton
  1976 "Religions of the Caribbean." In *The African Diaspora: Interpretive Essays.* Edited by Martin L. Kilson and Robert I. Rotberg. Cambridge: Harvard University Press.

  1978 *Black Religions in the New World.* New York: Columbia University Press.

Smith, Keithlyn B., and Fernando C. Smith, eds.
  1986 *To Shoot Hard Labour: The Life and Times of Samuel Smith an Antiguan Workingman 1877–1982.* Scarborough, Ontario: Edan's Publishers.

Smith, M. G.
  1962 *West Indian Family Structure.* Seattle: University of Washington Press.

  1965a "Social and Cultural Pluralism." In *The Plural Society in the British West Indies.* Berkeley and Los Angeles: University of California Press.

  1965b "Some Aspects of Social Structure in the British Caribbean about 1820." In *The Plural Society in the British West Indies.* Berkeley and Los Angeles: University of California Press.

  1965c "The Transformation of Land Rights by Transmission in Carriacou." In *The Plural Society in the British West Indies.* Berkeley and Los Angeles: University of California Press.

  1965d *Stratification in Grenada.* Berkeley and Los Angeles: University of California Press.

  1966 "Introduction." In *My Mother Who Fathered Me.* Edith Clarke. London: George Allen and Unwin.

Smith, Raymond T.
  1955 "Land Tenure in Three Negro Villages in British Guiana." *Social and Economic Studies* 4 (1):64–82.

  1956 *The Negro Family in British Guiana* London: Routledge and Kegan Paul.

  1966 "People and Change." *New World: Guyana Independence Issue* (May): 49–54.

  1967 "Social Stratification, Cultural Pluralism and Integration in West Indian Societies." In *Caribbean Integration: Third Caribbean Scholars Conference, Georgetown, Guyana.* Edited by Sybil Lewis and Thomas G. Mathews. Puerto Rico: University of Puerto Rico, Institute of Caribbean Studies.

  1973 "The Matrifocal Family." In *The Character of Kinship.* Edited by Jack Goody. Cambridge: Cambridge University Press.

  1976 "Religion in the Formation of West Indian Society: Guyana and Jamaica." In *The African Diaspora: Interpretive Essays.* Edited by Martin L. Kilson and Robert I. Rotberg. Cambridge: Harvard University Press.

1978 "The Family and the Modern World System." *Journal of Family History* 3 (4):337–60.

1982a "Family, Social Change and Social Policy in the West Indies." *Nieuwe West Indische Gids* 56 (3/4):111–42.

1982b "Race and Class in the Post-Emancipation Caribbean." In *Racism and Colonialism.* Edited by R. Ross. The Hague: Martinus Nijhoff.

1987 "Hierarchy and the Dual Marriage System in West Indian Society." In *Gender and Kinship: Essays Toward a Unified Analysis.* Edited by Jane Fishburne Collier and Sylvia Junko Yanagisako. Stanford: Stanford University Press.

1988 *Kinship and Class in the West Indies: A Genealogical Study of Jamaica and Guyana.* Cambridge: Cambridge University Press.

1992 "Race, Class, and Gender in the Transition to Freedom." In *The Meaning of Freedom.* Edited by Frank McGlynn and Seymour Drescher. Pittsburgh: University of Pittsburgh Press.

Smith, Raymond T., ed.
1984 *Kinship Ideology and Practice in Latin America.* Chapel Hill: University of North Carolina Press.

Smith, R. T., and C. Jayawardena
1959 "Marriage and the Family Amongst East Indians in British Guiana." *Social and Economic Studies* 8:321–76.

Snyder, Francis G.
1981 "Colonialism and Legal Form: The Creation of 'Customary Law' in Senegal." *Journal of Legal Pluralism and Unofficial Law* 9:49–90.

St. Johnston, Sir Reginal
1936 *From a Colonial Governor's Note-Book.* London: Hutchinson and Company.

Starr, June, and Jane F. Collier, eds.
1987 "Historical Studies of Legal Change." *Current Anthropology* 28 (3):367–72.

1989 *History and Power in the Study of Law: New Directions in Legal Anthropology.* Ithaca, N.Y.: Cornell University Press.

Starr, June, and Jonathan Pool
1974 "The Impact of a Legal Revolution in Rural Turkey." *Law & Society Review* 8 (4):533–60.

Stinchcombe, Arthur L.
1975 "Social Structure and Politics." In *Handbook of Political Science.* Vol. 3. Edited by Nelson W. Polsby and Fred Greenstein. Reading, Mass.: Addison-Wesley.

Stolcke, Verena
1984 "The Exploitation of Family Morality: Labor Systems and Family Structure on São Paulo Coffee Plantations, 1850–1979." In *Kinship Ideology and Practice in Latin America.* Edited by Raymond T. Smith. Chapel Hill: University of North Carolina Press.

Stoler, Ann L.
   1985 *Capitalism and Confrontation in Sumatra's Plantation Belt, 1870–1979*. New Haven: Yale University Press.

   1989a "Making Empire Respectable: The Politics of Race and Sexual Morality in 20th-century Colonial Cultures." *American Ethnologist* 16 (4):634–60.

   1989b "Rethinking Colonial Categories: European Communities and the Boundaries of Rule." *Comparative Studies in Society and History* 31 (1):134–61.

Sutton, Constance, and Susan Makiesky-Barrow
   1977 "Social Inequality and Sexual Status in Barbados." In *Sexual Stratification: A Cross-Cultural View*. Edited by Alice Schlegel. New York: Columbia University Press.

   1981 "Social Inequality and Sexual Status in Barbados." In *The Black Woman Cross-Culturally*. Edited by Filomina Chioma Steady. Rochester, Vt.: Schenkman Books.

Taussig, Michael T.
   1980 *The Devil and Commodity Fetishism in South America*. Chapel Hill: University of North Carolina Press.

   1987 *Shamanism, Colonialism, and the Wild Man*. Chicago: University of Chicago Press.

Thelwell, Michael
   1980 *The Harder They Come*. New York: Grove Press.

Thome, Jas. A., and J. Horace Kimball
   1839 *Emancipation in the West Indies. A Six Months Tour in Antigua, Barbados, and Jamaica, in the year 1837*. New York: Anti-Slavery Society.

Thompson, E. P.
   1967 "Time, Work-Discipline, and Industrial Capitalism." *Past and Present* 38:56–97.

   1975 *Whigs and Hunters: The Origin of the Black Act*. New York: Pantheon Books.

   1978 "Eighteenth-century English Society: Class Struggle without Class?" *Social History* 3 (2):133–65.

Trotman, David Vincent
   1986 *Crime in Trinidad: Conflict and Control in a Plantation Society 1838–1900*. Knoxville: University of Tennessee Press.

Trouillot, Michel-Rolph
   1992 "The Caribbean Region: An Open Frontier in Anthropological Theory." *Annual Review of Anthropology* 21:19–42.

Trubek, David M.
   1984 "Where the Action Is: Critical Legal Studies and Empiricism." *Stanford Law Review* 36:575–622.

Tunteng, P-Kiven
    1975 "Reflections on Labour and Governing in Antigua." *Caribbean Studies* 15 (2):36–56.

Turk, Austin T.
    1976 "Law as a Weapon in Social Conflict." *Social Problems* 23 (3):276–91.

Turner, Mary
    1982 *Slaves and Missionaries: The Disintegration of Jamaican Slave Society, 1787–1834.* Urbana: University of Illinois Press.

Van Velsen, J.
    1967 "The Extended-case Method and Situational Analysis." In *The Craft of Social Anthropology.* Edited by A. L. Epstein. London: Tavistock Publications.

Vincent, Joan
    1989 "Contours of Change: Agrarian Law in Colonial Uganda, 1895–1962." In *History and Power in the Study of Law.* Edited by June Starr and Jane F. Collier. Ithaca, N.Y.: Cornell University Press.

Wade, Richard C.
    1964 *Slavery in the Cities: The South 1820–1860.* New York: Oxford University Press.

Watkins, Frederick Henry
    1924 *Handbook of the Leeward Islands.* London: West India Committee.

Watters, David Roberts
    1980 "Transect Surveying and Prehistoric Site Locations on Barbuda and Montserrat, Leeward Islands, West Indies." Ph.D. diss., University of Pittsburgh.

Webb, Sidney, and Beatrice Webb
    [1910] 1963a *English Poor Law History: Part 1. The Old Poor Law.* Hamden, Conn.: Archon Books.

    [1910] 1963b *English Poor Law Policy.* Hamden, Conn.: Archon Books.

Weber, Max
    1958 *The Protestant Ethic and the Spirit of Capitalism.* Translated by Talcott Parsons. New York: Charles Scribner's Sons.

    1978 *Economy and Society.* 2 vols. Edited by Guenther Roth and Claus Wittich. Berkeley and Los Angeles: University of California Press.

Wedenoja, William
    1988 "The Origins of Revival, a Creole Religion in Jamaica." In *Culture and Christianity.* Edited by George Saunders. New York: Greenwood Press.

Weitzman, Lenore
    1985 *The Divorce Revolution.* New York: Free Press.

Wells, Robert V.
    1975 *The Population of the British Colonies in America before 1776: A Survey of Census Data.* Princeton: Princeton University Press.

Westermark, George D.

    1986 "Court is an Arrow: Legal Pluralism in Papua New Guinea." *Ethnology* 25 (2):131–48.

White, Averille

    1986 "Profiles: Women in the Caribbean Project." *Social and Economic Studies* 35 (2)59–81.

Williams, Brackette F.

    1991 *Stains on My Name, War in My Veins: Guyana and the Politics of Cultural Struggle.* Durham, N.C.: Duke University Press.

Williams, Eric

    1944 *Capitalism and Slavery.* New York: Capricorn Books.

    1962 *History of the People of Trinidad and Tobago.* London: Andre Deutsch.

Williams, Eric, ed.

    1952 *Documents on British West Indian History, 1807–1833.* Port-of-Spain, Trinidad: Trinidad Publishing Company.

Williams, Joseph J.

    1932 *Voodoos and Obeahs: Phases of West India Witchcraft.* New York: Dial Press.

Williams, Patricia J.

    1991 *The Alchemy of Race and Rights: Diary of a Law Professor.* Cambridge: Harvard University Press.

Williams, Raymond

    [1976] 1983 *Key Words: A Vocabulary of Culture and Society.* New York: Oxford University Press.

    [1977] 1988 *Marxism and Literature.* Oxford: Oxford University Press.

Wilson, Monica Hunter

    1951 "Witch Beliefs and Social Structure." *American Journal of Sociology* 56 (4):307–13.

Wilson, Peter J.

    1969 "Reputation and Respectability: A Suggestion for Caribbean Ethnology." *Man* 4:70–84.

    1973 *Crab Antics: The Social Anthropology of English-Speaking Negro Societies of the Caribbean.* New Haven: Yale University Press.

Wolfram, Sybil

    1955 "An Outline of English Divorce 1700–1857." MS.

    1983 "Eugenics and the Punishment of Incest Act 1908." *Criminal Law Review* (May): 308–16.

The World Bank

    1985 *Antigua and Barbuda Economic Report.* Washington, D.C.

Wright, Gavin

    1992 "The Economics and Politics of Slavery and Freedom in the U.S. South." In *The Meaning of Freedom*. Edited by Frank McGlynn and Seymour Drescher. Pittsburgh: University of Pittsburgh Press.

Yngvesson, Barbara

    1985 "Re-Examining Continuing Relations and the Law." *Wisconsin Law Review* 3 (1985): 623–46.

    1988 "Making Law At The Doorway: The Clerk, The Court, And The Construction Of Community In A New England Town." *Law & Society Review* 22 (3):409–48.

    1994 " 'Kidstuff' and Complaint: Interpreting Resistance in a New England Court." In *Contested States: Law, Hegemony, and Resistance*. Edited by Mindie Lazarus-Black and Susan F. Hirsch. New York: Routledge, Chapman and Hall.

❧ Index

347

Long, Edward, 32, 62, 64, 93, 236
Lowes, Susan, xxii, 82, 99, 100, 115, 129, 131, 132, 133, 134, 145, 177, 223, 226
Luffman, John, 36, 48, 67, 80--81, 94

Macfarlane, Alan, 29, 37, 252, 253
McGlynn, Frank, 103
Magistrates, 167–68, 190, 255–56
Magistrate courts: cases heard before, 166, 169–77, 193, 195–204, 205, 206, 208, 219, 253–54, 255–56; description of, 166–67
Makiesky-Barrow, Susan, 193, 212
Mansfield, Lord (William Murray), 32
Manumission, 70, 95, 98, 117
Marriage: Antiguan laws governing, 60–72, 121–22, 151, 245, 246, 247; British laws governing, 56–60, 121–22; common-law, 62, 72, 152, 249; and economic considerations, 77–80; of free persons, 60–67, 74, 75–86; of free persons of color, 81–86; of indentured servants, 63–64, 72, 76, 246; interracial, 7, 13, 14, 61, 80; of non-Anglicans, 121–22, 127, 134–39; rates of, 74, 76, 84–85, 92, 143–44, 146, 147–48, 162, 177, 247, 251–52; among slaves, 8, 63, 67–71, 92–93; and social class, 8, 61–67, 79–80, 133, 136, 143–46, 213–19, 251–52
Marshall, Woodville, 31, 107
Martin, Col. Samuel, 53, 77
Martinez-Alier, Verena, 7, 61
Marx, Karl, 46, 250
Massachusetts Bay Colony, 76
Massiah, Joycelin, 7, 37, 168, 193, 231
Mather, Lynn, 164
Mauss, Marcel, 218
Medicine. *See* Disease and medical care
Mercantilism, 17, 18–21
Merry, Sally Engle, 52, 164, 172, 186, 253
Methodist church, 88, 90, 91, 122, 150, 151, 155, 171

Mintz, Sidney W., 7, 15–16, 32, 36, 105
Miscegenation, 74, 81, 88, 93–100
Missionaries: influence on slaves, 88–92; in postemancipation period, 128, 129, 146–57
Monocrop economy, xiii, 27
Montesquieu, Baron, 58
Montserrat, 21, 62, 74, 88
Moore, Sally Falk, 103, 189, 199
Moravian church, 88, 89–90, 91, 150, 151, 155, 171
Morgan, Edmund S., 76
Morrish, Ivor, 45
Morrissey, Marietta, 7, 35, 45, 88
Mortality rates: of Europeans in the tropics, 13, 246; of infants, 112, 113; of slaves, 35
Moses, Yolanda, 8, 212
Moyne Commission (1938), 223
Mullin, Michael, 46
Myalism, 129, 146

Nader, Laura, 52, 189, 253
Nevis, 21, 33, 49, 77, 88, 91, 98
Nicholson, D. V., 19
Norms, meanings of, 5–6

O'Barr, William, 172, 253
Obeah, 4, 40, 42, 43–47, 53–54, 74, 110, 129, 146, 156, 157–61, 163, 256, 259
Oliver, Vere, 19, 27, 78, 82, 85, 97, 98
Olwig, Karen Fog, 7

Pares, Richard, 48, 49, 77, 78
Parham, 160, 166
Parham Plantation, 35
Passports, 108, 228
Patchett, K. W., 9, 20, 123
Paternity cases, 171–72, 219. *See also* Illegitimate children, maintenance of
Patterson, Orlando, 7, 45, 48, 212
Pentecostal Missions, 151, 155, 156
Philanthropy, 116